Global Financial Markets

Global Financial Markets is a series of practical guides to the latest financial market tools, techniques and strategies. Written for practitioners across a range of disciplines it provides comprehensive but practical coverage of key topics in finance covering strategy, markets, financial products, tools and techniques and their implementation. This series will appeal to a broad readership, from new entrants to experienced practitioners across the financial services industry, including areas such as institutional investment; financial derivatives; investment strategy; private banking; risk management; corporate finance and M&A, financial accounting and governance, and many more.

Sue Wright

The International Loan Documentation Handbook

Third Edition

Sue Wright
London, UK

Global Financial Markets
ISBN 978-3-031-38488-2   ISBN 978-3-031-38489-9   (eBook)
https://doi.org/10.1007/978-3-031-38489-9

1st edition: © Sue Wright 2006
2nd edition: © Sue Wright 2014
3rd edition: © The Editor(s) (if applicable) and The Author(s), under exclusive license to Springer
Nature Switzerland AG 2024

This work is subject to copyright. All rights are solely and exclusively licensed by the Publisher, whether
the whole or part of the material is concerned, specifically the rights of translation, reprinting, reuse
of illustrations, recitation, broadcasting, reproduction on microfilms or in any other physical way, and
transmission or information storage and retrieval, electronic adaptation, computer software, or by similar
or dissimilar methodology now known or hereafter developed.
The use of general descriptive names, registered names, trademarks, service marks, etc. in this publication
does not imply, even in the absence of a specific statement, that such names are exempt from the relevant
protective laws and regulations and therefore free for general use.
The publisher, the authors, and the editors are safe to assume that the advice and information in this book
are believed to be true and accurate at the date of publication. Neither the publisher nor the authors or
the editors give a warranty, expressed or implied, with respect to the material contained herein or for any
errors or omissions that may have been made. The publisher remains neutral with regard to jurisdictional
claims in published maps and institutional affiliations.

This Palgrave Macmillan imprint is published by the registered company Springer Nature Switzerland AG
The registered company address is: Gewerbestrasse 11, 6330 Cham, Switzerland

Paper in this product is recyclable.

For Dave, Amy, Leo, Hilary and Claude

Preface to the Third Edition

This third edition of *The International Loan Documentation Handbook* was largely prompted by the abolition of Libor and the fundamental changes to loan documentation which ensued. After a period of rapid development during the transition away from Libor, market practices for documentation of loans based on the new interest rate methodologies have started to emerge and the Loan Market Association now publishes a library of recommended forms of loan documentation appropriate for use with either (or both) term rates or compounded rates of interest based on risk free rates. This book provides a comprehensive overview of the concepts behind the interest rate provisions, an explanation of the mechanisms by which the raw data on risk free rates is converted into the interest rate charged to the borrower, and a clause-by-clause explanation of the drafting.

The book has also been updated to reflect the many other changes in the documentation and practice of international lending which have taken place since the second edition was published in 2014. These include new case law, accounting changes, Brexit, rise in ESG lending and a challenging commercial environment as a result of COVID, sanctions on Russia, rising geopolitical tensions, rising energy costs and inflation.

viii   **Preface to the Third Edition**

Thanks, as always, to the Loan Market Association, for giving me permission to use their documentation for the purpose of this book, and to the many delegates on my loan courses over the years, for their questions and inspiration.

London, UK   Sue Wright

Preface to the Second Edition

This second edition of *The International Loan Documentation Handbook* was prompted by the major changes in the documentation and practice of loan documentation that have occurred since the first edition was published in 2005.

The financial crisis of 2007–2008, and the increased regulation and litigation which followed it, gave rise to a host of new issues as well as some useful judicial decisions on the wording of the documents. Interest rates, in particular, became the subject of much discussion both as a result of concerns over the accuracy of LIBOR as a benchmark rate and as a result of changes in bank funding arrangements following the crisis. This has led to the substantial revision of the sections in the book dealing with interest.

There are also new sections on defaulting lenders; commodification of debt; the Euro crisis; FATCA; sanctions and anti-corruption legislation; and on the impact of recent court decisions on the loan agreement wording. I have also taken the opportunity to expand the sections of the book dealing with financial covenants and with other undertakings other than those contained in the investment grade LMA loan agreement.

x   Preface to the Second Edition

As ever my thanks go to the many delegates who have attended my loan documentation courses over the years. Their questions and comments have been invaluable in inspiring this book in the first place as well as in highlighting contentious issues. Thanks also are due to the partners, staff and clients at Norton Rose, where I gained my practical experience in international finance.

Sue Wright

Acknowledgements

This book was inspired by the questions and comments of the many delegates who have attended my loan documentation courses over the years. Their questions, often difficult and insightful, and based on their widely differing backgrounds and areas of expertise, have been indispensable in helping to widen my own perspective on the documentation, and in highlighting issues of concern. My thanks to those many delegates who have inspired me to investigate those issues which are discussed in this book. My thanks also go to the partners, staff and clients at Norton Rose, where I obtained my practical experience of international finance, without which this book would have been impossible. Thanks are also due to those who have been kind enough to spare their valuable time to review parts of the manuscript of this book at its various stages of development, and to provide comments and suggestions. In particular, I would like to thank Staffan Avenius (Nordea Bank), Anne-Marie Godfrey (Deacons), Kenneth Gray (Norton Rose), Alexey Ievlev (ING Bank), Jonathan Porteous (Stevens and Bolton LLP), Richard Powell (Mundays) and Paul Rogerson (ABN Amro) for their kind assistance. The comments, information and support provided have been enormously helpful in getting this book from conception to completion. Finally, of course, I would like to thank the Loan Market Association for their permission to use their primary form documents in this text, and the Dutch Bankers Association, for consenting to the use of their 'parallel debt' wording.

PS To Leo, thanks too for your comments, which will be included if a humorous version of this book is ever commissioned.

List of Statutes and Conventions

Statutes and Regulations

1890

s2 Partnership Act 1890   127
s3 Partnership Act 1890   127

1925

Law of Property Act 1925
s136   490

1967

s3 Misrepresentation Act 1967   478

1971

s1 Powers of Attorney Act
1971   477

1977

s2(2) Unfair Contract Terms Act
1977   478

xiv   **List of Statutes and Conventions**

s3 Unfair Contract Terms Act
1977   478
s27 Unfair Contract Terms Act
1977   479

1986

s123 Insolvency Act 1986   337, 503, 524
s214 Insolvency Act 1986   350, 540
s238 Insolvency Act 1986   503
s239 Insolvency Act 1986   530
Rule 12.3(2A) Insolvency Rules
1986   128

1989

Rule 4.90 Insolvency Rules
1986   375
s1(2) Law of Property (Miscellaneous Provisions) Act
1989   477

1999

Contracts (Rights of Third Parties) Act
1999   137

2000

Financial Services and Markets Act
2000   81

2002

Enterprise Act 2002   487

2003

Financial Collateral Arrangements (No 2) Regulations
2003   494

2006

s40(1) Companies Act 2006   420
s170(4) Companies Act 2006   504
s172 Companies Act 2006   504
s251 Companies Act 2006   260, 535

List of Statutes and Conventions xv

s474(1) Companies Act 2006 125

2009

Banking Act 2009 119
Bribery Act 2010 259

2011

Overseas Companies (Execution of Documents and Registration
of Charges) (Amendments) Regulations 2011 (SI 2011/
2194) 492

2016

Statutory Auditors and Third Country Auditors Regulation 2016 (SI
2016/649) 313

2017

Money Laundering, Terrorist Financing and Transfer of Funds
(information on the Payer) (regulations 2017 (SI 2017/692) (as
amended)) 270

2018

EU (Withdrawal Act) 2018 414

2019

The Law Applicable to Contractual Obligations and Non
Contractual Obligations (Amendments, etc.) (EU Exit) Regulations
2019 532

2020

Protecting against the Effects of Extraterritorial Application of Third
Country Legislation (Amendment) (EU Exit) Regulations 2020 (SI
2020/1660) 66

2021

Pension Schemes Act 2021 317

xvi List of Statutes and Conventions

EU Regulations and Directives

1996
Blocking Regulation 2271/96   66, 511

2007
Rome II 864/2007   414

2008
Rome I 593/2008   532

2013
Credit Ratings Agencies Regulation 462/
2013   127
Capital Requirements Regulation 575/2013
('CRRI')   207
Fourth Capital Requirements Directive 36/2013
('CRDIV')   207, 208, 516

2015
Recast Insolvency Regulation 2015/
848   314

2019
Sustainable Finance Disclosure Regulation ('SFDR') 2019/
2088   98
Second Capital Requirements Regulation 876/2019
('CRRII')   206
Fifth Capital Requirements Directive 878/2019
('CRDV')   206

2020
Taxonomy Regulation on establishment of a
framework to facilitate sustainable investment 852/
2020   98, 520, 537

List of Statutes and Conventions xvii

2022

Corporate Sustainability Reporting Directive 2464/ 2022	98
Pending—expected to become effective in January 2025	209, 211, 524
Third Capital Requirements Regulation ('CRRIII')	206–208
Sixth Capital Requirements Directive ('CRDVI')	206–208, 516

International Conventions

Brussels Convention of 1926 Relating to Maritime Liens and Mortgages	495
Geneva Convention of 1948 on the International Recognition of Rights in Aircraft	495
United Nations Convention on the Recognition and Enforcement of Foreign Arbitral Awards 1958—the 'New York Convention'	415
Hague Convention on the law applicable to trusts and on their recognition 1985	367
Cape Town Convention on International Interests in Mobile Equipment 2001	495
Hague Convention on Choice of Court Agreements 2015	416

Other

Model Laws

UNCITRAL Model Law on Cross-Border Insolvency	314

US Legislation and Rules

Employee Retirement Income Security Act 1974 ("ERISA")	310, 519
Foreign Account Tax Compliance Act 2010 ("FATCA")	119, 171, 187, 197-201, 209, 520, 524
Qualified Financial Contract Rules	68, 532

List of Cases

Argo Fund Ltd v Essar Steel Ltd [2006] 2 All E.R. (Comm) 104	78
ARM Asset Backed Securities SA (2013) EWHC 3351 Ch	338
Ashborder BV v Green Gas Power Ltd (2004) EWHC 1517	299, 306
Associated British Ports v Ferryways NV & anor (2009) EWCA Civ 189	220
Aviva Insurance Ltd v Hackney Empire Ltd [2013] 1 W.L.R. 3400	223
Badeley v Consolidated Bank (1888) LR 38 Ch D	128
The Bank of New York Mellon, London Branch v Essar Steel India Ltd [2018] EWHC 3177 (Ch)	416
Bank of Scotland Plc v Constantine Makris and Ben O'Sullivan (2009) EWHC 3869	221
Barclays Bank v Quistclose [1968] UKHL4	145
Belvedere case (French Supreme Court Sept 13, 2011)	370
BNP Paribas SA v Yukos Oil Co (2005) EWH C 1321 (Ch)	342
BNY Corporate Trustee Services Ltd v Eurosail- UK 2007- 3BL Plc [2013] UKSC 28	338

xx   List of Cases

Braganza v BP Shipping Ltd & anr [2015] UKSC
17   385, 464

British Waggon Co v Lea & Co (1879–80) LR 5 QBD
149   361

Buzzle Operations Pty Ltd (in liquidation) v Apple Computer Australia
Pty Ltd, [2011] NSWCA 109.   261

Carlill v Carbolic Smoke Ball Company (1892) 2QB
484   358

Cattles plc v Welcome Financial Services and others [2010] EWCA Civ
599   225

Cavendish Square Holding v Makdessi (2015) UKSC 67 and ParkingEye
Ltd v Beavis [2015] *UKSC 67*   177

Central London Property Trust Ltd v High Trees House Ltd (1947) KB
130   520

Charmway v Fortunesea (Cayman) Ltd & Ors [2015] HKCU
1717   141

Chemco Leasing SpA v Rediffusion plc (1987) 1 FTLR
201   503

Cherry v Boultbee (1839) 4 My & Cr
442   223

China & South Seas Bank Ltd v Tan (1990) 1 AC
536   220

Re Citibank August 11, 2020 Wire Transfers, 2nd U.S.
Circuit Court of Appeals, No. 21–487 (the "Revlon
case")   65, 392

Clayton's case (Devagnes v Noble 1816 1 Mer
572)   217

Close Bros v Ridsdale (2012) EWHC
3090   221

Concord Trust v The Law Debenture Corp plc (2005) 1 WLR
1591   342

Cukurova Finance International Ltd v Alfa Telecom Turkey Ltd 2013
UKPC 2   342, 494

Dearle v Hall (1828) 3 Russ 1   491

Director General of Fair Trading v First National Bank Plc 2002 1 AC
481   177

Enviroco Ltd v Farstad Supply [2011] 1 W.L.R.
921   133

Re Eurofood IFSC Ltd [2006] EUECJ C-341/
04   314

Fons HF (in liquidation) v Corporal Limited and Pillar Securitisation
[2014]EWCA Civ 304   82

Gabriel v Little and others [2013] EWCA Civ
1513   145

List of Cases   xxi

Goldsoll v Goldman (1915) 1 Ch 292 — 403, 464

Goodridge v Macquarie Bank Limited [2010] FCA 67 (Australian case) — 358

Griffith v Tower Publishing (1897) 1 Ch 21 — 361

Grupo Hotelero Urvasco SA v Carey Value Added SL [2013] EWHC 1039 — 336, 349

Habibsons Bank Ltd v Standard Chartered Bank (Hong Kong) Limited [2010] EWCA Civ 1335 — 358

Hedley Byrne & Co Ltd v Heller (1964) AC 465 — 479

Holme v Brunskill (1877) 3 QBD 495 — 220, 221

Hooper v Western Counties and South Wales Telephone Co Ltd (1892) 68 LT 78 — 169

Hughes v Metropolitan Ry (1877) 2 App Cas 439 — 404

Interedil Srl (in liquidation) v Fallimento Interedil Srl and another [2011] EUECJ C-396/09 — 314

Jet2.Com Limited v Blackpool Airport Limited [2012] EWCA Civ 417 — 262

Kleinwort Benson Ltd v Malaysian Mining Corp (1989) 1 AER 785 — 503

L Schuler AG v Wickman Machine Tool Sales Ltd [1974] AC 235 — 464

Lester v Garland (1808) 15 Ves 248 — 113

Lombard North Central Plc v European Skyjets Ltd [2022] EWHC 728 — 346, 405

Lordsvale Finance plc v Bank of Zambia (1996) QB 752 — 177

Mauritius Commercial Bank Ltd v Hestia Holdings [2013] EWHC 1328 (Comm) — 416

Maxted v Investec Bank Plc [2017] EWHC 1997 (Ch) — 221

McGuinness v Norwich and Peterborough Building Society [2011] EWCA Civ 1286 — 216

Re Mytravel Group [2004] EWCA Civ 1734 — 308

National Westminster Bank Plc v Spectrum Plus Limited (2005) 3 W.L.R. 58 — 488

NML Capital v Argentina (2013 US case) — 252

xxii   List of Cases

North Shore Ventures Ltd v Anstead Holdings (2011) EWCA Civ
230   221
ParkingEye see Cavendish
Square   177
Re PFTZM Ltd [1995] BCC
280   260
Red Sea Tankers v Papachristidis [1997] 2 Lloyd's
Rep. 547   389
Revlon case—see Citibank   65
Rolled Steel Products (Holdings) Ltd v British Steel Corp and others
(1986) Ch 246   504
Rothschild case (Cour de cassation in Mme X v
Rothschild Civil Division 1, 26 September 2012,
11–26022   416
Re SSSL Realisations (2002) Ltd [2006] EWCA Civ
7   223
Strategic Value Master Fund Ltd v Ideal Standard
International Acquisition S.A.R.L. & Ors [2011] EWHC 171
(Ch)   351
Sumitomo Bank v Banque Bruxelles Lambert (1997) 1 Lloyds Law
Reports 487   383
Tele2 International Card Co SA v Post Office (2009) EWCA Civ
9   404
Telefonnaya Kompaniya (RTK) v Sony Ericsson Mobile Communication
Rus (Russian case in 2012)   415
Thomas v Thomas (1842) 2 QB
851   476
Tolhurst v Associated Portland Cement Manufacturers (1900) Ltd
(1903) AC 414   361
Torre Asset Funding Ltd v The Royal Bank of Scotland (2013) EWHC
2670 Ch   384
Triodos Bank v Dobbs (2005) EWCA Civ
630   221
Twinsectra Ltd v Yardley [2002] UKHL
12   145
Ultraframe v Fielding [2005] EWHC 1638
(Ch)   260
White v Davenham Trust Ltd (2011) EWCA Civ
747   221
White Hawthorne llc v Argentina 16 -cv-1042 (TPG) -US
case   253
Wulff v Jay (1871–72) LR 7 QB
756   220

Contents

Introduction	1
General Introduction	1
1. How to use this book	1
2. What should I be looking for in this loan agreement? Why does it have to be so long?	3
Section 1: Principal Types of Loans	4
1. Classification on the basis of availability	4
2. Classification on the basis of the lenders' credit decision	6
3. Classification on the basis of the purpose of the loan	8
4. Classification on the basis of the number of lenders	11
5. Miscellaneous categories	12
Section 2: Loan Agreement Overview	13
1. The LMA recommended forms and exposure drafts	13
2. Loan agreement structure	16
3. Key concerns	19
4. Hazards in reviewing a loan agreement	24
Section 3: Risk Free Rates	27

xxiii

xxiv **Contents**

1. What replaced Libor and why?	27
2. Key issues when using rates based on risk free rates	29

Section 4: Documentary Complexity of Using RFR Rates — 37
    1. Key words — 38
    2. Fallback provisions and other changes to the calculation of interest. — 47

Section 5: Scope of the Loan Agreement — 51
    1. Who can make use of the facility? — 52
    2. Who are the lenders? — 52
    3. Who can be called on to repay? — 53
    4. Whose activities are restricted by the loan agreement? — 53

Section 6: Non Standard Provisions — 64
    1. Sanctions — 65
    2. Special resolution procedures for systemically important lenders — 68
    3. Additional debt flexibility — 69
    4. Borrowers and affiliates purchasing in the secondary market — 70
    5. Lehman provisions — 71

Section 7: Commodification and Digitization of Debt — 76
    1. Non-bank lenders as direct lenders — 77
    2. Direct lenders transferring credit risk — 79
    3. Convergence with capital markets — 80

Section 8: Asset, Project and Acquisition (or 'Leveraged') Finance — 82
    1. Asset finance — 82
    2. Project finance — 84
    3. Acquisition (or 'Leveraged' or 'Private Equity') finance — 87

Section 9: Quasi Security and Financial Indebtedness — 90
    1. Quasi security — 90
    2. Financial Indebtedness — 95

Section 10: Socially Responsible Lending (or 'ESG Lending') — 97
    1. What is ESG Lending? — 97
    2. Categories of ESG Lending — 99
    3. Key issues in ESG Lending — 99
    4. Documentation of Sustainability Linked Loans — 102

Administrative Provisions

Interpretation	107
Clause 1: Definitions and Interpretation—Section 1—An Introduction	107
1. Definitions out of context	108
2. Different meanings in different contexts	109
3. Circularity	110
4. Operative provisions	111
Clause 1: Definitions and Interpretation—Section 2—The LMA Definitions	111
Clause 1.1 Definitions	111
Clause 1.2 Construction	134
Clause 1.3 Currency symbols and definitions	136
Clause 1.4 Third party rights	137
The Facilities	139
Clause 2: The Facilities	139
Clause 2.1 The Facilities	139
Clause 2.2 Increase	140
Clause 2.3 Finance Parties' rights and obligations	141
Clause 2.4 Obligors' agent	144
Clause 3: Purpose	144
Clause 3.1 Purpose	144
Clause 3.2 Monitoring	146
Clause 4: Conditions of Utilization	146
Clause 4.1 Initial conditions precedent	146
Clause 4.2 Further conditions precedent	149
Clause 4.3 Conditions relating to Optional Currencies	151
Clause 4.4 Maximum number of Utilizations	151
Utilization	153
Clause 5: Utilization—Loans	153
Clause 5.1 Delivery of a Utilization Request	153

Contents

Clause 5.2 Completion of a Utilization for Loans Request	153
Clause 5.3 Currency and amount	154
Clause 5.4 Lenders' participation	154
Clause 5.5 Cancellation of Commitment	154
Clause 6: Utilization—Letters of Credit	155
Clause 6.1 Facility B	155
Clauses 6.2, 6.3 and 6.4 Delivery of a Utilization Request for Letters of Credit; Completion of a Utilization Request for Letters of Credit and currency and amount.	156
Clauses 6.5 and 6.6 Issue of Letter of Credit and Renewal of a Letter of Credit	156
Clause 6.7 Revaluation of Letters of Credit	156
Clause 7: Letters of Credit	157
Clause 8: Optional Currencies	157
Purpose of a multicurrency loan	157
Clause 8.1 Selection of currency	160
Clause 8.3 Change of currency	160
Clause 8.4 Same Optional Currency during successive Interest Periods	161
Repayment, Prepayment and Cancellation	163
Clause 9: Repayment	163
Clause 9.1 Repayment of Facility A Loans	163
Clause 9.2 Repayment of Facility B Loans	163
Clause 9.3 Reduction of Facility B Loans	164
Clause 10: Prepayment and Cancellation	165
Clause 10.1 Illegality	165
Clause 10.2 Illegality in relation to Issuing Bank	166
Clause 10.3 Change of control	167
Clause 10.4 Voluntary cancellation	168
Clause 10.5 Voluntary prepayment of Facility A Loans and Clause 10.6 Voluntary prepayment of Facility B Utilizations	169
Clause 10.7 Right of replacement or repayment and cancellation in relation to a single Lender or Issuing Bank	170
Clause 10.8 Restrictions	171
Costs of Utilization	173
Clause 11A: Rate Switch	173
Clause 11A.1 Switch to Compounded Reference Rate	173
Clause 11A.2 Delayed switch for existing Term Rate Loans	174
Clause 11: Interest	175

Contents   **xxvii**

Clause 11.1 Calculation of interest—Term Rate Loans and 11.2
Calculation of interest—Compounded Rate Loans   175
Clause 11.3 Payment of interest   176
Clause 11.4 Default interest   176
Clause 11.5 Notifications   178
Clause 12: Interest Periods   178
Clause 12.1 Selection of Interest Periods   178
Clause 12.2 Changes to Interest Periods   179
Clause 12.3 Non-business days   180
Clause 12.4 Consolidation and division of Facility A Loans   180
Clause 13: Changes to the Calculation of Interest   180
Clauses 13.1 and 13.2 Interest calculation if no Primary Term
Rate and Interest calculation if no RFR or Central Bank Rate   180
Clause 13.3 Market disruption and 13.4 Cost of funds   181
Clause 13.5 Break costs   184
Clause 14: Fees   184

Additional Payment Obligations   185
Clause 15: Tax Gross-Up and Indemnities Section 1—Introduction   185
1. Withholding tax   185
2. Double tax treaties   186
3. Gross-up   187
4. Categories of lenders   188
5. Double Tax Treaty Passport Scheme ('DTTP Scheme')   189
6. Documentation   190
Clause 15: Tax Gross-Up and Indemnities—Section 2—The Clause   190
Clause 15.1 Definitions   190
Clause 15.2 Tax gross-up   192
Clause 15.3 Tax indemnity   197
Clause 15.4 Tax credit   198
Clause 15.8 FATCA Information and 15.9 FATCA Deduction   199
Clause 16: Increased Costs—Section 1—Introduction   201
1. Who issues the Basel regulations?   201
2. What are the Basel Accords there for?   202
3. The Basel Accords   203
Clause 16: Increased Costs—Section 2—The Clause   206
Clause 16.1 Increased Costs   206
Clause 16.2 Increased Cost claims   209
Clause 16.3 Exceptions   209
Clause 17: Other Indemnities   210
Clause 17.1 Currency indemnity   210

xxviii   Contents

Clause 17.2 Other indemnities	210
Clause 18: Mitigation by the Lenders	211
Clause 19: Costs and Expenses	211

Guarantee, Representations, Undertakings and Events of Default

Guarantee	**215**
Clause 20: Guarantee and Indemnity	215
Clause 20.1 Guarantee and indemnity	215
Clause 20.2 Continuing guarantee	217
Clause 20.3 Reinstatement	217
Clause 20.4 Waiver of defences	218
Clause 20.5 Immediate recourse	221
Clause 20.6 Appropriations	221
Clause 20.7 Deferral of Guarantors' rights	222
Representations, Undertakings and Events of Default	**227**
Clause 21: Representations—Section 1—An Introduction	227
1. Purpose	227
2. Repetition of Representations	231
3. Qualifications	236
Clause 21: Representations—Section 2—The LMA Representations	238
Clause 21.1 Status	239
Clause 21.2 Binding obligations	240
Clause 21.3 Non-conflict with other obligations	242
Clause 21.4 Power and authority	243
Clause 21.5 Validity and admissibility in evidence	244
Clause 21.6 Governing law and enforcement	245
Clause 21.7 Deduction of Tax	246
Clause 21.8 No filing or stamp taxes	247
Clause 21.9 No default	247
Clause 21.10 No misleading information	249
Clause 21.11 Financial statements	250
Clause 21.12 Pari passu ranking	251
Clause 21.13 No proceedings	255
Clause 21.14 Repetition	257
Possible Additional Representations	258
Clauses 22–24: Undertakings—An Introduction	259
1. Purpose	259
2. Shadow Directors	260

3. Qualifications	261
4. Cumulative Nature	263
Clause 22: Information Undertakings	265
Clause 22.1 Financial statements	265
Clause 22.2 Compliance Certificate	266
Clause 22.3 Requirements as to financial statements	266
Clause 22.4 Information: miscellaneous	268
Clause 22.5 Notification of default	269
Clause 22.6 Direct electronic delivery by company	270
Clause 22.7 'Know Your Customer' checks	270
Clause 23: Financial Covenants	271
1. Purpose	271
2. Which aspects of the borrower's financial condition should be tested?	271
3. At which level of the Group should the tests be run?	278
4. In respect of what periods should the tests be run?	279
5. What should the consequences of breach of a ratio be?	280
6. Can a breach be cured?	281
7. How should the words used in the tests be defined?	282
Clause 24: General Undertakings—Section 1—The LMA Undertakings	287
Clause 24.1 Authorizations	288
Clause 24.2 Compliance with laws	289
Clause 24.3 Negative pledge	290
Clause 24.5 Merger	308
Clause 24.6 Change of business	308
Clause 24: General Undertakings—Section 2—Other Common Undertakings	309
1. Authorizations and Compliance with Laws	310
2. Restrictions on business focus	311
3. Restrictions on dealing with assets and security	311
4. Restrictions on movements of cash—cash out	312
5. Restrictions on movement of cash—cash in	313
6. Information	313
7. Granting powers to others.	314
8. Reflecting regulatory or legal risks	314
9. Undertakings relating to assets given as security	315
10. Miscellaneous	317
Clause 25: Events of Default—Section 1—Introduction	319
1. Purpose	319

xxx   Contents

2. Objective versus subjective	320
3. Control over the relevant events	321
4. From Default to acceleration	321
Clause 25: Events of Default—Section 2—The LMA Events of Default	324
Clause 25.1 Non-payment	324
Clause 25.2 Financial covenants	325
Clause 25.3 Other obligations	325
Clause 25.4 Misrepresentation	326
Clause 25.5 Cross default	327
Clause 25.6 Insolvency	335
Clause 25.7 Insolvency proceedings	338
Clause 25.8 Creditors' process	339
Clause 25.9 Ownership of the Obligors	340
Other Events of Default	340
Clause 25.12 Material adverse change	341
Clause 25.13 Acceleration	349

Boilerplate and Schedules

Changes to Parties	355
Clause 26: Changes to the Lenders—Section 1—Methods of Transfer	355
1. Novation	357
2. Assignment	360
3. Sub-participation	363
4. Credit derivatives	364
Clause 26: Changes to the Lenders—Section 2—Transfers of Secured Loans	366
1. Security to a trustee for the covenant to pay	367
2. Security to an Agent	367
Clause 26: Changes to the Lenders—Section 3—The LMA Clause	371
Consent to transfers	371
Clause 26.1 Assignments and transfers by the lenders	375
Clause 26.2 Company consent	376
Clause 26.3 Other conditions of assignment or transfer	376
Clause 26.4 Assignment or transfer fee	378
Clause 26.5 Limitation of responsibility of existing lenders	378
Clause 26.6 Procedure for transfer	378
Clause 26.7 Procedure for assignment	379

Clause 26.8 Copy of Transfer Certificate, Assignment Agreement or Increase Confirmation to Company	379
Clause 26.9 Security over lenders' rights	379
Clause 26.10 Pro rata interest settlement	380
Clause 27: Changes to the Obligors	380
Clause 27.1 Assignments and transfers by Obligors	380
Clause 27.2 Additional Borrowers	380
Clause 27.3 Resignation of a Borrower	382
Clause 27.4 Additional Guarantors	382
Clause 27.5 Repetition of representations	382
Clause 27.6 Resignation of a Guarantor	382

The Finance Parties — 383

Clause 28: Role of the Agent, the Arranger and the Issuing Bank	383
Clause 28.1 Appointment of the Agent	385
Clause 28.2 Instructions	385
Clause 28.3 Duties of the Agent	386
Clause 28.4 Role of Arranger	387
Clause 28.5 No fiduciary duties	387
Clause 28.6 Business with the Group	387
Clause 28.7 Rights and discretions	388
Clause 28.8 Responsibility for documentation	388
Clause 28.9 No duty to monitor	389
Clause 28.10 Exclusion of liability	389
Clause 28.11 Lenders' indemnity to the Agent	389
Clause 28.12 Resignation of the Agent	390
Clause 28.13 Confidentiality	390
Clause 28.14 Relationship with the Lenders	391
Clause 28.15 Credit appraisal by Lenders and Issuing Bank	391
Clause 28.16 Agent's management time	391
Optional provisions dealing with amounts paid in error	392
Lehman Provisions and the Agent	392
Clause 29: Conduct of Business by the Finance Parties	393
Clause 30: Sharing among the Finance Parties	393
Clause 30.1 Payments to Finance Parties and Clause 30.2 Redistribution of payments	393
Clause 30.3 Recovering Finance Party's rights	394
Clause 30.4 Reversal of redistribution	395
Clause 30.5 Exceptions	395

Administration — 397

xxxii Contents

Clause 31: Payment Mechanics	397
Clause 31.1 Payments to the Agent	397
Clause 31.2 Distributions by the Agent	398
Clause 31.3 Distribution to an Obligor	398
Clause 31.4 Clawback and pre-funding	398
Clause 31.5 Partial payments	399
Clause 31.6 No set off by Obligors	400
Clause 31.8 Currency of account	400
Clause 31.9 Change of currency	400
Clause 31.10 Disruption to payment systems, etc.	400
Clause 32: Set Off	401
Clause 33: Notices	401
Clause 34: Calculations and Certificates	402
Clause 34.1 Accounts	402
Clause 34.2 Certificates and determinations	402
Clause 34.3 Day count convention and interest calculation	403
Clause 35: Partial Invalidity	403
Clause 36: Remedies and Waivers	404
Clause 37: Amendments and Waivers	405
Clause 38: Confidential Information	408
Clause 39: Confidentiality of Funding Rates	410
Clause 40: Bail-In	410
Clause 41: Counterparts	411
Governing Law and Enforcement	413
Clause 42: Governing Law	413
Clause 43: Enforcement	414
Clause 43.1: Jurisdiction	414
Clause 43.2: Service of process	416
Schedules	419
Schedule 1: The Original Parties	419
Schedule 2: Conditions Precedent	419
Part I Conditions precedent to initial utilization	419
Part II Conditions precedent to additional Obligors	422
Schedule 3: Requests	425
Part 1—Utilization Request	426
Part 2—Selection Notice	426
Schedule 4: Form of Transfer Certificate	426
Schedule 5: Form of Assignment Agreement	427
Schedule 6: Form of Accession Letter	427

Schedule 7: Form of Resignation Letter	427
Schedule 8: Form of Compliance Certificate	428
Schedule 9: Existing Security	428
Schedule 10: LMA Form of Confidentiality Undertaking	428
Schedule 11: Timetables	429
Schedule 12: Form of Increase Confirmation	429
Schedule 13: Form of Letter of Credit	429
Schedule 14: Reference Rate Terms	429
1. Schedule for Compounded Rate Loans	430
2. Schedule for Term Rate Loans	435
Schedule 15: Daily Non-Cumulative Compounded RFR Rate	438
1. Principles of the calculation of the interest rate attributable to a given day	439
2. The formula for calculating the Annualised Cumulative Compounded Daily Rate	441
3. Deconstructing the formula and explaining its constituent parts	442
Schedule 16: Cumulative Compounded RFR Rate	445
Schedule 17: Legal Opinions	446
Schedule 17: Legal Opinions—Section 1—Introduction	447
1. Types of opinion	447
2. Limits on scope of opinion	447
3. Locations of opinions	449
4. Which lawyers?	450
Schedule 17: Legal Opinions—Section 2: Form of Opinion	451
1. Introduction	452
2. Assumptions	452
3. Opinions	453
4. Qualifications	462
Appendix 1: Some English Law Concepts	467
Glossary of Terms	507
Index	541

Introduction

General Introduction

1. How to use this book

0.001

A word of caution is necessary at the outset. This book seeks to give readers the tools to enable them to negotiate loan agreements efficiently (i.e. with minimum expense in terms of time and money) and effectively (i.e. to result in a document which closely suits their corporate needs, whether they are borrowers or lenders). For this book to succeed in its aim it must be used appropriately—that is, as an aid to, and not as a substitute for, proper understanding of the commercial position of the parties. Readers need to keep in mind that loan agreements are used in widely differing commercial situations.

0.002

Some examples (among the numerous possibilities) are:

* secured loans made to start-up companies owned by entrepreneurs;
* structured loans to special purpose companies, designed to achieve a particular tax effect or for the purpose of a particular project;
* loans to **investment grade** corporates designed to provide them with **liquidity**.

© The Author(s), under exclusive license to Springer Nature
Switzerland AG 2024
S. Wright, *The International Loan Documentation Handbook*, Global Financial Markets,
https://doi.org/10.1007/978-3-031-38489-9_1

2   Introduction

0.003

The basic precedent for all these situations will be remarkably similar, but the changes to that precedent which are appropriate in each case will vary enormously. Comments which are made in this book will only be appropriate in some (usually a minority) of the circumstances in which a loan agreement will be used. One size does not fit all. Moreover, there will be many comments which ought to be made in specific transactions which are not made in this book. The comments included are not intended to be (nor can they be) exhaustive. The comments in the book are intended to give the reader a better understanding of what the loan agreement does and does not say, and to provide readers with a full set of tools with which to ensure that the final agreement meets their commercial objectives.

0.004

However, the most important commercial objective of the parties to a loan transaction is to reach an agreement on the documents quickly (time is money) and in a way which gives all involved confidence in their ongoing relationship (and does not result in disproportionate legal fees). If this is to be achieved, parties must identify the points they wish to make with care, and only make comments which are commercially significant in the context of the particular transaction. Failure to do this will backfire as the **counterparty** will quickly lose patience, probably resulting in a negotiation which fails to achieve the parties' real commercial objectives.

0.005

Readers are therefore urged to ensure that they do not lose sight of the ultimate commercial objectives, and that they use this book only as an aid to better understanding of the agreements, not as a 'checklist' of comments—a purpose for which this book was not designed and is not appropriate.

0.006

This book is structured around loan agreements published by the Loan Market Association ('LMA')[1] as the starting point for its discussions. In general, discussions in this book are based on the LMA Multicurrency Term and Revolving Facilities Agreement incorporating Term SOFR for use in Investment Grade transactions, available to LMA members via www.lma.eu. com (the 'LMA Compounded/Term Rate Loan'), which also includes provisions for drawing the revolving credit by letters of credit. The book follows

---

[1] The Loan Market Association was established in 1996 as a forum for dealing with issues relating to the syndicated loan market. It was established to promote the trading of interests in loans.

the structure and numbering of the LMA Compounded/Term Rate Loan and references to clause numbers in this book are, unless otherwise stated, to clauses in LMA Compounded/Term Rate Loan.

While the Loan Market Association ('LMA') has consented to the quotation of, and referral to, parts of its documents for the purpose of this publication, it assumes no responsibility for any use to which its documents, or any extract from them, may be put. The views and options expressed in the publication are the views of the author and do not necessarily represent those of the LMA. Furthermore, the LMA cannot accept any responsibility or liability for any error or omission. ©2023 Loan Market Association. All rights reserved.

0.007

> The text also comments on situations and documents which differ from LMA Compounded/Term Rate Loan. Such comments are marked by an outline as indicated here.

2. What should I be looking for in this loan agreement? Why does it have to be so long?

0.008
This Introduction sets the scene for the discussion of the loan agreement by

- describing the main categories of loans (in Sect. 1 in 0.009);
- providing an overview of the loan agreement (in Sect. 2 in 0.037);
- looking at **risk free rates** (in Sect. 3 in 0.091);
- explaining the documentary complexity which results from the use of backward looking risk free rates and providing a roadmap for understanding those provisions (in Sect. 4 in 0.111);
- discussing the scope of the agreement, including who can be affected by it, and whose activities can have an effect under it (in Sect. 5 in 0.142);
- highlighting (in Sect. 6 in 0.179) common 'non standard provisions', which are commonly addressed in loan documentation but which, for various reasons, are not included in the standard LMA Compounded/Term Rate Loan including

4   Introduction

- sanctions provisions
- consequences (such as **bail-in clauses**) of special resolution procedures for systemically important lenders
- provisions (such as **accordions**) providing for loan flexibility
- provisions dealing with borrowers purchasing in the **secondary market**
- provisions for dealing with defaulting lenders;

- looking at the commodification and digitization of debt (in Sect. 7 in 0.227), including the influence of non-bank lenders and **credit derivatives**;
- providing a brief overview of asset, project and acquisition (or 'leveraged') finance (in Sect. 8 in 0.250);
- describing (in Sect. 9 in 0.286) various commercial arrangements which, while not amounting to borrowing or giving **security** in a legal sense, amount to the commercial equivalent and therefore have to be treated in a similar manner for the purposes of the loan agreement; and
- discussing environmental, social and governance linked loans ('**ESG lending**') including **green loans** and **sustainability linked loans** (in Sect. 10 in 0.312).

Section 1: Principal Types of Loans

0.009
Loans can be classified with reference to a number of characteristics. The principal categories are discussed here.

1. Classification on the basis of availability

0.010
Perhaps the main characteristic for categorizing loans is the issue of availability.

Term loan

0.011

A term loan is a loan which is made available to the borrower on the basis that it will be repaid by specified instalments over a set period of time. Once repaid it cannot be redrawn. It is generally used for a specific financing requirement such as an **asset** purchase. It is a long-term debt on the borrower's balance sheet.

Demand loan

0.012

A **facility** which the lenders make available but which the lenders are able to cancel or require repayment of at any time (or 'on demand') may be called an 'uncommitted facility' (because the lenders are not committed to maintain its availability) or a 'demand facility'. Facilities of this type do not require lengthy documentation as there is no need for **undertakings** or **Events of Default**, the lenders being free to terminate the facility at will. The lack of a commitment by the lenders is clearly a significant disadvantage to a borrower.

Overdraft facility

0.013

An overdraft facility is a facility that the borrower may draw on, repay and then draw on again. This is as distinct from a term loan which, once the borrower has repaid, cannot be reborrowed. An overdraft facility is used for situations where the borrower has fluctuating financing requirements (e.g. for **working capital**). By having the ability to repay and reborrow, the borrower is able to ensure that levels of borrowing at any time do not exceed the financial requirements of the borrower at that time. An overdraft facility may be committed or uncommitted. In a **committed facility**, the lenders would commit to lend up to a specified sum for a given period, for example, 12 months. The borrower could draw up to the limit at any time, repay as it wished and have the comfort of being able to draw again, up to the limit,

6   Introduction

at any time within the committed period.[2] If the facility is uncommitted or if the period of the commitment is short then the facility will be a **current liability** on the borrower's balance sheet, with the implications which that carries for the borrower's liquidity. Given its short-term (and in some cases, uncommitted) nature, lengthy documentation will not be required.

Revolving credit

0.014
A **revolving credit** is a committed facility which operates in a similar way to an overdraft (in that it may be repaid and reborrowed) but is of longer term and is fully committed. It is a long-term debt on the borrower's balance sheet. The documentation will be very similar to that for a term loan. The maximum amount available may remain the same throughout the facility period or it may reduce over time.

2. Classification on the basis of the lenders' credit decision

0.015
The second key characteristic of a loan is the question of the type of credit risk which the loan represents for the lenders. That is, what are they relying on in their assessment of the borrower's ability to repay the loan? Borrowers repay loans either by selling assets; by using income generated from a particular asset or project; or out of their general corporate resources. While this is a very broad generalization, these are the distinctions which underlie the classification of loans as 'corporate finance', '**asset finance**' and '**project finance**'.

---

[2] However, the borrower will need to pay a commitment fee to the lenders for any part of the facility which the borrower is not using at any time, and which the lenders remain committed to lend.

Corporate finance

0.016

A corporate finance transaction (when the expression is used in this context, not in its wider meaning which encompasses corporate financings based on the **capital markets**) is one in which there is neither a specific asset nor a specific stream of income on which the lenders' credit decision is based, but rather they are relying on the general financial position of the borrower. This is also known as '**balance sheet lending**'.

Asset finance

0.017

An asset finance transaction is one in which the future value of the asset concerned is a key factor in the lenders' credit risk. This, of course, has major implications for the security and the documentation, as discussed in Sect. 8 of this Introduction from 0.250 onwards.

Project finance

0.018

A **project finance** transaction is one in which the income generated by the project which is being financed is a key factor in the lenders' credit decision. It is described in more detail in Sect. 8 of this Introduction in 0.262.

0.019

In the context of asset and project financing, it should be noted that the lenders are often taking a mixture of asset risk, project risk and corporate risk. For example, lenders providing ship finance (which is regarded as asset finance) will not only assess the future value of the ship, they will often also look at the operator's balance sheet and financial ratios and at the likely income which the ship will generate. In other words, the lenders will take asset, project and corporate risk within a facility which is traditionally regarded as an asset finance transaction.

8   Introduction

Limited recourse financing

0.020
Some transactions (most commonly project finance) are put together on a '**limited recourse**' basis. This involves the lenders accepting that they will only be repaid out of specified assets. This may be done by having a contractual limitation on recourse (see Box 0.1).

> **Box 0.1**
> Under a contractual limitation on recourse, the lenders agree with the borrower only to pursue certain assets, such as income from the project in question, and that if the income in question is insufficient, the lenders will suffer a loss and will not be able to claim further repayment from the borrower.

0.021
Alternatively, and more commonly, it may be done structurally, by establishing a special purpose entity which will only own the assets (e.g. project assets and income) to which the lenders are intended to have recourse, with the lenders lending to that entity.

3. Classification on the basis of the purpose of the loan

0.022
The third major attribute of a loan for classification purposes is the question of its purpose. While there are as many purposes as there are borrowers those purposes fall into categories which are commonly used to describe loans.

Acquisition (or 'Leveraged') finance

0.023
Acquisition finance or leveraged finance is finance used to acquire a company. It has become a highly active market, particularly attractive to **hedge funds**. The financing arrangements are highly structured with a

Section 1: Principal Types of Loans 9

number of different tiers of lending and the relationship between the tiers regulated by an **intercreditor agreement**. The LMA produces template documents for the loan (which is referred to in this book as the 'Leveraged LMA') and for the intercreditor agreement.

Bridge finance

0.024

Bridge finance is finance made available to bridge a gap. For example, a company may require financing for a corporate acquisition. It may intend to raise the bulk of that finance through issuing bonds on the capital markets but need interim finance to cover the period during which circulars are issued to the public, etc. A bridge finance loan (which is usually high margin, short-term debt provided by the relationship bank) could bridge the gap.

Mezzanine finance or venture capital

0.025

Mezzanine finance or **venture capital** is finance used where traditional finance is not available in sufficient amounts to meet the borrower's needs. Generally, companies meet their financing requirements by a mixture of debt (borrowing from third parties) and equity (the company's own money, either as invested by shareholders or as profits which would otherwise be available to shareholders). Where the level of debt is high compared to the amount of equity, the company is described as 'highly **leveraged**' or 'highly geared'.[3] Where equity plus the amounts available from traditional lenders will be insufficient to meet the need, borrowers may approach mezzanine financiers to make up the difference. These financiers specialize in providing funds for a particular project, such as a major acquisition, which supplement moneys available from traditional lenders for that project. The finance they provide will be subordinate to the traditional loan. It will carry more risk and therefore the **Margin** will be higher. Often the mezzanine financier will also require some form of '**equity kicker**'—that is, in addition to the Margin they

---

[3] Hence the description of acquisition finance as 'leveraged' finance. There may be a 'senior' facility and a mezzanine facility or the financing may consist of a mixture of loan finance and capital markets finance.

10   Introduction

will require a share in any profits from the transaction. The finance may be provided by way of **subordinated debt** or by way of **preference shares**.

Refinancing

0.026
Refinancing is finance made available to repay existing debt. This may be done to achieve less onerous undertakings or more favourable Margins; to reflect new corporate structures; to increase leverage; as part of a restructuring following a default; or for numerous other reasons.

Mismatch facilities

0.027
These are facilities which seek to match the difference between what is available to a borrower from a given source and what the borrower needs. For example, in a **securitization** a borrower may require a mismatch facility to bridge the gap between dates of payment of **receivables** and due dates on **commercial paper** issued.

Swingline facilities

0.028
Swingline facilities are facilities which are available to meet short-term liquidity needs (such as to replace funds which, but for a market disruption, would have been available to a borrower by the issue of commercial paper). They will be available with minimum (same day) notice and only to cover short-term needs. They often have a maximum period for **advances** to be outstanding of 3–5 days.

Trade finance

0.029
Trade finance is the financing of the manufacturing and selling process and of international trade generally. It usually takes the form of short-term

or revolving facilities secured on inventory and/ or receivables. There are many different structures including **borrowing base finance; export finance; inventory finance and receivables financing**.

4. Classification on the basis of the number of lenders

Syndicated loans

0.030
Syndicated loans are made available by a number of lenders who all join together to make the loan. With the exception of certain fees, which are for the benefit of individual lenders in the syndicate, the basic principle[4] is that the lenders have equal rights (or rather, rights proportionate to the amount each has lent—i.e. **pro rata**) against the borrower under a single loan agreement.

Club loans

0.031
These are syndicated loans where there are few syndicate members. The lenders, who are called a **club** and who will participate in the loan, are known from the outset and there will be no need to market the facility to the wider banking community as with a large syndicate.

Bilateral facilities

0.032
Bilateral facilities are made by a single lender to a single borrower.

---

[4] Nevertheless it is common to have syndicated loans which involve numerous different facilities (revolving credit; term loan; ancillaries; etc.) or different tranches of facilities with different attributes (such as pricing and maturity) with different lenders participating in the different facilities or tranches. In these cases the various lenders will only have equal rights in relation to the particular facility or tranche which they are participating in.

12   Introduction

5. Miscellaneous categories

Sovereign debt

0.033
This is debt made available to a sovereign entity.

Export credit

0.034
Export credit is debt that is supported in some way (e.g. by some form of guarantee of payment) by a government in order to encourage exports from their country.

Acceptance credit facility

0.035
Under an **acceptance credit facility**, instead of the lenders agreeing to lend money to the borrower, they agree to accept[5] bills of exchange or letters of credit on behalf of the borrower. The terms of the facility document will be similar to the term loan with changes reflecting the mechanical differences in the forms of financial support.

PIK Financings

0.036
PIK financings are debts on which the borrower does not pay interest, but instead the interest is added to the **principal** amount of the debt. In other words, the interest is **capitalized**. The letters 'PIK' stand for payment in kind. There are many different types of **PIK** financings. They may have a '**toggle**' which means that the borrower has a choice—they can elect to pay interest or alternatively, choose to capitalize the interest, in which case the rate will be higher than if they elected for payment.

---

[5] In other words, to agree to make payment under.

Section 2: Loan Agreement Overview

0.037
The loan agreement is generally produced by the lenders' lawyer. Its purpose is to ensure that the lenders have all the rights and powers they require, bearing in mind that, at least in a simple, single drawdown, term loan, the lenders will have handed over a large sum of money and received in exchange, this document (plus perhaps security). Therefore, by custom, the lenders have what is a major negotiating advantage—the right to produce the first draft of the agreement.

1. The LMA recommended forms and exposure drafts

0.038
In London, LMA has produced a wide suite of recommended forms for different situations. These are now widely accepted as a common negotiating platform, albeit often with variations reflecting a law firm's own preferences.

0.039
The first LMA documents were introduced in 1999 with a number of aims, including, in particular, the aim of promoting efficiency in the original negotiation of the loan, and, subsequently, on its transfer, to facilitate review of the agreement by proposed investors. To a large extent, these documents have been very successful in their aims and it has become market practice to use the LMA documents as a basis for loan documentation in the London market and beyond.

0.040
The intention behind the drafting is that the recommended forms should be relatively even handed—not overly favourable to either borrowers or lenders—although the extent to which this has been achieved in any given form is a moot point. From time to time the Association of Corporate Treasurers publishes detailed commentary of issues for borrowers to look out for in specific examples of the recommended forms. These are available from the website of the Association of Corporate Treasurers at www.treasurers.org.

The transition to risk free rates (discussed in 0.091) was a hugely challenging task, not least in terms of crafting the appropriate documentation. The LMA served as a catalyst for the development of documentation by

14   Introduction

drafting numerous 'exposure drafts' of loan documentation for use with risk free rates, reflecting the recommendations of the various working parties tasked with leading the transition away from **Libor**. These 'exposure drafts' were different from the recommended forms in that they were designed to highlight the documentary issues and to help the market to coalesce around a favoured approach. Over time, as a market approach emerged, these exposure drafts were replaced by recommended forms although the documentation for risk free rates is still in its infancy and in some areas noted in this book, (such as **break costs**, market disruption and fallback provisions) a consistent market practice has yet to develop.

0.041

The LMA recognized, on launch of the recommended forms, that some provisions would need to be negotiated on a case-by-case basis. They therefore divided the loan into 'hard' and 'soft' provisions, with the soft provisions (**representations**, undertakings, financial covenants, Events of Default, transferability and **conditions** precedent) being put forward simply as a starting point, which would need negotiation on a case-by-case basis. The remainder of the agreement (the 'hard' provisions) was expected, in most cases, not to require adjustment.

0.042

A number of adjustments to the recommended form will need to be made in any given transaction, mostly in relation to the 'soft' provisions, but often also including adjustment to the 'hard' provisions.

0.043

- The documentation and use of risk free rates is in its infancy. Practice has yet to develop on topics such as **market disruption** and fallback options. Additionally, operational, procedural or regulatory developments can be expected as use of the rates increases. These developments may require adjustments to be made to the recommended forms.
- Some parts of the recommended form have been left blank as there is no standard market practice for these provisions. Such provisions need to be negotiated on a one-off basis. Examples are the financial covenants and the material adverse change clause.

Section 2: Loan Agreement Overview **15**

0.044

* If the loan is to be secured then a number of the provisions may be drawn more tightly than for the LMA Compounded/Term Rate Loan, which assumes an unsecured loan. The Leveraged LMA (designed for use in leveraged or acquisition finance) is often used as a prompt for the types of additional undertakings and Events of Default which may be needed for a secured loan, although this needs to be done with a significant degree of caution since many areas of the document are really not appropriate outside the leveraged market.[6]

0.045

* The document will need tailoring to reflect the credit decision—that is, additional representations, undertakings and Events of Default are likely to be necessary, reflecting specific concerns relating to the borrower's business. In particular, if the lenders are taking any project or asset risk in the transaction, substantial additions will be needed as discussed in Sect. 8 of this Introduction from 0.250 onwards.

0.046

* The lenders may have certain policy requirements, for example, as to transferability or sanctions which they wish to have incorporated.

0.047

* The borrower may have certain policy requirements, for example, as to agreeing cross acceleration clauses only, which they have agreed with the lenders.

0.048

* From time to time the LMA issues advice including optional riders to their recommended forms (such as the contractual recognition of bail-in clause following Brexit); which the parties may want to have incorporated.[7]

---

[6] An obvious example is the '**clean up period**' which gives the borrower a period of time after the loan is advanced (and the target company acquired) in which to comply with certain specified undertakings.

[7] See Sect. 6 of this Introduction in 0.179.

16   Introduction

0.049

- Other more detailed points may need to be adjusted as mentioned in the remainder of this book.

2. Loan agreement structure

Function of the clauses

0.050

Each provision of the agreement is of one of three types:

0.051

- first, there are the administrative provisions—dealing with calculation of interest, mechanics of advances, repayment, and the like[8];

0.052

- second are the information and business restriction provisions (see Box 0.2) such as representations, undertakings, and Events of Default[9];

0.053

- third, there are the boilerplate clauses dealing with important issues such as **indemnities**, notices, **jurisdiction**, and the relationship between the lenders (such as the agency clause).[10]

---

[8] In the LMA Compounded/Term Rate Loan, these provisions are in Clauses 1 (*Definitions and Interpretation*)–19 (*Costs and Expenses*).

[9] In the LMA Compounded/Term Rate Loan, these provisions are in Clauses 20 (*Guarantee and Indemnity*)–25 (*Events of Default*).

[10] In the LMA Compounded/Term Rate Loan, these provisions are in Clause 26 (*Changes to the Lenders*) to the end of the Agreement.

Section 2: Loan Agreement Overview   **17**

> **Box 0.2**
>
> Negotiation should usually focus on two areas of the agreement. First the business restriction provisions, since this is the part of the agreement which will have a significant ongoing effect on how the borrower conducts its business, and how much power the lenders can wield. The second key area is those parts of the administrative provisions under which the borrower may find that the ongoing cost of the loan is higher than expected. There are three areas of concern here: the interest rate fallback provisions; the increased costs clause; and the grossing up clause, all of which are discussed in some detail elsewhere.

Stages of the transaction

0.054

The business restriction provisions of the agreement seek to protect the lenders at three different stages of the transaction.

0.055

Before Drawing

First, the document protects the lenders before any money is lent, through those provisions which operate to release the lenders from their obligations to advance funds. At this stage, the lenders have three types of protection operating at the same time: the **due diligence** (which the lenders and their lawyer will conduct prior to signature of the loan agreement), the borrower's representations (in Clause 21 (*Representations*) and discussed in 8.001–8.074), and the conditions precedent (in Clause 4 (*Conditions of Utilization*) and discussed in 2.016–2.029) (see Box 0.3).

> **Box 0.3**
>
> In other words, the borrower is being asked to state that certain facts are true (in the representations), to prove that they are true (in the conditions precedent), and the lenders are also checking that they are true (in the due diligence).

18 **Introduction**

0.056

This triple layer of protection is designed to minimize the risk of error. As a practical issue it means that the conditions precedent, representations and legal opinions duplicate each other to a large extent, so that if adjustments are made to one area in a loan agreement, it will often be necessary to make corresponding adjustments to the other areas.

0.057

After Drawing

Second, the document protects the lenders after the money has been lent and while it is outstanding. This is the remit of the undertakings (or **covenants**). Their role is to ensure that the status quo (or something near to that) is maintained during the life of the loan and that the lenders are given the information they need (see Box 0.4).

Box 0.4

Except in limited recourse transactions such as some project finance, it makes little difference whether any particular issue is dealt with as an undertaking or as an Event of Default (in some cases, only after a **grace period** expires) since a breach of undertaking is an Event of Default. The tradition is to include as undertakings those things which the borrower can promise (e.g. not to grant security) and as Events of Default those which it cannot (e.g. material adverse change).

0.058

Termination

Third, the document sets out the circumstances which the lenders regard as changing the position so completely that they require the right to be repaid immediately. These are the Events of Default[11]—which give the lenders the right to accelerate the loan. In practice, often the result of an Event of Default

---

[11] Or compulsory prepayment events—see Clause 10.3 (*PREPAYMENT AND CANCELLATION: Change of Control*) in 4.011.

Section 2: Loan Agreement Overview **19**

is a renegotiation not an **acceleration**, but it is the existence of the right to accelerate which gives the lenders the necessary leverage to renegotiate.

3. Key concerns

Borrower's concerns

A borrower's key concerns in reviewing the documents are:

Control

0.059

* to what extent do they remain free to conduct their business as they see fit and to what extent do they require consent for their activities?

0.060

* if they need consent (see Box 0.5) for some acts—what level of consent is needed (e.g. Majority Lenders' consent or unanimous consent of all lenders) and might any requirement for consent impose unacceptable delays in their action (e.g. do they need freedom to act if there is no response to a request within a specified period of days)?

Box 0.5

At some point in the negotiations, the lender may make the point that the borrower should not be too concerned about giving the lenders rights to object to certain things, because the lenders will only use their rights when it is sensible to do so. Nevertheless, borrowers should treat this argument with caution and seek to negotiate an agreement which will enable them to conduct their business with minimum need to make requests for consents or waivers because

* requests for consent will involve the borrowers spending time and money (and, in some cases, the lenders charge a fee for consents);
* if consent is required, the lenders may take the opportunity to raise other issues of concern to them and link those to the issue of consent;

20   Introduction

> - there may be a change in personnel or policies at the lenders' office which may result in a different approach to the granting of waivers and consents;
> - wherever the lenders have the right to accelerate their loan then other lenders will have the same right under their **cross default** clauses.

0.061

- How easy will it be to get consent and does the agreement give them any flexibility to deal with the situation if they have difficulties getting the required level of consent? Hence the '**Snooze you lose**' and '**Yank the bank**' provisions discussed in Box 11.6 and 4.023.

0.062

- what companies within their group are restricted?[12]

Certainty of Funds

0.063

- in what circumstances might the loan cease to be available? This includes not only the undertakings and Events of Default but also the possibility of the lenders defaulting on their obligations[13];

0.064

- are all the Events of Default within the borrower's control (e.g. change of ownership of the borrower[14])?

0.065

- are all the Events of Default objectively tested or are some matters of opinion, and, if so, by what standards can an opinion be tested? For

---

[12] See discussion on the scope of the agreement in 0.142.

[13] See 0.204 for 'Lehman' or '**Defaulting Lender**' provisions.

[14] See discussion of Clause 10.3 (*PREPAYMENT AND CANCELLATION: Change of Control*) in 4.011 and see also the discussion of Clause 25 (*Events of Default*) in 8.222.

example, is the Event of Default limited by concepts of materiality or reasonableness?[15]

0.066

* should some of the events which are expressed to be Events of Default more properly result in a change in Margin rather than a right to accelerate, for example, minor breach of a financial ratio?[16]

Flexibility

0.067
How robust is the loan agreement in terms of giving the borrower flexibility to respond to changing circumstances such as Brexit, Covid and the war in Ukraine, and to adapt its business model accordingly? For example,

0.068

* how much headroom is there in the financial covenants?

0.069

* Do the financial covenants allow occasional breaches to deal with unusual market conditions?

0.070

* Is there flexibility in terms of maturity dates and loan amounts via extension options and accordions, so as to help bolster liquidity quickly if needed[17]?

---

[15] See the discussion of Clause 25 (*Events of Default*) in 8.223.
[16] See discussion of Clause 23 (*Financial Covenants*) in 8.122.
[17] As discussed in 0.197.

22   Introduction

0.071

- Is there flexibility to enter into **hedging** arrangements to protect against price movements?

0.072

- Are caps on **baskets** and the like fixed in amount or flexible either with reference to the company's results (such as **EBITDA**) or a price index, so as to protect against inflation erosion?

Pricing

0.073

In what circumstances will the ongoing cost of the loan be different to what was expected? The borrower will want to focus on the increased cost clause, the interest rate fallback provisions and the grossing up clause; and

Scope

0.074

- The scope of the agreement—as discussed in Sect. 5 of this Introduction in 0.142.

Lenders' concerns

0.075

Lenders' key concerns in reviewing the agreement are:

0.076

● equality with other creditors—if things go wrong, this lender wants to be in the driving seat. This is one of the reasons for the **pari passu** clause,[18] the **negative pledge**[19] and the cross default clause[20] in an unsecured facility:

0.077

● ensuring they are provided with sufficient information, in good time[21];

0.078

● protection of their profit (by the ability to pass on changes in costs such as changes in regulatory cost[22];

0.079

● certainty as to the effect of the agreement (hence the importance of the choice of law and jurisdiction clauses[23]);

0.080

● ability to withdraw (i.e. right to accelerate) if there is a change in circumstances which may affect the lenders' view of the credit risk involved[24];

0.081

● maintenance of the borrower's assets and income—hence financial ratios and asset or project specific covenants;

---

[18] Clause 21.12 (*REPRESENTATIONS: Pari passu ranking*) of the LMA Compounded/Term Rate Loan discussed in 8.052.

[19] Clause 24.3 (*GENERAL UNDERTAKINGS: Negative pledge*) of the LMA Compounded/Term Rate Loan discussed in 8.140.

[20] Clause 25.5 (*EVENTS OF DEFAULT: Cross default*) of the LMA Compounded/Term Rate Loan discussed in 8.238.

[21] Financial ratios and Clause 22 (*Information undertakings*) of the LMA Compounded/Term Rate Loan discussed from 8.081 to 8.100.

[22] Clause 16 ((*Increased costs*) of the LMA Compounded/Term Rate Loan discussed in 6.044.

[23] Clauses 42 (*Governing law*) and 43 (*Enforcement*) of the LMA Compounded/Term Rate Loan discussed in 12.001–12.007.

[24] Clause 25 (*Events of Default*) of the LMA Compounded/Term Rate Loan discussed in 8.222.

24   Introduction

0.082

* reputational, regulatory and political issues, including any policy requirements as to sustainability or green principles; the risk of imposition of exchange control regulations and risks of breaching sanctions, anti-corruption, money laundering or similar regulations or expectations.

0.083

* Syndicate democracy and the power of different groups of lenders.[25]

4. Hazards in reviewing a loan agreement

0.084

Five principal difficulties arise in reviewing a loan agreement, which are worth highlighting here. These are the difficulty of spotting what is not there; the potential for conflict between different parts of the agreement; the significance of the precise wording of the definitions; appreciating the impact of Repeating Representations; and the difficulty of negotiating a document which is presented as being a market standard. These issues are discussed in turn in the following paragraphs.

Spotting what is not there

0.085

It is easy to see and comment on what is there, but harder to spot what is not there. In order to see the wood for the trees it is often helpful to summarize the key issues before reading the draft agreement. This will help the reader to spot what is not there and minimize the risk of being drawn into making minor comments on what is there while failing to spot the bigger picture.

---

[25] Clause 37 (*Amendments and Waivers*) of the LMA Compounded/Term Rate Loan discussed in 11.025.

Potential conflict between provisions

0.086

Potential conflicts arise because, as discussed in 0.054–0.058, the agreement protects the lenders at three different stages.[26] Any particular issue is therefore touched on in a number of different places in the agreement, some of which may conflict with others (see Box 0.6).

> **Box 0.6**
>
> For example, to find out in what circumstances litigation against the borrower can impact on the loan, it will be necessary to look at the representations, conditions precedent, repeating representations, undertakings and the Events of Default.

0.087

It is therefore sensible, as well as reading the agreement from start to finish, to check, in relation to each key issue, how it is dealt with at each point of the agreement (conditions precedent, representations, repeating representations, undertakings and Events of Default) to get a complete picture and also to ensure that any conflicts between the provisions are ironed out. This is worth doing on later drafts as well as initially, because changes negotiated in one area of the document are often inadvertently missed in corresponding parts of the agreement.

Definitions

0.088

Loan agreements contain detailed definitions. There are a number of reasons for this. One reason is to keep the complexities out of the body of the agreement. Another is to avoid ambiguity. The difficulty for the reader is that it is hard to comment on (or to fully appreciate the implications of) any particular definition out of context. It is sensible to start reviewing any loan agreement, not at the definitions, but, instead, at the operative clauses (those which operate to actually do something as opposed to the definitions clause

---

[26] The provisions of the representations and conditions precedent, and the wording of any attached legal opinion, are also inter-related.

26   Introduction

which simply describes things). When a defined term (usually signified by capital letters, but see 1.004) is encountered, return to review its definition. This will make it easier to appreciate the detail of the definition.

Repeating Representations

0.089

A final word of caution relates to the Repeating Representations. As we will see when we discuss the representations (8.001 onwards), certain representations may be repeated during the life of the loan. After full **drawdown** on a term loan, the result of this is that, if a Repeating Representation becomes untrue, the lenders will be entitled to accelerate the loan. The same result would have been achieved by phrasing the issue as an undertaking (if it is something which the borrower can promise) or an Event of Default (if not). By using a Repeating Representation instead, the possibility of conflict between different parts of the document has been increased.[27]

Market practice

0.090

It can be difficult to negotiate a document which is presented as a market standard, particularly where lenders feel that suggested changes may hinder syndication, as this is not something which can readily be tested by the borrower. Similarly, borrowers will not wish to waste time, money and goodwill trying to achieve something which the lenders regard as non-negotiable. The best protection against this is to use lawyers who are active in the market and who know what can be achieved and what cannot. Nevertheless, regardless of whether any provision is market standard or not, borrowers need to ensure that they are happy with what the clause says and not accept risks simply because other borrowers have agreed to accept those risks. After all, not all borrowers have the same commercial constraints—there may be reasons why other borrowers found the risk acceptable which might not apply to this one.

---

[27] See further Sect. 1 of the commentary on Clause 21 (*Representations*) in 8.001.

Section 3: Risk Free Rates

1. What replaced Libor and why?

0.091

From the 1960s when **eurocurrency**[28] lending started, until 2022, the vast majority of international floating rate loans charged interest on the basis of Libor (representing the lenders' cost of funds) plus a Margin (representing the lenders' profit from the loan), although exactly what was meant by Libor changed during that period (see Box 0.7).

Box 0.7

When eurocurrency lending started, Libor was, for each lender, the price which it paid to borrow an amount equal to their participation in the loan in the wholesale money markets. So the loan was made on a true 'cost plus' basis—Libor was the lender's funding costs and the Margin was its profit. In 1986 the British Bankers' Association published the first official Libor rates (commonly referred to as **'BBA Libor'** or the 'screen rate'). The rates were based on estimates from a group of prime banks as to what rate they would have to pay to borrow in the wholesale markets. The intention was to set a benchmark rate—the rate obtainable by prime banks. From then on the vast majority of international loan agreements defined Libor as meaning these 'screen rates'. From that point onwards, Libor was simply a proxy for the lenders' funding costs—which might be more or less than the screen rate.

0.092

The problems inherent in this system started to become apparent when, in 2007, Barclays alerted US regulators that it believed that other banks had been submitting dishonestly low interest rates for the purpose of the calculation of the screen rates. A global probe into interest rate manipulation followed in 2010, resulting in fines, resignations, sackings and criminal proceedings, but, more importantly for our purposes, also in regulation of benchmarks generally and a comprehensive review of Libor which eventually, in 2017, resulted in the decision to scrap the benchmark rate (see Box 0.8 for the situation in relation to Euribor). In announcing the decision, the Financial Conduct Authority in the UK explained that the inherent flaw in the

---

[28] 'Eurocurrency' is used here in its historical sense of meaning a currency being traded outside its home country. It does not necessarily involve Europe or Euros.

28   Introduction

screen rate of Libor was that it was based on expert opinions, not transactions, and that there were not enough transactions underpinning the rates. For example, for one Libor variant, there were only 16 trades in 2016.

Box 0.8

It is worth noticing that, at the time of writing, there are no plans to discontinue Euribor—the methodology of which has been made more robust to comply with relevant benchmark regulation. Loan documentation using Euribor should nevertheless have robust fallback provisions to deal with the possibility of Euribor being temporarily unavailable, discontinued or becoming unrepresentative of the market which it seeks to measure.

0.093

The hunt was on for an alternative to Libor. There were no easy options. What was needed was an internationally available market driven rate, rooted in real transactions and in a market with sufficient liquidity to mean that the rate was truly representative of market sentiment—unaffected by lack of liquidity. Working parties were established in the major economies to identify potential successors to Libor.

0.094

Central Bank rates were ruled out firstly because they are not internationally available (they are the rates at which central banks will lend to banks in the country of the central bank); and secondly because they are influenced by political factors (fighting inflation, etc.) rather than being purely market rates. Banks' base rates are inappropriate because those are internal rates set by the bank in question, rather than market driven rates.

0.095

The working parties hunting for a replacement for Libor quickly focused on the highly liquid markets for overnight transactions which have long existed for most highly traded currencies.[29] The working parties settled on these markets as having the necessary attributes (liquidity and transparency—the markets are active and the rates are based on transactions, not opinions) to form the basis of a satisfactory alternative to Libor. The rates charged in these

---

[29] Sonia—or Sterling Over Night Index Average—for Sterling; Sofr—or Secured Overnight Financing Rate—for Dollars; €STR or Euro Short Term Rates—for Euros (although this market is more recent than the others); Tona or Tokyo Overnight Average Rate—for Yen and Saron—or Swiss Average Rate Overnight—for Swiss Francs.

markets are referred to as risk free rates because they are overnight rates so, unlike Libor, do not include any element of pricing for taking longer-term credit risk.

0.096

However, these are all overnight rates, reflecting market sentiment of pricing where interest is paid immediately (i.e. daily). For loan markets interest will not be paid daily so these rates need to be converted into a rate which would be appropriate where interest is paid less frequently. In other words they need to take account of interest on unpaid interest—they need to be **compounded**. The various working groups leading the transition away from Libor therefore recommended use of backward looking compounded rates[30] based on risk free rates to replace Libor. This rate is referred to in the LMA documents as the 'Cumulative Compounded RFR Rate' for an Interest Period.[31]

2. Key issues when using rates based on risk free rates

Forward looking or backward looking rates?

0.097

The concept of backward looking rates, where the interest rate would not be known until the end of the Interest Period, was a major shift for market participants, both operationally and from a business planning perspective. There was much discussion of the need for forward looking rates, not least because, operationally, they involve much less disruption to systems than backward looking rates (see Box 0.9).

---

[30] The idea is that you effectively work out the annual rate of interest which would have achieved the same result as investing a unit of money every day for a given period of time and earning interest on it (plus on the interest accrued on it) each day at the relevant risk free rate for that day.

[31] Actually, as we shall see, the rate for an **Interest Period** is rarely used in the loan agreement and instead, the agreement works on the basis of a calculation of a rate of interest for each day. This is referred to as the **Daily Non-Cumulative Compounded RFR Rate** and is explained further in 0.123.

30 Introduction

> **Box 0.9**
>
> Operationally, forward looking rates are closer to Libor than backward looking ones, because, like Libor, they are set in advance, and apply to a period of time, so for example, dealing with loan sales in the middle of an Interest Period is a simple matter of apportioning the interest with reference to the number of days accrued. Switching from Libor to these rates would be straightforward from both an operational and a documentary point of view as the basic structure of how interest is charged is so similar to Libor. The same can certainly not be said for switching to backward looking rates, which, as we shall see, posed formidable challenges.

0.098

In 2021 regulators in the US formally approved the use of **CME Term Sofr**—which is a forward looking term rate published by the Chicago Mercantile Exchange and based on Sofr—the risk free rate for USD. This rate is based on pricing in the Sofr linked **derivatives** market. This rate is specifically approved for use in mainstream business loans. The approach with other currencies is different. Forward looking term rates based on risk free rates are published for Sterling and Yen. These rates are based on derivatives markets and expectations about future rates.[32] However, regulators are wary of simply re introducing one of the problems with Libor—basing pricing on markets which have a lack of liquidity or on opinions rather than transactions. Hence for Euros, as at the time of writing, no forward looking Euro term rate is published, but there are plans to publish such a rate as soon as there is sufficient liquidity in the derivatives market for Euro risk free rates. Regulators are encouraging activity in these markets; no doubt with a view to introducing forward looking Euro term rates based on risk free rates as soon as possible. UK regulators have emphasized the importance of using the most robust alternative to Libor for any given use case and have largely limited use of forward looking term Sonia to limited, niche, specialist products such as project finance and export finance of large capital projects.

---

[32] Other ways of using risk free rates to fix forward looking rates are sometimes suggested. For example, one option would be to simply take a rate for a particular day or period (e.g. last week) and charge that rate for a future period (e.g. next month). However clearly these options expose lenders to risks in times of market stress when rates may change quickly.

How to calculate the Cumulative Compounded RFR Rate?

0.099

One of the main difficulties in using the compounded, backward looking risk free rates is that, unlike with Libor, there is no simple data source to refer to, so the loan agreement cannot simply refer the reader to a particular page on a particular screen where the relevant interest rate will be published. The loan agreement needs to 'look under the bonnet' and explain exactly how the raw data of the daily risk free rates will be converted into the interest rate which will be charged. The formula for making this calculation is complex (see the discussion in 13.073). Three practical problems make it more complex still. These are

0.100

- The need to be able to calculate how much interest is attributable to any given day—so that, for example, a lender selling part way through an Interest Period can be paid the appropriate amount of interest without reference to risk free rates after the date of sale. In LMA documents the rate attributable to any given day is referred to as the 'Daily Non-Cumulative Compounded RFR Rate' and it is discussed in more detail in 0.123).[33]

0.101

- The fact that the borrower will need some notice of the amount of interest due some days before the date on which it falls due. This is the reason for the 'Lookback Period' and the concept of 'Observation Shift'.

Lookback Period and Observation Period

0.102

If the interest rate applicable to an Interest Period was calculated with reference to risk free rates during that period, the rate would not be known until

---

[33] Incidentally, you may wonder, if we are looking for a rate attributable to any given day, why we do not simply use the RFR rate for that day? Of course that would be incorrect as it would not include the effect of the compounding which happened prior to that day—the relevant RFR rate on any given day will apply to a larger amount of principal (and so yield more interest) than the amount of principal at the start of the Interest Period.

32   Introduction

the last day of the Interest Period, and would fall due on the same day as the rate became known, which is impractical. To deal with this, the concept of an '**Observation Period**' has been introduced. The Observation Period is of the same length as the Interest Period, but starts a few days before the Interest Period does and ends the same number of days before the Interest Period does. This number of days is referred to as the '**lag time**' or the '**lookback period**' and is the period allowed for administering and arranging the payment of interest (see Box 0.10).

Box 0.10

The formula for calculating the interest rate which is discussed in detail in 0.065 onwards uses this expression to give effect to this concept of a lookback period.

*"**Daily Ratei-LP** means, for any RFR Banking Day "i" .... the Daily Rate for the RFR Banking Day which is the Lookback Period prior to that RFR Banking Day "i";*

*"**Lookback Period**" means [5] RFR Banking Days"*

In other words, for the purpose of the calculation, you do not use the Daily Rate on any given RFR Banking Day (referred to as RFR Banking Day 'i'), but instead you use the rate from a number of RFR Banking Days prior to that date.

0.103

The length of the lookback period is one of the detailed issues which needs to be decided in drafting the interest provisions. The longer the lookback period the more potential there is for a mismatch between the interest rates applicable to the Observation Period and the Interest Period.

Observation Shift

0.104

This concept of an Observation Period gives rise to another question— whether to use **observation shift** or not (see Box 0.11).

Box 0.11

An issue arises as to what to do about the fact that there will be a different number of RFR Banking Days in the Observation Period from the number in the Interest Period. This matters because when calculating a compounded rate, you can only compound on days when the relevant underlying rate (Sonia, Sofr, etc.) is published. That is, you can only compound on RFR Banking Days. So the different number of RFR Banking Days in the two periods results in a different amount of compounding and so affects the final figure. So the decision has to be made—when calculating the compounded rate—whether to use the number of RFR Banking Days in the Observation Period (i.e. to do the calculation 'with Observation Shift') or not. In the UK the working party recommendation is not to use Observation Shift but market participants are free to make their own choices.

0.105

* The third point which adds to the complexity of the calculation of interest based on risk free rates is the question of negative interest rates. Lenders are likely to want to ensure that, if the relevant risk free rate is negative on any given day, there is a zero **floor** on the rate input into the calculation for that day.

0.106

The complexities of the Observation Period and the zero floor explain why at the time of writing there is no simple data source to use to refer to for the figure for the Cumulative Compounded RFR Rate for a given Interest Period. To calculate that figure you would need to decide.

* How long the lookback period is;
* Whether to use observation shift or not; and
* Whether to apply a zero floor only to the rate for the whole period or to apply it to the daily input rate, or perhaps to apply it to the aggregate of the daily input rate and some other number as discussed in the context of credit adjustment spreads in Box 0.12.

34 Introduction

Credit Adjustment Spreads

0.107

Risk free rates are lower than Libor because the risk free rates are overnight rates so do not include the same pricing for credit risk as Libor—which is a term rate.[34] So, when legacy transactions (i.e. transactions which started off with Libor-based interest) switched to risk free rates, in order to maintain the same value for the lenders (and avoid 'value transfer'), the Margin had to increase or an extra **'credit adjustment spread'** needed to be charged to make up for this difference. In legacy transactions, this number was calculated at around the time of the switch and then fixed at that number for the rest of the loan period. It is sometimes referred to as the 'Rate Switch CAS'. The amount of the spread is a subject for negotiation. Commonly, when compounded rates started being used, the spread used was the median historic difference between Libor and the relevant risk free rate over a five year period ending on 5 March 2021. However, from time to time the result was that the RFR rate plus the spread was higher than Libor, demonstrating that any credit adjustment spread can only be an approximation of what it is trying to measure.

0.108

You may come across another type of credit adjustment spread—the 'Baseline CAS'. Because compounded risk free rates are lower than Libor, in order to make the same profit as previously, lenders have to charge higher Margins. From a presentational point of view, some lenders might like to have a transparent method of enabling borrowers to compare like with like when comparing Margins under the new regime with those which were charged previously. To do this, some lenders may choose to use the concept of a 'Baseline CAS'[35]—being effectively the additional charge which the lender needs to make to compensate it for the historical difference between Libor and interest calculated on the new basis. The interest rate would then be specified to be the relevant risk free rate calculation, plus a credit adjustment spread to compensate for the historical differences between that rate and Libor, plus a Margin. Given the inherent difficulty in calculating any credit adjustment spread as discussed in 0.107, the majority of loans at the time of writing do not include a Baseline CAS.

---

[34] It is also worth noticing that the same is true for CME Term Sofr, so the same issues about credit adjustment spreads arise with that as with use of backward looking compounded rates.

[35] Or, in the context of CME Term Sofr, a Term Reference Rate CAS—see Box 0.17.

Section 3: Risk Free Rates 35

> **Box 0.12**
>
> Returning then to the question of a zero floor discussed in 0.105, the question arises as to how to deal with the different credit adjustment spreads in setting that zero floor. For a legacy loan transitioning from a Libor loan with a zero floor on Libor—the floor should apply to the aggregate of the compounded risk free rate and Rate Switch CAS so as to avoid value transfer. To achieve a similar result in a loan which is documented on the basis of risk free rates from the start is more difficult if the loan does not include a Baseline CAS (or a Term Reference Rate CAS, in the context of CME Term Sofr).

0.109

There are numerous other types of credit adjustment spread which you may come across as a result of the various fallback provisions in the loan agreement discussed in 0.132 onwards.

As is clear from experience with Libor—nothing can be assumed to last forever. So the loan agreement needs to deal with what happens if the relevant risk free rate ceases to exist or is simply unavailable on any given day. In other words, it needs some fallback provisions. Lenders may choose what rate is appropriate for a fallback rate—commonly a Central Bank Rate is chosen, sometimes a Term Rate Loan will have a fallback to an 'Alternative Term Rate' and sometimes to a compounded risk free rate. Sometimes there is an ultimate fallback to cost of funds as discussed in 0.134–0.138. In each of these cases there may be an adjustment designed to protect lenders against any difference between that fallback rate and the relevant risk free rate. See 0.130.

Relevance of cost of funds

0.110

Libor-based loans were presented as representing lenders' cost of funds plus a Margin representing their profit (a "cost plus" basis) and this is the rationale behind some of their provisions—notably those dealing with break costs and market disruption as discussed in Box 0.13. However given that risk free rates are not designed to reflect funding costs many market participants expect that these clauses will be abandoned going forward.

36   Introduction

Box 0.13

There are two provisions in Libor-based loans which arguably have no role to play in loans based on risk free rates. These are the provisions relating to break costs and market disruption.

Break Costs
The original rationale for break costs was that the lender was funding itself for specified Interest Periods and early payment exposed them to potential loss (if the interest rate which they could earn on the money they received early was less than the interest rate which they had committed to pay for the rest of the Interest Period). In practice of course lenders did not actually fund themselves in that way and the rationale for charging Break Costs was often debated. Where interest is based on compounded backward looking risk free rates there is no element of fixing of rates in advance for a specified period so the original justification for charging Break Costs, and the traditional method of calculating the amount of Break Costs, do not apply. Nevertheless lenders may wish to negotiate prepayment fees to cover themselves for increased administrative costs and inefficiencies in reallocating the funds arising from unexpected early prepayment. Any calculation of the amount due would be unlikely to be based on the idea that the lender needs compensation for what they had expected to receive. In the case of forward looking rates such as CME Term Sofr, some concept of Break Costs may be more justifiable so as to prevent opportunistic prepayment (e.g. if rates unexpectedly dropped mid period). In either case, if Break Costs are not included the lender may wish to restrict prepayments during Interest Periods to avoid the issue arising.

Market Disruption
The market disruption clause was designed to protect lenders if Libor was no longer quoted (and this function of a fallback to the benchmark rate is preserved as discussed in []) or if their funding costs were significantly different from Libor. The clause provided that, if the lenders' funding costs was significantly different from Libor, the lenders could charge their cost of funds plus Margin instead of Libor plus Margin. It was rarely used in practice, as noted in Box 5.3.

The rationale for both the market disruption clause and the provisions on Break Costs in Libor loans is that they are there to ensure that the interest rate (excluding Margin) covers lenders' funding costs and the Margin is the profit. The theoretical justification for both clauses has been questionable for many years as lenders have not in practice funded themselves at Libor. With the move to risk free rates the historical link between the interest rate charged and lenders' funding costs is ever more clearly broken—making these clauses ever harder to defend.

Section 4: Documentary Complexity of Using RFR Rates

0.111

It will be clear from what has been explained so far that if you have a multi-curreny loan you will need different interest rate provisions for each of the currencies involved. The LMA Compounded/Term Rate Loan, for example, includes provision for Sterling, US Dollars, Swiss Francs, and Euros. The agreement assumes that the Dollars will bear interest on the basis of CME Term Sofr and may or may not include a Baseline CAS; the Euros may bear interest at Euribor and have no credit adjustment spread while the Swiss Francs and Sterling are assumed to bear interest on the basis of a backward looking compounded risk free rate calculation, either with or without a Baseline CAS (and if no Baseline CAS is included, the Margin will be likely to be different for Euros from what it is for Sterling and Swiss Francs[36]). The details of the fallback provisions for each currency are also different.

Using the LMA terminology explained in 0.114, Dollars and Euros are Term Rate Currencies and Sterling and Swiss Francs are Compounded Rate Currencies.

0.112

The LMA Compounded/Term Rate Loan envisages a separate schedule of provisions for each currency[37]—specifying such things as are currency specific for that currency: such as whether break costs apply to that currency; what the relevant risk free rate is (i.e. Sofr, Sonia, etc.); the applicable fallback rate (e.g. which central bank rate will apply); and the market conventions applicable to that currency (e.g. 360- or 365-day year) as discussed in more detail in relation to Schedule 14 (*Reference Rate Terms*).

To help navigate the documentation, this Sect. 4.

* Describes some key words used in the LMA Compounded/Term Rate Loan; and
* Describes the various fallback provisions which account for a lot of the complexity in the documentation.

---

[36] Because the interest rate baseline for Euros, being Euribor, includes pricing for an element of credit risk, while the baseline for Sterling and Swiss Francs do not, so to make the same profit on Sterling and Swiss Francs the lenders have to charge a higher Margin.

[37] Referred to as the 'Reference Rate Terms'.

38   Introduction

1. Key words

0.113

Understanding some key expressions will help navigate the complexity of the LMA documentation.[38]

Key words used to describe different tranches of the loan for the purpose of the interest rate provisions

0.114

Term Rate Currencies and Compounded Rate Currencies

These definitions reflect the position when the loan was signed. So, in the example multicurrency loan discussed in 0.111, Dollars and Euros would be Term Rate Currencies and Sterling and Swiss Francs would be Compounded Rate Currencies.

0.115

Rate Switch Currency[39]

This is a currency (such as perhaps Euribor) to which the rate switch clause applies—that is—clauses are hardwired into the document enabling the basis of interest calculation to be changed to a new, pre-agreed methodology on occurrence of a specified event (a 'Rate Switch Trigger Event').

---

[38] Note that not all these expressions are defined in the main definitions section: some are defined in the Schedules and others in the other clauses of the loan agreement.

0.116

Term Rate Loans and Compounded Rate Loans

These are the key definitions. At any given time a tranche of the loan may be bearing interest on the basis of a compounded rate—so it is a Compounded Rate Loan—or on the basis of a term rate—so it is a Term Rate Loan. So, in the example in 0.111, if the rate switch clause was triggered for Euros so that interest on Euros became chargeable on the basis of backward looking €str, Euros would join Sterling and Swiss Francs as a Compounded Rate Loan, leaving only Dollars as a Term Rate Loan.

Key words used to describe the rate charged

As you will see there are a number of expressions used in the LMA documents to refer to different rates of interest for different purposes, many of which are easily confused. Key expressions are explained below. See also Box 0.14 for a simplified summary of all the different expressions used to describe different interest rates.

Box 0.14

Summary of LMA definitions of different interest rates[40]

"Alternative Term Rate"
> A fallback rate to be used if the Primary Term Rate is temporarily unavailable (e.g. ICE Benchmarks term Sofr instead of CME Term Sofr).

"Annualized Cumulative Compounded Daily Rate"
> In respect of any given day, the rate of interest (expressed as a rate per annum) inherent in the amount of growth which an investment would have seen if invested at the beginning of the then current Interest Period and rolled over (together with **accrued interest**) daily since then until that day.

---

[40] In the interests of simplicity these explanations ignore the Lookback Period. It might help with some of these definitions to refer to the example in Box 0.16.

"Compounded Reference Rate"

In respect of any given day, the Daily Non-Cumulative Compounded RFR Rate for that day (or its substitute in accordance with any of the fallback options) plus all applicable adjustments and credit adjustment spreads.

"Cumulative Compounded RFR Rate"

The rate of interest (expressed as a rate per annum and applying to an Interest Period) inherent in the amount of growth which an investment would have seen if invested at the beginning of the Interest Period and rolled over (together with accrued interest) daily until the end of the Interest Period.

"Daily Non-Cumulative Compounded RFR Rate"

In respect of any given day, the rate of interest (expressed as a rate per annum) inherent in the amount of growth seen in the Unannualized Cumulative Compounded Daily Rate on that day.

"Market Disruption Rate"

The rate of interest (expressed as a rate per annum) used to determine whether the lenders' funding costs are excessive for the purposes of triggering the market disruption clause.

"Primary Term Rate"

The methodology for calculation of the rate of interest (e.g. Euribor or CME Term Sofr) which the parties intend to apply to any given Term Rate Loan in the absence of any rate switch or fallback.

"Term Reference Rate"

The Primary Term Rate or any fallback rate which has come into effect together with any applicable adjustment resulting from that fallback but excluding any Term Reference Rate CAS.

"Unannualized Cumulative Compounded Daily Rate"

In respect of any given day, the rate of interest inherent in the amount of growth which an investment would have seen if invested at the beginning of the then current Interest Period and rolled over (together with accrued interest) daily since then until that day. The rate of interest is expressed on the basis of the rate for the actual period of time covered by the calculation, as opposed to being expressed as a rate per annum.

0.117

Primary Term Rate

—this is whatever term rate (e.g. Euribor or CME Term Sofr) as is intended to apply to the relevant Term Rate Loan from the outset of the transaction (i.e. prior to any rate switch or fallback).

0.118

Term Reference Rate

—either the Primary Term Rate (e.g. Euribor—i.e. the rate which is intended to apply to the relevant Term Rate Loan) or its fallback for the relevant Interest Period.

0.119

Compounded Reference Rate

—on any given day—the Daily Non-Cumulative Compounded RFR Rate for that day (see 0.123) plus any applicable credit adjustment spread (see Box 0.15).

> **Box 0.15**
>
> There are two important points to notice about these two reference rate definitions.
>
> - First, note that the Compounded Reference Rate applies 'on any given day', unlike the Term Reference Rate which applies to an Interest Period. This is because the Compounded Reference Rate will change daily, while the Term Reference Rate will not, but will be fixed in advance of an Interest Period and apply to the whole Interest Period as explained in Box 0.9.
> - Second, note that the Compounded Reference Rate includes a credit adjustment spread but the Term Reference Rate does not. This is because some Term Rate Loans will [41] bear interest on the basis of a rate such as Euribor, which includes pricing for credit risk, (and therefore requires no credit adjustment spread) and others will be something like CME Term Sofr which does not. The interest clause for Term Rate Loans (see 5.005) therefore states that any applicable credit adjustment spread (other than those which apply

42   Introduction

> as a result of a fallback interest rate, such as an Alternative Term Rate Adjustment) will be payable IN ADDITION to the Term Reference Rate, unlike for Compounded Rate Loans where the credit adjustment spread (if any) is included in the Compounded Reference Rate.

Key words used in calculating the interest rates

0.120

<u>Daily Rate</u>

In a Compounded Rate Loan it all starts with this. This is the relevant risk free rate for the particular currency (e.g. Sonia or Sofr). The definition will also say that in the absence of a published rate, a different rate will be used— usually the central bank rate for the particular currency.

0.121

<u>Lookback Period</u>

Of course, as we saw in 0.102, the Daily Rate for any given day will be that for a few days earlier, so as to ensure that the borrower can be given some days' notice of the amount due before it actually falls due.

---

[41] (Provided the relevant fallback provisions do not apply).

0.122

[Annualized or Unannualized] Cumulative Compounded Daily Rate[42]

If you had invested a sum of money at the risk free rate (Sofr, etc.) and rolled it over daily (or on each day when the markets were open), this rate refers to the rate of growth inherent in the amount by which that sum would have grown over the period of time being measured (being the 'Cumulation Period' ending on that day[43]). See Box 0.16 for an example.

0.123

Daily Non-Cumulative Compounded RFR Rate

This refers to the amount by which the Unannualized Cumulative Compounded Daily Rate is higher at the end of one day than it was at the end of the immediately preceding day. This calculation is needed so that we can calculate the amount of interest attributable to any particular day for the purpose, e.g. of loan sales during an Interest Period.

This is the key rate as the loan agreement will describe the interest rate applicable to each day, and so this is the rate which will be used. See Box 0.16 for an example. It is explained in more detail in the discussion on Schedule 15 (*Daily Non-Cumulative Compounded RFR Rate*).

Box 0.16

It might help to see an example.

If a sum of 1000 would have grown to 1010 after three months and to 1009 the previous day, then the growth on the last day (i.e. the amount of interest attributable to that last day) was 1, which is a rate of growth of 0.1% in one day. On the basis of a 360 day year that equates to an annual rate of 3.6% per annum. So 3.6% per annum is the interest rate attributable to that last day.

The rate of growth for the 3 month period ending on that day on the other hand is 4% (the relevant sum grew by 1% over 3 months which is an annual rate of growth of 4%). (Notice here the difference between annualized rates and unannualized rates. In this example, 1% is the unannualized rate and 4% is the annualized rate).

---

[43] Note the difference between the Cumulation Period—which is used to calculate the interest rate attributable to any given day—as discussed in 0.122-3—and the Interest Period—which determines when interest is payable and which may also be used in those rare cases when an interest rate is needed for an Interest Period—as discussed in 13.045.

44 Introduction

> In this example the "Daily Non-Cumulative Compounded RFR Rate" on the day in question is 3.6%; the "Unannualized Cumulative Compounded Daily Rate" is 1% and the "Annualized Cumulative Compounded Daily Rate" is 4%.

0.124

Of course to get to the actual rate attributable to each day we will need to add any applicable credit adjustment spread plus the Margin. Hence there is also a definition of "Compounded Reference Rate" which is defined to mean the Daily Non-Cumulative Compounded RFR Rate plus any applicable credit adjustment spread.

Cumulative Compounded RFR Rate

0.125

This refers to the rate of interest applicable to an Interest Period for a Compounded Rate Loan. This rate is only used in the context of market disruption as discussed in relation to Schedule 16 (*Cumulative Compounded RFR Rate*).

Key words used to describe Schedules and supplements to the Agreement relevant for the interest rate clauses

0.126

Reference Rate Terms

This expression refers to the currency specific terms (such as the definition of the Daily Rate; is it Sonia, Sofr, etc.; the identity of the Central Bank for the purpose of the Central Bank Rate; Bank of England, US Federal Reserve, etc.; and the conventions; such as number of days in a year) used for that currency which are relevant to the calculation of interest and which are set out in the relevant part of Schedule 14 (*Reference Rate Terms*) for that currency.

0.127

Compounding Methodology Supplement and Reference Rate Supplement

It is envisaged that if different market practices develop in relation to interest rates, (whether as to how to do the calculation so as to turn the Daily Rate into an interest rate for the purpose of the loan, or more generally, e.g. in relation to conventions such as month ends) then supplemental documents can be signed updating this loan to the new methodology with a lower level of lender approval that would be necessary for other changes. These expressions refer to any supplements signed to effect these changes.

Key words used to describe different credit adjustment spreads

0.128

Baseline CAS

See the discussion in 0.108. Some lenders may choose to express the interest rate on a Compounded Rate Loan as including a Margin and a separate Baseline CAS for presentational purposes so that, for example, margins on a loan based on Euribor will be the same as margins on loans based on compounded rates. Inclusion of this separate spread enables like by like comparison of Margins regardless of whether the baseline includes some pricing for credit risk (e.g. Euribor) or does not (e.g. CME Term Sofr or compounded risk free rates) See also Box 0.17.

> **Box 0.17**
>
> "Term Reference Rate CAS". This may be used for term rates (such as CME Term Sofr) which are based on risk free rates. Since these rates do not include any element of credit risk they are lower than Libor, so some lenders might want to separate the Margin into separate elements for presentational purposes, in the same way as they might for Compounded Rate Loans. This credit adjustment spread therefore has the same function in relation to Term Rate Loans based on risk free rates as the Baseline CAS has in relation to Compounded Rate Loans.

46   Introduction

0.129

Rate Switch CAS

See the discussion in 0.107. Where interest was initially to be charged on an IBOR basis (such as Euribor) but was to change to another methodology on the occurrence of a specified event, a Rate Switch CAS would be added to the new rate. This was designed to compensate the lenders for the 'normal' difference between the pricing of the rate used at the start and the rate used after the rate switch happened.

0.130

There are then a number of different expressions for adjustments which may be necessary if a rate is unavailable and a fallback rate needs to be used. These are variously the "Central Bank Rate Adjustment" (where the Central Bank Rate is used as a fallback) the "Fallback CAS" (where a compounded rate is used as a fallback to a term rate[44]) and the "Alternative Term Rate Adjustment" (where the Reference Rate Terms for a Term Rate Currency provide for an 'Alternative Term Rate' to apply if the Primary Term Rate is unavailable).

Key words used in relation to business days

Different places need to be open for different purposes.

0.131

The LMA Compounded/Term Rate Loan has three definitions which describe days on which different markets and financial centres need to be open for the purpose of the loan agreement.

An 'Additional Business Day' in relation to any currency, is a date on which the relevant market for that currency is open for business. For example, for Euros, an Additional Business Day is a **Target Day**, while for Sterling based on Sonia, it is an RFR Banking Day for Sonia.

---

[44] But see also the discussion in relation to Schedule 14 (*Reference Rate Terms*).

Section 4: Documentary Complexity of Using RFR Rates   **47**

An RFR Banking Day for a given currency is a day when the market for the relevant risk free rate is open for business, so that data is available to be input into the calculation of the relevant compounded rate of interest.

A **Business Day**, then, is a flexible definition, the precise meaning of which will depend on the action which needs to happen on that day. It requires the place of business of the Agent and the borrower to be open, as well as other places as appropriate for the action concerned. See 1.010.

2. Fallback provisions and other changes to the calculation of interest.

0.132

Loan agreements need to include provisions dealing with what is to happen if a given piece of information which is necessary for the calculation of interest is temporarily unavailable or is permanently unavailable or inappropriate.

These provisions in the LMA Compounded/Term Rate Loan are long and complex, involving many detailed defined terms. LMA acknowledge that they are just options until market practice develops. They are described briefly here.

Temporary unavailability

0.133

The LMA Compounded/Term Rate Loan includes provisions dealing with temporary problems as follows.

Term Rate Loans

0.134

The LMA offers a waterfall of options (in Clause 13.1 (*CHANGES TO THE CALCULATION OF INTEREST*: *Interest calculation if no Primary Term Rate*)) so that if the first is unavailable, the next will be used and so on. In simple terms the waterfall is

* Primary Term Rate (e.g. Euribor or CME Term Sofr—the rate which the parties propose to use in the first instance).

48 **Introduction**

- Optional variations, e.g. interpolated, different Interest Period and historic rates.

- Alternative Term Rate (e.g. ICE Benchmarks Term Sofr for CME Term Sofr)

  – Optional variations, e.g. interpolated, different Interest Period and historic rates.

- The 'Term Fallback Option' which, if the parties elect for it to apply, will be specified in the Reference Rate Terms for the relevant currency and interest rate and, if applicable, will be either the Compounded Reference Rate for the relevant currency or a fixed Central Bank Rate.

- Cost of funds See 0.136.

0.135

Each of the Alternative Term Rate, Compounded Reference Rate/fixed Central Bank Rate and cost of funds fallbacks will only apply to a particular currency if the relevant Reference Rate Terms state they are to apply[45] and, in the case of a Compounded Reference Rate fallback, only if the agreement includes Reference Rate Terms for the compounded reference rate for that currency[46]). This allows different waterfalls to be specified for different currencies.

0.136

In Term Rate Loans using an IBOR methodology such as Euribor, use of cost of funds as an ultimate fallback option for temporary problems may be appropriate given pre-existing market practice and the limited other acceptable options. For Term Rate Loans based on CME Term Sofr the parties may be content not to include cost of funds as an ultimate fallback as the waterfall of options includes an Alternative Term Rate (e.g. Ice Benchmarks Term Sofr) and a Fallback Option of either the compounded reference rate or a fixed central bank rate. Given the viability of these other options and the practical difficulties of using cost of funds as a fallback as discussed in Box 5.3, parties may feel that it is unnecessary to include cost of funds as an ultimate fallback.

---

[45] In the case of Euribor, the Alternative Term Rate and Term Fallback Options are not intended to apply—the intention being that the fallback waterfall should be the same as that which applied in historic Euribor transactions. In particular LMA note that a compounded rate fallback is not intended to apply as a fallback to Euribor.

[46] The Reference Rate Terms will also identify any applicable adjustment or credit adjustment spread as discussed in relation to Schedule 14 (*Reference Rate Terms*).

Compounded Rate Loans

0.137

For Compounded Rate Loans the definition of the Daily Rate in the Reference Rate Terms will specify the rate to be used as a fallback on any given day if the relevant risk free rate (**Sonia**, **Sofr**, etc.) is unavailable (together with an optional credit adjustment spread). Invariably this will be a Central Bank Rate for the relevant currency with a fallback to use a recent Central Bank Rate if one is not available for that date. There is then an option to provide that cost of funds will apply as an ultimate fallback if there is no applicable Central Bank Rate.

0.138

In Compounded Rate Loans, given the difficulties in using cost of funds as a fallback (see Box 5.3) and the unlikelihood of the absence of a Central Bank Rate, in many loans no cost of funds fallback has been included.

Permanent unavailability, inappropriateness or decision to change

Anticipated Changes to a Different Rate—Rate Switch Provisions

0.139

A 'Rate Switch' clause may be included in the document if any part of the loan may be in a currency for which interest is initially calculated on the basis of a term rate but the parties anticipate that the interest calculation will change to another, pre-agreed methodology at some point during the life of the loan. The relevant currency will be defined as a 'Rate Switch Currency'. The clause will define the 'Rate Switch Trigger Event' on the occurrence of which the change will occur (see Box 0.18) and will specify the terms of the interest rate calculation which will apply after the occurrence of that event, including any applicable Rate Switch CAS.

50   Introduction

> **Box 0.18**
>
> A Rate Switch Trigger Event is intended to cover permanent problems with the relevant published rate for a given tenor (the "Quoted Tenor")—whether permanent unavailability, change in methodology on a long-term basis or regulatory advice that the rate is no longer accurate. There is an option to include a 'pre cessation trigger' to allow the borrower and a specified majority of the lenders to decide that the rate is no longer appropriate even in the absence of any of these more formal changes occurring.

Unanticipated Changes to a Different Rate

0.140

The agreement also deals in Clause 37.4 (*AMENDMENTS AND WAIVERS: Changes to reference rates*) with the question of how to replace a reference rate on a long-term basis, where the need for this (and the appropriate replacement) was not envisaged from day 1. There is an option to limit this provision so that it only applies in the event of a 'Published Rate Replacement Event'. The definition is very similar to the definition of a Rate Switch Trigger Event discussed in Box 0.18 and also includes an option for a 'pre cessation trigger'. The key point is that a lower proportion of lenders will be required to approve a replacement benchmark in these circumstances than in the case of other changes to the interest rate.

Changes in Methodology

0.141

At the time of writing it is normal for the loan agreement to include detailed explanations of how the interest rate will be calculated in the case of a Compounded Rate Loan. See commentary on Schedule 15 (*Daily Non-Cumulative Compounded RFR Rate.*) It is to be hoped that over time, this process will become simpler and that loan agreements will no longer need to 'look under the bonnet' and explain precisely how the daily risk free rate will be used in the calculation of the interest rate charged. The LMA includes the concept of a 'Compounding Methodology Supplement' and/or a 'Reference Rate Supplement' to describe any document entered into in future updating the methodology for calculating the compounded rate or the details (such as perhaps applicable conventions) set out in the Reference Rate Terms and provides for such a supplement to require approval by a lesser percentage of lenders than would normally be necessary in order to agree changes to the interest rate.

The agreement provides (in Clause 1.2 *DEFINITIONS AND INTERPRE-TATION*: *Construction*) that the terms of any such supplement will override the relevant Schedule of Reference Rate Terms or calculations of cumulative or non-cumulative compounded rates.

The concept is similar to the provisions of Clause 37.4 (*AMENDMENTS AND WAIVERS*: *Changes to reference rates*), discussed in 0.140, but is intended to be used for less drastic changes.

Section 5: Scope of the Loan Agreement

0.142
In every loan agreement, some fundamental issues relating to the scope of the agreement need to be addressed,

- Who can make use of the facility?
- Who are the lenders, the **Agent**, and the Security **Trustee**?
- Who can be called on to repay?
- Whose activities are restricted by the loan agreement?

See Box 0.19 for a description of the concepts used in the LMA Compounded/Term Rate Loan to address some of these issues discussed in the paragraphs below.

Box 0.19

The LMA structure
 The LMA Compounded/Term Rate Loan describes the various categories of persons affected by the agreement by the following definitions:

- *'Original Borrowers'*: These are the companies in the Group which are initially entitled to borrow as specified in a schedule to the agreement.
- *'Original Guarantors'*: These are the companies specified in a schedule to the agreement which are initially required to guarantee the loan.
- *'Company'*: This is the ultimate holding company of the Group or subgroup (which may or may not also be a Borrower or Guarantor).

52   Introduction

- *'Borrowers'*: These are the members of the Group which, at any particular time, have borrowed or remain entitled to borrow moneys under the facility. This will be the Original Borrowers plus any other company in the Group which has been accepted by the lenders as a Borrower but excluding any who are no longer entitled to borrow under the agreement.
- *'Guarantors'*: These are the members of the Group which, at any particular time, are liable under guarantees of the loan. This will be the Original Guarantors plus any additional group companies which have guaranteed the loan but excluding any whose guarantees have been released.
- *'Obligors'*: These are the Borrowers and the Guarantors.
- *'Group'*: This is the Company and all its Subsidiaries. [47] at any given time.

1. Who can make use of the facility?

0.143

In many loan agreements only certain named persons may use the facility. In other cases (including the LMA Compounded/Term Rate Loan) additional group companies may make use of the facility subject to certain conditions. Those additional companies will become party to the loan agreement at a future date by a mechanism agreed at the start.[48] Borrowers will wish to ensure that this process is a mechanical one, as far as possible, and that the conditions precedent do not effectively make the extension of the loan to new group members discretionary on the part of the lenders.

2. Who are the lenders?

0.144

Most commonly there will be a syndicate with the identity of lenders changing from time to time and new lenders becoming party to the agreement at a future date, by a mechanism agreed at the start.[49] Borrowers will wish to be sure that any changes in lenders or in the **lending office** do not cause any adverse consequences, such as additional costs under the **gross-up** clause,[50] for the borrower. The original Agent and Security Trustee will be

---

[47] See definition of 'Subsidiary' in 1.056.

[48] See Clause 27 (*Changes to the Obligors*) in 9.060.

[49] See Clause 26 (*Changes to the Lenders*) in 9.054-7.

[50] See Clause 15 (*Tax Gross Up and Indemnities*) in 6.021.

Section 5: Scope of the Loan Agreement   53

specified, but there may be provisions allowing these roles to be passed on to others over time.

3. Who can be called on to repay?

0.145

Often there will be specified guarantors in addition to the borrowers. The LMA Compounded/Term Rate Loan also contains a mechanism for guarantors to change[51] (subject to approval of the lenders) allowing flexibility, for example, if the holding company wishes to dispose of a group member which is a guarantor or to release it from those requirements of the agreement which relate to guarantors.

4. Whose activities are restricted by the loan agreement?

0.146

What is the scope of the loan agreement in relation to the group? For example, are there negative undertakings in relation to members of the group who are not Borrowers?

See Box 0.20 for a diagram of the position under the LMA Compounded/ Term Rate Loan.

---

[51] See Clause 27 (*Changes to the Obligors*) in 9.064 onwards.

Box 0.20

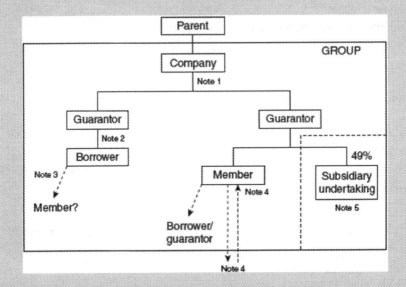

(Based on the assumption that selling of shares in group companies is permitted under the no disposals undertaking.)

Note 1 The 'Company' administers the facility. It assumes miscellaneous payment and other obligations. The loan must be prepaid if there is a change of control of the Company. Note that if the Company is not the ultimate holding company of the group it is important to ensure that a change of 'ultimate' control triggers the clause. Even if the borrower's shareholders do not change, if the shareholders of the shareholders change, the lenders will want that to trigger the clause.

Note 2 Guarantors must remain in the group, unless they resign as guarantors, which they can do with the consent of all lenders. They are bound by the undertakings relating to 'Obligors'.

Note 3 Borrowers must remain in the group unless they resign as borrowers. They may resign as borrowers if they repay those advances which were made to them and if there is no **Default** at the time of their resignation. They are bound by the undertakings relating to 'Obligors'.

Note 4 Members of the group are bound only by the 'group' undertakings, which are less extensive than the 'Obligor' undertakings. They need not remain in the group. They may become Borrowers or Guarantors subject to certain conditions, including delivery of a satisfactory legal opinion.

Note 5 If this company is effectively controlled by a group member it may be a 'Subsidiary Undertaking', and, if such companies are included in the definition of 'Subsidiary', it will be affected by the Loan Agreement in the same way as other group companies.

Section 5: Scope of the Loan Agreement   55

0.147

This issue of the scope of the Agreement is of particular importance to all parties:

0.148

● Lenders need to ensure that the agreement provides them with sufficient powers in relation to all those issues which are relevant to their credit decision, which may well extend to issues involving members of the group which are neither borrowers nor guarantors. See Box 0.21.

> **Box 0.21**
>
> This issue is well illustrated by a series of restructurings in the US leveraged market, starting in 2017 with a highly publicized restructuring by J Crew, where borrowers made creative (and aggressive) use of 'Unrestricted Subsidiaries' to transfer value away from the lenders' security package—referred to as 'collateral stripping'[52], and the mechanism by which they did it being commonly referred to as a 'trap door'. Valuable assets owned by Obligors were transferred to 'Unrestricted Subsidiaries' which then borrowed money using those assets as security thus giving these new lenders effective priority over the original lenders—see 0.162–3 and Box A1.10.

0.149

● Borrowers will be concerned to insulate themselves as far as possible from problems which may arise in other parts of the group. They will also want to avoid the possibility that activities of other group members, particularly those over which the borrowers have no control, may result in the withdrawal of the borrowers' funding.

0.150

● The ultimate holding company will want to maintain the flexibility to restructure the group and, if appropriate, sell parts of it, or develop new businesses within it, without interference by the various lenders to group members under their different financing arrangements.

---

[52] See "The Development of Collateral Stripping by Distressed Borrowers" by Mitchell Mengden in *Capital Markets Law Journal*, Volume 16, Issue 1, Jan 21 pp56–71.

56 Introduction

0.151

The parties therefore need to address the following questions, considered in turn here.

0.152

- Can group members be bought and sold?[53]

0.153

- Are some companies in the group entirely unrestricted by the loan agreement (sometimes called Excluded Companies or Unrestricted Subsidiaries)?[54];

0.154

- Which provisions (if any) should relate to group members who are neither borrowers nor guarantors?[55] and

0.155

- Are the lenders concerned to maintain value in certain specific companies (or categories of companies, such as borrowers and/or guarantors) in the group?[56]

Can group members be bought and sold?

0.156

Some loan agreements restrict the borrowers from forming subsidiaries[57] and restrict group members from being sold out of the group. A common way to achieve this is to attach a group structure chart to the agreement and require the borrowers to undertake to make no changes to the group structure from that indicated in the chart. Of course, the no disposals undertaking

---

[53] See 0.156.

[54] See 0.158.

[55] See 0.164.

[56] See 0.169.

[57] Indeed, in a loan to a single borrower which has no subsidiaries it is usually sensible to either include potential future subsidiaries in the undertakings or to include an undertaking against forming subsidiaries to ensure that the purpose of the negative undertakings cannot be avoided through activities of unregulated subsidiaries.

Section 5: Scope of the Loan Agreement   57

also prevents the disposals of subsidiaries unless appropriate carve-outs are negotiated.

0.157

Other loan agreements prevent sale of a subsidiary less explicitly, as they include undertakings relating to specific named group companies or companies which are members of the group on the day of the loan agreement's signature. The result is that such companies cannot be sold out of the group, since, if they were, the continued compliance with the relevant provisions would be outside the control of the group. See Box 0.22 for a description of the position under the LMA Compounded/Term Rate Loan.

Box 0.22

The LMA Compounded/Term Rate Loan requires Obligors to remain members of the group, [58] but, on the face of it, it allows other group members to be sold (although there needs to be an adjustment to the no disposals clause to achieve this), and allows new companies to become part of the group. Change in the control of the group gives lenders the right to require to be prepaid.[59] By virtue of the provisions allowing Obligors to cease to be Obligors,[60] even Borrowers can be sold out of the group as long as they first repay any loan they have borrowed and as long as that is not prohibited by the no disposals clause. Guarantors can only be released from their obligations (and hence become free to be sold) with consent of all lenders.

Are some companies in the group entirely unrestricted by the loan agreement (sometimes called Excluded Companies or Unrestricted Subsidiaries)?

0.158

Two types of companies are often excluded from the undertakings in the loan agreement, being insignificant companies and non-recourse companies.

---

[58] See Clause 25.9 (*EVENTS OF DEFAULT: Ownership of the Obligors*) in 8.270.

[59] See Clause 10.3 (*PREPAYMENT AND CANCELLATION: Change of control*) in 4.011.

[60] See Clause 27 (*Changes to the Obligors*) in 9.063.

58 Introduction

0.159

Insignificant Companies

Borrowers will often ask for insignificant companies to be exempted from the undertakings. Often the test of significance for this purpose looks at the **Tangible net worth** or EBITDA of the company concerned and exempts it if that represents a minor (e.g. less than 5%) part of the Tangible net worth or EBITDA of the group. This is often calculated with reference to the latest audited accounts at the relevant time.

0.160

Comment Borrowers need to be cautious with this approach as a company which was once exempt may be caught at a later point if its relative importance in the group changes. This may even result in an Event of Default by virtue of things done while the company was exempt. If this type of exception has been agreed, the group needs to keep a check on whether exempt companies might cross the threshold and cease to be exempt (see Box 0.23).

Box 0.23

An example might assist. Assume that a loan agreement includes a negative pledge clause saying '*The Company shall ensure that no ... [Material Subsidiary] shall ... permit to subsist any Security*'. Assume that

(a) the company grants security at a time when it is not a Material Subsidiary; and
(b) the value of the company increases relative to that of the group and it becomes a Material Subsidiary.

Unless the security falls within one of the exceptions to the negative pledge clause, the company will need to discharge the security before it becomes a Material Subsidiary in order to avoid being in breach, as the covenant is not to '*permit Security to subsist*'.

0.161

Non-Recourse Companies

The second type of company which is commonly exempted is a company which is established for the purpose of a particular non-recourse transaction. These companies are established as vehicles for particular projects. The argument for excluding them from the provisions of the loan agreement is that difficulties with the project vehicle are not the responsibility of the group and therefore should not impact on the group's commercial borrowing. (If excluded from the undertakings, they would also then be excluded for all purposes, including, e.g. financial ratios.) Hence a definition of 'Non-Recourse Company' is sometimes inserted (see Box 0.24).

Box 0.24

'Non-Recourse Company' means, at any relevant time, a company which, at such time, has no Financial Indebtedness other than Non-Recourse Indebtedness.

'Non-Recourse Indebtedness' means Financial Indebtedness incurred by a company (the 'Project Company') for the purposes of financing a particular project where

(i) the principal assets and business of the Project Company are constituted by that project; and
(ii) the provider of the Financial Indebtedness has no recourse against any member of the Group or its assets except the assets of the Project Company comprised in the project.

0.162

It is also worth noticing the concept of 'Unrestricted Subsidiaries' in the leveraged market. This concept is designed to give the borrower group flexibility to develop new lines of business or **joint ventures** outside the scope of the loan agreement. The borrower may be permitted to designate certain group members as being wholly unrestricted by the loan agreement, so that those unrestricted subsidiaries can operate on a standalone basis, raising their own finance and securing their own debt. Those Unrestricted Subsidiaries are then not included in calculation of financial ratios and dealings between them and the Restricted Subsidiaries are restricted so as to retain value in the Restricted Subsidiaries.

60   Introduction

0.163

The J Crew restructuring discussed in Box 0.21 highlighted the opportunities which this designation gives to borrowers of removing value from the lenders' security net because

- traditionally the loan agreements in the leveraged market have been less restrictive for investments in Unrestricted Subsidiaries than for transfers to third parties
- the assets transferred may be of particular value in the context of the restricted group (such as intellectual property rights) even though they fall within the thresholds allowed for permitted investments and
- once assets are in Unrestricted Subsidiaries there is no prohibition on distribution by way of dividends or on borrowing.

Which provisions (if any) should relate to group members who are neither borrowers nor guarantors?

0.164

Borrowers, as noted earlier, want the undertakings and other provisions to apply only to Obligors (or the Obligors and their Subsidiaries) and not to be extended to any other company in the group. There are three main reasons for this.

0.165

- The result of extending the provisions to a company which is not an Obligor means that, potentially, as a result of the cross default clause, a downturn in that other company's financial fortunes will cause a problem for the borrower.

0.166

- The borrower may not be in a position to control the activities of that other company, and therefore may be unable to prevent that other company from doing things which cause an Event of Default under the borrower's loan.

0.167

* The group may wish to maintain flexibility as to company sales and purchases.[61]

0.168

Given that lenders have no claim against group companies which are not Obligors it may be questioned why, for example, the negative pledge or the no disposals covenant extend to those companies. One argument of course is that subsidiaries of Obligors need to be included in the undertakings because they contribute to the financial strength of their parent, the Obligor.[62] Lenders may also want to restrict subsidiaries of Obligors from borrowing money so as to avoid structural subordination. Another justification may be that, whatever the legal situation, if a subsidiary were to have financial difficulties (such as those caused by cross default,[63] or which may be heralded by **asset stripping**[64] or a breach of the negative pledge[65]) the ultimate holding company may well find itself bound up with the financial difficulties of its subsidiary, even if not legally bound to support it. The solution needs to be agreed on a case-by-case basis and usually on a clause-by-clause basis, taking account of the credit decision. The result (as in the LMA Compounded/Term Rate Loan) may well be that some clauses will apply to all group members and others to Obligors only. However, any extension of any clause to companies which are not Obligors needs very careful consideration by the borrower, as to whether it is justified, and acceptable, in the context of the particular group.[66]

---

[61] See 0.156.

[62] If that is the case, you might expect the subsidiaries themselves to be Obligors but this may not be possible in all cases in view of local laws on upstream guarantees.

[63] See Clause 25.5 (*EVENTS OF DEFAULT: Cross default*) in 8.238.

[64] See Clause 24.4 (*GENERAL UNDERTAKINGS: Disposals*) in 8.180.

[65] See Clause 24.3 (*GENERAL UNDERTAKINGS: Negative pledge*) in 8.140.

[66] If the eventual agreed position is that some provisions extend beyond the Obligors, the borrower may seek to mitigate this by providing for extended grace periods for Events of Default which relate to companies that are not Obligors.

62 Introduction

Are the lenders concerned to maintain value in certain specific companies (or categories of companies, such as borrowers and/ or guarantors) in the group?

0.169
It will be apparent from the above that there are at least three different categories of group company for the purpose of the loan agreement.
0.170

* Borrowers and guarantors (in LMA terminology the 'Obligors'). Even within this category the lenders may want to treat some Obligors differently from others if, e.g. there are some upstream guarantees in the structure which might be problematic in the jurisdiction of the guarantor or of its assets.[67]

0.171

* Non Obligors which are restricted by various provisions in the loan agreement (e.g. by restrictions which extend to group members). Within this category there may also be a distinction to be made between Material Subsidiaries and other group members if there are Material Subsidiaries which are not Obligors and

0.172

* Non Obligors which are not restricted by the loan agreement (such as Non-Recourse Companies or Unrestricted Subsidiaries).

0.173
The interaction between these different categories of group members needs to be considered. For example, the lenders may be concerned to ensure that value is maintained in the Borrowers, or they may be happy as long as value is maintained in the Obligors. Alternatively they may be content to see value moved around the group as long as the value is maintained in those group members which are subject to the restrictions in the loan agreement.

---

[67] See the discussion in A1.081.

Section 5: Scope of the Loan Agreement 63

0.174

For certain provisions (such as perhaps sanctions) the lenders will want the relevant clause to operate if ANY relevant company is affected, while for other provisions (such as perhaps the test of change of business) the lenders might be prepared to assess the situation on the basis of the relevant category (e.g. Obligors) taken as a whole.

0.175

The answers to these questions will impact (among other things) on the following questions:

0.176

* whether any relevant limits, such as the effect which is to be treated as material for the purpose of the definition of 'Material Adverse Effect'[68] or the threshold amount for the negative pledge,[69] or the test of change of business,[70] is set on a company-by-company basis (and then, whether it is set with reference to any Borrower, or any Obligor or with reference to any group member, or perhaps any restricted group member) or with reference to the position of the group (or a sub-category) as a whole.

0.177

* negative undertakings—the borrowers may request that these relate to the group as a whole and that transactions between group members should be excluded from, for example, the no disposals clause. The lenders, on the other hand, may be happy to permit such transactions as between Obligors, or between Borrowers but not between other group members (see Box 0.25).

---

[68] See definition of 'Material Adverse Effect' in 1.048.

[69] See Clause 24.3 (*GENERAL UNDERTAKINGS*: *Negative pledge*) subclause (c)(x) in 8.174.

[70] See Clause 24.6 (*GENERAL UNDERTAKINGS*: *Change of business*) in 8.197.

64 Introduction

> **Box 0.25**
>
> For example, in relation to the no disposals undertaking in Clause 24.4 (*GENERAL UNDERTAKINGS: Disposals*), [71] the borrower may request the ability to transfer assets between group members without the restrictions of that clause. The lenders, on the other hand, may be concerned to ensure that specific assets remain within a company to which the lenders have direct access, in which case they may agree to the exception, but only in relation to transactions between Obligors.

0.178

- at which levels the financial ratios are tested. The lenders may require ratios to be tested both at a consolidated level (excluding any companies such as non-recourse companies or Unrestricted Subsidiaries which have been excluded from the undertakings), and also for particular Obligors or borrowers.

Section 6: Non Standard Provisions

0.179

There are many issues which are not addressed in the LMA Compounded/ Term Rate Loan, but which may merit inclusion in any given loan agreement. LMA may provide optional provisions for inclusion in the documents to address some of these issues and for others it may add provisions to some, but not all, of its suite of documents. In some cases LMA does not provide clause wording but issues guidance and advice. These non standard provisions may address

0.180

- issues such as sanctions and anti-corruption where there is no standard market practice and any appropriate drafting will need to reflect the make up of the syndicate and the nature of the borrower's business;

---

[71] See 8.180.

Section 6: Non Standard Provisions **65**

0.181

* a specific event which creates concern (such as the publication of an erroneous payment clause after the Revlon case[72] in the US in which an agent intending to distribute a payment of interest only to syndicate members mistakenly paid them the entire outstanding principal and interest);

0.182

* a regulation which affects loan agreements with certain characteristics only (such as the contractual recognition of bail-in provisions discussed in 0.196); or

0.183

* a market practice which has become sufficiently common, or sufficiently common in some markets, to merit provision of drafting (such as the **Lehman provisions** or provisions dealing with accordions and structural adjustments).

0.184

Some of the most important issues are discussed separately here in order to give an overview of some issues to consider in addition to the 'standard' provisions in the LMA recommended forms. Where appropriate, they will also be discussed in more detail in the clauses where they appear.

1. Sanctions

0.185

Lenders are commonly concerned to ensure that the loan specifically addresses sanctions, rather than leaving the issue to be dealt with by the lender's due diligence at the outset of the transaction and the general undertaking by the borrower to comply with the law (discussed in 8.139) and the prepayment obligation in the event of illegality (discussed in 4.007).

---

[72] In re: Citibank August 11, 2020, No 21-487 (2nd Cir.2022).

66   **Introduction**

0.186

Having specific sanctions provisions gives a mechanism for monitoring the borrower's ongoing compliance and helps lenders to comply with their reporting obligations to sanctions authorities. Additionally, lenders may want to impose stricter terms on the borrower group than they are subject to as a matter of law. For example it may be perfectly legal for a borrower in country A to trade with an entity in country B, and for the lender to provide finance for that trade, but, if the finance is made available in US Dollars, and the financed activity breaches US sanctions, the US has the ability to freeze loan payments going through its payment system.

0.187

There are no standard provisions in the LMA documents as precisely what is required will need to reflect the borrower's business and the make up of the syndicate.

0.188

There will commonly be detailed discussion around the scope of the sanctions provisions—that is—precisely what issues need to be addressed. The borrower is likely to be aware of, and to have policies and procedures ensuring its compliance with, sanctions provisions of key jurisdictions relevant to its business and its financing arrangements, but will be keen to ensure that the loan agreement provisions do not expose it to additional sanctions-related risks. For example, trade sanctions may be imposed which make it illegal for a borrower to trade in certain goods in a sanctioned country, or illegal to do so without a licence. If the loan agreement prohibits any group member from doing any business with a sanctioned country, this is clearly far more restrictive than the sanctions themselves and will require the borrower to obtain lender consents for activities which do not breach sanctions laws.

0.189

Another complexity of sanctions is that in some cases compliance with the sanctions regime of one country may be prohibited by a **blocking law** in a second country.[73] To deal with this it is common to include a clause which states that, to the extent that any sanctions provisions in the loan agreement

---

[73] So, for example, the European Blocking Regulation (EC) 2271/96 of 22 November 1996 prohibits European operators from complying with specified US sanctions without consent. The purpose of the regulation is to limit the extraterritorial impact of US sanctions. The English regulation having this effect is The Protecting against the Effects of Extraterritorial Application of Third Country Legislation (Amendment) (EU Exit) Regulations 2020 (SI 2020/1660).

would cause a lender to breach any local law, that provision will not apply in favour of the relevant lender. Partly to facilitate this, it might be appropriate to provide that breach of any sanctions provision should be a compulsory prepayment event rather than an Event of Default—as discussed in 4.009.

0.190
The sanctions against Russia arising from the war in Ukraine also highlighted the fact that sanctions issues can also arise if a member of the syndicate becomes a target of sanctions. Depending on the make up of the syndicate and its transferability, Borrowers may want to include provisions protecting the loan from disruption in the event that a lender becomes sanctioned. Issues to address might include

0.191

* A provision that no participation in the loan may be transferred to a sanctioned lender.

0.192

* A provision that any amounts payable by the borrower for the benefit of a sanctioned lender may instead be paid to a suspense account, or, if paid, must be held in a suspense account by the Agent.

0.193

* An exception to the illegality clause so that the borrower is not obliged to prepay a sanctioned lender as a result of it becoming a sanctioned lender.

0.194

* A general provision that no Event of Default shall occur as a result of the consequences of a lender becoming a sanctioned lender.

0.195

* Some loan agreements have included clauses (inspired by the Lehman Provisions discussed in 0.204) requiring a sanctioned lender to transfer its participation in the loan to a lender nominated by the borrower, although this may be impractical as the sanctions may prevent any purchaser from completing the purchase.

68   Introduction

2. Special resolution procedures for systemically important lenders

0.196

Post financial crisis many jurisdictions (including the US and the EU) introduced laws allowing regulators to take control of failing financial institutions which are deemed 'too big to fail', rather than having them undergo a traditional winding up process.[74] The aim of these regulations is to make systemically important financial institutions more resilient and to provide a more orderly resolution of their affairs than in a traditional winding up. The bail-in legislation in the EU (which allows regulators to convert claims against the relevant institutions into equity claims) and the Qualified Financial Contract Rules (the '**QFC Rules**') in the US (which require counterparties to certain financial contracts to agree not to exercise their default rights or transferability restrictions under those contracts in certain circumstances) are examples. Syndicated loans may need to include provisions acknowledging and agreeing to these special regulations. For example, post Brexit, financial institutions in the EU contracting with an English counterparty under an agreement governed by English law will need to incorporate a provision into the contract under which the English counterparty expressly agrees to the bail-in powers and this is the reason for Clause 40 (*Bail-in*) of the LMA Compounded/Term Rate Loan. The US QFC Rules similarly require affected financial institutions to include provisions in relevant contracts under which the counterparties expressly agree to the restrictions on their rights as required by the QFC Rules. LMA has issued advice and appropriate clauses addressing these requirements. These are available to LMA members only on the LMA website.

---

[74] Fallout from the collapse of Silicon Valley Bank in 2023 may trigger a review of the scope of these requirements. Silicon Valley Bank was not viewed as systemically important but was a key lender to an important growth industry. Its collapse spooked markets and was followed by UBS purchasing Credit Suisse in a government brokered deal which wiped out tier AT1 bondholders (i.e. bondholders whose debts can be converted to equity) but left shareholders not completely wiped out. This reversal of the usual insolvency waterfall—where shareholders are expected to absorb losses before bondholders—in turn spooked markets, increasing pricing for AT1 bonds.

Section 6: Non Standard Provisions 69

3. Additional debt flexibility

0.197

A trend which started after the financial crisis of 2008/9 has been to increase flexibility for borrowers to incur additional debt under the terms of the existing loan agreement—which can be significantly faster and cheaper than negotiating new loan documentation. The classic ways in which this is done is to are

0.198

* Include an uncommitted 1 year extension option in a revolving credit— usually specifying a window in which the option must be exercised and limiting the number of times it can be exercised.

0.199

* Include 'accordion' provisions—(also called 'Incremental Facilities'[75]). These are uncommitted facilities for the provision of further funds to the borrower on request, benefitting from the same guarantees and security as the existing debt. If the required amount is not forthcoming from the existing syndicate, new lenders may be brought into the loan agreement to make up the shortfall. In loans where syndicate consent is needed for additional borrowing, a key factor in the attractiveness of these facilities is the fact that such consent is not required for drawing the incremental facility, as long as the facility fulfils certain criteria as to, e.g. maturity, **yield**, most favoured nation terms and pari passu status (including preserving the pro rata payment mechanism on payments).

0.200

* Allow for certain 'structural adjustments' to be made with a lower level of consent from the existing syndicate than would normally be necessary for increasing the loan amount. So for example the addition of a new tranche with a later maturity than the original loan may be permitted with consent of Majority Lenders and all lenders in the new tranche, provided the new tranche meets certain criteria similar to those for an Incremental Facility.

---

[75] Although it would appear that in the US market, the two expressions are not used interchangeably—see LSTA's *Handbook of Loan Syndications and Trading*, 2nd edn, 2022, pp111–114.

0.201

- The LMA has included optional provisions for accordions and structural adjustments into its leveraged facilities. Where the original loan agreement restricted further borrowing it is worth the syndicate reviewing the various different clauses under which additional debt may be incurred (e.g. incremental, structural adjustment, debt permitted if certain incurrence ratios are met, etc.) to iron out any unintentional inconsistencies in the conditions on which such debts may be incurred. Existing Lenders may also want to cap the amount of debt which can be incurred by non guarantor subsidiaries, given concerns about structural subordination to loans to such subsidiaries.

4. Borrowers and affiliates purchasing in the secondary market

0.202
Optional wording dealing with this was introduced after a Danish telecom company—TDC—bought 200 million Euros of its debt in the secondary market at a discount of 90–95%. The LMA provides two options as to how to deal with this. The first option prohibits transfers to borrowers or their Affiliates. The second option permits it but provides that the purchaser's offer to purchase must be capable of being accepted by all the lenders pro rata so that the borrower cannot pick and choose which lender to buy out (just as they cannot choose who to prepay). This option also provides that the purchaser will not have any voting rights in relation to its share of the loan.

0.203
Comment Where there is a senior and junior loan, senior lenders might also want to consider adding similar provisions preventing the junior lenders or their affiliates from buying into the senior loan and influencing voting there primarily to protect their own position in the junior loan.

Section 6: Non Standard Provisions   **71**

5. Lehman provisions

0.204

In June 2009, as a result of the 2008 financial crisis, the LMA published (and subsequently updated) a number of clauses addressing lender default. These clauses (which the LMA refer to as the 'LMA Finance Party Default and Market Disruption Clauses' and which are commonly referred to as the 'Lehman Provisions'[76]) deal with:

0.205

* how to deal with the position where a lender is in financial difficulty;

0.206

* what to do if the Agent were in financial difficulty—and in particular how to ensure that this does not interfere with the flow of payments between the borrower and its lenders; and

0.207

* how to deal with a lender which is in financial difficulties when the facility provides for **letters of credit** to be issued, with the Issuing Bank relying on indemnities from syndicate members.

We will deal with each of the defaulting lender issues in turn.

Lender Default

0.208

The main consequences which the LMA clauses provide for are that:

---

[76] They are also known as 'Defaulting Lender provisions'.

72 **Introduction**

0.209

* The borrower ought not to be obliged to pay a **commitment fee** to a lender which is unlikely to be able to comply with its obligation to advance the undrawn **commitment**[77];

0.210

* The borrower ought to be able to bring in a different lender (referred to in the LMA Compounded/Term Rate Loan as an 'Increase Lender') to commit to advance the sums which the defaulting lender has not yet advanced[78];

0.211

* The defaulting lender's vote in syndicate meetings should be calculated on the basis of amounts it has actually advanced and should not take into account its undrawn commitment (since it may well not be able to comply with its obligations to advance that)[79];

0.212

* The borrower ought also to be able to remove the defaulting lender from the facility entirely (i.e. also in relation to sums already drawn) and replace it with a more acceptable lender[80];

0.213

* The borrower ought not to be obliged to repay that lender's participation in a revolving credit until the end of the **availability period** for that revolving credit[81];

---

[77] See 5.030.
[78] See 2.003.
[79] See 11.031.
[80] See 4.022.
[81] See 4.004.

0.214

* If the defaulting lender fails to respond promptly to requests for consent and the like, then its vote should be disregarded; and[82]

0.215

* The Agent may disclose the identity of the defaulting lender to the borrower.

0.216

Of course the documents also need to address the question of what is a defaulting lender and the Lehman provisions define this to mean a lender which fails to advance moneys when due or which makes it clear that it will not perform its obligations under the agreement or in relation to which **insolvency** procedures are commenced.

Impaired Agent

0.217

Next the Lehman provisions deal with the situation where problems arise in relation to the Agent. This would be of concern to all parties because the lenders take a credit risk on the Agent, in relation to monies paid through the Agent; and also because the Agent may become unable to continue to perform its communication role for the syndicate.

0.218

The Lehman provisions deal with this by providing that[83]:

0.219

* The Majority Lenders can remove the Agent and replace him with a new Agent;

---

[82] See 11.031.

[83] See 10.020.

74 Introduction

0.220

● Payments need not be made through Agent, but may either be made direct to the appropriate recipient or may be paid to a **trust** account with a third party bank (having a specified minimum credit **rating**) to be held on trust for the relevant recipient; and

0.221

● Communications need not be made through Agent but may be given directly between the parties.

0.222

The concept which is used to define a problem Agent is that of an 'Impaired Agent'. The idea is similar to that of a defaulting lender but recognizing the many different circumstances in which payments need to be made by Agents. So it is defined to mean an Agent which fails to make a payment when due or which makes it clear that it will not perform its obligations under the agreement (in each case, whether in its capacity as Agent, or, if applicable, as a lender) or in relation to which insolvency procedures are commenced.

Letter of Credit Facilities

0.223

The next area of concern is the situation where a defaulting lender participates in a letter of credit facility (see Box 0.26).

Box 0.26

A letter of credit is a method of payment used, for example, in export finance. A buyer wants to be sure that he only pays for goods when they have been shipped, but the seller does not want to ship them until he knows he will be paid. So the buyer's bank issues a letter of credit, which is essentially a promise by the bank to make payment on behalf of its customer, once proof of shipment is given. Once payment is made by the bank issuer it is entitled to receive repayment from its customer.

Under a letter of credit facility, the bank agrees that it will not require immediate repayment but that the amount paid on behalf of the customer will take the form of a loan, repayable over time. If the facility is syndicated then, once the Issuing Bank makes payment under the letter of credit, it will

Section 6: Non Standard Provisions   **75**

> require each syndicate member to reimburse it for that lender's share of the sum paid.

0.224

The problem here is that it is common for a single lender to issue the letter of credit and to rely on indemnities from syndicate members in respect of any payments made by the issuing lender under the letter of credit. Of course, if a syndicate member gets into financial difficulties the Issuing Bank will be concerned about—

- existing letters of credit—will the defaulting lender make payment when required? as well as about
- future letters of credit—it will not want to be obliged to issue additional letters of credit when it knows there is a problem with a syndicate member.

0.225

The general position should be, just as in a syndicated loan, that it is the borrower who is taking the credit risk on the syndicate members. To achieve this, the Lehman provisions provide that: the Issuing Bank may require a defaulting lender to provide cash **collateral** for its participation in the facility, but that, if it fails to provide that, the borrower has the option to provide cash collateral (or can be required to do so if the letter of credit has already been issued). The document goes on to provide that if no cash collateral is provided, the Issuing Bank can reduce amounts of unissued letters of credit by the amount of that lender's **participation**.

Note also that these provisions apply not only to defaulting lenders but also to lenders of below a specified rating.

0.226

The Lehman provisions also include optional provisions allowing the borrower to appoint more than one bank as the bank which will issue letters of credit under the loan agreement. The purpose is to allow a fallback position if one of the banks appointed to that role gets into financial difficulties.

76   Introduction

Section 7: Commodification and Digitization of Debt

0.227
The credit crunch of 2007–2008 was widely seen as resulting from the massive commodification of debt which happened since the invention of securitization and credit derivatives. These instruments gave rise to the growth of the so-called 'shadow banking system'—with all the challenges which give rise to for regulators and for borrowers.

More recently the rise of fintech and blockchain technology has revolutionized consumer finance and is beginning to take hold in key areas of commercial finance such as trade finance. At the same time there has been increasing digitization of the processes used in syndicated loans, from kyc, initial marketing, and through to secondary sales. The trend of commodification and digitization of debt looks set to continue.

0.228
This part of the Introduction gives a brief description of the growth and influence of non-bank lenders on the loan market and highlights some of the complications which this creates for the documents.

0.229
There are three key issues to consider.

0.230

- The first is the fact that there may be lenders in the syndicate which are not banks.

0.231

- The second issue is that the lenders of record may not have retained the credit risk in relation to the loan, but may have sold it on. Moreover, some lenders may have purchased the debt at a discount in the secondary market. These factors may influence the lenders' motivation when it comes to requests for consent and the like and can lead to considerable complexity in the context of restructuring distressed debt.

Section 7: Commodification and Digitization of Debt 77

0.232

* The third issue is that the increased trading of loans has led to a convergence between market practices in the loan markets and capital markets, as investors increasingly participate in both markets.

We will look at each of these issues in turn

1. Non-bank lenders as direct lenders

0.233

Pension funds, insurance companies, hedge funds and 'CLOs'[84] all participate in loans. This has been the case for many years but the increased regulation and state of the financial markets after the financial crisis (in Europe at least), added impetus to this as banks retrenched and companies had to look elsewhere for funds. The LMA Compounded/Term Rate Loan allows interests in the loan to be transferred to any entity which is '*regularly engaged in ... investing in ... financial assets*'.[85] So there is very broad scope for different types of entities to buy into the loan. See Box 0.27 for a discussion of the expression 'financial institution'.

Box 0.27

Even if the borrower restricted the loan agreement so that the loan could only be transferred to a bank or financial institution, in two cases in 2006 and 2017[86] in the UK it was held that the expression 'financial institution' encompassed 'a legally recognised form or being which carries on its business in accordance with the laws of its place of creation and whose business involves commercial finance'. The 2017 case went on to clarify that an entity could be a 'financial institution' without being involved in lending money and without operating on its own behalf in the field of regulated finance. On the other hand, a US case has held that a distressed debt fund was not a 'financial institution'.[87] If the borrower does want to restrict transferees, these cases highlight that the interpretation of any expression depends on the facts of the case and therefore any restrictions must be carefully worded.

---

[84] CLO stands for **Collateralised Loan Obligation**. It is an investment which can be issued to purchasers, giving them a share in the **pool** of assets (loans) underlying the CLO.

[85] LMA Compounded/Term Rate Loan Clause 26.1 (*CHANGES TO THE LENDERS*: *Assignments and transfers by the Lenders*) discussed in 9.043.

78 **Introduction**

0.234

Involvement of non-banks as direct lenders has a number of consequences:

0.235

- Some of these entities may also trade in shares so they may not want to receive non-public information from the borrower as that may restrict their ability to trade the shares. The LMA Compounded/Term Rate Loan has addressed this by allowing lenders to nominate a third party to receive information on their behalf so as to filter out any non-public information[88];

0.236

- Some of these entities may not have the duties of confidentiality which a bank has—hence the introduction of a confidentiality clause in the LMA Compounded/Term Rate Loan imposing duties of confidentiality on lenders[89];

0.237

- Some of these lenders may have a different business model and strategy from traditional banks, and so may adopt a different approach in any proposed restructuring

0.238

- Many of these lenders do not want to be consulted on anything other than major issues—they do not have the manpower to deal with requests and are used to investing in bonds which have much less restrictive undertakings than loans. This gives rise to two issues:

  - they may not respond to requests for consent (making consent harder to achieve unless there is a snooze you lose clause[90]) and

---

[86] Argo Fund Ltd v Essar Steel Ltd [2006] 2 All E.R. (Comm) 104 and Grant and others v WDW 3 Investments Ltd and another [2017] EWHC 2807 (Ch).

[87] *Meridian Sunrise Village v NB Distressed Debt Investment Fund Ltd (2014) WL 909219.*

[88] See 10.016.

[89] See 11.034.

[90] See Box 11.6.

Section 7: Commodification and Digitization of Debt — 79

– They may prefer the loan to have less onerous undertakings (the so-called '**covenant lite**' transactions discussed in 8.073, which were criticized as being part of the issues behind the credit crisis and which remain common).

2. Direct lenders transferring credit risk

0.239

Turning to the second issue—lenders may not have kept the credit risk of the loan but may have sold that on through credit derivatives. The most popular form of **credit derivative** is a **credit default swap** (or 'CDS'). It is effectively rather like insurance in that the lender of record, in exchange for a fee, receives compensation if there is a 'Credit Event' such as failure to pay, **bankruptcy** or restructuring. The **lender of record** is known as the 'purchaser'—buying credit protection; and the counterparty is the 'seller'— selling credit protection (see Box 0.28).

> **Box 0.28**
>
> A credit default swap may be issued in relation to a particular debt, or in relation to a bundle of debts of a given type. For example, they could relate to debts of a particular borrower or from a particular country or with some other particular characteristic (such as sub-prime mortgage debt). A buyer of protection does not need to hold the debt to enter into such an arrangement. A seller of protection may also offer protection against different tranches of risk—such as the first 5% of loss. credit default swaps are discussed in more detail in relation to Clause 26 *(Changes to Lenders)* in 9.021.

0.240

The result of this is that there is an active market for credit risk which can be traded without trading the underlying debt itself. A lender which has purchased credit protection may have little motivation to support the company in difficult times, and borrowers are unlikely to know whether their lenders have purchased credit protection or not.[91]

---

[91] See further 9.035 onwards.

80   Introduction

0.241

The market for **distressed debt** also leads to difficulties in organizing restructurings not only because of the difficulty in identifying all the relevant stakeholders but also because of their different incentives. Some investors in distressed debt may be following a 'loan to own' policy—with the intention of taking over the company or its assets in a restructuring. Others may have purchased at a discount and have a very different perspective to the original lenders on any proposed restructuring.[92]

0.242

The upside of all this is increased sources of funds, particularly in times when banks are retrenching. The downside is increasing difficulties in organizing restructurings, or even just in obtaining consents, and stress on the documentation which was drafted to deal with relationships in a very different financial landscape from that which exists today.

3. Convergence with capital markets

0.243

It is also worth noting that this commodification of debt has increased the liquidity of loan investments, leading to some convergence between practices in the loan markets and the capital markets—(see Box 0.29) particularly in the leveraged acquisition market where investors commonly invest in both types of debt—that is, they take participations in traditional loans and also invest in debt instruments in the capital markets. One well-known example is the so-called 'covenant lite' loan—a loan with less onerous undertakings than has been traditional in the loan market, but which is acceptable to investors who traditionally invest in the capital markets.

Box 0.29

For some companies needing to raise money, they have the option of raising it from the public, instead of approaching banks or other lenders. This is what is meant by the 'capital markets'. The most familiar form is for a listed company to issue shares, but the capital markets deal in many forms of investments, including debt instruments, commonly referred to as bonds or notes. From the borrowers' point of view, issuing bonds is similar to raising money through a loan from banks, in that the bond issue will raise a given amount of funds,

---

[92] See LSTA's *Handbook of Loan Syndications and Trading*, 2nd edn, 2022, Chapter 10.

Section 7: Commodification and Digitization of Debt   81

> on which the borrower must pay interest, and which must be repaid on specified dates. In the meantime the borrower will need to comply with various undertakings which they have agreed to in the documentation.

0.244

There are still significant differences between financing in the loan markets and in the capital markets, principally in:

0.245

- the amount of publicity involved—loans are confidential while bond issues involve the provision to the public of extensive amounts of information;

0.246

- the amounts of money which can be raised (and its cost)—the size and liquidity of the capital markets enables borrowers to raise more money more cheaply than by using loan finance;

0.247

- less restrictive terms of financing in the capital markets in terms of the undertakings and Events of Default;

0.248

- raising money in the capital markets is not possible for all companies as they need to be large enough, and sufficiently creditworthy to be able to attract the investors;

0.249

- the degree of regulation involved—the accepted view (uncertainty around which was clarified to a certain extent in 2014, see Box 0.30) has been that loan agreements are not specified investments under the Financial Services and Markets Act 2000, whereas bonds and similar instruments issued in the capital markets are regulated.

82 Introduction

> **Box 0.30**
>
> The case of Fons HF (in liquidation) v Corporal Limited and Pillar Securitisation [2014] EWCA Civ 304 however held that, contrary to the accepted view, loan agreements are **debentures** (defined as an instrument which evidences a debt). The case did not concern regulatory issues but the implications of the decision are that if a loan agreement is a debenture then it is a regulated investment. Nevertheless the Financial Conduct Authority has confirmed that they do not regard the case as having altered the previously accepted position.[93]

Section 8: Asset, Project and Acquisition (or 'Leveraged') Finance

1. Asset finance

0.250
Asset finance is financing of an asset where the lender regards the value of the asset being financed as a significant factor in its credit assessment. The expression is commonly used for ship finance, aircraft finance, financing of rolling stock, satellites, containers and other major assets.

0.251
Key issues in asset finance, which need to be addressed by the documents[94] and by due diligence, include:

0.252

* conflict of law (e.g. the law chosen for the loan agreement, the law applicable to the security, and the law in the place where the asset is at the time any security comes to be enforced);

---

[93] The letter explains the implications of the case and is available from the website at www.citysolicitors. org.uk (search 'Fons').

[94] See, for example, Sect. 2 of the commentary on the undertakings in 8.208 onwards.

Section 8: Asset, Project and Acquisition (or 'Leveraged') Finance 83

0.253

- whether to structure the transaction as a **mortgage** financing or as a **title financing**[95];

0.254

- liabilities of a financier (such as the issue of whether the financier will be exposed to environmental liabilities, either simply as a result of taking security over the asset, or as a result of ownership of it in a title finance arrangement, or as a result of the enforcement of security over the asset);

0.255

- detention rights of third parties relating to the asset, if it is a moveable asset. The issue here is to identify what parties may be entitled to detain the asset and prevent its profitable use. Examples are the **lien** which a repairer has on an asset until the repair bill is paid and the right of port states to detain vessels for safety reasons;

0.256

- maintenance of the asset—the lenders will want to be sure that the asset is properly maintained and, perhaps, that funds are set aside for this purpose;

0.257

- preservation of the value of the asset generally, including loan to value ratios[96];

0.258

- insurance—the lenders will want to have security over the asset's insurance so that, if there is damage to it, the lenders have replacement security. They will also want to be satisfied as to the insurance for potential liabilities to third parties arising in respect of the use of the asset;

---

[95] See 0.289.

[96] See commentary on Clause 23 (*Financial Covenants*) in 8.128.

84   Introduction

0.259

- impact of insolvency—are there risks that enforcement of security on the asset may be impeded as a result of insolvency proceedings such as **administration** in England, or that transactions such as guarantees may be vulnerable to be unwound in the event of an insolvency?

0.260

- registration—where does the asset and any security on it need to be registered and what are the consequences of non-registration?

0.261

- ability to sell the asset free of liens and other interests—and can the lender exercise self-help remedies, or will any sale have to be effected by a court?

2. Project finance

0.262

Project finance consists of lending against the income of a project. It usually involves:

- the development or exploitation of a right, natural resource or other asset;
- limited recourse lending;
- income capture with the debt being repaid out of the revenue generated by the project.

0.263

In relation to the loan agreement, key characteristics will be:

0.264

- strict undertakings in relation to the key contracts in the project, (see Box 0.31) for an illustration of some common key contracts) for example, undertakings not to amend them, **assignments** of these contracts to the lenders, and direct agreements between lenders and the counterparties to those contracts—allowing the lenders **step-in rights** (i.e. the right to step in and perform the contract on behalf of the borrower);

Section 8: Asset, Project and Acquisition (or 'Leveraged') Finance 85

Box 0.31

Typical Project Finance Contracts

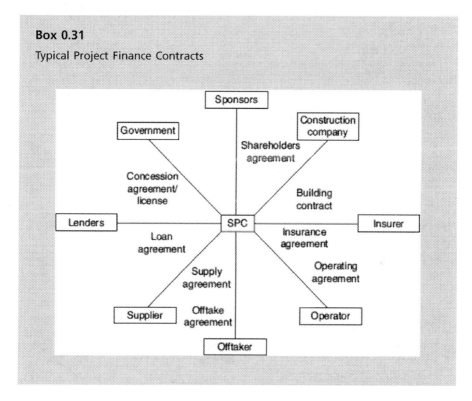

0.265

- the availability of funds from the lenders will be dependent on the rateable contribution from other lenders and/or **sponsors**;

0.266

- extensive information provision for the lenders;

0.267

- detailed project forecasts and budgets agreed in a financial model before the loan agreement is signed, with variations from the base case having numerous consequences, such as restricting drawings of the loan; restricting payment of **dividends**; changing the Margin; setting the amounts of repayments; and ultimately, triggering an Event of Default;

86   Introduction

0.268

- long drawdown period during construction, with interest possibly being capitalized, and drawings paid to a **disbursement account**;

0.269

- detailed expert evidence required as to the state of the project at various points during the drawdown period, as conditions precedent to further drawing;

0.270

- 'waterfall' for payment (see Box 0.32) of project income;

Box 0.32

The 'waterfall' is the expression commonly used to describe the series of accounts used to hold income generated in a project finance transaction. Typically these include:

- The revenue or operating account, into which income is paid and which is used to hold up to an agreed sum to pay for ordinary operating expenses;
- The debt service reserves account, which builds up an agreed cushion to pay for future **debt service**;
- The maintenance reserves account, which builds up an agreed cushion to pay for major maintenance costs;
- The distribution account—available to pay dividends to sponsors, subject to certain conditions.

0.271

- often, release of certain security (e.g. completion guarantee) once evidence of completion of the construction phase is provided;

0.272

- special purpose company undertakings—restricting the ability of the borrower to undertake other activities[97];

---

[97] See Sect. 2 of the commentary on Clause 24 (*General Undertakings*) from 8.199 onwards.

Section 8: Asset, Project and Acquisition (or 'Leveraged') Finance 87

0.273

* security over all project assets;

0.274

* limited recourse to sponsors (shareholders in the project company);

0.275

* extensive insurance undertakings;

0.276

* additional Events of Default if:
    - remaining development cost exceeds available funding;
    - ratios are not met;
    - insurance becomes voidable;
    - any relevant consent or licence is altered;
    - any physical damage occurs to project assets;
    - the project is abandoned;
    - **force majeure** occurs under a project document in excess of a specified period;
    - the project is expropriated;
    - completion is delayed; or
    - any project document is terminated.

3. Acquisition (or 'Leveraged' or 'Private Equity') finance

0.277

Acquisition finance is the provision of finance to enable the acquisition of a 'target' company, which may be a private or a public company. The acquisition loan will be secured by security and guarantees given by the target group to the extent that is possible without breaching financial assistance rules.

Some of the challenges which need to be addressed in acquisition finance are

0.278

Financial assistance

- In many countries directors' duties or statute restricts companies from providing financial assistance, such as loans, security or guarantees, for the acquisition of their own shares. There may be exceptions for private companies, or exceptions subject to certain conditions.

0.279

Certain funds

- Takeover regulation typically requires the bidder in a takeover of a public company to have '**certain funds**' (i.e. cash or fully committed funding) at the time they make an offer and this requirement has also become common in acquisitions of private companies. To meet this requirement, the loan agreement will include a 'Certain Funds Period' in which the lenders' ability to refuse to advance funds will be severely restricted and exercisable only in the event of certain 'Major Defaults'.

0.280

Loan purpose

- Given financial assistance restrictions the lenders would prefer to lend directly to the target company, as far as possible, rather than to the shareholders. The lenders are also likely to want to be the sole lenders for the group. As the group is likely to need working capital, foreign exchange and overdraft facilities, the acquisition loan will need to cover all these requirements. So the loan will need to include provision for refinancing existing debt, (which will probably have a change of control clause so that the acquisition will trigger a requirement for prepayment) a revolving credit for working capital; and 'ancillaries' for the sort of banking services, such as foreign exchange and overdraft facilities, normally provided by relationship banks.

Section 8: Asset, Project and Acquisition (or 'Leveraged') Finance 89

0.281

Leverage

* A key driver in acquisition finance is leverage. That is, the parties want to use as little equity as possible and as much debt as possible. See Box 0.33 to see the impact of leverage on sponsors' profits and losses. Leverage is key to the transaction. To achieve this and attract as much debt as possible there will be different layers of debt. Typically there will be more than one tranche of senior debt (with tranches having different maturity dates to attract lenders who need senior status but want to take different degrees of risk) as well as junior debt and perhaps shareholder and other tiers of debt. This gives rise to issues in the loan agreement around the relationship between the different tranches of debt in terms of, e.g. application of prepayments and voting rights.

Box 0.33

For example loan finance might be 100 and equity may be 1. If the company makes a profit of 2 then the shareholders have doubled their money. If the company becomes insolvent the shareholders have only lost 1.

0.282

Conditions subsequent and clean up

It is usually impractical to investigate the legal obstacles—such as financial assistance, directors' duties and tax consequences—of the target and its subsidiaries giving guarantees and security before the point at which the lenders need to commit to the loan for the purpose of the certain funds requirement. Therefore it is common to simply take security on the shares in the target at the time of the loan by the arrangers, and to deal with security and guarantees from the target group as a condition subsequent.

90 Introduction

0.283

Given that the lenders will be aware from the start that there will be limits on the ability of the target group to give security and guarantees, the condition subsequent will limit the target's obligation to provide such security with reference to the '**Agreed Security Principles**'—which essentially say that the lenders will not request security or guarantees to the extent that the costs and legal and tax consequences involved would be disproportionate to the benefits.

0.284

The lenders will protect themselves by requiring a 'guarantor coverage ratio'—requiring that at all times they have guarantees from companies in the target group which generate a specified percentage of consolidated EBITDA as well as from all Material Subsidiaries.

0.285

Similarly, it may be impractical for the target group to ensure that the target company is in full compliance with the terms of the loan agreement immediately as of the date of the acquisition. To deal with this the loan agreement may include a clean up period (not to be confused with a **clean down** period) during which the lender agrees it will not have acceleration rights for Events of Default caused by breaches of undertakings at the target group level.

Section 9: Quasi Security and Financial Indebtedness

1. Quasi security[98]

0.286

Quasi security means arrangements which have the same commercial effect as security. It comprises both title financing and other arrangements.

0.287

Title financing is using title (or ownership to property) instead of security, such as is done in **finance leases** or **hire purchase agreements** (as discussed here). Most title financing arrangements involve the separation of

---

[98] See, for example, Ross Cranston et al., *Principles of Banking Law*, 3rd edn, 2018 at pp553–555.

Section 9: Quasi Security and Financial Indebtedness 91

legal ownership (or title) to an asset from the economic ownership of the asset (or the commercial risks and rewards which go with ownership such as the risk or reward of a loss or gain in value of the asset). There are many different reasons for using title finance. In some cases, a tax or accounting advantage is sought. In others, the structure is used as an alternative to security because of unavailability of satisfactory security in the relevant jurisdiction. Whatever the purpose of the arrangements, their commercial effect is equivalent to the effect of security (but see also Box 0.34). Therefore any provisions in a loan agreement which deal with security must also deal with these arrangements.

Box 0.34

Title financing is often used as an alternative to security but careful **due diligence** is necessary, not only as to the legal effect but also as to the tax, accounting, and regulatory effect. The person who is treated as the 'owner' of the asset for accounting purposes may be different from the 'owner' for tax purposes; the 'owner' for regulatory purposes[99]; and the owner for other legal purposes. In some countries, the structure will not be treated, for legal purposes, in accordance with its apparent effect, but will be **'recharacterized'** in accordance with its substantive effect. This may lead to a requirement that such arrangements be registered as though they were security (as in New York) or to the arrangements not being effective at all.

0.288

Other arrangements, such as rights of **set off**, do not amount to title financing but can also have a similar impact on security and therefore are discussed together with title financing in this Sect. 9.

0.289

Examples of title financing include the following:

---

[99] For example, is a temporary owner of shares under a **repo** treated as the owner for regulatory purposes such as duty to disclose major shareholdings?

0.290

Hire purchase, conditional sale and similar arrangements

These are arrangements under which the owner of the asset is simply a financier and the other party to the transaction has the commercial risks and benefits of ownership. They have the commercial effect of borrowing.

0.291
In a hire purchase arrangement, the owner (financier) funds the purchase of the asset and receives rent through the hire purchase sufficient to pay off the funding cost plus interest. Once paid, the ownership of the asset is transferred to the other party for a nominal price. The effect is as though the owner had lent the funds to the other party and had been given security over the asset. In a conditional sale the owner (financier) sells the asset on the basis that the price can be paid over time but, until paid in full, the ownership of the asset remains with the seller. Until 2019 International Financial Reporting Standards drew a distinction between these sorts of transactions (where the risks and rewards were not with the owner and which were referred to as 'finance leases') and other arrangements in which the owner retained the risks and rewards of ownership, which were referred to as '**operating leases**' (such as short-term rentals of assets). US Generally Accepted Accounting Principles still make that distinction for some purposes. See also the discussion on the definition of 'Financial Indebtedness' from 1.025 onwards.

Title retention

0.292
If a seller gives credit to the purchaser of an asset and retains title to the asset until paid, the commercial effect is as if the purchaser had given security over the asset for the amount of the credit.[100]

0.293
Another example is an instalment sale agreement, or a conditional sale agreement under which title only passes on payment of the final purchase instalment or fulfilment of other conditions.

---

[100] In some countries, the seller is automatically given a security interest for unpaid purchase moneys so that title retention would be unnecessary.

Section 9: Quasi Security and Financial Indebtedness 93

Selling receivables but keeping the associated risk (as in some securitizations)

0.294

A distinction needs to be drawn between situations where the receivables are sold together with the risk[101] and where they are sold but the risk is retained by the seller.

0.295

For example, compare the situation where

0.296

- debts with a face value of $10 million are sold for $8 million and

0.297

- the same debts are sold at the same price but the seller keeps the risk (e.g. by giving a **guarantee** to the buyer of the payment of the debts).

Assume the debtors pay only $6 million. In the first case, that is of no concern to the seller. In the second, the seller must compensate the buyer. The commercial effect of the second case is as though the seller had borrowed $8 million from the buyer and given security over the receivables.

Forward sale

0.298

This may be illustrated by an example. Let us assume that a manufacturer of watches, in order to raise finance, agrees with a 'lender' in January, for a price paid by the 'lender' at that time, that the next 500 watches produced will belong to the 'lender'. In other words, the 'lender' will purchase the watches in advance of their manufacture.[102] The 'lender' may then appoint the manufacturer as his agent to sell the watches with a requirement that a certain part

---

[101] Often referred to as a 'true sale', and, depending on the purpose of the securitization, the requirement of a true sale may be key to its effectiveness.

[102] To be effective, the relevant jurisdiction would need to recognize agreements to sell future property as being binding.

94   Introduction

of the sale proceeds be paid over to the 'lender' and with the manufacturer guaranteeing to make up any shortfall between the proceeds of sale recovered by the 'lender' and the advance price originally paid by the 'lender' plus 'interest'. The commercial effect is as though the manufacturer had given security over the watches to raise a loan.

Forward purchase (as in repos)

0.299
This is an arrangement where a company owns an asset, such as shares, and, in order to raise finance, sells those shares to a financier for, say, $5 million, and agrees to repurchase them in six months' time for $6 million. The commercial effect is very similar to the situation if the company had borrowed $5 million and given the shares as security.

Set off

0.300
Set off is a procedural rule which allows a party which owes money to another to reduce the amount he pays to that other by an amount which that other party owes to him.

0.301
The availability of this right of set off is a matter of law in the courts in which it is asserted. It may have the same commercial effect as security in some cases. For example, if a borrower of a loan of $10 million has a bank account with its lender with $5 million deposited, and the lender, if unpaid, can set off the amount in the bank account (leaving it with no obligation to pay over the deposit and with the amount of its loan reduced to $5 million), the commercial effect is as though the lender had security over the bank account.[103]

---

[103] But a right of set off is not as good as security in all cases (and may even be better than security in some instances). See A1.066.

Cash deposits

0.302
Depositing money with a party could have the same commercial effect as security either because of the set off rights which will arise or because of formal or informal arrangements allowing that other party to forfeit the sums deposited in certain circumstances or because those sums are part of a payment mechanism.[104]

Trust arrangements

0.303
If a company holds an asset on trust for others then that asset is, just as it would be if security had been given over it, not available to that company's creditors generally in the insolvency of the company. If the trust is for the purpose of securing an obligation it may amount to a form of security[105]

2. Financial Indebtedness

0.304
In considering quasi security it is also useful to look at the breadth of arrangements by which finance can be raised and which can have the same commercial effect as borrowing money. Examples of such arrangements are described here.

Acceptance credit facility

0.305
This is an agreement by a lender to accept (or become liable for) bills of exchange issued by the company. Under this arrangement the lender agrees

---

[104] See Goode and Gullifer, '*Legal Problems of Credit and Security*' 7th edn, 2022, in 1.55.

[105] In fact, it may amount to a registrable security interest—see Goode and Gullifer '*Legal Problems of Credit and Security*' 7th edn, 2022, in 1.39.

96   Introduction

to make payment to a third party under the **bill of exchange** on behalf of the company. The effect is as if the lender lent the equivalent amount to the company.

Bonds (like notes or commercial paper)

0.306
Bonds are simply promises to pay, which are traded in the capital markets. A company will issue a bond (or note, or paper) which will be purchased in the capital markets and then traded. The purchase price will be paid to the company. The company has effectively borrowed the amount paid to it.

Note purchase facility

0.307
This is a facility under which a financier agrees to buy **promissory notes** issued by the company.

Loan stock

0.308
Money borrowed from investors and represented by certificates which can be sold by the investors in whole or in part. Loan stock may be secured, in which case it is known as debenture loan stock. It may be convertible into shares on terms specified in the stock, in which case it is known as convertible loan stock.

Seller's credit

0.309
Where a seller sells goods but agrees to delayed payment.

Forward sale

0.310

Selling assets which are not owned yet may amount to borrowing money. For example, assume a furniture store sells furniture and requires payment in advance of the purchase of that furniture by the store. The store has effectively borrowed money from its customers.

Other title financing

0.311

Other methods of title financing discussed above amount to borrowing on a secured basis, being finance leasing, forward purchase (e.g. repos) and selling receivables on recourse terms.

Section 10: Socially Responsible Lending (or 'ESG Lending')

1. What is ESG Lending?

0.312

Socially responsible lending has a long history with environmental and social policies having been included in the loan documentation of many development banks since at least the beginning of the century. The **Equator Principles**, first published in 2003 and the **Poseidon Principles**, first published in 2019, are examples of frameworks designed to promote and facilitate socially responsible lending in their respective financing sectors. In 2011 the UN published its Principles for Responsible Investment and in 2018/2019 the LMA/ LSTA published the first set of Green Loan Principles and Sustainability Linked Loan Principles, aimed at the lending market generally, followed by the Social Loan Principles in 2021. (together the 'Loan Principles'). Popular with investors, lenders, companies, ratings agencies and regulators, 'ESG' (or environmental, social and governance) lending caught on with rapid increases in 2020 and 2021.

98   Introduction

0.313

Ensuring continued popularity of ESG lending will require that it maintains a reputation for effectiveness and avoids any hint of **greenwashing**. The Loan Principles therefore have a heavy focus on transparency, verification and challenging targets. At the time of writing, when ESG lending is in its infancy, there are many inherent challenges to the development of a robust framework for the industry, which regulators are grappling with. See Box 0.35.

Box 0.35

Challenges to the development of ESG Lending include:

- the breadth of activities which ESG lending seeks to encourage;
- the moral judgements involved (e.g. is a windfarm which powers increased fossil fuel extraction green?);
- the lack of a single body responsible for setting criteria for establishing exactly what qualifies as sustainable;
- scientific developments resulting in changing standards and different expectations as to what counts as sustainable, and
- the absence of consistency in measurement of targets. The ESG ratings which different agencies award to companies rarely agree—since they use inconsistent criteria to reach their conclusions.

0.314

The EU regulations have been introduced to increase transparency and standardization. The principal regulation is the **EU Taxonomy Regulation**[106] which outlines six environmental objectives for an activity to qualify as being environmentally sustainable and states that, for an activity to be environmentally sustainable it must make a substantial contribution to one of those objectives and not cause significant harm to any of the others. This regulation is supported by the disclosure regulations of The EU Corporate Sustainability Reporting Directive[107] and the Sustainable Finance Disclosure Regulation.[108] Meanwhile, elsewhere the International Sustainability Standards Board (founded in 2021 as an arm of the **IFRS**—or International Financial Reporting Standards Foundation) aims to make sustainability reporting as consistent as financial reporting.

---

[106] Regulation (EU) 2020/852 on the establishment of a framework to facilitate sustainable investment.

[107] Directive (EU) 2022/2464, amending earlier directives.

[108] Regulation (EU) 2019/2088 on sustainability-related disclosures in the financial services sector (**SFDR or Disclosure Regulation**).

2. Categories of ESG Lending

0.315
Two distinct categories of ESG Lending have emerged. These are

0.316

Sustainability Linked Loans

- which are available for use for any purpose and under which borrowers are incentivized (invariably through a reduction in the Margin) to achieve specified sustainability targets (such as reduced emissions); and

0.317

Green Loans and Social Loans

- These are loans which are provided for a green purpose (e.g. renewable energy) or a social purpose (e.g. affordable housing) respectively.[109] Use for a different purpose would be an Event of Default and the borrower should no longer be permitted to describe the loan as 'Green' or 'Social'.

3. Key issues in ESG Lending

0.318
The core objective of ESG lending is to make a difference. Achieving that requires the application of rigorous processes in the following areas[110]:

- Choice of project/ targets;
- Reporting;
- Updating; and
- Verifying.

---

[109] The Loan Principles include a non exhaustive list of the types of projects which will be regarded as Green or Social.

[110] Given that the Sustainability Loan Principles, Green Loan Principles and Social Loan Principles have different objectives, each set of Loan Principles has a different degree of focus on these core topics reflecting the different purposes of the loans which they relate to.

100 Introduction

We look at each of these in turn

Choice of project/targets

0.319

Given the fact that there is no one single body for establishing criteria; and that standards change over time, lenders need to be particularly rigorous in their choice of projects to fund or targets to incentivise. They need to be careful to ensure that they pay close attention to the latest guidelines, regulations and best practices. They are also likely to want to take the broader picture into account. For example, they may decide not to categorize a loan as Green if the borrower has a poor sustainability profile generally, even though this project on its own might fulfil the criteria specified in the relevant Loan Principles.

0.320

In relation to Sustainability Linked Loans, the relevant Loan Principles emphasize the need for setting ambitious sustainability goals, aligned to the borrower's overall sustainability strategy. To achieve this the Principles focus on two key issues:

0.321

* The choice of sustainability goals (such as reduced water consumption or improved energy efficiency)—referred to as key performance indicators or **KPI's**. These need to be material to the borrower's core business and to address significant challenges faced by the business. They also need to be measurable against a known baseline and benchmarked against an industry standard.

0.322

* The calibration of targets—referred to as sustainability performance targets or **SPT's**. In other words, identifying how ambitious the borrower wants to be in achieving its sustainability goals—what does it want to achieve and by when? These targets need to be ambitious and not just to be 'business as usual'. They need to be benchmarked against the borrower's past

Section 10: Socially Responsible Lending (or 'ESG Lending') 101

performance, that of its peers and/or against official targets such as the Paris Agreement on Climate Change.

0.323

Lenders may not have the internal expertise to address the detailed issues involved in agreeing KPI's and SPT's, so as to ensure that they are sufficiently challenging without being unrealistic, or in evaluating the merits of any proposed Green or Social Loan or framework for future drawings under a Green or **Social Loan**. They may want a 'second party opinion'[111] from experts assessing the alignment of the loan with the Loan Principles. In the case of Sustainability Linked Loans this opinion may assess the relevance and ambitiousness of the KPI's and SPT's. In the case of Green and Social Loans it may assess the borrower's overall strategy and the benefits (and risks) anticipated from the financed project/the suitability of any framework for identifying future projects. See Box 0.36 for a discussion of the use of third party ESG ratings as KPI's.

Box 0.36

Third party ESG ratings could be used as a KPI but the methodologies used by third parties in determining ratings is inconsistent, resulting in significantly different ratings being allocated to the same company by different agencies. The Loan Principles therefore discourage their use on their own. Steps are underway in the EU to regulate ESG ratings agencies which may in time result in more consistency.

Reporting

0.324

Green and Social Loans may be made to finance a single project or to finance numerous different projects; commonly with a framework included for identifying further projects to be funded. Lenders will want regular reporting on the use of loan proceeds and on the impact of the project(s) funded.

---

[111] See further LMA's Guidance for Green, Social, and Sustainability-Linked Loans External Reviews available from their website.

102 Introduction

0.325

For Sustainability Linked Loans the relevant Loan Principles state that borrowers should report to lenders at least annually with enough information to allow lenders to monitor progress against targets and whether the targets are still relevant. Borrowers are also to be encouraged to make the relevant information publicly available.

Verifying

0.326

In the context of Green or Social loans, this involves an independent expert auditing standards or claims made by the borrower or its method of tracking use of the loan proceeds. In the context of Sustainability Linked Loans it involves an independent expert auditing performance against the KPI's at least annually, so as to enable the lenders to determine whether or not the Margin reduction has been earned.

Updating

0.327

In Sustainability Linked Loans lenders will need to ensure that the targets remain relevant and challenging as science changes; as the borrower's business may change; and as benchmarks and data availability for measuring performance changes. The documents will commonly include a review process to address this. Lenders may also want to include an 'ESG Controversy' clause allowing them to disallow the relevant Margin adjustment even if the KPI's are met, in the event of an adverse ESG incident, such as an environmental incident.

4. Documentation of Sustainability Linked Loans

0.328

At the time of writing there are no standard documents for these loans and the market is in its infancy. Some themes are worth highlighting.

Appointment of a Sustainability Co-ordinator

0.329

A lender may be appointed as Sustainability Coordinator for the syndicate. The role of the Sustainability Coordinator (in general terms) is to assist with the negotiation and monitoring of KPI's and SPT's and to deal with queries arising in relation to ESG issues.[112] They will commonly seek to ensure that their liability is limited in the same way as the Agent's liability (as discussed in 10.010) and that they are just an intermediary between the syndicate and the experts giving ESG advice such as those providing the second party opinions.

Reporting, verifying and updating

0.330

Lenders are likely to require a second party opinion as a condition precedent, with at least annual reporting and external verification of success or otherwise in achieving the KPI's. The identity of the third party providing the verification and the form of the verification will need to be documented. The loan agreement will also be likely to include provisions enabling the targets to be reviewed in the event of changes.

Consequences of meeting or not meeting the ESG provisions

<u>Green and Social Loans</u>

0.331

Use of the loan for a purpose which does not qualify is an Event of Default. Breach of reporting requirements may be an Event of Default or may result in declassification of the loan (potentially resulting in reporting requirements for the borrower) as it affects the lenders' ability to ensure the loan is indeed achieving its objective.

---

[112] See LMA's Introduction to the Sustainability Coordinator Role issued in July 2022.

104   Introduction

Sustainability Linked Loans

0.332
If there is more than one KPI do they all have to be met in order to achieve a Margin reduction or does each KPI operate independently?

0.333
Should failure to meet KPI's result in a Margin increase? Lenders are unlikely to want to be seen to profit from failure to meet the relevant targets. Mechanisms where the Margin is increased and the increase donated to a relevant charity or retained for release against expenses of improving performance against the targets may be considered.

0.334
What are the consequences of a breach of the reporting requirements?

- There should be a requirement to repay any reduction in Margin attributable to any inaccurate reporting.
- Should failure to report

  - be an Event of Default or
  - simply result in the Margin benefit not being awarded or
  - result in declassification of the loan (possibly after some negotiation period) so that the Margin benefits will no longer be available and the borrower may have reporting obligations in relation to the declassification?

Administrative Provisions

This Part deals with those parts of a loan agreement which are mechanical in nature: the definitions, procedures for drawdown, calculation of interest and the like.

Interpretation

Clause 1: Definitions and Interpretation—Section 1—An Introduction

1.001

Loan agreements contain detailed definitions. This helps

- to ensure consistency between different provisions of the document;
- to avoid ambiguity; and
- to keep the complexities out of the body of the agreement (see Box 1.1).

> **Box 1.1**
>
> For example, in the operative provisions, a simple statement can be made, such as *The Borrower shall not create any Encumbrances other than Permitted Encumbrances.* The general purpose of this provision is easily understood, while its application, and therefore its impact on the borrower, is only understood by reviewing the detail in the definitions.

1.002

There are traps for the unwary in using definitions. Principally these are:

© The Author(s), under exclusive license to Springer Nature Switzerland AG 2024
S. Wright, *The International Loan Documentation Handbook*, Global Financial Markets, https://doi.org/10.1007/978-3-031-38489-9_2

108   Interpretation

- reading (or not reading) the definitions in context;
- appreciating (or failing to appreciate) that the definitions may need different meanings in different contexts;
- avoiding circular definitions; and
- avoiding including operative provisions.[1]

We look at each of these issues here.

1. Definitions out of context

1.003

It is hard to comment on, or to fully appreciate the implications of, any particular definition out of context (see Box 1.2).

Box 1.2

For example, appreciating whether the definition of 'Financial Indebtedness' should or should not include **derivative** transactions depends on the reader knowing where the definition will be used and with what purpose.[2]

It may therefore be sensible to skip the definitions clause and start reading from the operative clauses starting in Clause 2 (*The Facilities*) of the LMA Compounded/Term Rate Loan[3] (or, rather, in Clause 1.2 *(DEFINITIONS AND INTERPRETATION: Construction)*, for reasons discussed here). When a defined term is encountered, its definition can then be reviewed in context. This makes it easier to appreciate the detail of the definition.

The suggestion is to commence reading in Clause 1.2 *(DEFINITIONS AND INTERPRETATION: Construction)*, so as to be aware of any words which have been defined by that clause without that fact being flagged by the use of capital letters.

---

[1] Provisions which 'operate' or actually do something as opposed to the provisions of the definitions in the definitions clause which are merely descriptive.

[2] See comments on the definition of Financial Indebtedness in 1.026 for a discussion on the inclusion of derivatives in this definition.

[3] References in this book to the LMA Compounded/Term Rate Loan are to the LMA Multicurrency Term and Revolving Facilities Agreement incorporating Term Sofr for use in Investment Grade transactions, available to LMA members via www.lma.eu.com

Clause 1: Definitions and Interpretation—Section 1—An Introduction 109

1.004

Clause 1.2 *(DEFINITIONS AND INTERPRETATION: Construction)*, is intended to deal with references to *concepts* (such as a person) as opposed to *specific words* (such as '**Encumbrance**'). In this interpretation clause, concepts are broadened without their being given capital letters (see Box 1.3).

Box 1.3

So you can see there is no attempt to define 'person'—instead of saying 'person **means** ABC' the statement is that 'person **includes** ABC'. The idea is to **extend** the ordinary meaning, not to provide a complete definition.

This can lead to the existence of the wider meaning which has been given to the concept being overlooked. It is therefore sensible to read Clause 1.2 *(DEFINITIONS AND INTERPRETATION: Construction)*, before reviewing the operative clauses and to make special note of the words and concepts which have been defined without being capitalized (see Box 1.4).

Box 1.4

For example, assume the acceleration clause is drafted to say 'On, and at any time after, the occurrence of an Event of Default which is continuing, the Agent may... [accelerate the Loan]'.

On its own, this appears clear. However, it needs to be read in the context of Clause 1.2 *(DEFINITIONS AND INTERPRETATION: Construction)* which defines the word *'continuing'*.[4] When that meaning is taken into account, the reader will appreciate that the acceleration clause has a somewhat different meaning than would have been understood from reading the acceleration clause alone.

---

2. Different meanings in different contexts

1.005

While the definitions help to ensure consistency throughout the document it may be that consistency is not required in some cases.

Borrowers frequently request that adjustments be made to a definition which, on consideration, the lenders may wish to make in some instances

---

[4] See comments on Clause 1.2 *(DEFINITIONS AND INTERPRETATION: Construction)* in 1.065.

110   Interpretation

(e.g. the negative pledge) but not others (e.g. the conditions precedent) (see Box 1.5).

> **Box 1.5**
>
> For example, the borrowers may request a definition of 'Permitted Encumbrances' which allows the creation of a wide variety of security interests over the company's property. The lenders may be willing to agree to this request in the context of the negative pledge but may want to be more restrictive as to the security interests which may exist at the date of the first **advance** of the loan. In that case changing the operative clauses would be a better option than changing the definition.

It is therefore advisable to leave the definitions alone and make changes as appropriate in the operative clauses. Similarly, when reviewing the definitions, it is important to review them in each context in which they are used, as the definition may be appropriate in some circumstances but may require adjustment in others.

3. Circularity

1.006

It is not unusual to find that a defined term itself refers to another defined term. This, if carried to extremes, can make the definitions very difficult for readers to understand. In some cases, it might make the definitions meaningless (see Box 1.6).

> **Box 1.6**
>
> An example of a meaningless definition is, '"Outstanding Indebtedness" means all moneys outstanding under the Security Documents' while '"Security Documents" means all documents executed as security for the Outstanding Indebtedness'.

4. Operative provisions

1.007

The definitions are there to explain what particular expressions mean. They should not include any operative provisions, such as positive or negative undertakings or conditions. The main hazard of including operative provisions in the definitions is that they are harder to find there. At the extreme they may also be ineffective.

Clause 1: Definitions and Interpretation—Section 2—The LMA Definitions

Clause 1.1 Definitions

The following definitions in the LMA Compounded/Term Rate Loan deserve particular attention.

Additional Business Day see 0.131

Alternative Term Rate see 0.134

Alternative Term Rate Adjustment see 0.130

Base Currency

1.008

This definition is used in a facility which may have outstandings in different currencies from time to time (e.g. a multicurrency loan or a loan which may include letters of credit or ancillary facilities in different currencies). The Base Currency is the currency in which the loan is denominated for the purpose of calculating available amounts, thresholds, financial ratios and the like.[5]

---

[5] See ACT Borrower's Guide to the LMA's Investment Grade Agreements Part III at 1.4 for a commentary on the effect of exchange rate movements.

112   Interpretation

Base Currency Amount

This definition is used in multicurrency loans as a reference point for the lenders to determine from time to time what the amount of the loan would have been had it always been drawn in a single currency and remained in that currency.[6]

Baseline CAS see 0.128

Break Costs

1.009
The Reference Rate Terms for each currency will specify whether Break Costs apply and if so, how they are calculated. At the time of writing there appears to be a general acceptance that Break Costs should not apply to Compounded Rate Loans (in some cases, at the expense of restrictions on voluntary prepayments during Interest Periods). See Box 0.13. There is more justification for Break Costs in Term Rate Loans, although the method of calculation is likely to be different for a Term Rate Loan based on an IBOR (such as Euribor) and one based on Risk Free Rates (such as CME Term Sofr).

Comment. If Break Costs (or prepayment fees) apply to any currency then borrowers often argue that they should only apply to voluntary prepayment.

Business Day

1.010
The LMA definition reads
    "'Business Day" means a day (other than a Saturday or Sunday) on which banks are open for general business in London[, []] and:

a) *(in relation to any date for payment or purchase of a currency other than euro) the principal financial centre of the country of that currency;*
b) *(in relation to any date for payment or purchase of euro) which is a TARGET Day; and*
c) *in relation to:*

---

[6] See the commentary on Clause 8 *(Optional Currencies)* 3.013 onwards.

Clause 1: Definitions and Interpretation—Section 2—The LMA Definitions 113

i) *the fixing of an interest rate in relation to a Term Rate Loan;*

ii) *any date for payment or purchase of an amount relating to a Compounded Rate Loan; or*

iii) *the determination of the first day or the last day of an Interest Period for a Compounded Rate Loan, or otherwise in relation to the determination of the length of such an Interest Period),*

which is an Additional Business Day relating to that Loan or Unpaid Sum'.

The LMA definition of Business Day has different meanings in different contexts. The reason for these distinctions is that different places and markets need to be open for different purposes. The LMA reflects these differences by use of a flexible definition of Business Day and by the introduction of the concept of an Additional Business Day to define a day when the relevant underlying markets are open for rate fixing as discussed in 0.131. See Box 1.7.

Box 1.7

Paragraph c of the LMA definition of Business Day is designed to reflect the fact that the actions which require a rate fixing (and so require the underlying markets to be open) for Term Rate Loans (as referred to in (c)(i)) are less extensive than for Compounded Rate Loans (as referred to in (c)(ii) and (iii)).

1.011

Often the loan agreement does not explicitly state whether references to a number of Business Days are intended to mean 'clear' days, that is, excluding the first and last day, or periods of 24 hours (see Box 1.8). General principles of interpretation will treat it as clear days.[7]

Box 1.8

For example, if three Business Days' notice of drawdown is required and notice is given on Monday at 10 a.m. when will that notice expire? If the intention is to refer to 'clear' days, it will expire on Thursday at midnight (so that drawing will be available on Friday). If it is to periods of 24 hours then it will expire at 10 a.m. on Thursday (so that drawing will be available on Thursday). This example assumes that Monday to Friday are all Business Days.

---

[7] This is because a 'day' is treated as meaning a calendar day and a period of days after an event occurs excludes the day on which the event occurred. Lester v Garland (1808) 15 Ves 248.

114 Interpretation

Central Bank Rate

1.012

This rate will be specified in the Reference Rate Terms for each currency. It will be used as a fallback (together with any Central Bank Rate Adjustment) if the Daily Rate is unavailable on any given day as discussed in 0.136. It may also be used as a fallback if the Primary Term Rate and its early fallbacks are unavailable as discussed in 0.134.

Central Bank Rate Adjustment see 0.130

Compliance Certificate

1.013

Generally, financial covenants are tested by requiring periodic certificates confirming compliance.

The LMA precedent gives the draftsperson a choice here of attaching the form or referring to a form 'satisfactory to the Agent'. Attaching the form is preferable for both parties (and syndicate members) for the certainty it gives as to precisely what will be required. Some flexibility is introduced by saying the document is to be 'substantially' in the form attached, allowing for minor modifications which may prove to be necessary between the date of signing the loan agreement and the date of production of the relevant document.

A third alternative which is sometimes used is to require the document to be substantially in '*agreed form*' and define '*agreed form*' as referring to the forms of documents attached to a particular letter, for example. This has the advantage of keeping the loan agreement itself shorter, and is particularly useful for items which will only be required to be produced once at the start of the loan period.

Compounded Rate Currency see 0.114

Compounded Rate Loan see 0.116

Compounded Reference Rate see 0.119

Compounding Methodology Supplement see 0.127

Confidentiality Undertaking

This is the form of undertaking which a prospective purchaser will be required to sign before receiving confidential information.

Daily Non-Cumulative Compounded RFR Rate see 0.123

Daily Rate see 0.120

Default

1.014

'Default' means an Event of Default or any event or circumstance specified in clause [] (Events of Default) which would (with the expiry of a grace period, the giving of notice, the making of any determination under the Finance Documents or any combination of any of the foregoing) be an Event of Default.

The term 'Default' is used to mean the occurrence of any event which might mature into an Event of Default. An example is a breach of covenant which, if not remedied within any applicable grace period, would become an Event of Default. The breach of covenant would be a 'Default'. Some loan agreements use the concept of 'Potential Event of Default' to describe this.

The concept is used throughout the agreement and in the security documents. It is not the same as an Event of Default, in that occurrence of a Default does not give the lenders the ability to accelerate the loan. However, the existence of a Default causes concern for the lenders and therefore the borrower's rights after a Default and before an Event of Default will be more restricted than they were previously. For example, a lender will usually require that its commitment to lend new money (in a term loan) or to increase the amount outstanding (in a revolving credit) is suspended while there is a Default. It will also often place restrictions on things which would otherwise be permitted (e.g. payment of dividends, or application of insurance moneys or earnings may be prevented after a Default and before an Event of Default) (see Box 1.9).

1.015

It is important to look carefully at the words in brackets in the definition. The LMA Compounded/Term Rate Loan provides for three possibilities: expiry of grace periods; making determinations; and giving of notice, or any combination of these.

116 Interpretation

> ### Box 1.9
>
> DEFAULTS AND EVENTS OF DEFAULT
> Default = Breach of covenant or similar occurrence
> → Term loan—no obligation to advance new money
> → Revolving credit no obligation to advance loans which are not Rollover Loans[8]
> Event of Default = Default which remains unremedied on expiry of grace period (or similar)
> → no obligation to advance new money
> → Entitled to demand immediate repayment of outstanding sums

1.016

Expiry of Grace Periods

This part of the definition is to cover circumstances (e.g. a breach of certain undertakings) which will become Events of Default if those circumstances still exist when a **grace period** expires.

1.017

Comment The question might arise as to whether an event which is about to be remedied is a 'Default' as defined in the LMA Compounded/Term Rate Loan (see Box 1.10).

> ### Box 1.10
>
> For example, assume that a particular loan agreement states that it is an Event of Default if there is a judgement against the borrower in an amount in excess of $1 million and that judgement is not satisfied within 30 days. Assume also that a judgement has been made against the borrower in an amount of $2 million, and the borrower is making arrangements to pay it. It will take the borrower ten days to access the necessary funds. Until the payment has been made, the intention behind the drafting of the LMA Compounded/Term Rate Loan is that these events should constitute a 'Default'. The borrower might argue that in these circumstances there is no 'Default' because a Default is defined as an event that 'would', on expiry of a grace period, constitute an Event of Default. The judgement will not result in an Event of Default because it will be paid.

---

[8] See comment on Clause 4.2 *(CONDITIONS OF UTILIZATION: Further Conditions Precedent)* in 2.025

Clause 1: Definitions and Interpretation—Section 2—The LMA Definitions 117

> Given that, if the borrower's argument succeeded, it would render the definition of 'Default' meaningless, it is reasonably clear that Defaults which are about to be remedied remain Defaults until they have actually been remedied.

1.018

Making a Determination

* This is to cover those circumstances that will become an Event of Default if a party makes an adverse decision. An example is where it is an Event of Default if circumstances occur which, in the opinion of the Majority Lenders, are material. While they consider materiality there is a Default.

1.019

Comment As discussed in relation to the Events of Default,[9] one issue of concern to the borrower is to avoid subjective Events of Default as far as possible. If Events of Default are included which are to be determined in the opinion of some or all of the lenders, the impact of this definition should be considered. Payments (such as further drawings) are generally frozen on a Default and lenders may well be more willing to exercise their rights to freeze drawings than to exercise their rights of acceleration. By virtue of the definition of 'Default' their right to freeze drawings would arise whenever circumstances occur which *might* fall within the Event of Default, even if, on consideration, it would not do so. However strongly the wording of the Event of Default may be drafted, the ability to freeze future drawings is slightly more easily triggered because of the definition of 'Default' (see Box 1.11). As a result, some borrowers might want to request deletion of the words 'making a determination'. Nevertheless, lenders will want to resist this as they will not want to be obliged to advance further funds while there is any uncertainty as to whether an Event of Default is imminent or not. This is particularly important in the context of financial ratios as discussed in Chapter 8 in 8.121.

> **Box 1.11**
>
> For example, there may be an Event of Default if there is *'litigation against the Borrower which, in the opinion of the Majority Lenders, would have a*

---

[9] See Sect. 1 of the discussion of Clause 25 *(Events of Default)* in 8.223.

118 Interpretation

> *Material Adverse Effect'.* The word 'would' in that Event of Default makes it very difficult for the lenders to use the Event of Default because a high degree of certainty is necessary. Nevertheless, if litigation arises which *might* have a Material Adverse Effect, by virtue of the definition of 'Default', the lenders will be entitled to freeze drawings while they consider whether or not the circumstances fall within the wording of the Event of Default.

1.020

Giving of Notice

● This wording is to cover any Events of Default that are triggered by the giving of notice. It is unusual for Events of Default to be triggered by notice alone, but often notice is required in addition to the expiry of a grace period or the making of a determination. For example, some breaches of covenant (in the LMA Compounded/Term Rate Loan, breaches of undertaking which are capable of remedy[10]) may only be Events of Default if a certain period of time expires after the lenders give notice to the borrower of the existence of a breach. The definition of 'Default' therefore includes the three issues outlined here *and* any combination of them.

> Some definitions of 'Default' or 'Potential Event of Default' include words such as 'or any other occurrence'. This should be resisted as too broad. It could, for example, include the occurrence of a breach of covenant.

Defaulting Lenders

1.021

A definition of "Defaulting Lenders" may be included if the Lehman provisions are inserted. A Defaulting Lender is a lender which fails to lend, rescinds

---

[10] Clause 25.3 (*EVENTS OF DEFAULT: Other obligations*) subclause b states "No Event of Default will occur if the failure to remedy is capable of remedy and is remedied within ... in relation to [Clause] [] Business Days ... of the Agent giving notice to the Company ... of the failure to comply".

Clause 1: Definitions and Interpretation—Section 2—The LMA Definitions **119**

the agreement, or in respect of which an Insolvency Event occurs. There is a similar concept of 'Impaired Agent' to deal with an Agent in financial difficulty. The consequences of being a defaulting lender or Impaired Agent are discussed in the discussion on the Lehman provisions in Section 6 of the Introduction in 0.204.

It is worth noting that in practice the insolvency limb of these definitions may not work as stated since the authorities may be able to disapply these provisions (as would be the case under the Banking Act 2009 in England) in the event of a bank stabilization or similar procedure.

Eligible Institution

1.022
This expression is used to describe the types of entities which the borrower can bring in under clauses 2.2 (*THE FACILITIES*: *Increase*) or 10.7 (*PREPAYMENT AND CANCELLATION*: *Right of replacement or repayment and cancellation in relation to a single Lender or Issuing Bank*) to replace, for example, defaulting lenders or lenders who are prepaid because of extra costs of servicing their participation as a result of grossing up, etc.

Facility Office

1.023
'Facility Office' means, in respect of a Lender or the Issuing Bank, the office or offices notified by that Lender or Issuing Bank to the Agent in writing on or before the date it becomes a Lender or the Issuing Bank (or, following that date, by not less than five Business Days' written notice) as the office or offices through which it will perform its obligations under this Agreement.

The plural ('office or offices' in the first line of the definition) is deliberate so as to allow any lender to service different tranches of the loan from different Facility Offices.[11]

Fallback CAS see 0.130

FATCA see 6.038

---

[11] The borrower is concerned to ensure it does not have to gross-up payments. The protection in Clause 26.3 (*CHANGES TO THE LENDERS*: *Other conditions of assignment or transfer*) at subclause (d) is important here as discussed in 9.047.

120   Interpretation

Finance Document

1.024

'Finance Document' means this Agreement, any Fee Letter, any Accession Letter, any Resignation Letter, any Reference Rate Supplement, any Compounding Methodology Supplement and any other document designated as such by the Agent and the Company.

Many of the borrower's undertakings and representations relate to the Finance Documents. These should not be extended to include lenders' documents such as any document used to transfer interests in the loan to new lenders. Such documents are solely a concern for the lenders and, for example, the obligation of the borrower to pay any stamp duty in relation to the Finance Documents should not extend to these transfer documents. Note that by including Reference Rate Supplements and Compounding Methodology Supplements in this definition, any costs associated with those documents fall on the borrower (see 6.073).

Financial Indebtedness

1.025

The purpose of this definition is to distinguish between ordinary trade debts (e.g. debts to suppliers and employees) and debts in the nature of a financing. The definition needs to be broad to pick up activities having the commercial effect of borrowing, such as repos (short for repurchase agreements) or selling receivables on recourse terms.[12]

The definition is used in the negative pledge and in the cross default clause in the LMA Compounded/Term Rate Loan and may be used elsewhere in any given loan agreement. In the negative pledge the definition is used to distinguish between permitted and prohibited transactions.[13] In the cross default clause only defaults under arrangements that constitute Financial Indebtedness are Events of Default.[14] The LMA Compounded/Term Rate Loan does not include a covenant to incur no Financial Indebtedness although

---

[12] See 0.286 for a discussion of transactions having the commercial effect of borrowing and giving security.

[13] See commentary on the negative pledge in 8.149.

[14] See commentary on para (a) of the cross default clause in 8.239.

Clause 1: Definitions and Interpretation—Section 2—The LMA Definitions **121**

the relative level of Financial Indebtedness (or something akin to Financial Indebtedness[15]) may well be regulated by the financial ratios.

1.026

'Financial Indebtedness' means any indebtedness for or in respect of: ...

1.027

Comment It might be sensible to add the words 'without double counting' at the start of this definition. This ensures that there is no duplication for the purpose of the thresholds.

1.028

a) *moneys borrowed;*
b) *any amount raised by acceptance under any acceptance credit facility or dematerialised equivalent;*
c) *any amount raised pursuant to any note purchase facility or the issue of bonds, notes, debentures, loan stock or any similar instrument;*
d) *the amount of any liability in respect of any lease or hire purchase contract which would, in accordance with GAAP, be treated as a balance sheet liability [(other than any liability in respect of a lease or hire purchase contract which would, in accordance with GAAP in force [prior to [January 2019][20] have been treated as an operating lease;*

1.029

Note here that IFRS 16 required most leases to appear on the balance sheet of the lessee regardless of whether they are operating leases or finance leases with effect from January 2019. Under IFRS the lessee accounts for leases as a 'right of use' asset with a corresponding liability. This is more transparent than the previous system under which companies with significant lease liabilities for assets used on operating leases did not account for those liabilities on their balance sheet even though those assets might well have formed a fundamentally necessary part of the lessee's business—aircraft for an airline; hotels for a hotel chain, etc. Lenders are given the option, under the LMA drafting, of whether to include all long-term leases as Financial Indebtedness or only to include leases which, under the old system, would have been treated as finance leases. Lenders may prefer the former: for the negative pledge and the cross default clauses, giving security for long-term operating leases or default

---

[15] Commonly a different definition will be used in any financial ratios (such as 'Borrowing') so as to enable it to be more finely tuned and more readily measured.

122   Interpretation

under them would be of concern to the lenders regardless of whether they would have been classified as operating leases under the pre 2019 rules.

1.030

e) *receivables sold or discounted (other than any receivables to the extent they are sold on a non-recourse basis);*

This para deals with receivables discounting and debt **factoring** and draws a distinction between the situation where the receivables purchaser has recourse to the borrower (which counts as Financial Indebtedness) and the situation (often referred to as a 'true sale') where they do not (which does not count as Financial Indebtedness).

1.031

f) *any amount raised under any other transaction (including any forward sale or purchase agreement) of a type not referred to in any other paragraph of this definition having the commercial effect of a borrowing;*
   This is intended to catch those various other arrangements described in 0.286 having the same commercial effect of borrowing. If there is a prohibition on incurring Financial Indebtedness borrowers need to review their affairs to identify anything which might fall into this category.
g) *any derivative transaction entered into in connection with protection against or benefit from fluctuation in any rate or price (and, when calculating the value of any derivative transaction, only the marked to market value ... shall be taken into account);*

1.032
Including derivatives in the definition of Financial Indebtedness causes a number of difficulties for the borrower:

- First, for the purpose of the cross default clause, the current drafting has the effect that early termination of the derivative due to default of the swap counterparty is an Event of Default under the loan—which ought not to be the case.
- Second, the borrower will want to be clear on what types of credit support they are allowed to give for derivatives as discussed in 8.155 in relation to the negative pledge.
- Third if, as is common, ability to incur Financial Indebtedness is restricted, derivatives will use up the cap and reduce the amount available for

Clause 1: Definitions and Interpretation—Section 2—The LMA Definitions   123

borrowing. If the derivative was entered into to hedge against a particular risk such as interest rate movements, the hedge ought to have a neutralizing effect on the borrower's financial position, and so should have no impact on available borrowing limits or other financial parameters.

- Last, because derivative values fluctuate, including them in thresholds, (such as the threshold in the negative pledge which specifies that security can be given if the total 'Financial Indebtedness' secured is less than a specified amount) makes compliance with those thresholds difficult.

1.033

Lenders want the definition to include derivatives partly to ensure that any credit support arrangements which create security or quasi security are prohibited (see the discussion on the negative pledge from 8.155 onwards) and partly because, for the purpose of the cross default clause, non-payment of a derivative can trigger a large unexpected payment in the same way as non-payment of financial debt can. Therefore lenders want to ensure that the borrower's breach of a derivative is an Event of Default. Including derivatives in the definition of Financial Indebtedness achieves these two aims.

A better solution may be to exclude derivatives from the definition of Financial Indebtedness but deal with them separately in each place where the expression 'Financial Indebtedness' is used (see Box 1.12).

Box 1.12

If derivatives were to be excluded from the definition of Financial Indebtedness then one way to reconcile the concerns of both parties could be as follows

- Negative pledge
    - prohibit giving quasi security for Financial Indebtedness
    - prohibit giving Quasi Security for Derivatives (if appropriate—see the discussion in 8.155)
- Prohibition
    - on incurring Financial Indebtedness
    - on incurring speculative derivatives if appropriate
- Cross default clause triggered by
    - breach relating to Financial Indebtedness or
    - borrower breach in relation to Derivatives,

124 Interpretation

h) *any counter-indemnity obligation in respect of a guarantee, indemnity, bond, standby or documentary letter of credit or any other instrument issued by a bank or financial institution; and*

i) *the amount of any liability in respect of any guarantee or indemnity for any of the items referred to in paragraphs (a) to (h) above.*

1.034

Comment Borrowers may wish to exclude Non-Recourse Indebtedness if any company in the group[16] has or is likely to have any limited recourse indebtedness, since failure to pay such debt should not trigger the cross default clause and security over the project assets for such indebtedness should not cause a breach of the negative pledge.

Borrowers will commonly want to exclude intercompany debts from this definition. Lenders need to be cautious here as they may want to prohibit intercompany debts, or the giving of security for intercompany debts, even if perhaps they agree to allow debts between Obligors (see 0.177)

GAAP

1.035

'GAAP' means generally accepted accounting principles in [] [(including IFRS)].

Some, but not all, companies are required to produce accounts in accordance with International Financial Reporting Standards.[17] Even where companies are required to produce accounts in accordance with some version of IFRS, they must also comply with local legal requirements (GAAP) in their own jurisdiction. If the company is not required to comply with IFRS, lenders need to be satisfied that they have sufficient understanding of local GAAP in the relevant country to be able to interpret the accounts correctly. If different companies in the group use different GAAP to others, this definition will need amending.

---

[16] Which is not a limited recourse company excluded from the provisions of the loan agreement as discussed in 0.161.

[17] And what IFRS means is also different in different countries—see the comments in 1.037 on IFRS.

Clause 1: Definitions and Interpretation—Section 2—The LMA Definitions

1.036

Group

See the discussion on the scope of the agreement in the Introduction from 0.142 onwards.

IFRS

1.037

means UK adopted international accounting standards within the meaning of Sect. 474(1) of the Companies Act 2006 to the extent applicable to the relevant financial statements.

Since Brexit, there has been a difference between UK adopted International Financial Reporting Standards and those adopted in the EU. The LMA definition of IFRS refers to the UK adopted international financial reporting standards and so that definition may need amending if non UK companies are involved.

Interpolated Primary Term Rate

This is a rate which may be used in the fallback provisions discussed in 0.134. If no rate of interest is available for the specific period of time required (e.g. a rate is required for a one month Interest Period) the Interpolated Primary Term Rate is calculated from the rates available for the nearest shorter period (e.g. perhaps an overnight rate is the nearest shorter rate available) and the nearest longer rate available, e.g. perhaps a 3 month rate is available). The interpolated Primary Term Rate is then calculated by assuming the rate changed on a straight line basis between those two available dates.

Lookback Period see 0.102

Majority Lenders

1.038

'Majority Lenders' means a Lender or Lenders whose Commitments aggregate more than [66^2/$_3$]% of the Total Commitments (or, if the Total Commitments have been reduced to zero, aggregated more than [66^2/$_3$]% of the Total Commitments immediately prior to the reduction).

One of the basic principles of a syndicated loan is that the lenders will be treated equally and that the syndicate will act in accordance with the wishes of a 'Majority'. The lenders need to decide what they mean by a Majority. Commonly, the level is set at 66.66% of the loan by contribution. A different level may be appropriate in a club deal, particularly if the usual level would give one lender (e.g. the Agent) a blocking vote.

1.039

It is worth noting that this definition has changed over time. Originally, the definition looked at the amounts actually outstanding (ignoring amounts committed but not yet lent). It is now calculated with reference to the total of amounts advanced and committed to be advanced. In a loan where all lenders share all parts of the facility in the same proportion, the distinction makes no difference. In a loan such as the LMA Compounded/Term Rate Loan, where there is a term loan and a revolver, with lenders able to have a different level of participation in the different parts of the facility, the new formulation of the definition is preferable, because with the previous formulation, lenders under the revolving credit may be effectively disenfranchised if their facility was undrawn at the time consent was sought.

1.040

It is also worth noticing that Majority Lenders are not able to amend all terms of the agreement. Some changes require all lender consent. This is particularly important for those clauses which amount to credit committee issues (such as the Margin) and clauses dealing with the relationship between the tranches (e.g. any clause which requires one tranche to be repaid in full before prepayment of another tranche is permitted). See the discussion in Clause 37 *(Amendments and Waivers)*.

Clause 1: Definitions and Interpretation—Section 2—The LMA Definitions   127

Margin

1.041

The Margin will be specified in the Reference Rate Terms for the particular currency, so allowing different Margins for different currencies as discussed in 0.111.

In Sustainability Linked Loans the Margin will adjust with reference to the performance of the borrower against its targets as discussed in 0.316.

1.042

If the Margin is adjusted with reference to the financial performance of the borrower (e.g. by reference to financial ratios or the rating of the borrower[18]) there may be

* an implication that the lender is a partner in the business[19]
* tax issues to consider (e.g. might the payment be treated as a distribution of profits of the company, as opposed to a payment of interest?) and/or
* issues as to the priority of the loan in an insolvency of the borrower (see Box 1.13).

These will be issues for due diligence in the country or countries in which the borrower conducts business and in which an insolvency of the borrower may occur. This sort of arrangement is referred to as a '**Margin ratchet**' or '**pricing grid**'.

Box 1.13

S3 Partnership Act 1890[20] states *In the event of any person to whom money has been advanced by way of loan upon such a contract as is mentioned in the last foregoing section.*
[this reference is to s2(3)(d) Partnership Act which reads 'the advance of money by way of loan to a person engaged ... in any business on a contract

---

[18] It is worth noting that contractual provisions such as Margin ratchets which are triggered by changes in ratings have been the subject of numerous investigations over the years, as concerns arise over the consequences of over-reliance on corporate ratings. For example, in 2013, the Credit Ratings Agencies Regulation—EU regulation 462/2013—required public authorities which supervise certain financial institutions to 'encourage the supervised entities to ... reduce automatic reliance on ratings issued by recognised agencies'.

[19] Under English law, entitlement to a share in the profits is not conclusive as to the existence of a partnership—s2 Partnership Act 1890.

128   Interpretation

> with that person that the lender shall receive a rate of interest varying with
> the profits ... arising from carrying on that business']
>   *being adjudged bankrupt ... the lender of the loan shall not be entitled to*
> *recover anything in respect of his loan ... until the claims of the other creditors*
> *of the borrower ... have been satisfied.*
>   This English provision does not, however, affect a lender's right to recover
> under any security held for the loan.[21]

1.043

Where, as is common, the Margin changes with reference to financial ratios, a question arises as to the date on which the revised Margin will take effect. The lenders will want any increased Margin to take effect retrospectively, from the date the ratios were tested, rather than from the (later) date on which any Compliance Certificate is delivered. Borrowers are likely to also want downward adjustments to the Margin to be retrospective although lenders are likely to resist that so as to incentivize the borrower to produce the Compliance Certificate (and hence get the benefit of the reduced Margin) as quickly as possible.

1.044

Sometimes the Margin is stated to increase if a Default occurs. The effect, of course, is to allow a higher interest rate to be charged even for Defaults which are not related to non-payment. This may be a useful provision, especially for minor Defaults.

Comment The borrower should object—the Margin should only increase on an Event of Default. See comments on 'Default' at 1.014. This is particularly important where there is a Margin ratchet which restricts the amount and frequency of reductions in the Margin so that it can take a number of years for the Margin to step down from its highest figure to its lowest.

---

[20] This section of the Partnership Act probably applies to companies as well as to persons by virtue of Rule 12.3(2A) Insolvency Rules 1986.

[21] See Badeley v Consolidated Bank (1888) LR 38 Ch D 238.

Market Disruption Rate

1.045

If the agreement, for any currency, is to protect the lender against the possibility that their cost of raising funds is excessive,[22] then the Market Disruption Rate is the rate which will be used as a benchmark for the relevant currency, to decide if there is an excess. It will be specified in the Reference Rate Terms for the relevant currency.

1.046

For a loan with interest rates based on Euribor, the Market Disruption Rate (if any) will be Euribor. To achieve the same economic affect with a Compounded Rate Loan, or with a Term Rate Loan where the rate is based on risk free rates (such as CME Term Sofr) the Market Disruption Rate may need to include the Rate Switch, Baseline, Term Reference Rate or Fallback CAS if there is one or to make some other appropriate adjustment, if not. See the discussion of the Market Disruption Rate in 13.044 and 13.058. See also Box 0.12 where a similar issue arises with reference to zero floors.

1.047

It is also worth noticing that the Market Disruption Rate is the rate applicable to the Interest Period, rather than a daily rate.[23] This means, in relation to a Compounded Rate Loan, that it will not be known until shortly before the end of the Interest Period. See further 0.097.

Material Adverse Effect

1.048

This definition is used as a qualifier to undertakings, representations and Events of Default (see Box 1.14), as well as in the material adverse change Event of Default itself (if there is one). The definition is discussed in 8.281.

---

[22] As to which see 5.023.

[23] This is the only circumstance in which a rate for a whole Interest Period needs to be calculated in relation to Compounded Rate Loans and is the reason for Schedule 16 (*Cumulative Compounded RFR Rate*).

130   Interpretation

> **Box 1.14**
>
> For example there may be a representation that
> *No Environmental Claim has been commenced... where that claim would be reasonably likely ... to have a Material Adverse Effect*
> The relevant Event of Default could say that it is an Event of Default if *any event or circumstances occurs which is reasonably likely to give rise to a Material Adverse Effect.*

Month

1.049

The definition of 'month' needs to reflect the practice in the relevant market. The definition states that a period of a month starting on say the eighth day of a particular month will end on the eighth day of the following month but subject to the Business Day Conventions for the relevant currency which are set out in the Reference Rate Terms for that currency.

Optional Currency

1.050

'Optional Currency' means a currency (other than the Base Currency) which complies with the conditions set out in clause [] (Conditions relating to Optional Currencies).

It is normal to provide that every new currency not agreed in the original loan agreement must be approved by every lender. If the borrower is likely to need to have parts of the loan available in currencies other than the Base Currency, it is sensible to ensure that the loan agreement includes Reference Rate Terms for each such currency and does not require any further lender approvals for its availability.

Original Financial Statements

1.051

Consolidated statements are required from the Company as the ultimate holding company. Given that the lenders do not have recourse to assets

Clause 1: Definitions and Interpretation—Section 2—The LMA Definitions 131

which are in group members which are not Obligors, it may be that financial covenants will be tested with reference to the Obligors as opposed to (or as well as) the entire group.[24] In this case the lenders will need a method to assess the financial position of each Obligor, in addition to that of the group as a whole. For this reason (and also because lender policy generally requires this) audited statements are usually required from each Obligor in addition to the consolidated statements.

Primary Term Rate see 0.117

Published Rate Replacement Event see 0.140

Quotation Day

1.052
The Quotation Day for each currency takes into account the amount of notice required to book funds in that currency. As it is currency specific it will be defined in the Reference Rate Terms for the relevant currency.

Quoted Tenor

1.053
This is used in the Rate Switch Trigger Event if there is one. See 5.003

Rate Switch CAS see 0.129

Rate Switch Currency

see 0.115. This is defined in Clause 11A (Rate Switch).

Reference Rate Supplement see 0.127

Reference Rate Terms see 0.126

---

[24] See discussion on scope of the agreement in 0.178.

132   Interpretation

Repeating Representations

1.054

It is advisable that the Repeating Representations should consist only of those which are not already covered by an undertaking or an Event of Default or alternatively, that they do not conflict with them.[25]

RFR Banking Day see 0.131

Rollover Loan

1.055

A Rollover Loan is an advance of the revolving credit facility which does not increase the total amount outstanding (usually because there is a repayment of an existing advance at the same time as discussed in Box 2.1). Because a Rollover Loan does not involve an increase in the lenders' exposure, the conditions precedent to drawing a Rollover Loan are more relaxed than for other loans. See 2.025.

Subsidiary

1.056

The draftsperson may choose whether to define 'Subsidiary' with reference to subsidiary undertakings or to subsidiaries (see Box 1.15). Lenders may wish to include subsidiary undertakings because they will have been included in the consolidated accounts. Depending on the group, borrowers may wish to exclude them from the undertakings and other provisions if the borrower does not have full control over them.

Box 1.15

A is a subsidiary undertaking of B if, effectively, B has the right to exercise, or actually exercises, a dominant influence or control over it, or the right to remove or appoint a majority of the board of directors or if it may exercise the majority of the voting rights, or if the two companies are managed on a

---

[25] See commentary on Clause 21 *(Representations)* from 8.010 onwards.

Clause 1: Definitions and Interpretation—Section 2—The LMA Definitions 133

> unified basis, regardless of the fact that B may not own the majority of the shares in A.

It is also worth noting the decision in Enviroco Ltd v Farstad Supply [2011] 1 W.L.R. 921. In that case, a company (A) owned the majority of the shares in another company (B), but not the majority of the voting rights. The Supreme court held that, despite the majority ownership of shares, B was not a 'Subsidiary' of A as defined in the Companies Acts because its shares were subject to a legal mortgage (because a legal mortgage is created by transferring ownership of the mortgaged asset to the mortgagee for the duration of the security, see A1.042 and to achieve that, in the case in question, the security holder had been registered as a member of the company in place of the security provider[26]).

Target Day

1.057
This is any day when the payment system for Euros (TARGET2), is open.

Term Rate Currency see 0.114

Term Rate Loan see 0.116

Term Reference Rate see 0.118

Termination Date

1.058
This is intended to refer to the final date for each of the Facilities by which that Facility must be repaid.

---

[26] The case turned on the definition of 'Subsidiary' in the Companies Acts which, on the rather unusual facts of the case, where A did not have the majority of the voting rights, required the company in question to be a registered member of the company, which it was not.

134   Interpretation

Clause 1.2 Construction

1.059
This clause sets out some rules of interpretation (not quite the same as definitions,) It is worth reading this clause particularly carefully as it can contain some important surprises and is an area of the loan agreement where it is not unusual to see divergence from the LMA forms. For example this section may contain rules of interpretation dealing with the meaning of the word 'reasonable' or the word 'knowledge' which will clearly have an important impact on the meaning of the operative provisions of the loan agreement.

Some common provisions worthy of note are addressed here.

Clause 1.2 (*Construction*) subclause (a) (iii)

1.060
This subclause defines cost of funds to mean

'*the average cost (determined either on an actual or a notional basis) which that Lender would incur if it were to fund, from whatever source(s) it may reasonably select, an amount equal to the amount of that participation in that Loan for a period equal in length to the Interest Period of that Loan*'.

This expression may be used if cost of funds is to be used in the waterfall dealing with unavailability of specified interest rates—as discussed in 0.134–0.138—or if the lenders are to be compensated if their cost of raising funds is excessive as discussed in 5.020. This definition was introduced at the same time as the compounded rate loan forms, to help combat some of the practical difficulties experienced by lenders in applying earlier versions of the cost of funds provisions as discussed in Box 5.3. Relevance of cost of funds in relation to compounded rate loans is debatable—see 5.024.

Clause 1.2 (*Construction*) subclause (a) (x)

1.061
This subclause gives a broad statement about the interpretation of the word 'regulation'.

Clause 1: Definitions and Interpretation—Section 2—The LMA Definitions 135

a 'regulation' includes any regulation, rule, official directive, request or guideline (whether or not having the force of law) of any governmental, intergovernmental or supranational body, agency, department or of any regulatory, self-regulatory or other authority or organization.

1.062

This broad meaning is principally due to the use of the word 'regulation' in the increased cost clause[27] and in the context of capital adequacy rules.

1.063

Comment Some like to add the words 'but compliance with which is customary' after the words 'whether or not having the force of law', so as to introduce some level of objectivity.

1.064

Clause 1.2 (*Construction*) subclause (a) (xii)

This subclause states that a reference to a law is intended to refer to that law as it may be amended from time to time. This rule needs to be considered whenever a reference to a statute or other legal reference is made in the agreement since it may not be appropriate in each case to have the reference treated as a reference to the **statute** as amended from time to time. For example, a reference to a particular tax provision would often be intended to refer to that particular provision, not that provision as it may change from time to time.

1.065

Clause 1.2 (*Construction*) subclause (e)

This subclause reads
A Default (other than an Event of Default) is 'continuing' if it has not been remedied or waived and an Event of Default is 'continuing' if it has not been [remedied or waived][waived]

Particularly important is the definition given to the word 'continuing'. A Default continues until remedied or waived. Under the LMA Compounded/Term Rate Loan, two alternatives are provided in relation to an Event of Default. The first alternative is that the Event of Default is continuing unless 'remedied or waived'. So, following an Event of Default, the lenders lose their rights of acceleration not only if they waive them, but also if the borrower

---

[27] Clause 16 (*Increased Costs*).

136 **Interpretation**

remedies the Event of Default before the loan is accelerated. In the second alternative the Event of Default will continue unless waived (i.e. the remedy of it will not terminate the lenders' acceleration rights). The reason some lenders require this is that they take the view that the Default should have been remedied while it was a Default and before it became an Event of Default. Moreover, if the borrower could unilaterally cure Events of Default it would reduce the borrower's incentive to inform the lender of them (see Box 1.16).

Box 1.16

For example, assume that the loan agreement provides that the existence of a potential environmental liability against the borrower is an Event of Default. Assume that such a **liability** arises. The borrower may feel that, if they can deal with the issue (e.g. by arranging for the clean up or whatever else is necessary to discharge the liability) the best course for them would be not to notify the lenders, but simply to satisfy the liability, thereby remedying the Event of Default.

If this clause provides that an Event of Default is continuing unless 'waived' (as opposed to saying that it is continuing unless 'remedied or waived') then if the borrower were to pursue their proposed course of action in this case, they would run the risk that the lenders subsequently might discover what had happened, and, since the Event of Default had not been 'waived', the intention is that the lenders would be entitled to accelerate the loan even though the Event of Default had been remedied. In other words, if the clause specifies that an Event of Default is continuing unless waived, this gives the borrower an incentive to advise the lenders of Events of Default so as to obtain waivers.

This is particularly important in the context of the obligation to notify of a Default. If that can be remedied at any time prior to acceleration, the obligation has no teeth.

Clause 1.3 Currency symbols and definitions

1.066

It became common to add a clause dealing with currency definitions as a result of the crisis over the Euro during 2011 (and this clause now optionally extends to include definitions of other relevant currencies). Concerns arose that some countries might exit the Euro, and that payments denominated in Euros might, as a result, be 'redenominated' into whatever new currency the departing country adopted in place of the Euro. A related concern was that countries might impose exchange control restrictions (as both Iceland and

Clause 1: Definitions and Interpretation—Section 2—The LMA Definitions   **137**

Cyprus did following their currency crises) which might prevent the borrower from fulfilling its repayment obligations in the due currency.

1.067

To protect against these risks, amendments were made to the LMA loans to clarify that the expression 'Euro' meant the common currency of the participating member states. LMA also focused on lenders' ability to take legal and enforcement action in some countries other than the 'departing' country. So they focused on the choice of law clause and the jurisdiction clause, in particular

* making the change of these clauses require unanimous lender approval (as opposed to Majority Lender)[28]
* ensuring that lenders had the ability to require payment in a country other than one of the Euro countries[29]

Clause 1.4 Third party rights

1.068

This clause deals with the position of third parties. It is intended to clarify the intention of the parties in relation to the rights that third parties may acquire as a result of the agreement, as envisaged by the Contracts (Rights of Third Parties) Act 1999. The LMA Compounded/Term Rate Loan provides for two options. First, the parties may elect that no third parties[30] are intended to have enforceable rights under the agreement. Alternatively, they may select that enforceable rights will arise where specifically stated—this choice will be made if it is preferred to have the Act regulate the position in relation to the exclusion clause in Clause 28.10 *(ROLE OF THE AGENT, THE ARRANGER AND THE ISSUING BANK: Exclusion of liability)*, rather than rely on the common law (see Box 1.17).

---

[28] See 11.025.

[29] See 11.001.

[30] Meaning, in the context of the LMA Compounded/Term Rate Loan, by virtue of the definition of 'Party' in Clause 1.2 *(DEFINITIONS AND INTERPRETATION: Construction)*, persons who are not assignees or transferees—see Box 1.17.

138   Interpretation

> **Box 1.17**
>
> The Contracts (Rights of Third Parties) Act 1999 was introduced to remove some of the difficulties which the common law doctrine of **privity** of contract had given rise to. That doctrine has the effect that no person is entitled to enforce a contract or to take a benefit under it unless that person is a party to the contract. There are a number of exceptions to the doctrine, notably the law relating to assignments of contracts and the law in relation to the taking of the benefit of **exclusion clauses**.[31] The Act did not abolish the doctrine of privity but it did supplement it, allowing third parties to enforce terms of a contract and to take the benefit of those terms if the contract intended (expressly or by its proper construction) that those third parties should have the benefit of the relevant terms of the contract. The Act expressly preserved the rights of persons who could take the benefit of exceptions to the privity rule (such as assignees) under the common law. However, how the common law and the Act interrelate in such circumstances is a complex issue.[32] Given this uncertainty, some prefer to provide that no third parties (other than assignees and transferees, who will become 'Lenders' as defined in the agreement when the assignment or transfer is effected) are intended to take the benefit of the contract. Others prefer to provide specifically that employees may take the benefit of the exclusion clause in Clause 28.10 *(ROLE OF THE AGENT, THE ARRANGER AND THE ISSUING BANK: Exclusion of liability)* in accordance with the Act (rather than under an exception to the privity rule), in order to avoid the complexities of the common law in this area.[33]

---

[31] Treitel *The Law of Contract*, 15th edn, 14.063–14.098.

[32] Treitel *The Law of Contract*, 15th edn, 14.102 onwards.

[33] If any third party is intended to have the benefit of any provision of the contract, the Act (s2) also allows that third party to prevent amendment of the contract to their detriment in certain circumstances. This right is subject to any express term of the contract to the contrary. This is the reason that Clause 1.4 *(DEFINITIONS AND INTERPRETATION: Third Party Rights)* optionally provides that '....*the consent of any Person who is not a Party is not required to rescind or vary this Agreement at any time*'.

The Facilities

Clause 2: The Facilities

Clause 2.1 The Facilities

2.001

This clause in the LMA Compounded/Term Rate Loan[1] contains the lenders' agreement to provide the facilities.

Facility A is a term loan repayable either in instalments or in a single instalment.

Facility B is a revolving credit, under which moneys can be repeatedly advanced and repaid throughout the term of the facility, with commitment fees being paid on undrawn amounts. Drawings under Facility B can also be made in the form of letters of credit as discussed in 3.006. When the borrower requests an advance they will choose its Interest Period and the advance will be repaid (subject to the cashless rollover provisions which we look at in Box 2.1) at the end of its Interest Period. This avoids having frequent changes in the outstanding amounts so as to keep administration to a minimum, and distinguishes a revolving credit from an overdraft, under which outstanding amounts can change daily.

---

[1] References in this book to the LMA Compounded/Term Rate Loan are to the LMA Multicurrency Term and Revolving Facilities Agreement incorporating Term SOFR for use in Investment Grade transactions, available to LMA members via www.lma.eu.com

© The Author(s), under exclusive license to Springer Nature Switzerland AG 2024
S. Wright, *The International Loan Documentation Handbook*, Global Financial Markets, https://doi.org/10.1007/978-3-031-38489-9_3

140   The Facilities

> **Box 2.1**
>
> In practice of course, often at the end of an Interest Period for an advance, the borrower will want to keep the funds for a further period rather than repay them. In this case, on the date of repayment of the first advance, the borrower will redraw a new advance, possibly in a different amount from the maturing advance—that is, the funds will be 'rolled over'. In practice then, instead of repaying the first advance and drawing the second, the borrower will simply pay (or receive, depending on which of the two advances is larger) the difference. This commercial practice of simply paying the net amount is included in the 'cashless rollover provisions' in the repayment provisions discussed in relation to Clause 9 (*Repayment*).

2.002

The flexibility which the borrower wants in terms of having the ability to draw and repay as and when their commercial requirements merit doing that is achieved by the fact that the borrower can draw additional advances while the first is outstanding (but note Clause 4.4 *(CONDITIONS OF UTILIZA-TION: Maximum number of Utilizations)* discussed in 2.030) as well as having the ability to prepay at any time (subject to any restrictions agreed as discussed in the context of Break Costs in 1.009).

Clause 2.2 Increase

2.003

Next comes a clause dealing with the situation where the borrower has cancelled the Commitment of a lender (or in some cases, an Issuing Bank) which requires additional payments under the gross-up, increased costs or tax indemnity clauses, or which requires to be prepaid as a result of illegality. Where the loan deals with defaulting lenders it also extends to lenders whose participations have been cancelled as a result of those provisions. It allows for the borrower to bring in another lender to lend the missing part. It is discussed further in the comments on Clause 10.7 *(PREPAYMENT AND CANCELLATION: right of replacement or repayment and cancellation in relation to a single Lender or Issuing Bank)* in 4.020.

Clause 2: The Facilities   **141**

Clause 2.3 Finance Parties' rights and obligations

2.004

This clause provides that the obligations of the lenders are several.[2] The lenders are not underwriting each other and, if one lender fails to advance funds when due, the others are not responsible. This is so even if, at the time the syndicate was being put together, one or more lenders underwrote the syndication. That underwriting related to the syndication process only—that is the ability to obtain sufficient take up of the loan—and not to the creditworthiness of the participants.

The borrower is not, of course, at the complete mercy of the Arranger in terms of the identity of lenders to be invited into the syndicate (and therefore, whose credit risk the borrower will be exposed to). The borrower and Arranger will have agreed principles relating to the syndication process, and the types of lenders who can be invited to join the syndicate, at an early stage in the syndication process.

2.005

The Lehman provisions referred to in the Introduction in 0.204 are the usual way to mitigate the problems which would arise if a lender defaulted. Those provisions do not reduce the possibility of a lender default, but simply provide a mechanism to ameliorate the results for the borrower, provided a substitute lender can be found.

2.006

Clause 2.3 (*Finance Parties' rights and obligations*) (b) and (c) provide that the rights of the lenders are separate[3] and they may take independent action to enforce their rights subject as otherwise stated (see Box 2.2).

Box 2.2

Generally, the loan agreement will state that acceleration and enforcement of security given for the loan require Majority Lender consent. Those rights therefore cannot be exercised independently as envisaged by this clause. The most likely enforcement action available to be exercised independently pursuant to

---

[2] For a discussion of the difference between several, joint, and joint and several obligations, see A1.016.

[3] The clause was extended to make this abundantly clear after a case under Hong Kong law (Charmway v Fortunesea (Cayman) Ltd & Ors [2015] HKCU 1717) raised doubts about the efficacy of the earlier version of the clause.

142   The Facilities

> this clause is the right of set off and/or the ultimate sanction which unsecured creditors generally have, which is to petition for the winding up of the company.

2.007

This may seem an unusual provision, inconsistent with two basic concepts in a syndicated loan:

- that all lenders are equal and will achieve equal levels of return (subject to fees, etc.);
- that the syndicate will be run in accordance with the wishes of the 'Majority'.

These subclauses represent one of the limits on these concepts of joint action in a syndicated term loan.[4] Its effect in a fully drawn term loan is that, even though Majority Lender approval is needed for acceleration of the loan and enforcement of security, and even though it is not possible for a single lender to accelerate its portion of the loan independently of the rest; nevertheless there will come a time when the loan advanced by each lender will fall due, regardless of the views of the rest of the syndicate. If the borrower fails to pay any amount which has fallen due this clause ensures that each lender has the same rights as any other unsecured creditor in relation to its share in that instalment.

2.008

This can be a useful right in a **workout** if some lenders do not want to go ahead with a **rescheduling** which the Majority are pursuing, but would prefer to enforce their rights. Clause 2.3 (*THE FACILITIES*: *Finance Parties' rights and obligations*) (c) gives the individual lenders at least some leverage in that situation (but see Box 2.3).

---

[4] See below in 2.009 for revolving credits.

Clause 2: The Facilities   **143**

> **Box 2.3**
>
> For this right to be effective, lenders must ensure that
>
> - any recovery they make is not required to be shared with the syndicate under Clause 30 *(Sharing among the Finance Parties)*[5]; and
> - the due date for payments cannot be altered by the Majority Lenders.[6]
>
> The right to petition to wind up the company may well turn out only to be a temporary advantage since in many countries, creditors can be forced to agree to restructuring and rescheduling proposals in a potential winding up, if those proposals are approved by a certain percentage of the creditors, with the aim of allowing the company to continue as a going concern. Depending on the percentages involved, the creditor which initiated the process may find itself bound by a rescheduling in any event.

2.009

In the case of a term loan which is not fully drawn (or a revolving credit), these provisions of Clause 2.3 (*THE FACILITIES: Finance Parties' rights and obligations*) (c) give little comfort to lenders because, although an individual lender can take action to enforce amounts due, they can also be forced by the Majority Lenders to advance further funds, despite the existence of a Default or an Event of Default. See commentary on Clause 4.2 *(CONDITIONS OF UTILIZATION: Further conditions precedent)* in 2.023.

2.010

In some circumstances the borrower or the lenders may wish to negotiate amendment of this clause precisely to protect themselves against being held to ransom by individual 'rogue' lenders. In this case deletion of the right of independent action may not be sufficient. It would be sensible to expressly exclude individual lenders' rights to petition to wind up the borrower (i.e. to include a 'non petition clause') as, if the rights owed to each lender are indeed separate, then each lender has its own right to take action against the borrower and to petition for winding up for its own portion of the debt even if the agreement did not specifically provide for this.

---

[5] This is achieved by Clause 30.5 *(SHARING AMONG THE FINANCE PARTIES: Exceptions)*. See 10.027.

[6] This is achieved by Clause 37.2 *(AMENDMENTS AND WAIVERS: All Lender matters)*. See 11.026.

144 The Facilities

Clause 2.4 Obligors' agent

2.011
It is not uncommon to include a clause under which each Obligor appoints one group member—the 'Company' to provide information and to sign documents and generally to communicate with the lenders on its behalf, and to agree to be bound by all such communications as though they had been made by the Obligor itself.

Clause 3: Purpose

Clause 3.1 Purpose

2.012
The borrower undertakes to use the loan for the specified purpose. This does not, of itself, provide a great deal of protection for the lenders for three reasons:

* first, the borrower may disregard the clause, using the money for unauthorized purposes (and putting the lenders in the position of, at best, having assumed a different credit risk from that intended);
* second, the loan may be used for the purpose intended (e.g. general corporate purposes), but its availability results in other moneys being able to be diverted to a purpose which the lenders would not have funded; and
* third, the purpose stated is often quite vague, for example, 'general corporate purposes', leaving a lot of room for interpretation.

Nevertheless, the purpose clause is of some value. It may assist in good faith arguments by the lenders (e.g. to demonstrate their lack of awareness of any illegal use or use in contravention of a regulation). It will, in most cases, be likely to trigger discussions about intended use of the facility, which may then be more specifically detailed. It can, in the worst cases, assist in establishing a claim in fraud if the borrower uses the funds for an unauthorized purpose.

2.013

In some cases the purpose clause may also give rise to a 'Quistclose trust' so that the moneys can only be used for the specified purpose and if that purpose fails (for example, if the loan was to finance construction of a factory but the borrower became insolvent before construction was completed) then any loan proceeds which were still in the hands of the borrower would be held on trust for the lenders (and therefore would not fall into the insolvency of the borrower). This can only be achieved if it is clear (both in the document and commercially) that the loan is to be used exclusively for the specified purpose.[7]

Some lenders use the clause to specify prohibited uses, for example, to say that it is not available for any purpose which would constitute (illegal) financial assistance in England.[8]

It is also worth noting that under **Basel III** regulations, facilities which may be used for liquidity purposes attract a different (more onerous) regulatory treatment for the purpose of the **liquidity coverage ratio** (see Clause 16 *(Increased Costs)* in 6.054) than other facilities. Lenders may therefore want to prohibit the use of the loan to refinance debt.

Clause 3.1 (Purpose) in other commercial circumstances

2.014

In an asset finance transaction (or indeed a corporate loan in some instances such as a refinancing), the loan agreement will provide that advances will be made to a specified account (e.g. the account of the seller of the asset or the lender to be refinanced) and that will be treated as an advance to the borrower. In a project finance transaction, the agreement will provide for the loan to be advanced to a disbursement account (charged to the lenders) with provisions for drawings on that account against invoices and/or other certification.

---

[7] See Barclays Bank v Quistclose [1968] UKHL 4, Twinsectra Ltd v Yardley [2002] UKHL 12 and Gabriel v Little and others [2013] EWCA Civ 1513.

[8] If it were to be used for such a purpose, the clause would not protect the lenders from the consequences, so this is no substitute for proper due diligence including investigating any debt which is to be refinanced.

146   The Facilities

Clause 3.2 Monitoring

2.015

This clause provides that the lenders are not required to verify the application of moneys lent under the agreement.

Clause 4: Conditions of Utilization

Clause 4.1 Initial conditions precedent

This clause reads *No Borrower may deliver a Utilization Request unless the Agent has received all of the documents and other evidence listed in Part I of Schedule 2 (Conditions precedent) in form and substance satisfactory to the Agent. The Agent shall notify the Company and the Lenders promptly upon being so satisfied.*

2.016

Before the loan can be advanced, the borrower must provide certain documentary conditions precedent as listed in Schedule 2 (*Conditions Precedent*) and discussed in relation to that schedule from 13.002 onwards. Satisfaction of these conditions precedent supplements the lenders' own due diligence procedures and the borrower's representations set out in Clause 21 (*Representations*), so that, before the loan is advanced, the lenders have three independent checks on each important issue: the borrower's statement in the representations; the lenders' independent review (encapsulated, in the case of legal issues, in its lawyer's legal opinion); and the evidence presented in satisfaction of the conditions precedent. As a drafting matter, changes negotiated in any one of these areas of the document may need to be reflected in the others.

2.017

Comment Borrowers need to review the list of conditions precedent to ensure that they are able to satisfy them. They will need to be particularly careful with any conditions which are not within their control, such as consents and licences, particularly if there is a reasonable risk that they will not be forthcoming (for example, acknowledgements of notices of assignment, if a contract is being assigned).

2.018

One issue here is what instructions (if any) the Agent needs from the lenders to approve the conditions precedent. Clause 4.1 *(CONDITIONS OF UTILIZATION: Initial conditions precedent)* requires the conditions precedent to be met to the satisfaction of the Agent, while Clause 37.1 *(AMENDMENTS AND WAIVERS: Required consents)* requires the consent of the Majority Lenders (or, in the case of matters covered by Clause 37.2 *(AMENDMENTS AND WAIVERS: All Lender matters)*, all the lenders) for waivers and amendments.

2.019

In exercising its discretion as to whether to approve a condition precedent or not, the Agent is entitled to rely on its lawyers' advice on legal issues (see Clause 26.2 *(Instructions)* and Clause 28 *(ROLE OF THE AGENT, THE ARRANGER AND THE ISSUING BANK)* at subclauses 2 *(Instructions)* and 7 *(Rights and discretions)*, discussed in 10.007 and will usually require the lawyer to confirm satisfaction of those legal conditions precedent in writing.[9] For other issues, such as satisfactory reports from experts (surveyors, environmental experts and the like) or, as in legal opinions, or reports on title, where the lawyer gives advice but the lenders need to assess that advice, the Agent will invariably circulate drafts round the syndicate in advance, for their approval, rather than taking that decision on its own shoulders. Taking the decision without involving the syndicate would go beyond the 'purely mechanical and administrative' role of the Agent described in Clause 28.3 *(ROLE OF THE AGENT, THE ARRANGER AND THE ISSUING BANK: Duties of the Agent)* and discussed in 10.006 and, while it is authorized to take such decisions, doing so could expose the Agent to liability as discussed in 10.003. See also Box 2.4.

Box 2.4

This is the reason for the following provision in Clause 4.1 *(CONDITIONS OF UTILIZATION: Initial conditions precedent)*. It is designed to exclude liability for the Agent arising in relation to satisfaction of the conditions precedent. The usual clause reads

Other than to the extent that the Majority Lenders notify the Agent in writing to the contrary before the Agent gives the notification described in paragraph (a) above, the Lenders authorize (but do not require) the Agent to

---

[9] See Wood, International Loans, Bonds, Guarantees, Legal opinions, 3rd edn at 5–016 for a specimen of a letter which lawyers might give in relation to satisfaction of conditions precedent.

148   The Facilities

> *give that notification. The Agent shall not be liable for any damages, costs or losses whatsoever as a result of giving any such notification.*

Clause 4.1 *(Initial conditions precedent)* in other Commercial Circumstances

The following commentary looks at this clause in situations not involving loans to investment grade borrowers

Asset Finance Transactions

2.020
For transactions where the loan is to finance the purchase of an asset and security is to be taken over that asset, the conditions precedent will fall into two categories: those required before notice of drawdown can be given; and those (the conditions related to the establishment of the security) which are required on drawdown. There will be practical difficulties in satisfying the conditions precedent to drawdown.[10]

Multiple Drawdown Facilities

2.021
The conditions precedent will require adjustment where there is a term loan with multiple drawdowns (and possibly an extended drawdown period). There will be different conditions precedent for the first drawdown from those which apply to subsequent drawings.

Documentary conditions precedent to subsequent drawdowns clearly need to reflect the purpose of the drawdown. So, for example, a loan for construction of a given project, such as an airport, may provide for drawdowns matching stages of construction—in which case the conditions precedent will relate to evidence of achievement of the relevant stage of the project. Often the lenders are also concerned that the ratio of debt to equity is maintained and will therefore require evidence that the relevant amount of equity has been injected.

---

[10] See Box 13.1.

Clause 4: Conditions of Utilization 149

> **Backstop Facilities**
>
> **2.022**
> **Backstop Facilities** are intended to be a backstop only—it is not intended that they be drawn except in exceptional circumstances. For these it will be sensible to have key conditions precedent (such as board resolutions and legal opinions) satisfied either before the loan agreement is signed or as a condition precedent to the lenders' commitment to lend (as opposed to being a condition precedent to the actual advance of funds, as would normally be the case) and perhaps to require those conditions precedent to be satisfied within a fairly short period after signing the facility. There may then be a separate clause with any other conditions precedent required for an advance to be made (such as, perhaps, a condition precedent that there is no Default).

Clause 4.2 Further conditions precedent

2.023
Here is the Clause from the LMA Compounded/Term Rate Loan
'*Further conditions precedent*
The Lenders will only be obliged to comply with Clause [ ] (Lenders' participation) if on the date of the Utilization Request and on the proposed Utilization Date:

a) *in the case of a Rollover Loan, no Event of Default is continuing or would result from the proposed Loan and, in the case of any other Loan, no Default is continuing or would result from the proposed Loan; and*
b) *the Repeating Representations to be made by each Obligor are true in all material respects'.*

This clause requires certain factual conditions precedent to be satisfied in addition to the documentary conditions precedent referred to in the previous clause. These are a requirement that the Repeating Representations are true and, (except in relation to Rollover Loans discussed in 2.025) that there is no 'Default'[11].

---

[11] See commentary on the definition of 'Default' at 1.014.

150   The Facilities

2.024

The reason for the requirement that there should be no 'Default' is that, if circumstances exist which may mature into an Event of Default, the lenders should not be obliged to advance additional money and thereby increase their exposure to the borrower during the period of uncertainty.

2.025

In relation to Rollover Loans, the condition is more relaxed. For these loans, the condition is that there is no 'Event of Default', as opposed to the condition that there is no 'Default', which applies to other Loans. This is because a Rollover Loan does not result in the lender having an increased exposure to the borrower—see Box 2.5

Box 2.5

The concept of 'Default' involves drawing a distinction between the lenders' right to require repayment of moneys already advanced (which arises on an Event of Default) and their right to be relieved of their obligation to lend new money (which arises on a Default). This distinction is more difficult to make in a revolving credit facility than in a term loan. The mechanics of a revolving credit facility are that a loan is advanced for a relatively short period, for example, three months. It is repaid in full at the end of that period and the borrower may then redraw whatever available amount it requires for a new period. The new advance on a **rollover** may technically be regarded as 'new money', but in commercial terms, it is only any additional money over and above the amount outstanding immediately prior to the rollover, which is really new. So a Rollover Loan does not involve the lender incurring any additional exposure to the borrower.

2.026

The condition is that no Default (or Event of Default, in the case of a Rollover Loan) is 'continuing'. This requirement should be read together with Clause 1.2 *(DEFINITIONS AND INTERPRETATION: Construction)* at subclause (e) (which defines 'continuing' and is discussed in 1.065) and Clause 37 *(Amendments and Waivers)* (which sets out the level of consent required to grant waivers). The result is that, for most Defaults, it is a decision for the Majority Lenders as to whether or not to advance the loan, despite the existence of a Default.

2.027

In addition, Clause 4.2 *(CONDITIONS OF UTILIZATION: Further conditions precedent)* at subclause (a)(ii) requires all Repeating Representations to be true (and this applies to all advances of a term loan and to all rollovers of a revolving credit—whether or not they are simply 'Rollover Loans') '*in all material respects*'. The reason is to ensure that certain very basic issues (such as the ability to borrow the loan) remain as they originally were. It is up to the draftsperson to specify which of the representations are to be 'Repeating Representations' and are therefore to be conditions precedent to advances. This is a complex area, discussed in detail from 8.007 onwards in relation to Clause 21 (*Representations*).

Clause 4.3 Conditions relating to Optional Currencies

2.028

This clause sets out additional **conditions** for drawing in a currency other than the Base Currency. These include a requirement that the currency has been approved, is freely convertible to the Base Currency, and is readily available in the amount required. Once a currency is agreed the Agent must notify minimum drawing amounts.

2.029

Comment It may be helpful for borrowers to have a list of pre-approved Optional Currencies, not least to avoid delay if the borrower wants to draw or convert the Loan into a currency other than the Base Currency. The lenders have the protection of Clause 8.2 *(OPTIONAL CURRENCIES Unavailability of a currency)* which provides that if the relevant currency is not available to that lender or it is illegal to fund in that currency, they can fund in the Base Currency instead.

Of course if the loan provides for different currencies it will also need to contain different interest rate mechanisms appropriate to each currency—see 0.112.

Clause 4.4 Maximum number of Utilizations

2.030

This clause limits the number of loans that may be outstanding. This limits the administrative requirements in servicing the loan for the lenders. In the case of a loan such as the LMA Compounded/Term Rate Loan, which allows for different loans to different group members, the number of loans allowed must of course be sufficient for the anticipated number of borrowers.

2.031

The maximum number of loans also needs to be set at a high enough number to ensure that the borrower is not effectively unable to borrow any balance of Facility B—the revolving credit—(while still paying a commitment fee on it) until the end of the then current Interest Period (see Box 2.6).

> ### Box 2.6
>
> So, for example, assume that Facility B is for $50 million but only one loan at a time is available under it. Assume that the borrower has borrowed $20 million under Facility B for a six-month Interest Period. The result is that, during that six-month period, the borrower will be paying a commitment fee on the unused part of Facility B ($30 million) but will be unable to draw any of that commitment.

Utilization

Clause 5: Utilization—Loans

Clause 5.1 Delivery of a Utilization Request

3.001

This clause in the LMA Compounded/Term Rate Loan[1] requires a drawdown notice to be given at a 'Specified Time'. The precise period of time required for notice of drawdown depends on the currency, and on the market in which the loan is being funded, as well as on the size and logistics of the syndicate, and is set out in a schedule.

Clause 5.2 Completion of a Utilization for Loans Request

3.002

This clause requires the borrower to deliver a utilization request specifying the amount required, the date on which it is required, (which must be a date within the Availability Period for the relevant Facility) and the Interest Period,

---

[1] References in this book to the LMA Compounded/Term Rate Loan are to the LMA Multicurrency Term and Revolving Facilities Agreement incorporating Term SOFR for use in Investment Grade transactions, available to LMA members via www.lma.eu.com.

© The Author(s), under exclusive license to Springer Nature Switzerland AG 2024

S. Wright, *The International Loan Documentation Handbook*, Global Financial Markets, https://doi.org/10.1007/978-3-031-38489-9_4

154 Utilization

for any loan as well as identifying whether the drawing relates to Facility A or Facility B.

The clause provides that only one Loan may be requested in one Utilization Request but there are no restrictions on how many utilizations may be made on the same day (hence a number of currencies may be drawn).

Sometimes, there will be requirements as to frequency of drawdowns.

Clause 5.3 Currency and amount

3.003
This clause sets out the minimum amounts of any drawdown, with a different minimum for Facility A (the term loan) and Facility B (the revolving credit). This is for the administrative convenience of the lenders. There is an option to express this minimum both in the Base Currency and in a different Optional Currency, which may be useful for the borrower if a particular Optional Currency is likely to be used regularly, as this will avoid risks of the minimum amount in the relevant Optional Currency becoming impractical due to exchange rate fluctuations.

This clause also caps the drawings so that, using current exchange rates for drawings in Optional Currencies, no Utilization can exceed the Available Commitment. See further 3.013 onwards.

Clause 5.4 Lenders' participation

3.004
This clause requires the lenders to lend through their Facility Office.[2]

3.005

Clause 5.5 Cancellation of Commitment

This clause cancels any part of either facility as is unused at the end of its Availability Period.

---

[2] See however the definition of 'Facility Office' discussed at 1.023.

Clause 6: Utilization—Letters of Credit

3.006

The borrower may request Facility B to be made available by the issue of **letters of credit**. The form of letter of credit is 'standby' in nature—i.e. it is the functional equivalent of a guarantee. The form is set out as a schedule to the loan agreement.

The letter of credit will be issued by one of the lenders identified as Issuing Banks in the loan agreement, relying on an indemnity from the borrower in the event that a claim is made under the letter of credit. The Issuing Bank also has the benefit of indemnities from the lenders—pro rata to their commitments to Facility B—and the lenders in turn rely on counter indemnities from the borrowers.

3.007

If an Event of Default occurs before demand is made on the Issuing Bank under the letter of credit, the Agent has the right under Clause 25.13(d) *(EVENTS OF DEFAULT: Acceleration)* to require the borrowers to provide cash security to the Issuing Bank in an amount equal to the potential liability of the Issuing Bank under the letter of credit.

3.008

From the perspective of the Issuing Bank, it is relying on the borrower's credit risk, but also, to the extent that other lenders have committed to share the risks in the facility, the lender is relying on the credit risk of those other lenders—that is, will they make payment when due under their indemnities? For this reason the Issuing Bank is given the right (in Clause 26.3(a) *(CHANGES TO THE LENDERS: Other conditions of assignment or transfer)* to give or withhold consent to any proposed transfer of Facility B.

The Issuing Bank may also want to consider whether they need to add the protections for Issuing Banks which are included as part of the Lehman provisions and which are discussed in 0.224.

Clause 6.1 Facility B

3.009

This states that Facility B may be used to draw letters of credit.

156 Utilization

Clauses 6.2, 6.3 and 6.4 Delivery of a Utilization Request for Letters of Credit; Completion of a Utilization Request for Letters of Credit and currency and amount.

These clauses mirror the equivalent provisions in Clause 5 (*Utilization – Loans*). They require a drawdown notice to be given at a 'Specified Time', giving details of the requested letter of credit, and specifying the requirements as to minimum and maximum amounts of the letter of credit.

3.010

Clauses 6.5 and 6.6 Issue of Letter of Credit and Renewal of a Letter of Credit

Letters of credit will be issued for a specified period of time. Under Clause 6.6, the borrower may request that an existing letter of credit be renewed for a new period of time. Clause 6.5 states that the obligation of the Issuing Bank to issue a letter of credit is conditional on there being no Default at the time of issue, and that the obligation to renew a letter of credit is conditional on no Event of Default existing at the time of the renewal. This distinction between a Default and an Event of Default mirrors the position with Rollover Loans discussed in 2.025.

3.011

Clause 6.7 Revaluation of Letters of Credit

This clause requires any letters of credit which are outstanding in an Optional Currency to be revalued at regular intervals at current exchange rates and, if as a result Facility B outstandings exceed the maximum Commitment, the borrower is required to make a prepayment.

Clause 7: Letters of Credit

3.012

This clause provides for the indemnities described in 3.006 in relation to the letters of credit.

Clause 7.2 Claims under a Letter of Credit is where the borrower undertakes to reimburse the Issuing Bank immediately if the Issuing Bank makes payment under a letter of credit.

Clause 7.3 Indemnities is where the lenders indemnify the Issuing Bank and the borrower in turn indemnifies the lenders.

Clause 8: Optional Currencies

Purpose of a multicurrency loan

3.013

All companies need to ensure, as part of their normal financial management, that the currencies in which their income is denominated matches the currencies in which their liabilities are denominated or that they have resources available to manage any exposure which they have, resulting from a mismatch. The currencies which borrowers decide to borrow in will therefore normally (but not necessarily—e.g. see Box 3.1) be chosen to match the currencies in which they generate income.

Box 3.1

The borrower may also own assets which have a worldwide market and which are generally bought and sold in a specific currency. Examples are ships and aircraft, which are normally traded in Dollars. Here, the borrower, or the lenders, may wish to see the loan denominated in the currency in which the assets are normally bought and sold (even if income is earned in a different currency), so as to ensure the relative value of the security is maintained.

Multicurrency loans may be drawn in one or more specified currencies, or switched from one specified currency to another after drawdown. This ability to draw in and convert into different currencies assists the borrower in

158   Utilization

matching income and liabilities (particularly in a revolving credit), and can also be used as a tool to access the interest rate applicable for borrowings in different currencies.

3.014
Whatever the borrower's reason for wanting to have the ability to switch currencies, or to draw in a number of different currencies, it needs to consider also the questions of how its repayment obligations will be calculated and how the amount of the available facility will be calculated. They need to consider, for example, whether it is better for them to have.

- a Dollar-based loan which is available for drawing in, or conversion into, Euro or Yen;
- a Euro-based loan which is available for drawing in, or conversion into, Dollars or Yen; or
- three separate facilities, one in Dollars, one in Euros, and one in Yen.

The first two examples would normally be described as multicurrency loans. The third example is not normally described as a multicurrency loan.

The different impact of the three options depends on whether the facility in question is a term loan or a revolving credit facility.

Revolving credit

3.015
The key differences between the three examples, in the case of a revolving credit, relates to the calculation of how much remains for drawing. If the borrower had three separate facilities in different currencies, it has the security that those facilities will remain available, in their specified amounts, regardless of exchange rates. If, on the other hand, the borrower relied on a Dollar-based loan to finance its need for Euros, it would be exposed to the possibility that the available Euros would be reduced, due to their appreciation against the Dollar—because the amount available at a given drawdown date would be fixed at a Dollar sum. If that sum afforded fewer Euros than at the start, that risk is for the borrower.

Clause 8: Optional Currencies **159**

Term loan

3.016

In the case of a term loan, the principal difference relates to calculation of repayments. In the first example (a Dollar-based loan), repayment will be required to be made in amounts which keep the value of the loan, in Dollar terms, in line with a schedule fixed at the start of the loan (see Box 3.2). If income is in a currency other than Dollars, the risk is that exchange rates will move such that there will be insufficient income to fund the repayment instalments. In the second case (a Euro-based loan), fixed Euro repayments will be required. Again, the borrower will take the exchange rate risk in relation to the currency outstanding. In the third case, repayment of every facility will be in its outstanding currency, regardless of any movement of exchange rates relating to that currency.

Box 3.2

Taking a simple example. Assume a multicurrency loan of $10 million is available in Dollars or Euros and has a Base Currency of Dollars. It is repayable by 20 equal instalments, one every six months. It is drawn in Euros at a time when exchange rates are 1:1. Hence, 10 million Euros are drawn. On the first repayment date, the exchange rate has moved to 1:1.5. The borrower must repay 10 million Euros (i.e. the full amount it has drawn, in the currency in which it has drawn it) and redraw the then equivalent of $9.5 million (the 'Base Currency Amount' at that time, that is, the amount which would have been outstanding if the loan had always been denominated in Dollars). The amount the borrower can redraw is therefore 9.5 × 1.5 (the current exchange rate) = 14.25 million Euros. The borrower repays 10 million Euros and redraws 14.25 million Euros (but is still treated as having made a repayment of $0.5 million). On the next repayment date, exchange rates have returned to 1:1. The borrower must now repay 14.25 million Euros and can redraw the then equivalent of $9 million (the Base Currency Amount at that time). The then equivalent of $9 million is 9 × 1 = 9 million Euros. The borrower repays 14.25 million Euros and redraws 9 million Euros.[3] A multicurrency loan therefore involves an exchange rate risk for the borrower.

---

[3] The agreement may include provisions allowing these amounts to be netted so that only the difference between the two amounts is paid.

160 Utilization

3.017

Multicurrency facilities can give numerous different options, for example, as to which currencies are permitted and whether more than one currency is available at any one time.

Note that in relation to the revolving credit created by Facility B, the repayment mechanics are straightforward since each advance will be made in a particular currency and repaid in that currency.[4] In a term loan it is more complex since the loan can be converted from one currency to another while it is still outstanding.

Clause 8.1 Selection of currency

3.018

This clause allows the borrower to choose the currency of the loan on drawdown or, in relation to Facility A, at the start of an Interest Period, in each case from the pre-agreed Optional Currencies.

Each utilization under the LMA Compounded/Term Rate Loan must be in a single currency. However, borrowers may request more than one utilization at the same time, each of which may be in different currencies.

The loan agreement needs to deal with what happens if a borrower asks to convert a part of Facility A from one currency to another on a day which is not a Business Day for both currencies concerned (the loan normally remains in the existing currency and is rolled over on a daily basis until a day which is a Business Day for both currencies). The agreement also needs to deal with the situation where some syndicate members are unable to fund in the requested currency (they would then normally be required to fund in the Base Currency).

Clause 8.3 Change of currency

3.019

This clause deals with the situation if a utilization of Facility A is to be converted from one currency to another at the end of an Interest Period.

---

[4] Although for drawings of Facility B which are made by letters of credit, there is a requirement to revalue the amount of the letter of credit from time to time if it was issued in an Optional Currency, as discussed in 3.011.

A multicurrency facility has a Base Currency, with reference to which the amount of the loan available in any given currency will be calculated. This is the concept of the 'Base Currency Amount'. It is the amount that would have been outstanding in the Base Currency if the loan had always been denominated in that currency. The loan may be drawn in a different currency—in which case the amount advanced will be the equivalent of the Base Currency Amount on the drawdown date. This clause provides that, if a utilization of Facility A is to change currency, then, at the end of the Interest Period when that change is to occur, the amount drawn, in the currency originally drawn, will be repaid in full. The borrower will redraw (in whatever currency is permitted) the Base Currency Amount (or its then equivalent in the new relevant currency).

Clause 8.4 Same Optional Currency during successive Interest Periods

3.020

This clause applies a similar procedure (without the repayment and re-advance) for Interest Periods for Facility A where there is no change of currency (see Box 3.2).

There are often provisions (in sub clause (b) of this clause in the LMA Compounded/Term Rate Loan) that if there is no change of currency and the difference between the amount due to be repaid and the amount due to be re-advanced is minimal then no adjustment will be needed.

These mechanics mean that the lenders may be required to advance further funds even when the loan is being repaid.[5]

The mechanics of repayment and re-advance of the loan can cause difficulties with secured loans as it may inadvertently have the effect of repaying the loan which the security secures.[6]

---

[5] This has implications for the method of transfer of a multicurrency loan—see 9.015.
[6] See further A1.068.

Repayment, Prepayment and Cancellation

Clause 9: Repayment

Clause 9.1 Repayment of Facility A Loans

4.001

This clause in the LMA Compounded/Term Rate Loan[1] specifies the repayment schedule for Facility A (the term loan) and states that moneys repaid are not available for reborrowing.

Clause 9.2 Repayment of Facility B Loans

4.002

This clause reads …

…*(a) Each Borrower which has drawn a Loan shall repay that Loan on the last day of its Interest Period.*

A revolving credit involves the advance of a loan for a chosen Interest Period, with the loan being repaid in full at the end of its Interest Period.

---

[1] References in this book to the LMA Compounded/Term Rate Loan are to the LMA Multicurrency Term and Revolving Facilities Agreement incorporating Term SOFR for use in Investment Grade transactions, available to LMA members via www.lma.eu.com.

© The Author(s), under exclusive license to Springer Nature Switzerland AG 2024
S. Wright, *The International Loan Documentation Handbook*, Global Financial Markets, https://doi.org/10.1007/978-3-031-38489-9_5

164   Repayment, Prepayment and Cancellation

Additional loans may be advanced from time to time (up to a maximum number of loans at any one time).

4.003

Paragraph b of this clause is optional. This is the 'cashless rollover' provision referred to in Box 2.1, which provides that if an advance is being made under Facility B (the revolving credit) at the same time as an advance is being repaid under that facility, the two payments can be netted off against each other rather than having a repayment and readvance. This cashless rollover is market practice but at the time of the 2008 financial crisis, the need to formalize the market practice in the documents became apparent as concerns arose that liquidators of banks with revolving credit participations might insist on full repayment as per the documentation, but not have the funds to re-advance. Although the cashless rollover provisions are optional, they are invariably included and will apply on all rollovers of Facility B.

4.004

Clause 9.3 Reduction of Facility B Loans

This is an optional provision for inclusion if the amount of the Facility B loan (the revolving credit) is to be reduced over time.

If the Lehman provisions are included in the loan agreement then, in addition to cashless rollover provisions, there will be a provision which will automatically '**term out**' the participation of any Defaulting Lender in Facility B (see Box 4.1 for specimen wording).

Box 4.1

Specimen wording reads '*At any time when a Lender becomes a Defaulting Lender, the maturity date of each of the participations of that Lender in the Facility B Loans then outstanding will be automatically extended to the Termination Date and will be treated as separate Loans ('the Separate Loans') denominated in the currency in which the relevant participations are outstanding'.*

The issue is that a defaulting lender is unlikely to be able to fulfil its commitment to lend under the revolving credit. This optional clause is designed to ensure that, if at the time a lender becomes a defaulting lender it has already advanced funds under the revolving credit, the borrower is not

obliged to repay those monies until the end of the Commitment Period—
that is, those moneys will be 'termed out' (or effectively, converted into a
term loan).

4.005

> If there is an extension option for the revolving credit (as discussed in
> 0.198) then this clause will describe how the option works. The borrower
> will have a specified period in which it can invite lenders to participate
> in the extension, but the extension is typically uncommitted.

Clause 10: Prepayment and Cancellation

4.006

Clause 10 (*Prepayment and Cancellation*) deals with **prepayment** and cancellation. It falls into three sections: compulsory prepayment (in the first three
clauses dealing with illegality and change of control); voluntary cancellation
and/or prepayment (in the next three clauses); and voluntary prepayment of
a single lender (in the last clause).

Clause 10.1 Illegality

4.007

This clause requires compulsory prepayment and termination of the commitment in relation to a single lender if it becomes illegal for that lender to
continue to fund the loan. This covers not only illegality due to political
events but also illegality due to imposition of exchange control regulations
(for example). This clause is intended to deal with situations such as outbreak
of war and to allow a mechanism for the lenders to comply with any relevant
law. While it may be wishful thinking to expect the participation in the loan
to be prepaid in these circumstances, the right not to advance new moneys
will be effective and the right to require repayment may enable enforcement
action to be taken if the borrower has assets in jurisdictions which are not
tainted by the illegality.

4.008

Comment A borrower may, in certain circumstances, argue that

- the obligation to fund the loan should be suspended during the period of the illegality, but not cancelled, particularly if there is a long drawdown period;
- the obligation to prepay should not arise if the situation is capable of remedy, for example, by obtaining necessary licences or exemptions;
- the relevant lender should have an obligation to try to obtain any permits, etc., which may be available to cure the problem (although they probably already have this obligation under Clause 18 (*Mitigation by the Lenders*) discussed in 6.070) and/or
- they should not be obliged to prepay a sanctioned lender.

Sanctions

4.009

As discussed in 0.185, lenders will want to have specific clauses addressing sanctions affecting the borrower rather than rely on this illegality clause to deal with the issue. Lenders and borrowers may also want to provide that breach of any sanctions provision is not an Event of Default (which would result in a potential requirement for repayment of the whole loan), but instead, is a compulsory prepayment event, requiring prepayment of the affected lender. This may be particularly helpful where some lenders may be prohibited from giving effect to sanctions laws of other countries as discussed in 0.189.

Clause 10.2 Illegality in relation to Issuing Bank

4.010

This clause states that if it is illegal for an Issuing Bank to issue letters of credit or to keep them outstanding then its obligations to issue them will come to an end and the borrower will use its best endeavours to procure the release of any letters of credit then outstanding.

Clause 10.3 Change of control

4.011

This clause requires compulsory prepayment of the whole loan and release of all lenders from their obligation to fund if there is a change of control in relation to the borrower and the Majority Lenders require prepayment. The argument is that they have relied on continuity of ownership and management in their credit decision. The commercial effect of this is the equivalent of an Event of Default but it is framed as a compulsory prepayment to avoid triggering cross default clauses.[2] See Box 4.2.

> **Box 4.2**
>
> There may also be a concern that some countries would regard a provision which gives one party a right to terminate a contract early even when the other party is not in breach of any obligation under the agreement, as being repugnant to local law either because of its one-sided nature or because it is seen as an unfair forfeiture. By framing the clause as an obligation to prepay in certain circumstances, failure to pay when required will be a breach, and this may reduce the legal risks.

4.012

There is an option to draft this clause so as to require compulsory prepayment of individual lenders (as opposed to having the decision made by Majority Lenders and relate to prepayment of the whole loan). Many lenders will require this option, enabling them to require prepayment regardless of the views of the Majority in those cases where the identity of the shareholder is critical to their lending decision, even though a guarantee may not have been sought from the shareholder.

4.013

A key issue is what constitutes a change of control. Commonly it is defined to mean the power to control more than a stated percentage (often 50%) of the company, either through shares or through control of the board of directors. It is also worth noticing that lenders may be concerned about two different things here. Lenders may be concerned that if new controlling shareholders came in, then those new shareholders might have a different business strategy

---

[2] See commentary on the cross default clause in 8.256 'Compulsory prepayment events'.

168   Repayment, Prepayment and Cancellation

from the original shareholders. Additionally, lenders may want to ensure that specified existing shareholders keep their stake in the company—that they have 'skin in the game' so to speak. So some change of control clauses focus on a new entity gaining control of the borrower, while others will also require continued ownership of a specified percentage by the original sponsors.

Borrowers will want to negotiate a long period for prepayment to give time to arrange alternative funding.

Lenders will want to ensure that the clause relates to the ultimate control of the holding company.

4.014

Comment The borrower may wish to ask for compulsory negotiation and/or a grace period.

Some loans contain other circumstances in which a compulsory prepayment is required. These may include cash sweeps if results for a given period are better than expected, prepayment with the proceeds of permitted disposals, or prepayment out of insurance proceeds in an asset finance, or out of post-completion price adjustments, or on flotation in an acquisition finance.

Other issues which arise in relation to prepayments out of disposal proceeds are discussed in 8.183.

Commonly the clause allows the right to require prepayment to be exercised independently from the right not to lend new money. It may be that lenders will be reluctant to call for prepayment of moneys already advanced but will want to stop future drawings.

Clause 10.4 Voluntary cancellation

4.015

This clause gives the borrower the right to reduce the amount of the facility. This right to reduce the **commitment** is a useful additional right to the right to prepay, particularly in a revolving credit or a term loan with a long drawdown period, as in these cases the **commitment fee** will be payable during

Clause 10: Prepayment and Cancellation   **169**

the whole drawdown period and cancellation allows the borrower a method to bring these fees to an end.

Lenders often require the minimum amount for cancellation to be significant.

Comment The notice period for cancellation should be short so as to bring the commitment fee to an end as soon as possible.

Clause 10.5 Voluntary prepayment of Facility A Loans and Clause 10.6 Voluntary prepayment of Facility B Utilizations

4.016

These clauses give the borrower the right to prepay the loan.[3] Prepayment must be in minimum amounts.

4.017

Given that accrued interest will need to be made together with the prepayment, then for a compounded rate loan, lenders usually require that notice of prepayment should be given at least as long as the lookback period before the prepayment so as to enable the lenders to make the calculation of the amount of interest which is due.

4.018

There may be a prepayment fee (although this is unusual) or Break Costs (relevance of which to compounded rate loans is debatable—see Box 0.13) in respect of a prepayment. If so, then the borrower should consider whether that fee is appropriate in circumstances where there is a compulsory prepayment or a voluntary prepayment of part of the loan under Clause 10.7 (*PREPAYMENT AND CANCELLATION: Right of replacement or repayment and cancellation in relation to a single Lender or Issuing Bank.*) If there are no Break Costs for a particular currency, the lenders may prohibit prepayment during Interest Periods to avoid the administrative costs and inefficient use of funds involved in receiving unexpected payments.

---

[3] Without this express right, the borrower would probably not be entitled to prepay. See Hooper v Western Counties and South Wales Telephone Co Ltd (1892) 68 LT 78.

170 Repayment, Prepayment and Cancellation

4.019

Generally, in relation to term loans, the prepayment will be applied against the last instalments of the loan—to reduce its life. The lenders prefer this, not least as it is easier to assess risk over the shorter term.

Comment Borrowers may wish to have prepayments applied pro rata against repayment instalments in certain circumstances so as to see immediate benefit from any prepayment. This would be particularly important in an asset finance where the prepayment was made from the sale of an asset which would otherwise have generated part of the income required for the loan repayment.

Clause 10.7 Right of replacement or repayment and cancellation in relation to a single Lender or Issuing Bank

4.020

This clause allows voluntary prepayment, cancellation and/or replacement of an individual lender in the following circumstances

1. Where there is an additional cost attached to the participation of that lender or Issuing Bank, either as a result of a gross-up or where that lender or Issuing Bank is entitled to payment under the increased cost clause or the tax indemnity and
2. Where a lender or the Issuing Bank is required to be prepaid under the illegality clause

4.021

Comment Commonly borrowers ask to extend the right to other circumstances including

4.022

* Where the lender is a defaulting lender.

4.023

- Where the lender votes against granting a waiver or consent required where a certain specified minimum percentage of lenders have given approval. This is the so-called 'yank the bank' provision and such a lender is often defined as a 'Non Consenting Lender'.

4.024

- Where a lender is entitled to be prepaid as a result of sanctions or change of control.

4.025

Note also that the borrower cannot usually remove the Agent. There are separate provisions dealing with Agents in financial difficulty (Impaired Agents) and Agents affected by **FATCA** withholding.[4] These give the primary power of removal to the syndicate as it is they who take the credit risk on the Agent. Note however that this provision refers to the Agent in its capacity as Agent— it does not prevent the borrower from prepaying the Agent in its capacity as lender.

4.026

Comment Sometimes there are time limits within which these various rights must be exercised. Borrowers should bear in mind that of course it can take some time to negotiate a transferee.

Clause 10.8 Restrictions

4.027

This clause provides for notice of cancellation and prepayment to be irrevocable and for payment to be accompanied by payment of interest and **Break Costs** if applicable.

Comment If Break Costs apply to any currency the borrower may argue that they should only apply to voluntary prepayment, not to compulsory prepayment or situations where a lender is being replaced, e.g. because they are a defaulting lender as per 4.020 above.

---

[4] The provisions on FATCA withholding sometimes give borrowers as well as lenders the power to remove the Agent if it becomes likely that payments to the Agent will need to be made subject to a deduction for FATCA.

Costs of Utilization

Clause 11A: Rate Switch

Clause 11A.1 Switch to Compounded Reference Rate

5.001

If any part of the loan is made in a currency for which there is to be a change in the method of calculation of interest during the life of the loan, (for example, if the agreement is to charge interest on the basis of compounded rates in due course but lenders are not operationally ready to do so at the start of the loan agreement) then that currency will be defined as a 'Rate Switch Currency' and the agreement will contain a rate switch clause which will automatically convert the loan onto the new basis from the relevant Rate Switch Date as discussed in 0.139.

The LMA clause in the LMA Compounded/Term Rate Loan[1] reads

> *Subject to Clause [] (Delayed switch for existing Term Rate Loans), on and from the Rate Switch Date for a Rate Switch Currency:*

---

[1] References in this book to the LMA Compounded/Term Rate Loan are to the LMA Multicurrency Term and Revolving Facilities Agreement incorporating Term Sofr for use in Investment Grade transactions, available to LMA members via www.lma.eu.com.

© The Author(s), under exclusive license to Springer Nature Switzerland AG 2024
S. Wright, *The International Loan Documentation Handbook*, Global Financial Markets,
https://doi.org/10.1007/978-3-031-38489-9_6

174   Costs of Utilization

(a) *use of the Compounded Reference Rate will replace the use of the Term Reference Rate for the calculation of interest for Loans in that Rate Switch Currency*

(b) ....

Clause 11A.2 Delayed switch for existing Term Rate Loans

5.002
Clause 11A.2 then deals with the situation if the Rate Switch Date falls in the middle of an Interest Period for a Term Rate Loan. In those circumstances, the Term Rate Loan will continue to bear interest at its current rate for the rest of the Interest Period and convert to the compounded rate at that point.

5.003
The definition of the Rate Switch Trigger Event will determine the date on which any switch onto a compounded rate of interest will happen. As discussed in Box 0.18, the intention is that the switch will happen in the event of permanent problems with the relevant published rate—whether permanent unavailability, change in methodology on a long-term basis or regulatory advice that the rate is no longer accurate, or if a particularly important **tenor** (the 'Quoted Tenor') of the relevant published rate stops being published. There is an option (referred to as a 'pre cessation trigger') for the parties to agree that the switch can happen at an earlier point.

5.004
The LMA clause also includes a definition of 'Rate Switch Backstop Date'. The idea behind this definition is that the parties might wish to have a definite end date by which the rate switch must happen—either pre-agreed or agreed after signing. The switch will then happen on the earlier of the Rate Switch Backstop Date and the date of any Rate Switch Trigger Event.

Clause 11: Interest

Clause 11.1 Calculation of interest—Term Rate Loans and 11.2 Calculation of interest—Compounded Rate Loans

5.005

The interest rate for a loan bearing interest at a term rate will be specified to be a rate for an Interest Period whereas interest calculated on the basis of compounded risk free rates will specify what the rate is for each day. See Box 5.1.

> **Box 5.1**
>
> Compare the clauses below dealing with interest
>
> *'Calculation of interest — Term Rate Loans*
> *The rate of interest on each Term Rate Loan **for an Interest Period** is......'*
> *'Calculation of interest — Compounded Rate Loans*
> *The rate of interest on each Compounded Rate Loan **for any day during an Interest Period** is ....'*

The rate for Term Rate Loans will be the Margin for the relevant currency plus the Term Reference Rate and any applicable Term Reference Rate CAS.[2] The daily rate for Compounded Rate Loans will be the relevant Margin for the relevant currency plus the Compounded Reference Rate for that day (which itself is the Daily Non-Cumulative Compounded RFR Rate for that day plus any applicable credit adjustment spread as discussed in Section 4 of the Introduction).

---

[2] Note that the Term Reference Rate itself includes any adjustment or credit adjustment spread resulting from the fallback mechanisms such as any Central Bank Rate Adjustment or Alternative Reference Rate Adjustment. On the other hand any Term Reference Rate CAS is not included in the Term Reference Rate itself, but needs to be added to it when interest is charged. This is different from the situation with the Compounded Reference Rate which includes all applicable credit adjustment spreads, including any applicable Baseline CAS.

176 Costs of Utilization

Clause 11.3 Payment of interest

5.006

This clause deals with the timing of payment of interest. Interest will be due on the last day of each Interest Period.

Clause 11.4 Default interest

5.007

This clause provides that if any amount is not paid on its due date, the rate of interest applicable to it will be increased to a default rate. This is usually the rate which would otherwise have applied plus Margin plus an uplift. This is intended partly to give the borrower an incentive to pay in full and on time and partly to compensate the lenders for the additional credit risk and for the additional management time involved in lending to a borrower which is in default. The increase in the interest rate must be such that the overall default interest rate is higher than the rate a borrower could normally expect to have to pay if their financial fortunes reversed and obtaining funds was difficult, so as to make non-payment an unattractive form of financing in those circumstances.

5.008

The obligation to pay default interest arises whenever a payment is overdue, regardless of whether or not that non-payment constitutes an Event of Default. So, for example, if (as is common) the agreement provides that failure to pay principal is not an Event of Default if caused by technical error and remedied within a given period of time, nevertheless, default interest will start to accrue on the date of non-payment. Default interest is normally[3] only charged when payment is overdue. Hence, if there is an Event of Default other than as a result of non-payment, default interest will only start to accrue if the loan is accelerated.

---

[3] In some cases, lenders choose to require the loan agreement to allow them to charge a higher rate of interest on the occurrence of any Event of Default, even if there are no moneys overdue, as an added encouragement to the borrower to avoid Events of Default, particularly those which are minor where the lenders may be thought unlikely to exercise their right to accelerate. This would usually be achieved in the definition of 'Margin'.

5.009

The default interest clause provides for the default interest to be paid both before and after judgement. This is because many jurisdictions specify a statutory rate of interest to apply to amounts that the court has determined to be due and has issued a judgement for. That rate would apply from the date of the judgement until the judgement had been enforced, but often only applies if no other rate has been agreed. Given that the statutory rate is not regularly updated, the lenders prefer to know that, during that period, default interest will still be based on market rates.[4]

5.010

Default interest is one of the areas that can cause difficulty in a number of jurisdictions. In some jurisdictions there is a limit on the duration for which such interest can be charged or secured. In some there is a limit on the amount which can be charged, or secured. In England the provision will be void and unenforceable if it is a **penalty**. The law on penalties was clarified by a case in 2015.[5] That case determined that a clause which seeks to provide for the consequences of a breach of contract[6] will only be set aside as a penalty if the consequences which the clause provides for are 'out of all proportion to the legitimate interest' of the non-defaulting party.[7]

Clause 11.4 (*INTEREST: Default Interest*) at subclause (b) reads

5.011

If any overdue amount consists of all or part of a Term Rate Loan and became due on a day which was not the last day of an Interest Period relating to that Loan:

(i) *the first Interest Period for that overdue amount shall have a duration equal to the unexpired portion of the current Interest Period relating to that Loan and*

---

[4] A contractual choice of interest rate post-judgement is effective under English law. See Director General of Fair Trading v First National Bank Plc 2002 1 AC 481. Such a provision may not be effective in the place of enforcement of a judgement.

[5] Cavendish Square Holding v Makdessi (2015) UKSC 67 and *ParkingEye Ltd v Beavis [2015] UKSC 67* (the 'ParkingEye' Case).

[6] Which is what default interest clauses do, by stating that in the event of a breach of contract—non-payment when due—the consequences will be an increased interest rate.

[7] Lordsvale Finance plc v Bank of Zambia (1996) QB 752 considered an increase of 1% on a default and found it enforceable in the circumstances of the case. This case preceded the ParkingEye case.

178 Costs of Utilization

(ii) *the rate of interest applying to the overdue amount during that first Interest Period shall be [one] per cent higher than the rate which would have applied if the overdue amount had not become due.*

This subclause deals with principal falling due during an Interest Period in relation to a Term Rate Loan—(usually a loan which has been accelerated). It provides that, for the rest of the Interest Period, the increase in interest rate which is charged because of the Event of Default will be added to the existing rate applicable to the balance of that Interest Period (rather than being reset on the date of the acceleration). This is not necessary in the context of a Compounded Rate Loan because there is no element of pre-fixing of an interest rate.

Clause 11.5 Notifications

5.012
This clause provides for the Agent to notify all parties of interest rates for Term Rate Loans when they are determined.

For Compounded Rate Loans the requirement is to notify the amount of interest due (and the amount due to each lender and the rates used to make the calculation) as soon as the amount due is capable of calculation.

Clause 12: Interest Periods

Clause 12.1 Selection of Interest Periods

5.013
The tenors of available Interest Periods will be specified in the Reference Rate Terms for the relevant currency. For Term Rate Loans Interest Periods will need to reflect market availability for the relevant currency. Interest Periods will normally be limited to a maximum of six months as lenders will require to be paid six monthly as a minimum. Although with Libor-based loans, twelve-month Interest Periods were sometimes allowed, with interest being paid after six months, this is not possible with Compounded Rate Loans. For these, receiving interest part way through an Interest Period would make the interest calculation even more complicated than it already is!

Lenders may also want to restrict the borrower's choice of Interest Periods to match the lenders' operational capabilities.

This clause also provides that no Interest Period can overrun the final maturity of the Loan.

5.014

If there is a repayment of Facility A (the term loan) or of Facility B (the revolving credit) then outstanding Interest Periods at the date of the repayment or reduction need to end in sufficient amounts to ensure that the repayment or reduction can be effected. The borrower may therefore want the option (an optional provision in the LMA Compounded/Term Rate Loan) to choose Interest Periods of less than a month to achieve this.

Clause 12.2 Changes to Interest Periods

5.015

Clause 12.2 also permits the lenders to adjust Interest Periods to be of different durations to the standard if that is necessary to ensure sufficient Interest Periods end on Repayment Dates or dates for reduction of Facility B as discussed in 5.014.

See Box 5.2 for other circumstances in which unusual Interest Periods may be necessary.

Box 5.2

If the loan is advanced by instalments lenders will want to reduce the administrative burden and ensure that the first Interest Period for later instalments ends at the same time as the first Interest Period for the first instalment (so that, from that point onwards, there will be one Interest Period for the whole Loan).

5.016

These provisions mean that, in a Term Rate Loan, there may well be Interest Periods of a tenor which is not available in the market. In these circumstances, the interest rate fallback provisions discussed in 0.134 will come into effect and interest will be calculated on the basis of an Interpolated Rate.

180   Costs of Utilization

Clause 12.3 Non-business days

5.017

This clause deals with the position if an Interest Period ends on a non-business day—does the period get extended or shortened? As the conventions on this may be different for different currencies, the clause will apply the Business Day Convention for the relevant currency as specified in the Reference Rate Terms.

Clause 12.4 Consolidation and division of Facility A Loans

5.018

This clause allows loans to be consolidated if they are in the same currency, with the same **maturity** and to the same borrower. It also allows loans to be split into parts on the borrower's request.

Clause 13: Changes to the Calculation of Interest

Clauses 13.1 and 13.2 Interest calculation if no Primary Term Rate and Interest calculation if no RFR or Central Bank Rate

5.019

These Clauses deal with what happens if the benchmark interest rate (whether that is an IBOR or a risk free rate such as Sonia or Sofr) is temporarily unavailable. It is discussed from 0.133 onwards, together with other fallback provisions dealing with permanent unavailability of rates (see 0.139 onwards) and changes in the details of the calculations of the rates (see 0.141).

Clause 13: Changes to the Calculation of Interest **181**

Clause 13.3 Market disruption and 13.4 Cost of funds

5.020
These clauses deal with what happens if the lenders' actual funding costs for a currency are higher than the relevant Market Disruption Rate as defined in the Reference Rate Terms for that currency.

The Market Disruption Rate is intended to reflect a rate which is economically akin to Libor for the relevant Interest Period and so it may need to include a Rate Switch CAS, Baseline CAS, Fallback CAS or Term Reference Rate CAS, if there is one, or to include some other adjustment if there is not. It is discussed in more detail in 13.044 and 13.058.

5.021
The issue here is—who should bear the risk of the lenders' funding costs exceeding the relevant Market Disruption Rate?

5.022
The background to the clause relates to the Japanese banking crisis in the 1990s, shortly after the introduction of the screen rate of Libor. Japanese banks were involved in many syndicated loans under which interest was due at the screen rate of Libor plus a Margin. However, the Japanese banking crisis resulted in significant increases in the borrowing rates for Japanese banks, such that their funding costs for the loan exceeded their income from the loan and they were forced to sell their participations at a discount to lenders with lower funding costs. This clause was introduced to protect against this risk in the future. The current (optional) version of the clause reads.

5.023

13.3 Market disruption
If:

(a) *a Market Disruption Rate is specified in the Reference Rate Terms for a Loan and*
(b) ....*the Agent receives notifications from a Lender or Lenders* ....*[* making up a specified percentage of the Loan*] that its cost of funds relating to its participation in that Loan would be in excess of that Market Disruption Rate,*

182   **Costs of Utilization**

then Clause [] (Cost of funds) shall apply to that Loan for the relevant Interest Period.

5.024
There are many reasons to suggest that the risk of lenders' funding costs exceeding the relevant 'Market Disruption Rate' is a risk which should be borne by the lenders and not passed on to the borrower through the market disruption clause. Arguments include the fact that

- the lenders do not match fund, in a Compounded Rate Loan, so their funding costs will inevitably differ from the Market Disruption Rate from the outset.
- Calculating any credit adjustment spread for the purpose of defining the 'Market Disruption Rate' will never be able to be precise see 0.107.
- Any cost of funds clause is inherently hard to use—see Box 5.3.
- In a Compounded Rate Loan, it will not be known until the end of the Interest Period whether any lender's funding costs exceed the Market Disruption Rate as the Market Disruption Rate will not be known until the end of the Interest Period. It is unreasonable to retrospectively change the interest rate calculation.

5.025
Moreover, from the borrower's perspective, the clause as it has existed for some time in IBOR-based loans, (and as it has been transposed into loans with interest based on risk free rates) allows lenders to trigger the clause even if they could not fund themselves at the relevant Market Disruption Rate at the outset, and even if the reason they cannot fund at the Market Disruption Rate is personal to them.

Box 5.3

While this clause has been a feature of Libor loans since the 1990s, in practice, when circumstances arose which might have justified its use during the 2007 financial crisis, numerous problems arose with the operation of the clause in practice. These included:

- Lenders being reluctant to use the clause for fear of the effect on their reputation;
- Problems in lenders determining their 'cost of funds';
- Competition law problems in disclosing 'cost of funds';
- Lack of transparency for borrowers who simply have to rely on the lenders' statement of their 'cost of funds';

> - If the clause is triggered then a different interest rate is due to each lender and
> - If the clause is triggered it could result in any lenders who could fund below the screen rate receiving less interest as they would only be entitled to charge their cost of funds plus Margin.

5.026

In the new drafting the LMA has addressed some of these issues. In particular

- a clause has been included (13.4 (*CHANGES TO THE CALCULATION OF INTEREST: Cost of funds*) subclause (d)) stating that if a lender fails to provide information about its cost of funds, or its cost of funds is below the relevant benchmark, then its cost of funds will be deemed to be the 'Market Disruption Rate',
- a definition of 'cost of funds' has been introduced in Clause 1.2 (*DEFINITIONS AND INTERPRETATION: Construction*), to give lenders more guidance—see 1.060 and
- an optional provision has been included (in Clause 13.4 (*CHANGES TO THE CALCULATION OF INTEREST: Cost of funds*) subclause (a)) to allow for any substitute rate to apply to the whole loan rather than to each lender's share.

5.027

It is for the Reference Rate Terms for a particular currency to specify whether the market disruption clause will apply or not. See the discussion on Schedule 14 (*Reference Rate Terms*). If it is included, borrowers will want to restrict its operation so that

- a large percentage (by participation) of lenders have to be affected (so it is more likely to be a market problem than a problem which is personal to some lenders) and
- those affected are only taken into account to the extent that their funding costs have changed since the date on which they took up their participation in the loan.

184   Costs of Utilization

Clause 13.5 Break costs

5.028

This clause deals with Break Costs in relation to payments made in the middle of an Interest Period. The LMA provides for the issue to be addressed (and for the definition of 'Break Costs', which may need to be a simple fee if anything at all) in the Reference Rate Terms for the particular currency so that it can be dealt with on a currency by currency basis.

Clause 14: Fees

5.029

Common fees are a commitment fee, an arrangement fee, fees for letters of credit and an **agency fee**. The commitment fee is payable to all lenders in relation to the amount the lenders are committed to lend but which has not been drawn. It is calculated on a daily basis and payable at regular intervals during the drawdown period. The fee usually starts to accrue once the loan agreement is signed and the lenders are legally committed. Some lenders (particularly in club deals) will charge this fee from the date of the acceptance of the offer letter. Some borrowers request it should only start to accrue once the conditions precedent are satisfied.[8] This is an issue for the offer letter.

5.030

If the loan agreement deals with defaulting lenders then there is normally a provision here which provides that no commitment fee is due to a defaulting lender in relation to its undrawn commitment.

5.031

The agency fee and arrangement fee are stated to be as specified in a fees letter. The amount of these fees is confidential to the Agent/Arranger. Their existence needs to be disclosed to ensure that the obligation to pay them is secured by any security, that non-payment would constitute an Event of Default and to ensure that the Agent/Arranger is under no obligation to share those fees with participants on the basis that they are undisclosed profits.

---

[8] This argument might be made if there are conditions to the lender's commitment, as opposed to the drawing (and the amount of the loan is sufficiently high to justify the point). See commentary on conditions precedent to backstop facilities in 2.022.

Additional Payment Obligations

Clause 15: Tax Gross-Up and Indemnities
Section 1—Introduction

1. Withholding tax

6.001

Many countries (including England) require that, if a payment of interest (or other payments, such as rent under a lease, or payments of royalties) is paid by a resident of that country, the resident must, in certain circumstances, first deduct tax from that payment and account for that tax to the appropriate tax authorities. Any obligation to deduct tax in this way is referred to as 'withholding tax'. The tax is a tax on the recipient and the payer of interest is, in effect, acting as a tax collector on behalf of the tax authority. See Box 6.1.

> **Box 6.1**
>
> So, for example, if the **withholding tax** rate was 20% and the resident was due to pay 100, then the resident would only pay 80, paying the other 20 to the tax authorities. This 20 is tax on the recipient, in the country of the resident.

© The Author(s), under exclusive license to Springer Nature
Switzerland AG 2024
S. Wright, *The International Loan Documentation Handbook*, Global Financial Markets,
https://doi.org/10.1007/978-3-031-38489-9_7

186 Additional Payment Obligations

2. Double tax treaties

6.002

The result of the imposition of a withholding tax in relation to a cross-border payment may be that the recipient is taxed twice on the same income: once in the country of the source of the income and again in the country of the recipient. This may be avoided if the recipient is a resident of a country with which the payer's country has a **double taxation treaty**. Broadly speaking, (but see 6.009–10), such a recipient is referred to in the LMA Compounded/Term Rate Loan[1] as a 'Treaty Lender'. Such treaties may either remove or reduce the requirement to withhold tax on payments to residents of the country concerned (see Box 6.2). It may also be the case that, if tax is deducted at source, the country of the recipient will grant a tax credit in respect of tax paid in the country where tax has been deducted.

Box 6.2

Usually, in deciding which double tax treaties might be relevant, the countries concerned are those in which the income from which the interest is paid is earned—being the relevant place of business of the borrower (which is not necessarily the same as its place of incorporation) and the country of residence of the lender which is beneficially entitled to the interest—that is, entitled to use it as its own money and not simply as an agent for someone else.[2] Often there are administrative requirements which need to be complied with to get the benefit of the treaty.

6.003

However, it is worth noting that even if there is a double tax treaty which removes the need to withhold tax on payments to the relevant lender, the borrower often needs to deduct tax pending receipt of authorization from the local tax authorities, permitting payment to be made without deduction, and that can be a very slow process.

---

[1] References in this book to the LMA Compounded/Term Rate Loan are to the LMA Multicurrency Term and Revolving Facilities Agreement incorporating Term SOFR for use in Investment Grade transactions, available to LMA members via www.lma.eu.com

[2] Nevertheless, there may be tax consequences in the country of the Agent simply as collecting and/ or distributing agent.

3. Gross-up

6.004

Lenders generally expect to receive their full interest without deduction. In a cross-border case, absent a double tax treaty, the lender's obligation to pay tax in the borrower's jurisdiction is not part of the lender's ordinary corporation tax bill but is an additional cost incurred by the lender as a result of the location of the residence of the borrower. The LMA Compounded/Term Rate Loan (at Clause 15.2, *(TAX GROSS UP AND INDEMNITIES: Tax gross up)* subclause (c)) therefore states that if any withholding tax has to be paid in relation to payments under the loan, (other than in relation to FATCA, as discussed from 6.038 onwards) then, in certain circumstances,[3] the amount of the payment will be increased to whatever amount as, after deduction of the withholding tax, will leave the lender with the amount of interest originally due. This is referred to as 'grossing-up'. See Box 6.3.

> **Box 6.3**
>
> So, taking the example from Box 6.1, if the borrower is obliged to gross up, they must ensure that, after taking tax off the payment, the net sum received by the recipient will be 100. Assuming the withholding tax rate is 20%, that will require a total payment of 125, with 25 going to the tax authorities and 100 to the recipient.

6.005

Note that the arguments in relation to the gross-up obligation will be different if the borrower and lender are located in the same jurisdiction and the local law imposes a withholding tax on the payments. In this case the borrower is in effect simply acting as a tax collector, ensuring that the lender pays the tax which the lender is in any event due to pay in the local country.[4] The difference from a cross-border payment is that, in the case of a cross-border payment, the tax on the lender in the country of the borrower is an additional tax on the lender incurred solely because of the location of the borrower.

---

[3] Essentially, the borrower does not have to gross up if the lender was not entitled to receive payment without deduction in the first place or if the reason for the deduction was an issue relating to the lender's circumstances, acts or omissions.

[4] It is just the same as the withholding tax which employers are usually required to apply on payments to their employees—the employer is simply helping to ensure that the employee pays their tax. The employee would in most cases be unlikely to succeed in a request that their employer 'gross up' their salary.

188   Additional Payment Obligations

6.006

It is also worth bearing in mind that there is a personal obligation on the borrower to make the tax deduction and pay it to the relevant tax authorities. This means that if the borrower is unaware of the fact that they should have deducted tax (e.g. because the borrower incorrectly believes that the recipient is entitled to receive the funds without deduction), then the borrower still has to make payment of the tax. Unless the document provides for the borrower to have a claim against the lender in those circumstances (which it usually doesn't), then that cost will need to be borne by the borrower. See Box 6.4. This is discussed further in 6.031–2.

> **Box 6.4**
>
> So, taking the example from Box 6.1, if the resident failed to make any deduction and paid the full 100 of interest to the recipient, then the resident would have a personal obligation to pay tax (still tax on the recipient) of 25.

4. Categories of lenders

6.007

The LMA uses the expression 'Qualifying Lenders' to describe the types of lenders who could normally be paid free of deduction for UK tax in accordance with UK tax law at the time of the loan agreement.

Comment Of course if any of the borrowers are not UK tax resident, this clause will need to be adjusted to reflect the tax law in the borrower's jurisdiction.

6.008

It goes on to say that the borrower does not have to gross up to lenders which are not Qualifying Lenders at the date the payment was made unless they stopped being Qualifying Lenders as a result of a change in law since the date on which they became a lender. So, at a basic level, if the borrower is UK tax resident and all lenders are Qualifying Lenders, it might appear that the borrower need only be concerned about having to gross up interest if there is a change in law. As always however, the devil is in the detail. The question arises, in what circumstances might tax deductions be required to be made from payments to lenders despite their being Qualifying Lenders?

The principal circumstances in which this may occur are:

Clause 15: Tax Gross-Up and Indemnities Section 1—Introduction

6.009

* Some lenders (usually Treaty Lenders) are only entitled to receive payment without deduction once approval has been obtained from the relevant tax authorities. This may take some time and until the relevant procedures have been completed, the borrower must gross up. See 6.026 and 6.027.

6.010

* If the definition of Treaty Lenders includes lenders which, in practice, do not qualify to receive payment without deduction. The most likely circumstances in which this may occur arises from the definition of Treaty Lenders. This is discussed in 6.016.

6.011

* For some categories of lenders, borrowers can be prohibited by the revenue from paying gross or can only pay gross if they have a reasonable belief that the recipient qualifies to receive payment gross. The LMA includes specific provisions dealing with these cases as discussed from 6.028 onwards.

5. Double Tax Treaty Passport Scheme ('DTTP Scheme')

6.012

Before turning to the clause itself it is worth mentioning the DTTP scheme in the UK. This was introduced to try to alleviate some of the problems which arise in relation to Treaty Lenders, where borrowers have to withhold tax on payments until they receive authorization from the tax authorities allowing them to make payment without deduction.

6.013

The DTTP Scheme is an arrangement in the UK under which lenders may apply for a passport, which is valid for five years, (and applies to all loans they enter into during those five years) confirming their eligibility for treaty relief. The use of this passport significantly speeds up the process of obtaining clearance to pay without deduction. If a lender holds a passport and wants to use the passport for this loan then if it gives the borrower its scheme reference

190 **Additional Payment Obligations**

number and the borrower submits the relevant form to the UK authorities within 30 working days of the lender joining the loan then clearance to pay without deduction can be obtained more speedily.

The LMA Compounded/Term Rate Loan requires the original lenders to confirm the relevant DTTP information in the original agreement (in the schedule of lenders), and transferees to give the DTTP information in the form of a transfer certificate under which they purchase the loans, if they wish to use the scheme.

6. Documentation

6.014

In the context of withholding tax, the provisions of the LMA Compounded/ Term Rate Loan are highly jurisdiction specific. The standard provisions include wording (e.g. in the definition of 'Qualifying Lender'), which reflects the requirements of the UK tax authorities relating to withholding tax. They assume that, as at signing, all lenders are eligible to receive interest without tax deduction (albeit, in some cases, only after receipt of a direction from the tax authorities), or, if not, that the borrower will not be obliged to gross up.

6.015

Significant changes will be needed dependent on the tax residence of the borrowers and the lenders, the provisions of any relevant double tax treaty and the risk allocation between the parties. It is worth noting that many loan agreements designed for use outside the UK have much simpler tax provisions than those we discuss here. Superficially, that may seem attractive to borrowers, but they will usually find that the simplicity in the wording results in significant tax risks being taken by the borrower which ought more appropriately to be borne by the lenders.

Clause 15: Tax Gross-Up and Indemnities—Section 2—The Clause

Clause 15.1 Definitions

6.016

This clause sets out some definitions used in the tax gross-up clause. Particular attention needs to be given to the definitions of Qualifying Lenders and Treaty Lenders. The intention is that these definitions should only include

Clause 15: Tax Gross-Up and Indemnities—Section 2—The Clause 191

categories of lenders who can be paid without deduction under the laws of the country of the borrower's tax residence. The criteria for determining whether a lender in another country can be paid without deduction or not will be set out in the relevant double tax treaty. Double tax treaties do not come in one standard form, so, depending on the location of the lenders, there may be different requirements which need to be fulfilled in order for payment to be made without deduction. The definition of Treaty Lender therefore needs to reflect those criteria in all the double tax treaties applicable to all the lenders. However, given that there is no geographical limit on lender participation in the loan, general wording will be needed to ensure that the Treaty Lender definition only includes lenders who are entitled to receive payment gross under whatever double tax treaty happens to apply. Without such general wording, there is a risk that the borrower will be required to gross up payments to lenders who do not satisfy the requirements of any applicable double tax treaty. See Box 6.5 for sample wording.

Box 6.5

The LMA Compounded/Term Rate Loan leaves a placeholder for the parties to add additional criteria to reflect the requirements of applicable tax treaties. The Association of Corporate Treasurers provides two sets of suggested wording[5] to include in the definition of Treaty Lenders to address this. The relevant part of the simpler version is set out here

'Treaty Lender' means a lender which...

(i) ...
(ii) ... *and*
(iii) *meets all other conditions in the Treaty for full exemption from UK taxation on interest which relate to the Lender (including its tax or other status, the manner in which or the period for which it holds any rights under this Agreement, the reasons or purposes for its acquisition of such rights and the nature of any arrangements by which it disposes of or otherwise turns to account such rights).*

---

[5] In its 'ACT Borrower's Guide to LMA Loan Documentation for Investment Grade Borrowers', available from the website of the Association of Corporate Treasurers at www.treasurers.org.

192   **Additional Payment Obligations**

Clause 15.2 Tax gross-up

6.017

This clause is the clause dealing with tax gross-up.

Subclauses (a) and (b) require the borrower to advise the Agent if it becomes obliged to make tax deductions from payments and to make payments free of such deductions unless it is obliged to make deductions by law. Subclause (b) also requires a lender to notify the Agent if it becomes aware that the borrower must withhold tax on a payment to it.

6.018

Subclause (c) is the gross-up clause. It reads:

> *If a Tax Deduction is required by law to be made by an Obligor, the amount of the payment due from that Obligor shall be increased to an amount which (after making any Tax Deduction) leaves an amount equal to the payment which would have been due if no Tax Deduction had been required.*
>
> *'Tax Deduction' means a deduction or withholding for or on account of Tax from a payment under a Finance Document, other than a FATCA Deduction.*

6.019

In some countries, there are doubts as to the enforceability of this clause on the basis that an agreement by one person to pay another person's tax is unenforceable and this is a mandatory principle of public policy which cannot be avoided by a choice of law.[6] This is an issue for due diligence (see Box 6.6).

Box 6.6

If a gross-up clause is unenforceable then, if there is an actual withholding tax issue on the commencement of the transaction, the Margin will need to be higher to enable the transaction to proceed.

6.020

The grossing-up clause is generally included in the loan agreement even where there is no withholding tax obligation on payments between the relevant parties—so as to ensure that, if withholding tax is subsequently imposed,

---

[6] Enforcement of judgements which included payments of another tax may also therefore be affected.

Clause 15: Tax Gross-Up and Indemnities—Section 2—The Clause **193**

the lenders will be protected. The borrower's escape route in this event is the right to prepay the affected lender (see Clause 10.7 (*PREPAYMENT AND CANCELLATION*: *Right of replacement or repayment and cancellation in relation to a single Lender or Issuing Bank*) in 4.020).

Clause 15.2 *(Tax gross up),* subclause (d) Limitations on the gross-up obligation.

6.021

For the borrower, the obligation to gross up clearly makes a significant difference to the cost of the loan. The borrower will therefore wish to limit its gross-up obligations. As far as practical they will wish to ensure that they do not borrow money from lenders in respect of whom there would be an obligation to withhold. This will be achieved by agreement with the Arranger on the types of lenders to be invited into the syndicate in the first place, and by Clause 26.3 (*CHANGES TO THE LENDERS: Other conditions of assignment or transfer*) at subclause (d), discussed in 9.047, which limits the borrower's gross-up obligations in the event of a change in Facility Office or a change in lender.

6.022

The LMA Compounded/Term Rate Loan contains fairly comprehensive restrictions on the obligations of the borrower to gross up, if the borrower is a UK borrower. The key limitations on the gross-up obligation are contained in subclause (d) of the grossing-up clause, which reads

> *(d) A payment shall not be increased under paragraph (c) above for a Tax Deduction in respect of tax imposed by the UK from a payment of interest on a Loan, if on the date on which the payment falls due:*

6.023

Comment The first thing to notice about this limitation is that it only applies to the UK withholding tax (the wording reads—'*A payment shall not be increased ... for a Tax Deduction in respect of tax **imposed by the United Kingdom**'* ...). If any likely Obligor is a resident outside the UK and may be required to pay withholding tax in a different jurisdiction, the parties will need to consider whether there should be similar restrictions on the gross-up obligations of that Obligor in addition to the provisions of subclause (d) of the grossing-up clause. In other words, where Obligors may be from

194 **Additional Payment Obligations**

different tax jurisdictions, there may need to be a number of clauses dealing with withholdings imposed by different countries. In the case of the LMA Compounded/Term Rate Loan, the group needs to consider not only the jurisdictions of the original Obligors, but also of any likely future Obligors.

6.024
The clause continues, by saying there is no gross-up obligation if:

(i) *the payment could have been made to the relevant Lender without a Tax Deduction if the Lender had been a Qualifying Lender but on that date that Lender is not or has ceased to be a Qualifying Lender other than as a result of any change after the date it became a Lender under this Agreement in (or in the interpretation, administration, or application of) any law or Treaty, or any published practice or concession of any relevant taxing authority.*

6.025
Under this first exception to the gross-up obligation, it is stated that there is no gross-up obligation if

* the lender is not a 'Qualifying Lender' (as discussed in 6.007) in the first place or
* the lender ceased to be a Qualifying Lender (and so ceased to be eligible to receive payments without deduction) for reasons other than as a result of a change of law or similar. In other words, if a change of facts (e.g. tax residence of the lender) results in a change of its status for the purpose of withholding tax the borrower will not be required to gross up as a result.

6.026
It is also worth noticing that this exception for payments to Qualifying Lenders quoted in (d)(i) above only applies 'if *the payment could have been made to the relevant Lender without a Tax Deduction if the Lender had been a Qualifying Lender'*. In the UK, borrowers are obliged to deduct tax on interest payments to Treaty Lenders until they receive a direction from the UK tax authorities allowing them to make payment without deduction. So, until the borrower receives that direction, they are required to deduct tax on interest payments to those lenders, despite the fact that they are Qualifying Lenders, and the exception does not apply.

6.027
Unless the DTTP Scheme is used the procedure for obtaining a direction to pay without deduction can be slow so that gross-up may well be triggered at

least on the first interest payment, or, if the loan is transferred, on the first interest payment following transfer. See Box 6.7 for some ways in which the borrower may be protected.

Box 6.7

The borrower's position may be alleviated by

- trying to ensure that the first payment of interest falls due as late as possible so as to give time to complete the process for the initial lenders;
- use of the DTTP Scheme;
- relying on the clause dealing with tax credits discussed in 6.035—although, as mentioned there, that clause is not very borrower friendly and
- historically, in relation to transferees, relying on the provision in Clause 26.3 *(CHANGES TO THE LENDERS: Conditions of assignment or transfer)* at subclause (d), discussed in 9.047, to the effect that a transferee could not claim a payment under the gross-up clause unless the transferor could have done so. However, since the introduction of the DTTP Scheme an exception has been made to that clause, to the effect that the borrower cannot claim the benefit of the protection if their delay resulted in the expedited procedure being unavailable. See further the discussion in 9.049.

6.028

The clause then continues with the next exception to the gross-up obligation, stating that there is no gross-up obligation if:

(ii) *the relevant Lender is* [a non-bank lender] *and*

(A) *an officer of HM Revenue and Customs has given (and not revoked) a direction (a 'Direction') under Section 931 of the ITA which relates to the payment and that Lender has received from the Obligor making the payment or from the Company a certified copy of that Direction and*

(B) *the payment could have been made to the lender without any Tax Deduction if that Direction had not been made.*

6.029

So under this second exception to the gross-up obligation, there is no obligation to gross up if the tax authorities have required payment to be made subject to deduction of tax where the lender is resident or taxable in the UK but not a bank. (The tax authorities may do this if they believe that the payment in question is not actually eligible to be paid without deduction).

196 Additional Payment Obligations

6.030

There are then two further exceptions to the gross-up obligation (in subclauses (d)(iii) and (iv)) which state that there is no obligation to gross up if payment could have been made without deduction to the lender if it had delivered a Tax Confirmation (where the LMA requires one) or complied with certain necessary administrative requirements—See Box 6.8.

> **Box 6.8**
>
> - In the case of non-bank lenders—borrowers can only make payment gross to non-bank lenders if they 'reasonably believe' that the payment is exempt. So this clause says that the borrower does not have to gross up to non-bank lenders unless they have delivered a 'Tax Confirmation' to the borrower, so as to enable the borrowers to reach that reasonable belief.
> - Obtaining the approval from the tax authorities enabling the borrower to pay Treaty Lenders without deduction (whether through the DTTP Scheme or otherwise) requires the cooperation of the lender. So this clause says that the borrower does not have to gross up to a Treaty Lender which has not complied with its (limited) obligations to cooperate.[7]

Confirmation of tax status

6.031

Subclauses (k) and (l) of the grossing-up clause require UK lenders which are not banks and which are party to the loan agreement at the start, to confirm their tax status. A similar provision is included in the transfer certificates signed by incoming lenders, but in this case there is an express provision preventing the borrower from relying on the confirmation.

6.032

Comment Borrowers may wish to extend this provision (and the definition of 'Tax Confirmation') to all original lenders and to require a similar confirmation (and the ability to rely on that confirmation) from buyers in the secondary market, as well as undertakings to advise the borrower if the position changes. This is because the borrower may not be able to identify whether any particular lender is entitled to receive payment without deduction or not because this depends on issues which are only within the

---

[7] For more detail see ACT Borrowers Guide to the LMA's Investment Grade Agreements, 6th ed 2022.

Clause 15: Tax Gross-Up and Indemnities—Section 2—The Clause 197

knowledge of the lender (such as whether the lender is 'beneficially entitled' to the interest and whether it is liable to UK tax on the interest). If the borrower pays the lender without a deduction when it should have made a deduction, the borrower will have a personal liability to account for the tax which should have been deducted. Under the LMA Compounded/Term Rate Loan, the borrower will have no recourse to the lenders except for those who have been required to give a confirmation under this clause or in the transfer certificates.

Clause 15.3 Tax indemnity

Subclause (a) tax indemnity

6.033
The tax indemnity reads as follows.

(a) *The Company shall (within three Business Days of demand by the Agent) pay to a Protected Party an amount equal to the loss, liability or cost which that Protected Party determines will be or has been (directly or indirectly) suffered for or on account of Tax by that Protected Party in respect of a Finance Document.*

Comment Some borrowers may request the removal of the words 'which that Protected Party determines' to make this indemnity less one sided.

Subclause (b) exceptions

6.034
This subclause sets out some exceptions to the tax indemnity which effectively ensure that the borrower does not compensate the lenders for ordinary income tax on their profits in their countries of normal tax residence or with respect to FATCA claims (as discussed in 6.038).

198   **Additional Payment Obligations**

Clause 15.4 Tax credit

6.035
This clause provides that, if a lender receives a tax credit as a result of the tax withheld, the benefit of this tax credit will be passed back to the borrower. This is commonly referred to as the '**clawback clause**'. This clause should be read in conjunction with Clause 29 (*Conduct of Business by the Finance Parties*), which provides that the lenders can arrange their tax affairs as they see fit; they are not obliged to investigate or claim any relevant tax reliefs and they are not obliged to disclose their financial affairs or tax computations to the borrower.

6.036
The existence of a tax credit and a clawback clause is of limited value to the borrower because:

* the timing of any payment under the tax credit clause could well be some years after the gross-up payment was made. It will take some time for the financial year to end and then for the tax position for that financial year to be finally settled;
* a tax credit is not usually specifically attributed to any particular loan;
* the tax credit clause only applies if the lender *decides that* there has been an applicable tax benefit;
* the lender must have *used* and *retained* the benefit (i.e. it depends on the lender being profitable) and
* the clause provides that the borrower will be given whatever amount *the lender decides* will result in the lender being in the same after tax position as if there had been no gross-up.

6.037
Despite these limitations, there is little improvement that a borrower can realistically hope to achieve through negotiation in most cases. Lenders cannot permit borrowers to get involved in the lenders' tax affairs. Nevertheless, where the parties enter into the loan knowing that a gross-up will apply and perhaps that the effects of that will be lessened by an applicable double tax treaty, these standard provisions will not necessarily be applicable and the document will need to be adjusted to reflect each party's responsibilities in relation to claiming, and making use of, whatever relief is available.

Clause 15.8 FATCA Information and 15.9 FATCA Deduction

FATCA

6.038

Potential withholding tax issues also arise as a result of the US legislation commonly referred to as 'FATCA'.[8] This stands for the Foreign Account Tax Compliance Act. This legislation enacted in 2010 is designed to assist US tax authorities in ensuring that its citizens disclose (and pay tax on) all their worldwide income. The purpose of the legislation is to gather information about the foreign income of US citizens. It achieves this purpose by requiring foreign financial institutions (commonly referred to as 'FFIs') which receive US source income to provide information on their US customers to the US tax authorities or face a 30% withholding on their US source income. Interest under a loan agreement would be US source income if it comes from a US borrower or a US trade or business or from a guarantee of the payment of such income.

6.039

FATCA initially caused widespread concern, partly because of concerns about how to reconcile FATCA's reporting requirements with local bank confidentiality laws, partly because of uncertainty as to which payments would be affected, and partly as the market grappled with the allocation of FATCA risk between lenders and borrowers.

Intergovernmental Agreements

6.040

The growth of intergovernmental agreements (or **'IGA's'**) did much to allay these concerns. An intergovernmental agreement is an agreement entered into between the US and another country, making compliance with FATCA much easier for FFIs in that country and enabling them to receive US source income in full, without the deduction, and without breaching local bank confidentiality laws. The UK version of this agreement requires financial institutions in the UK (and UK branches of financial institutions elsewhere) to provide

---

[8] More information on the regulations is available from the US tax authorities website at www.irs.gov.

200 Additional Payment Obligations

the requisite information to the UK tax authorities (which will then pass it on to the US), and, provided they do so, they will be treated as being 'FATCA compliant'. The UK intergovernmental agreement is an example of a 'Model 1 IGA'. Some countries have a different arrangement (a 'Model 2 IGA') under which FFIs are required to register with the US tax authorities and report directly to them and only to open accounts for US entities which consent to disclosure of information to the US tax authorities.

Which payments are affected?

6.041

The issue of uncertainty as to which payments would be affected arose because of the concept of 'foreign passthru payments' which FATCA introduced. These are foreign (i.e. non-US) payments to the extent they are 'attributable' to US source payments—a difficult concept to pin down. Initially, the rules on passthru payments were stated not to come into effect until 2017 at the earliest and as at the time of writing, they have still not been implemented. Moreover the Model 1 IGA provides that the rules on 'foreign passthru payments' will not apply to those institutions which are deemed to be FATCA compliant as a result of the IGA.

What FATCA provisions are needed?

Turning then to the loan agreement—the question is—how should FATCA withholding be dealt with?

6.042

Where the lenders are in countries with an IGA, market practice is that the borrower does not bear FATCA risk as FATCA compliance is not within the control of the borrower. The FATCA provisions included in the LMA recommended forms provide that:

- All parties can make any FATCA withholding which is required and no party will be obliged to gross up for that (nor will any claim be made under any of the general indemnities);
- All parties will disclose their FATCA status to all other parties to facilitate compliance and
- The Agent may be replaced if there is a risk that payments to it may be subject to a FATCA withholding.

6.043

Where lenders are in countries with no IGA and cannot lend through branches in countries which have an IGA, they may seek to pass some FATCA risk to the borrowers in which case borrowers may need to take US tax advice to enable them to evaluate the degree of FATCA risk involved in the transaction.

Clause 16: Increased Costs—Section 1—Introduction

6.044

Historically, Libor-based lending was provided on a 'cost plus' basis. That is, the lenders charged the borrowers Libor, (which was originally the interest rate which the lenders paid to borrow money in the wholesale market), plus a fixed Margin. The Margin was the lenders' profit, and was sacrosanct, in that, with few exceptions, if the lenders suffered additional costs or reduced profits from the loan, those extra costs or losses were passed on to the borrower through the so-called 'yield protection clauses' such as the market disruption clause and the provisions on Break Costs discussed in Box 0.13. This historical background continues to inform market expectations, and therefore loan pricing, today. The increased costs clause is one of these yield protection clauses. It provides that any change in regulation which increases the lenders' costs or reduces their profits, must be compensated for by the borrower. The regulations which are most likely to result in a claim under this clause are the Basel regulations, so we start with a very brief description of these regulations.

1. Who issues the Basel regulations?

6.045

Actually, it is worth noticing that the Basel regulations are not regulations at all (and from here on we will refer to them by their accurate name—the 'Basel Accords'). They are recommendations issued by the Basel Committee on Banking Supervision. The Basel Committee is a forum for cooperation between central banks on banking supervisory matters. It was initially established by the G10 (a group of major economies) in 1974 following major disturbances in international financial markets and at the time of writing has 45 members from 28 jurisdictions. The Basel Accords are highly influential

202   **Additional Payment Obligations**

and have formed the basis of banking regulations on capital requirements in its member states and beyond.

2. What are the Basel Accords there for?

6.046
The work of the Basel Committee focuses on promoting international financial stability by encouraging standard regulation of internationally active banks worldwide. In particular, their recommendations have focused on capital adequacy and liquidity.

Capital adequacy

6.047
One reason why banking is a risky business is that banks are highly geared. That is, most of the money they lend is borrowed from someone else. This means that a comparatively small loss can wipe out the banks' capital and result in the bank being unable to repay those from whom they have borrowed money—that is, the deposit holders. Put simply, banks are taking risks with other people's money. This is the reason for the recommendations relating to capital adequacy.

6.048
These recommendations require banks to have a minimum amount of capital, with reference to the risks involved in their particular business. The riskier the business, the more of their own money (as opposed to money borrowed from depositors) must be used. In other words, more shareholders' funds (or capital) are required for more risky types of business.

Liquidity

6.049
The second key risk which a bank runs is liquidity risk. The role of a bank is to transform short-term debt (customer deposits) into long-term debt (loans

to customers)—which is an inherently risky activity.[9] Banks borrow money from deposit holders but allow them to withdraw funds with little or no notice—in other words, the banks borrow on a short-term basis from their deposit holders, supplementing this by short-term borrowing in the interbank markets and longer-term borrowing in the capital markets. The bank then lends that money to their customers on a long-term basis. This of course gives rise to the risk that customers will require repayment at a time when there are insufficient new deposits from other customers, insufficient maturing loans and insufficient ability of the banks to borrow the necessary funds elsewhere—this is liquidity risk.

6.050
This liquidity risk is something peculiar to financial institutions—outside the financial sector, firms invariably match the **tenor** of their financing to the tenor of the asset being financed. In other words, if they wanted to fund long-term assets, they would borrow money on a long-term basis to do that, rather than doing what banks do—and borrow on a short-term basis thus incurring the liquidity risk.

6.051
The Basel Accords are designed to try to reduce these two risks—the capital adequacy risk and the liquidity risk. It is worth noting at this stage that one effect of these recommendations is to encourage banks to have a variety of sources of funds and to reduce the extent to which they raise funds in the interbank markets so as to reduce their liquidity risk. This is one of the reasons for the reduced liquidity in the interbank markets discussed in 0.092 and resulting eventually in the cessation of Libor.

3. The Basel Accords

BASEL I

6.052
The first focus of the Basel Committee was on levels of capital. Capital ratios of international banks had been eroding, leading to increased risks of bank insolvency in the event of borrower defaults. The Committee was concerned

---

[9] It is similar in nature to financing a long-term asset, such as a house, by borrowing on a credit card—when the credit card bill arrives, the bill can only be paid by borrowing again.

204   **Additional Payment Obligations**

to avoid a race to the bottom—with banks in lightly regulated countries having the competitive advantage of being able to operate with less capital than banks in other countries.

Basel I therefore recommended that internationally active banks should be required to have a standard (8%) minimum amount of capital, with reference to the risks involved in their particular business. The riskier the business, the more of their own money (as opposed to money borrowed from depositors) was required to be used. The value of the bank's assets, such as outstanding loans yet to be repaid, adjusted to reflect the degree of risk involved in those assets, is referred to as the bank's 'risk-weighted assets'.

BASEL II

6.053

Basel II is the capital adequacy regime agreed in 2004. One main purpose of Basel II was to make the regulatory requirements for capital reflect market perception of risk more accurately than was the case under Basel I. The previous system was recognized as a blunt instrument that required more capital than generally thought necessary for some risks and less than necessary for others. The Basel II system relies on three elements (known as the three 'pillars').

Pillar 1 is similar to Basel I rules in that it requires banks' capital to be at least 8% of risk-weighted assets but operating risk (the risk of mistakes and wrongdoing) was added to the risks to be taken into account, in addition to credit risk and market risk included under Basel I. In measuring credit risk, banks were also given an option to use their own internal methods of risk assessment as the basis of the weighting.

Pillar 2 of the Basel II framework allowed national regulators the discretion to adjust the requirements of Pillar 1 to reflect the different track records of different banks in recovering losses.

Pillar 3 required greater disclosure of the risks to banks' profitability so as to expose them to the discipline of market reaction.

Clause 16: Increased Costs—Section 1—Introduction **205**

BASEL III[10]

6.054

Shortly after Basel II became effective the financial crisis of 2007–2008 hit. The sudden demise of Northern Rock in England highlighted the dangers of the model they used, of funding themselves mostly in the London interbank markets. It was clear that the existing bank regulatory framework was not sufficiently robust and in particular, that liquidity risks were not sufficiently regulated.

Basel III ensued. It contains a number of provisions including requiring affected banks to maintain countercyclical buffers (putting funds aside in good times which can be used to absorb losses in difficult times) and capital conservation buffers (which will be imposed if a bank is in difficulty, so as to prevent payment of dividends) and imposing more stringent rules on what counts as capital for the purpose of the existing capital adequacy rules. It also introduced a new leverage ratio which compares the bank's assets (without any risk weighting) to its Tier 1 capital (essentially, the core capital). Basel III also introduced two new ratios focusing on liquidity

- a minimum liquidity ratio, the **Liquidity Coverage Ratio**, intended to ensure banks have enough cash to cover funding needs over a 30-day period of stress and
- a longer-term ratio, the **Net Stable Funding Ratio**, intended to address maturity mismatches over the entire balance sheet. This requires banks to ensure they have a sufficiently stable mix of funding sources to fund the types of assets they have invested in, with equity being very stable and funds borrowed in interbank markets being far less stable. The idea is that meeting the ratio is more expensive with less stable funding sources than with stable sources such as equity.

---

[10] It should be noted that 'Basel III' is not a single set of rules but comprises a number of documents issued by the Basel Committee on Banking Supervision, which, in the EU, was implemented into law via the Fourth Capital Requirements Directive and the Capital Requirements Regulation ('CRD IV') in July 2013. Some parts of Basel III take effect as amendments to Basel II.

206   Additional Payment Obligations

Post-Crisis Reforms (sometimes informally referred to as 'Basel IV' or 'Basel 3.1')

6.055

Substantial refinements to the Basel III requirements were published by the Basel Committee in 2017 in 'Basel III: Finalising post-crisis reforms'. The main aim of this change was to enhance the credibility of the calculation of risk-weighted assets given concerns that the internal modelled approach permitted by Basel II gave highly variable results. A key feature of these post-crisis reforms is an output floor (which is being introduced in stages and will not be fully effective in the EU or UK until 2025) limiting the internally modelled calculation of risk-weighted assets to be no less than 72.5% of the amount of risk-weighted assets using the standardized approach to calculating risk.

6.056

As the recommendations of Basel III were refined over time, changes were made in the implementation of those recommendations in Europe by CRR II Regulation (2019/876) and the CRD V Directive (2019/878/EU) (and in the UK by a package of measures). The process is ongoing, with CRR III and CRD VI making further refinements and having been published in 2021 and expected to come into force in 2025.

Clause 16: Increased Costs—Section 2—The Clause

Clause 16.1 Increased Costs

6.057

The increased costs clause reads as follows

(a) *Subject to Clause [ ] (Exceptions) the Company shall, within three Business Days of a demand by the Agent, pay for the account of a Finance Party the amount of any Increased Costs incurred by that Finance Party or any of its Affiliates as a result of (i) the introduction of or any change in (or in the interpretation, administration or application of) any law or regulation or (ii) compliance with any law or regulation made after the date of this Agreement.*

Clause 16: Increased Costs—Section 2—The Clause **207**

6.058

Generally lenders are expected to fix their Margin at a rate that covers them for the cost of complying with existing capital adequacy and liquidity requirements. The increased cost clause deals with the possibility of a regulatory change, after the date of signing, in these capital adequacy, liquidity and regulatory costs and of any other costs, and passes these on to the borrower (which also has the right to prepay affected lenders under Clause 10.7 *(PREPAYMENT AND CANCELLATION: Right of replacement, repayment and cancellation in relation to a single Lender or Issuing Bank))*.

Under this clause the borrower agrees to compensate the lenders for any additional costs or lost profits (for any lender or any member of a lender's group of companies) attributable to the loan, resulting from changes in the regulatory[11] environment. The clause applies to increased costs arising as a result of regulations made after the loan agreement is signed and also as a result of existing regulations where a change occurs (such as a change in interpretation or a compliance date) after the loan agreement is signed.

6.059

Given that Basel II and Basel III (as initially published) have been implemented in Europe (the CRD IV package[12] which transposes—via a Regulation and a Directive—the initial Basel III standards on bank capital into the EU legal framework entered into force in July 2013), you might expect that they could be ignored for the purpose of this clause as the clause only deals with new regulations or changes in existing ones. However there are a number of issues to be cautious about.

6.060

* Firstly, names. Some parts of Basel III are actually changes to the detail of Basel II and although the original version of Basel III has been implemented, it has also been revised and those revisions (sometimes informally referred to as **Basel 3.1** or as **Basel IV**) will not be fully implemented in Europe until 2025 at the earliest. So, if making drafting changes to the clause it is unwise to include or exclude Basel II or Basel III without being very precise as to exactly which Basel Accords or regulations resulting from them are being included or excluded. For example, if you excluded 'Basel

---

[11] The word 'regulation' in this context needs to be read in the light of Clause 1.2 *(DEFINITIONS AND INTERPRETATION: Construction)* at subclause (a)(x) discussed in 1.061.

[12] The fourth Capital Requirements Directive (Directive 2013/36/EU) and the Capital Requirements Regulation (Regulation 575/2013).

208   **Additional Payment Obligations**

II costs' this might inadvertently exclude some Basel III costs as well and if you excluded 'Basel III costs' you would need to be clear whether you intended to exclude costs relating to Basel III as initially envisaged or also as subsequently amended via CRD V and/or CRD VI in Europe and/or to exclude the impact of the Post-Crisis Reforms.

6.061

• The clause covers changes in the 'application' of regulations. This could have a very broad meaning including changes in facts or changes in lenders' internal risk assessment procedures resulting in a different application of the regulations. This is why some borrowers ask for Basel II to be excluded from the clause—so that if lenders change their methodology of risk assessment for the purpose of Basel II, they cannot then make a claim under this clause as a result.

6.062

• The clause needs to reflect the borrower's reasonable expectations about what is included in the Margin and what is not. Three issues are relevant here

  – Regulations which are known about but not yet (fully) implemented (as with some of the Post-Crisis Reforms and CRR III and CRD VI).
  – Unknown future refinements to the regulations.
  – Lenders based in jurisdictions where the speed of implementation, or the details, are different to the borrower's expectations.

6.063

Commonly the expectation is that the impact of all known regulations and Basel Accords (whether implemented or not in the lender's jurisdiction) should have been taken into account. Reflecting this it is not uncommon to add a general provision to the clause to specify that lenders can only claim for costs which are not reasonably foreseeable at the time the agreement is signed. Given the difficulties discussed in 6.060 with the precise meaning of expressions 'Basel II' and 'Basel III' it is not uncommon to make specific reference to the underlying publications or regulations (CRDIV, CRDV, CRDVI, etc.) so as to clarify precisely what has and has not been taken into account in agreeing the Margin.

6.064

On a practical note, it is worth bearing in mind that the clause may prove difficult for lenders to implement in relation to any given regulation for two reasons.

- the lenders will only be able to claim compensation from the borrower if the additional cost results from the introduction of the relevant regulation or any part of it, or from a change in its operation or application. Proving this causation may be difficult—what changes in the bank's funding structure or capital base have been made as a result of the new regulations, and what changes happened as a result of prudent banking practice?
- the clause only allows lenders to pass on those additional costs or lost profits which are attributable to this loan—but in many cases it would be hard to allocate costs to particular loans.

Clause 16.2 Increased Cost claims

6.065

This clause provides for the affected lender to notify the Agent, which will then notify the borrower, before making a claim.

Clause 16.3 Exceptions

6.066

The Increased Cost clause does not deal solely with capital adequacy rules: it compensates the lenders for any reduction in their anticipated profits resulting from a change in regulation. This clause cuts back the scope of the clause to ensure that it does not compensate the lenders for ordinary tax on their profits (in subclause (a)(iii)), for FATCA deductions, or for issues such as withholding tax which is covered elsewhere in the agreement or for losses or costs incurred by a lender as a result of their 'wilful breach' of any law or regulation.

Comment Many borrowers might want to amend this so that the breach does not need to be 'wilful' for it to be excluded from the indemnity.

210   Additional Payment Obligations

Clause 17: Other Indemnities

Clause 17.1 Currency indemnity

6.067
This clause is the **judgement currency indemnity**. This deals with the situation which may arise if, in order to make a claim against the borrower or any of its assets in a particular country, the claim needs to be denominated in the local currency. In this event, the final judgement will be for an amount which, when converted back to the currency of the debt, will give a profit or a loss. This clause provides for the borrower to indemnify the lenders for any loss in this situation. This provision may not be enforceable in some countries and is an area for due diligence.

Clause 17.2 Other indemnities

6.068
This clause is a general indemnity to the lenders in respect of the occurrence of any Event of Default and in respect of funding costs. This indemnity applies whether or not the lenders exercise their right to accelerate. Note also that Clause 17.3 *(OTHER INDEMNITIES: Indemnity to the Agent)* indemnifies the Agent for expenses incurred in investigating a Default. Subclause (d) of that clause also indemnifies the Agent for the cost of instructing professional advisers, even where there is no Default.

6.069
Comment There is a risk of the indemnity in respect of professional advice cutting across what has been agreed in relation to costs and expenses (see 6.071 onwards) or in relation to any professional advice which has been specifically provided for (e.g. provisions for annual valuations at the borrower's expense, or legal fees in relation to Libor transition). Borrowers may want to restrict the indemnity in respect of professional advice so as to only apply where the Agent reasonably believes that there is a Default or where the borrower has requested a waiver or amendment. Agents are likely to be reluctant to agree this given that the general thrust of the agreement is that the Agent is protected from liability where it is relying on professional advice. As a result, the Agent will want to be able to obtain the protection afforded to it by getting advice whenever it thinks that is appropriate.

Clause 18: Mitigation by the Lenders

6.070

Under this clause, the lenders and Issuing Bank agree to try to minimize any additional costs to the borrower under the illegality, gross-up and increased costs clauses. They need not, however, take steps which, in their opinion acting reasonably, might be prejudicial to them. One possible way of mitigating these additional costs and other difficulties might, in certain circumstances, be to lend through a different branch.[13]

Clause 19: Costs and Expenses

6.071

Clause 19.1 (*Transaction expenses*) deals with the costs of putting the transaction together (including costs relating to all Finance Documents, whether signed at the start or at some later stage), Clause 19.2 (*Amendment costs*) deals with costs of amendments and Clause 19.3 (*Enforcement costs*) deals with costs of enforcement. In the first two cases, the borrower pays only the costs of the Agent and the Arranger, while in the case of enforcement expenses, the expenses of all lenders are to be covered. At the enforcement stage, lenders may well wish to have independent advice and even to take independent action[14]; whereas at the transaction stage, lenders are largely content to rely on the advice given to the Agent supplemented by the individual participant lenders' in-house lawyer's views, since, at this point, the interests of all the lenders are (almost) identical. This is often not the case in enforcement.

6.072

It is also worth noticing that, generally speaking, in the case of amendments and consents, the borrower is only required to pay for the costs of amendments and consents which it requests. This was important in the context of the Libor transition, where, commonly, borrowers were able to resist any suggestion that they should pick up the lenders' costs.

---

[13] See commentary on Clause 26.3 *(CHANGES TO THE LENDERS: Other conditions of assignment or transfer)* at subclause (d) in 9.051.

[14] See commentary on Clause 2.3 *(THE FACILITIES: Finance Parties' rights and obligations)* from 2.006 onwards.

212   Additional Payment Obligations

6.073

Going forward it is noticeable that the future proofing supplements included in the documentation to deal with changing interest rate methodologies[15] are included in the definition of Finance Documents so that costs in relation to agreeing those documents will fall on the borrower.

6.074

A number of comments may be made on this clause.

Comment Commonly borrowers ask for a **cap** on transaction expenses. It is unlikely that lenders would agree to any such cap or other restriction in relation to enforcement expenses. However, perhaps in a workout loan, a borrower may argue that they should only pay the expenses of the Agent in relation to any enforcement. The argument would be that the risk of multiple actions by different lenders could be reduced if only the Agent's legal expenses were covered and that this would effectively help protect all parties from 'rogue lenders'.

6.075

Comment In relation to Clause 19.2 *(COSTS AND EXPENSES: Amendment costs)* lenders may argue that all lenders' expenses should be covered, not just the Agent as they may wish to be advised separately from the other lenders.

6.076

Comment The requirement in Clause 19.1 *(COSTS AND EXPENSES: Transaction expenses)* is to pay 'promptly'; while in most other cases (including clauses 19.2 *(COSTS AND EXPENSES: Amendment costs)* and 19.3 *(COSTS AND EXPENSES: Enforcement costs)*) payment is required within three Business Days of demand. A borrower may wish to clarify the timing of the obligation in Clause 19.1 *(COSTS AND EXPENSES: Transaction expenses)* and to negotiate a longer time period for the expenses in relation to amendments and consents, to ensure they have a reasonable period to consider, and if appropriate, challenge any particular expense before default interest starts to be chargeable. Lenders may also prefer greater certainty on the timing of these obligations.

---

[15] The Reference Rate Supplement and Compounding Methodology Supplement.

Guarantee, Representations, Undertakings and Events of Default

This Part deals with the guarantee (if there is one, and if it is included in the loan agreement); representations; undertakings; and Events of Default. This is the part of the agreement that regulates the working relationship between the lenders and the borrower, and hence is often the most heavily negotiated part of the document.

Guarantee

Clause 20: Guarantee and Indemnity

Clause 20.1 Guarantee and indemnity[1]

7.001

The guarantee itself in the LMA Compounded/Term Rate Loan[2] is contained in three separate provisions. First comes subclause (a) which reads as follows.
Each Guarantor irrevocably and unconditionally jointly and severally[3]:

(a) *Guarantees to each Finance Party punctual performance by each Borrower of all that Borrower's obligations under the Finance Documents;*

7.002

This subclause (a) is sometimes referred to as a 'see to it' guarantee. It is a promise that each borrower will fulfil its obligations. If the borrower fails to fulfil its obligations, the guarantor is immediately in breach of this 'see to it' promise and will be liable for damages. A **guarantee** may be an 'all moneys'

---

[1] See A1.070 onwards for a brief commentary on some important aspects of English law on guarantees.

[2] References in this book to the LMA Compounded/Term Rate Loan are to the LMA Multicurrency Term and Revolving Facilities Agreement incorporating Term SOFR for use in Investment Grade transactions, available to LMA members via www.lma.eu.com

[3] See A1.016.

© The Author(s), under exclusive license to Springer Nature Switzerland AG 2024
S. Wright, *The International Loan Documentation Handbook*, Global Financial Markets, https://doi.org/10.1007/978-3-031-38489-9_8

216 **Guarantee**

guarantee—guaranteeing whatever the borrower owes the lenders from time to time; or it may relate to a specific transaction. In the context of major financings, all moneys guarantees are unusual.

Next comes subclause (b) which reads:

(b) *undertakes with each Finance Party that whenever a Borrower does not pay any amount when due under or in connection with any Finance Document, that Guarantor shall immediately on demand pay that amount as if it was the principal obligor;*

7.003
This subclause (b) is a conditional payment obligation. It is a promise to pay if the underlying debtor fails to pay. This gives the beneficiary of the guarantee a claim in debt against the guarantor (as opposed to the claim in damages under subclause (a)).

The third part of the guarantee clause is in subclause (c) which reads.

(c) *agrees with each Finance Party that if any obligation guaranteed by it is or becomes unenforceable, invalid or illegal, it will, as an independent and primary obligation, indemnify that Finance Party immediately on demand against any cost, loss or liability it incurs as a result* ....

7.004
This subclause (c) constitutes a primary obligation[4] on the guarantor to pay sums expressed to be due under the loan agreement if unpaid by the borrower. The intention is to ensure that any difficulties with the underlying debt (e.g. invalidity, illegality or release by variation) do not affect the guarantor's liability.[5]

---

[4] See A1.073.

[5] In McGuinness v Norwich and Peterborough Building Society [2011] EWCA Civ 1286; the court held that a single guarantee could create different rights for the beneficiary with one clause giving rise to a claim in damages and another giving rise to a separate (and more valuable) claim in debt.

Clause 20: Guarantee and Indemnity **217**

Clause 20.2 Continuing guarantee[6]

7.005

This clause states that the guarantee is a continuing guarantee. It is particularly important in a revolving credit, but is often also necessary in a term loan if, for example in a multicurrency loan, it is treated as being repaid in full and re-advanced from time to time.[7] The intention is to clarify that the guarantee relates not only to the original loan (which may well have been repaid)[8] but also to the re-advanced loans from time to time. The clause is also useful even in a single currency term loan, in order to clarify that the guarantee is not limited to moneys advanced at the start of the transaction but also includes future moneys under the loan such as interest and indemnities.

Clause 20.3 Reinstatement

If any discharge, release or arrangement (....) is made by a Finance Party in whole or in part on the basis of any payment, security or other disposition which is avoided or must be restored in insolvency, liquidation, administration or otherwise, ..., then the liability of each Guarantor under this Clause [ ] will continue or be reinstated as if the discharge, release or arrangement had not occurred.

7.006

This clause deals with the possibility of clawbacks. Most jurisdictions allow for certain transactions[9] which a company has entered into, to be 'clawed back' or reversed, if the company becomes insolvent within a certain period (commonly referred to as the **'hardening period'** or the 'suspect period') after the transaction occurred, subject to various criteria. The clause provides that if the loan is repaid, but the lenders subsequently have to reimburse that payment because it is clawed back in an insolvency, the liability of the borrowers and guarantors shall remain in place as though there had been no repayment of the loan in the first place.

---

[6] See A1.077.

[7] See comments on Clause 8.3 (*OPTIONAL CURRENCIES*: *Change of currency*) in 3.019.

[8] Or treated as repaid by virtue of the rule in Clayton's case (Devagnes v Noble 1816 1 Mer 572).

[9] Under English law, these include preferences and transactions at an undervalue. In some countries, set offs exercised shortly before winding up may also be clawed back.

218   Guarantee

7.007

> *Comment* This issue is not too contentious in an unsecured guarantee. However, if the guarantor has given security for their guarantee obligations, and that security had been discharged on repayment of the loan, such a provision would not be effective to reinstate the security. Therefore, secured guarantees often allow the lenders to retain the security for a period (matching the longest hardening period) after repayment of the loan. This, of course, can be commercially difficult for a guarantor. They are likely to want to be sure that, when the loan is repaid, any security they have given for the guarantee will be released. Any right to retain the security may have the effect of preventing a refinancing (see Box 7.1).

Box 7.1

It can be hard to find a compromise between the position of the lenders and the guarantor on the point in 7.007. Ideally, the likelihood of a clawback occurring might need to be assessed and, if the lenders perceive this as a real risk, provisions may need to be included in the original documents to the effect that security will only be released if evidence is provided, at the time of the repayment and requested release of the security for the guarantee, that there is no risk of clawback given the law in relevant jurisdictions (e.g. because the person making payment of the loan is not insolvent therefore no question of clawback arises).[10]

Clause 20.4 Waiver of defences

7.008

This clause is designed to ensure that acts or omissions which might otherwise discharge the guarantee or reduce the amount of the lenders' claim under it do not have that effect. It states that the guarantee will remain effective despite any amendments or waivers granted by the lenders, despite any release of

---

[10] This clearly depends on the relevant jurisdiction of potential insolvency. If proof of solvency is a solution, it should not be sought lightly. It would be time consuming and expensive on any given date to prove solvency.

Clause 20: Guarantee and Indemnity   **219**

security held by the lenders and despite any failure to enforce other rights or any problems with the borrowers' authorization of the loan.

Subclause (e) states that the guarantee shall remain valid despite.

(e) *any amendment, novation, supplement, extension, restatement (however fundamental and whether or not more onerous) or replacement of a Finance Document or any other document or security including without limitation any change in the purpose of, any extension of or increase in any facility or the addition of any new facility under any Finance Document or other document or security;*

7.009

Comment This subclause (e) provides that the guarantee will extend to increases in the facility, new facilities and more onerous obligations assumed by the borrower without the need for the guarantor to give its consent to those changes. The wording of this clause results from the series of cases on amendments discussed in Box 7.3 and is intended to avoid the need to obtain guarantor's consent even for significant variations. This can be useful where the agreement contemplates accordions, extensions and structural adjustments as discussed in 0.197, although in practice lenders may still request guarantor consent to significant amendments, because of the legal uncertainties in this area. Where the loan does not contemplate additional or restructured lending, some guarantors may wish to restrict subclause (e) so as to only give pre-approval of changes which are not more onerous and are not for a different purpose than the original loan.

7.010

Under English law, guarantors can raise numerous defences to a claim under the guarantee. The rationale for most of these defences comes from the guarantor's right of **subrogation**. This is the right of the guarantor, when they have paid under the guarantee, to stand in the shoes of the lenders and take over their rights against the borrower. If lenders alter their rights and thereby change the rights which the guarantor will obtain through subrogation, in certain cases, unless the guarantor has agreed otherwise, this will be a good defence for the guarantor to a claim for payment under the guarantee. In some cases, it will completely release the guarantor from liability, while in others it will reduce their liability (see Box 7.2).

220   Guarantee

> **Box 7.2**
>
> Cases include where
>
> - the lenders give time to pay[11];
> - the lenders alter or release their rights against, or any security is given by, the debtor[12];
> - the lenders negligently fail to protect the value of their security, for example, by non-registration[13];
> - the loan terms are amended (see Box 7.3) and
> - the lenders sell their security without taking proper care to obtain the current market value.[14]

7.011

This is the reason for Clause 20.4, *(GUARANTEE AND INDEMNITY: Waiver of defences)* which provides that the guarantors' liability will remain unaffected. In practice and as a matter of risk avoidance, lenders should not rely on this clause to be effective. There is always a risk that, on the facts of the case, what has happened is construed as not falling within the clause (e.g. a variation of the loan may be held to be so substantial as to result in a new loan, not the subject of the original guarantee. See Box 7.3). Therefore, in practice, whenever amending a guaranteed loan (or one where any party other than the borrower has given security, where the same principles apply) consent of the guarantor and third party security providers should be sought, together with their written confirmation, before the change is made, that the guarantee and security will remain effective following the change.

---

[11] Associated British Ports v Ferryways NV & anor (2009) EWCA Civ 189.

[12] Holme v Brunskill (1877–78) LR 3 QBD 495.

[13] Wulff v Jay (1871–72) LR 7 QB 756, but see also General Mediterranean Holding SA SPF v QucomHaps Holdings Ltd [2018] EWCA Civ 2416.

[14] Although (in the absence of bad faith) there is no positive duty to maximize the price obtained. See comments in China & South Seas Bank Ltd. v Tan (1990) 1 AC 536.

Clause 20: Guarantee and Indemnity 221

> **Box 7.3**
>
> There have been a number of cases on the effect of these clauses where the guaranteed obligation is amended. The basic principle (absent these clauses) was set out in Holme v Brunskill (1877) 3 QBD 495. That case held that amendments to the guaranteed debt would discharge the guarantee unless the guarantor consented to the variation or the variation is patently insubstantial. A later case[15] held that a clause consenting to future amendments of the guaranteed debt would be effective to allow changes as long as those changes did not amount to a replacement debt and as long as the amended agreement was within the general scope of the original contract. Unsurprisingly, there have been a number of cases[16] on what amounts to a variation, and what is a new loan. Each case is decided on its facts, so, if in doubt, the sensible approach remains to obtain the written approval of the guarantor before effecting amendments.

Clause 20.5 Immediate recourse

This clause allows the lenders to claim against the guarantor without first having to take action against any other party. It is, in any event, the case under English law that claims against a borrower do not need to be exhausted before a claim can be made on a guarantor,[17] but this express clause clarifies that position.

7.012

Clause 20.6 Appropriations

7.013

Subclause (a) of this clause allows the lenders to enforce security and apply proceeds they have available for the loan in whatever order they choose. This freedom can significantly affect recoveries.

---

[15] Triodos Bank v Dobbs (2005) EWCA Civ 630.

[16] See for example North Shore Ventures Ltd v Anstead Holdings (2011) EWCA Civ 230; Bank of Scotland Plc v Constantine Makris and Ben O'Sullivan (2009) EWHC 3869; Aviva Insurance Ltd v Hackney Empire Ltd (2012) EWCA Civ 1716; Close Brothers Ltd v Ridsdale (2012) EWHC 3090. and Maxted v Investec Bank Plc [2017] EWHC 1997 (Ch).

[17] The Court of Appeal confirmed in White v Davenham Trust Ltd (2011) EWCA Civ 747, that a beneficiary can enforce a guarantee even where they have security for the same loan from the principal debtor.

222 **Guarantee**

7.014

Subclause (b) of this clause allows the lenders to recover money from the guarantor and not apply it in the reduction of the debt. Instead the money can be placed in an interest-bearing account, allowing the lenders to claim in the insolvency of the borrower for the full debt and only apply the guarantee proceeds after the winding up has been completed. This will benefit the lender if the payment from the guarantor is less than the debt outstanding. In those circumstances, after payment under the guarantee, the lender is left with a claim against the borrower. The ability to put the guarantee payment in a suspense account increases the amount the lenders can claim for in an insolvency, which, in turn, increases their recovery in the insolvency.

Clause 20.7 Deferral of Guarantors' rights

7.015

This clause provides that the guarantor will not exercise its rights of subrogation and reimbursement until the lenders have been paid in full because lenders do not wish to have to share their security, or face competing claims with the guarantor in the insolvency of the borrower, or of any other guarantor, if the lenders have not been paid in full.

7.016

There are three separate rights that are being deferred here:

- first, the right of subrogation;
- second, the right of reimbursement (including its enforcement rights such as set off and insolvency proof in relation to the right of reimbursement) and
- third, the right of contribution from other guarantors (again, including enforcement rights).

7.017

Lenders are concerned to ensure that, until they are repaid, guarantors do not compete with them, whether in the insolvency of the borrower or in the insolvency of other guarantors, to the extent that guarantors have a claim in any insolvency arising by virtue of payment under the guarantee. See Box 7.4.

Clause 20: Guarantee and Indemnity 223

> **Box 7.4**
>
> The effectiveness of clauses deferring the right of reimbursement and non-competition clauses was considered in a number of cases between 2009 and 2011.[18] Such clauses have been upheld as not being contrary to public policy.[19] For a while there were concerns that the wording at the time did not go far enough and left the guarantor able to exercise rights under a rather obscure legal rule known as the rule in Cherry v Boultbee.[20] As a result, the LMA added subclauses (d) onwards to the clause to try to clarify that that rule was also being excluded. The conclusion of the cases was that as long as the guarantee is of the whole loan, the guarantor would not be entitled to claim in the insolvency under the rule in Cherry v Boultbee anyway,[21] even without the clauses. Nevertheless the practice is to retain the clauses, and this is particularly important in the case of partial guarantees.

Subordination

7.018

Some guarantees go considerably further than Clause 20.7 (*GUARANTEE AND INDEMNITY: Deferral of Guarantors' rights*). An example follows (Box 7.5).

> **Box 7.5**
>
> *Until all the Guaranteed Liabilities have been paid, discharged or satisfied in full ... the Guarantor agrees that it will not*
>
> a) *exercise its rights of subrogation, reimbursement and indemnity against any Obligor;*
> b) *demand or accept repayment in whole or in part of any Indebtedness due to the Guarantor from any Obligor ...;*
> c) *claim any set off or counterclaim against any Obligor or prove in competition with the Lender in the liquidation of any Obligor ... but so that, if so directed by the Lender, it will prove for the whole or part of its claim in such liquidation and hold all recoveries in trust for the Lender.*

---

[18] Mills and others v HSBC Trustee (C.I) Ltd and others [2009] EWHC 3377 (Ch).

[19] See Re SSSL Realisations (2002) Ltd [2006] EWCA Civ 7.

[20] See Cherry v Boultbee (1839) 4 My & Cr 442.

[21] See Cattles plc v Welcome Financial Services and others [2009] EWHC 3027 (Ch).

Subordination Before Winding Up

7.019

In this (not uncommon) example, the guarantor is being asked to agree to make *no claim whatsoever* against the borrower (or any other guarantor) until the loan is repaid. All sums due to the guarantor from time to time are being subordinated to the loan. This clearly depends on the commercial position and what cashflows exist within the group. In many cases, the guarantor and borrower (and other Obligors) have trading relationships which require inter-company payments to be made and should not therefore agree to such a broad subordination. It may well be that the free flow of moneys between the debtor and the guarantor should be permitted prior to winding up.

Subordination on Winding Up

7.020

A separate issue is subordination on a winding up. This is achieved by subclause (c) in the example. This prohibits the guarantor from putting in a claim in the insolvency of the borrower (or other Obligor such as a co-guarantor) in competition with the lenders. Alternatively, if the lenders direct, they may require the guarantor to claim in the insolvency and hold the proceeds on trust for the lenders. The argument for inclusion of this provision is that the guarantor should be supporting the borrower and not doing anything that would reduce the lenders' recovery. If the guarantor does not claim in insolvency or holds its claim in trust for the lenders, the lenders' recovery will be greater.

Guarantors should be wary of agreeing to such a clause. The difficulty is that the guarantor cannot agree two such clauses in different guarantees with different lenders to the same borrower. One lender may direct them to make no claim in the insolvency while the other directs them to claim and hold the claim in trust for them. The guarantor cannot comply with both directions. In most cases therefore, the agreement of the guarantor not to claim in the insolvency either of the borrower or of any other Obligor should apply only (as in the LMA Compounded/Term Rate Loan) to any claim which the guarantor has which arises from payment under the guarantee in question.

Interest

7.021

When moneys have been paid under the guarantee and not applied against the debt (in accordance with Clause 20.6 *(GUARANTEE AND INDEMNITY: Appropriations)* at subclause (b)) the guarantee should provide for that money to be placed in an interest-bearing account (see Box 7.6).

Box 7.6

Some guarantors, where the amounts at stake are high, may wish to specify in the guarantee that where moneys are placed on deposit as envisaged by Clause 20.6 *(GUARANTEE AND INDEMNITY: Appropriations)* at subclause (b), any additional claim for interest accruing under the loan will be limited to an amount equal to the interest accruing on the suspense account. This would be most likely to be an issue in cases where a guarantor provides a guarantee for less than the full amount of the loan. If the guarantor guarantees the whole loan, the suspense account issue will not arise since, assuming the guarantor pays in full, there will be no need for money to be applied otherwise than in immediate satisfaction of the debt.

Representations, Undertakings and Events of Default

Clause 21:
Representations—Section 1—An Introduction

1. Purpose

8.001
The loan agreement contains representations which are required to be made on the date of the agreement. It also often contains representations which are required to be made on other dates (typically, on each drawing and on the first day of each Interest Period). The purpose of the representations is:

* in the case of representations required to be made on the date of the agreement, to trigger disclosure of information; and
* in all cases, to give the lenders the contractual right not to advance additional monies (i.e. to act as a drawstop) and/or to accelerate the loan if the specified statements are untrue on the date they are made.

There may also be a liability in misrepresentation (as opposed to liability in contract) for the borrower if the statement is untrue.

We look at each of these functions of the representations in more detail here.

© The Author(s), under exclusive license to Springer Nature
Switzerland AG 2024
S. Wright, *The International Loan Documentation Handbook*, Global Financial Markets,
https://doi.org/10.1007/978-3-031-38489-9_9

Disclosure

8.002

The representations form a checklist of basic propositions which the lenders expect to be true. The borrower and its lawyer, in commenting on the draft agreement, will read through the representations and disclose further information on any which are not accurate. They form part of the three sets of checks which the lenders make before advancing the loan (representations, due diligence and conditions precedent).[1]

Drawstop/Acceleration

8.003

The representations ensure that the lenders have a remedy against the borrower (drawstop and/or acceleration) if any of the stated facts are untrue when the representation was made. They ensure that it is the borrower, not the lenders, who take the risk of any of them being untrue on that date (see Box 8.1).

Box 8.1

Take, for example, the representation in Clause 21.12 (*REPRESENTATIONS: Pari passu ranking*) of the LMA Compounded/Term Rate Loan[2] which states:

Its payment obligations under the Finance Documents rank at least pari passu with the claims of all its other unsecured and unsubordinated creditors, except for obligations mandatorily preferred by law applying to companies generally.

The borrower may not know whether this statement is true or not and may object to being asked to make it, on the grounds that it is not something which the borrower should be expected to know and, in any event, the lenders should rely on advice from their lawyers on this point.[3] Nevertheless, in most cases, the representation should be retained to ensure that, if the statement is not true and the loan does not rank pari passu, the lenders have the right not to advance the funds. Similarly, the lender would not want this representation qualified with reference to the borrower's belief. What matters is not the state

---

[1] See commentary on Clause 4.1 (*CONDITIONS OF UTILIZATION: Initial conditions precedent*) at 2.016.

[2] Multicurrency Term and Revolving Facilities Agreement incorporating Term SOFR for use in Investment Grade transactions, available to LMA members via www.lma.eu.com

[3] There are a number of other clauses in relation to which a similar point could be made, including Clause 21.6 (*REPRESENTATIONS: Governing law and enforcement*) and 21.8 (*REPRESENTATIONS: No filing or stamp duties*), leading some borrowers to make a broad objection that they should not be required to make representations on matters of law.

Clause 21: Representations—Section 1—An Introduction 229

of the borrower's knowledge, but rather, what remedy the lender has if the statement is untrue.

8.004

It is therefore important to focus on the risk allocation role of the representations in any negotiation of them, and to focus on the question 'Should the lenders have the right not to advance the loan if this statement is not true?' (i.e. who should take the risk of the statement being untrue?) and not on the question 'Is it reasonable to ask the borrower to represent that?' (see Box 8.2).

> **Box 8.2**
>
> The answer to the question of who should take the risk of a particular representation being untrue will depend (as always) on the nature of the transaction. In straightforward situations, the borrower is expected to take all risks including the risk that the initial legal situation is not as it had been expected. In complex cases, for example where the transaction is structured to take advantage of particular tax, accounting, or regulatory rules in different jurisdictions, it is not necessarily the case that the borrower should take risks relating to the existing or future legal position. In these cases, certain representations on matters of law may need to be deleted to reflect the agreed risk allocation. See also the discussion in Box 8.8.

Sometimes borrowers' lawyers object to this because of their client's potential liability for misrepresentation. In practice this ought not to be a concern for two reasons. First, as noted shortly, lenders are rarely interested in suing borrowers for misrepresentation—they simply want to rely on their contractual right to be repaid. Second, in order to have a claim in misrepresentation (certainly under English law, at least), the lender needs to have relied on the representation which they will not have done in those circumstances where the borrower is making this argument.

Nevertheless, sometimes borrowers' lawyers remain uncomfortable with the concept of representations being used for risk allocation. In this case an alternative approach is to recast the issu e in question as an Event of Default. So, for example, if the borrower is uncomfortable with making the pari passu representation, an alternative, which would avoid the borrower having potential liability for misrepresentation, would be to recast it as an Event of Default. The disadvantage of this alternative approach is that it is more cumbersome and involves more drafting, so that it is more expensive in terms of legal fees.

Liability in misrepresentation

8.005

The contractual rights which the agreement contains (the right not to lend if any representation is untrue, and the right to demand early repayment of the loan) are in addition to the remedies for misrepresentation and breach of warranty given by English law (see Box 8.3).

> **Box 8.3**
>
> Under English law, a person may be liable if he makes an incorrect statement which another relies on and which induces that other to enter into a contract.[4] That statement may be written or verbal and liability may arise even if the person making the statement was simply negligent in doing so. So, statements made by the borrower during negotiation of the loan could give rise to subsequent liability for the borrower, independently of any claim under the loan agreement itself. The lender will need to show, among other things, that the lender relied on the representation in deciding to advance the funds.

8.006

The lenders may be able to make an independent claim for misrepresentation in relation to the representations contained in the agreement if they relied on the representation and did not, for example, do their own due diligence. However, even if the lender could show the requisite reliance, their remedy, in a claim for misrepresentation, would be the amount of damages suffered as a result of the misrepresentation (unlikely to exceed the loan amount plus interest, etc.). There would also be numerous legal hurdles to jump in terms of proving the amount of damages. The lender's contractual remedies (acceleration, default interest and the indemnity in Clause 17.2 *(OTHER INDEMNITIES: Other indemnities)*) would be far simpler to pursue as they are claims in debt rather than damages.

Lenders pursuing a claim in misrepresentation against borrowers is therefore unlikely unless, for some reason, the contractual claims under the loan agreement are unenforceable against the borrower. The most likely situation in which this might arise is if the loan has been made to the borrower on a limited recourse basis, such as in a project finance. In these circumstances, borrowers need to take special care with the representations to ensure

---

[4] See Goode, *Commercial Law*, 6th edn, 2020, 3.98 et seq.

2. Repetition of Representations

8.007

The LMA loan agreements require certain of the representations to be repeated after the date of the agreement. This is usually required as a condition precedent to drawdown (Clause 4.2 (*CONDITIONS OF UTILIZA-TION: Further conditions precedent*) subclause (a)(ii), often also confirmed in the drawdown notice itself) and at the beginning of Interest Periods (Clause 21.14 *(REPRESENTATIONS: Repetition)*). The LMA Compounded/Term Rate Loan also requires repetition as a condition for the addition of a new Obligor.

Introduction—purpose of repetition

8.008

Clause 21.14 *(REPRESENTATIONS: Repetition)* reads as follows.

The Repeating Representations are deemed to be made by each Obligor by reference to the facts and circumstances then existing on:

(a) *the date of each Utilization Request and the first day of each Interest Period; and*

(b) *in the case of an Additional Obligor, the day on which the company becomes (or it is proposed that the company becomes) an Additional Obligor.*

Clause 21.14 *(REPRESENTATIONS: Repetition)* states that the 'Repeating Representations' are deemed repeated on (among other dates) the date of each new drawing and the first day of each Interest Period. The purpose of this is to ensure that, if any of the Repeating Representations become untrue, the lenders may refuse to advance new money and demand immediate repayment of moneys already advanced. The LMA Compounded/Term Rate Loan does not define 'Repeating Representations' and there may be much negotiation over which representations should fall into this category.

232   Representations, Undertakings and Events of Default

Hazards of repetition of representations

8.009

The effect of Repeating Representations is far reaching, particularly when considered in conjunction with other provisions of the agreement. The main problems which this simple clause creates are:

- it makes it hard to avoid inconsistencies in the document which will lead to uncertainty in its application; and.
- it makes it difficult (particularly for the principals involved) to understand the precise implications of the document.

Given these drawbacks, the simplest solution, for the person reading the loan agreement, is to avoid repetition of representations (at least after the first drawdown) and to deal with the relevant issues by specific conditions precedent, undertakings, compulsory prepayment events and Events of Default, as discussed in the summary to this introduction in 8.015. Nevertheless, it is often not possible, or worthwhile in terms of legal fees, to make such a change to the structure of the agreement, so all concerned need to be alive to the difficulties which repeating representations create and take extra care in reviewing these provisions. These main difficulties with repeating representations are therefore discussed in more detail here.

Inconsistencies

8.010

What the lenders want to achieve by the repetition is to ensure that if one of the specified representations is no longer true on one of the specified dates, then the lenders will be entitled to accelerate the loan. However, if a Repeating Representation covers a topic which is also covered by an undertaking or an Event of Default, any difference in the wording of the provisions will create uncertainty (see Box 8.4).

Box 8.4

An example may illuminate the problem. Assume that a loan agreement includes the following Event of Default:

Clause 21: Representations—Section 1—An Introduction 233

> '[It is an Event of Default if] the Borrower defaults under any material contract by which it is bound and such default could reasonably be expected to have a Material Adverse Effect.'
>
> Assume the agreement also contains a representation, which is repeated on the first day of each Interest Period, as follows:
>
> 'The Borrower is not in default under any material agreement by which it is bound'.
>
> Given that it is invariably expressed to be an Event of Default if a representation is untrue when made or repeated, the effect of repeating that particular representation would be to remove the Material Adverse Effect carve-out which had been negotiated into the Event of Default.
>
> In practice, were the borrower to default under a material contract in circumstances where the result was unlikely to have a Material Adverse Effect the borrower would be likely to contest the right of the lenders to demand immediate repayment of the loan because the Event of Default and the repeating representation are in conflict.

8.011

It is important to ensure that the agreement does not contain conflicting provisions. Some of the practical difficulties which such inconsistencies give rise to are:

- Neither party will be certain as to the real intention. Did the parties really intend, in the example at Box 8.4, to have the right to accelerate the loan even if the default in question clearly would not give rise to a material adverse effect?
- The Agent may feel that the inconsistency is unintentional and that there is simply a 'technical' Event of Default but not one which any of the lenders really intended to amount to a real Event of Default. However, if there is any doubt about this, the best practice would be for the Agent to advise the syndicate nevertheless and obtain instructions, rather than to take decisions itself, on behalf of the syndicate—see 10.002 onwards. It would have been better to avoid the need for syndicate consent in such circumstances because

  - unnecessary time and expense will be incurred in debating the issue.
  - if circumstances have changed (including change in market conditions generally or change in lender's policies), the lenders may have incentives to withhold consent, or they may want to link consent to other issues.[5]

---

[5] See Box 0.5.

234   Representations, Undertakings and Events of Default

– The syndicate may be influenced by concerns about the reaction of other lenders to the borrower. Assuming that other loans include a cross default clause, other lenders will have the right to accelerate their loans as a result of the fact that the syndicate has the right to accelerate this loan (whether or not that right was included intentionally).

8.012

The simplest way to avoid inconsistencies between the Repeating Representations and other parts of the agreement, and the problems which such inconsistencies cause, is to ensure that those representations which deal with issues which are commercially significant (e.g. default under other contracts or litigation) are not repeated, but that the relevant issue is dealt with instead by the undertakings and Events of Default. This will usually result in those representations which relate to matters of law being the ones which will be repeated (see commentary on the individual representations from 8.021 onwards).

8.013

> However, in different markets where there is a significant cross-border element such as in structured or project finance, it may not always be appropriate that a change in law which results in representations becoming untrue should result in an Event of Default. It may be better for them to result in a positive obligation on some party (perhaps a lender) to seek necessary consents or licences to cure the problem, and, if not curable, it may result in compulsory prepayment. The simplest way to achieve these objectives is not to repeat the representations, but instead, to ensure that the undertakings, conditions precedent, Events of Default and compulsory prepayment events deal with all issues as necessary.

Comprehensibility

8.014

As might be apparent from the discussion on this topic, another difficulty with Repeating Representations is that it makes the document hard to understand (and to draft correctly). Extra care must be taken in reviewing the Repeating Representations and it is often not immediately obvious to the

Clause 21: Representations—Section 1—An Introduction **235**

borrower what the effect of the repetition is. For example, will repeating a given representation detract from what has been discussed in relation to the Events of Default? Or will it result in a difference in relation to the opportunity which the borrower has to cure the problem? In the LMA Compounded/ Term Rate Loan, the borrower has no ability to remedy an Event of Default which is triggered by a misrepresentation while it may be given the possibility of curing other Events of Default.[6]

Summary

8.015

If any representations are to be repeated on dates after the first advance of the loan, some guidelines may help to reduce the difficulties that this concept can give rise to. Some suggested guidelines (bearing in mind that there is no consensus on this issue) are:

* Whichever representations are to be repeated, they should be the same ones for the purpose of drawdown and for Interest Periods (see Box 8.5).
* No representation should be repeated if it covers a topic which has been dealt with in the undertakings or the Events of Default, or if it deals with a commercially significant issue which should more appropriately be dealt with by the undertakings or Events of Default (or, if such a representation is repeated, it should be checked against the relevant undertaking and/or Event of Default to ensure the provisions do not conflict).
* A representation should not be repeated if the risk which that representation addresses should not fall on the borrower or should not constitute an Event of Default (e.g. if the risk of change of law should fall on the lender or if the relevant issue should give rise to a compulsory prepayment event instead of an Event of Default).
* Consider grace periods in relation to the misrepresentation Event of Default—see Clause 25.4 *(EVENTS OF DEFAULT: Misrepresentation)* in 8.232.

---

[6] See Clause 25.4 (*EVENTS OF DEFAULT: Misrepresentation*) in 8.232.

236 Representations, Undertakings and Events of Default

> **Box 8.5**
>
> Some argue that certain representations should be repeated in relation to new money advanced by the lender but not at any other time because the circumstances in which the lenders are relieved of their obligations to advance new money should be more stringent than the circumstances in which they are entitled to demand immediate repayment of moneys already advanced. This objective cannot be achieved by stating that Repeating Representations are only to be repeated on dates on which new drawings are to be made and not at any other time (e.g. by requiring repetition on drawdown dates but not on the first day of all Interest Periods). This is because, if on such repetition on a proposed drawdown date, the representation were to be untrue, it would result not only in a right not to advance additional money, but also in a right to accelerate the outstanding debt. A rather peculiar situation would result in which the lenders would be entitled to accelerate outstanding sums if certain circumstances (the facts specified in a Repeating Representation being untrue) happened to coincide with an attempted drawdown, but not if the same circumstances occurred at any other time.
>
> If lenders do want to draw a distinction between the obligation to advance additional funds and the right to accelerate existing moneys, this can be done by including a condition precedent that the Repeating Representations are true, but without actually requiring them to be repeated in Clause 21.14 *(REPRESENTATIONS: Repetition)*.[7] However in many cases lenders will not want to find themselves in a position where they are not obliged to advance further funds but cannot demand repayment of sums already advanced. They will usually prefer to have a complete exit route if problems arise.
>
> For this reason, it is unusual[8] to draw a distinction between the representations which are required to be true for the purpose of the lenders' obligation to advance funds and those which are required to be true for the purpose of giving rise to their right to accelerate.

3. Qualifications

8.016

Commonly, borrowers seek to qualify the representations in important respects. We look at some of the most common qualifications requested below:

---

[7] This is the approach taken with a 'Default'. Existence of a Default allows lenders not to advance funds but does not give rise to the right to accelerate.

[8] Outside project finance, where the limited recourse nature of the loan makes a significant difference.

Who is making the representations about whom?

8.017
See comments from 0.164 onwards for a discussion of whether provisions should extend to group members who are not Obligors and the concept of 'Material Subsidiaries'. Additionally, in some cases, borrowers may want to resist having to make representations relating to companies over which they have no control—that is, companies higher up the corporate structure or subsidiary undertakings (see the discussion on the definition of 'Subsidiary' at 1.056).

Inclusion of materiality thresholds

8.018
Borrowers are likely to want certain representations, for example, representations relating to compliance with laws, such as environmental laws, to be limited so as to represent that they are in compliance 'in all material respects'. Alternatively, they may request that the qualification says they are not in breach in a way which could be expected to have a 'Material Adverse Effect'. Note, except for very strong credits, lenders will want to restrict the second formulation. Some issues will be important to lenders for reasons other than credit risk. For example, lenders may require their borrowers to have sound environmental policies simply as part of the lenders' own internal policies, regardless of the credit risks involved.

Limitations with reference to knowledge

8.019
Borrowers commonly request the insertion of words such as 'to the best of their knowledge'. There are issues here for both lenders and borrowers. Borrowers need to consider precisely whose knowledge would be relevant. There may be people in the company who have the relevant knowledge, but if management does not, they will not want that to trigger the clause. It is common to specify that the reference is to the actual knowledge of specified persons, such as the board of directors. Lenders, if they agree to a qualification with reference to knowledge, frequently require the addition of the expression 'having made due enquiry'. Lenders also need to ensure, whenever they agree to a limitation with reference to the knowledge of the borrower, that they accept that the given set of circumstances is not an Event of Default

238 Representations, Undertakings and Events of Default

if the borrower was not aware of it at the time the representation was made. See the discussion in Box 8.1.

Geographical limitations

8.020
Some of the representations relate to specified countries, defined in the Leveraged LMA as 'Relevant Jurisdictions'. In an unsecured transaction such as the LMA Compounded/Term Rate Loan, the representations are usually restricted to the place of incorporation of the borrowers. In a secured transaction 'Relevant Jurisdictions' usually include the countries where the security is located and anywhere any Obligor conducts business. So, for example, the representation in Clause 21.5 *(REPRESENTATIONS: Validity and admissibility in evidence)* to the effect that the borrowers have all desirable authorizations is often extended to give that confirmation in 'all Relevant Jurisdictions'; similarly with the representations as to stamp duties and registration requirements in Clause 21.8 *(REPRESENTATIONS: No filing or stamp taxes)*. For international groups, this may be impossible to ascertain and borrowers may therefore want to restrict the representation to their countries of incorporation or to request a materiality qualification.

Clause 21: Representations—Section 2—The LMA Representations

8.021
21 Representations
   Each Obligor makes the representations and warranties set out in this clause 21 to each Finance Party on the date of this Agreement
   See Box 8.6.

Box 8.6

There is a technical difference between a representation and a warranty. The remedies for breach of the two types of provision are different and there are different requirements before a claim for breach can be founded. For most practical purposes, if any of the statements listed in this clause is untrue, the lenders will rely on their contractual rights (not to lend and/or to accelerate) which arise as a result. These rights are the same for a misrepresentation as for a breach of warranty.

Clause 21: Representations—Section 2—The LMA Representations 239

8.022

Turning then to the content of the representations. The LMA Compounded/ Term Rate Loan contains certain fairly standard representations relating to legal issues such as the power and authority of the borrower. It also contains a few representations relating to the borrower's business. It is likely that these business-related representations will need to be supplemented in many cases by additional representations relating to the business issues of concern to the lenders.[9]

8.023

This section reviews each representation in turn, first with reference to the statement required to be made on the date of the loan agreement, and second in the context of its potential inclusion in the definition of 'Repeating Representation'. In this second context, it should be emphasized that there is no consensus on which representations should be defined as 'Repeating Representations' and the suggestions made here are designed to help readers to identify and avoid conflicts between different parts of the document. In most cases, where this book suggests that a particular representation should not be a Repeating Representation, an alternative (but more cumbersome) approach would be for that representation to be a Repeating Representation, but also to identify any undertaking or Event of Default which deals with the same issue and ensure that these various provisions do not conflict.

Clause 21.1 Status

8.024

This clause is a representation that the company exists, is a limited liability company and has power to carry on its business.

Sometimes the words 'in goodstanding' are added. This will be relevant when the borrower is incorporated in a jurisdiction which requires annual payments or filings to maintain **goodstanding**, lack of which may result in fines or restrictions on business activities.

The representation will of course need adjusting if any relevant Obligor is not in fact a company (e.g. if there are limited partnerships in the group).

---

[9] See Sect. 2 of the commentary on Clause 24 (*General Undertakings*) from 8.199 onwards.

Should Clause 21.1 *(Status)* repeat?

8.025

It is possible (if not likely in most cases) that the borrower could cease to be duly incorporated, validly existing or have power to carry on its business. Licences to conduct the relevant business may be withdrawn or taxes unpaid may lead to the company being struck off the register. If it did so, the lenders would wish to have the right to accelerate the loan. Given the unlikelihood of this occurrence, any potential conflict with other provisions of the agreement is usually commercially insignificant. Therefore this representation is one which can be repeated in normal circumstances.

> In a more complex transaction, if the risk of change of law is not to fall simply on the borrower, it might be appropriate to recast this (or at least to ensure that the Event of Default relating to misrepresentations is not an automatic Event of Default but allows a period for remedy as discussed in the context of Clause 25.4 *(EVENTS OF DEFAULT: Misrepresentation))* to give appropriate possibilities to the borrower to remedy the situation.

Clause 21.2 Binding obligations

8.026

In this clause, the borrower represents that the agreements are *valid, binding and enforceable* obligations subject to principles of law specifically referred to in the legal opinion (see Box 8.7).

Box 8.7

There is an issue here as to whether the lenders' legal opinion should be disclosed to the borrower. The main argument against disclosure is that disclosure will highlight any areas of perceived legal risk, which the borrower may take advantage of at a later date. This is most likely to be a real issue for the lenders in circumstances where the opinions in question would not readily be apparent to the borrower or their advisers. This may be the case in innovative transactions involving legal issues on which lawyers may have differing opinions. It is less likely to be a significant issue in a straightforward unsecured loan. It would be hard for the borrower to make the representation as drafted here if they had not seen the legal opinion!

Clause 21: Representations—Section 2—The LMA Representations **241**

> An alternative way of dealing with this which is used in some of the other LMA documents is to make certain of the representations subject to the 'Legal Reservations' and to define these.

8.027

The limitation on the representation with reference to a legal opinion (or to 'Legal Reservations') is necessary because, of course, there are circumstances (administration or **Chapter 11** for example) which would freeze enforceability. Any such issues should have been addressed in the legal opinion and accepted by the lenders. The question, as discussed in 8.003–4, is which risks should fall on the borrower, and which on the lender? See Box 8.8.

> **Box 8.8**
>
> Most of the reservations will be issues which lenders accept—such as the impact of insolvency on the enforceability of the borrower's obligations. There may occasionally be others that highlight areas of legal uncertainty, of which lenders are aware but will want to ensure that they have the right to exit the transaction if they materialize; an example might be the issue of the effectiveness of the parallel debt structure discussed in 9.030. Lenders may be aware of the issue, still, if it were to become clear that the parallel debt structure was ineffective, lenders would want the right to accelerate the loan. To achieve this, if the representation is expressed to be subject to legal reservations then lenders need to ensure that the 'Legal Reservations' are limited and only include those legal issues in respect of which it is agreed that the risk should fall on the lender, not the borrower. An example would be the limits on enforceability of foreign judgements.

8.028

Comment If security is given, the representation may also need adjusting to refer to the need for registration, notice to third parties, or similar requirements.

Should Clause 21.2 *(Binding obligations)* repeat?

8.029

It is possible (if not likely in most cases) that the borrower's obligations under the loan agreement could cease to be binding and enforceable. There may be a change of law which has this effect. The same arguments apply as in relation to Clause 21.1 (*REPRESENTATIONS: Status*).[10] Therefore, again, this is a representation which can be repeated after drawdown in normal situations.

> In a more complex transaction, if the risk of change of law is not to fall simply on the borrower it might be appropriate to recast this[11] to give appropriate possibilities to the borrower to remedy the situation.

Clause 21.3 Non-conflict with other obligations

8.030
In this clause the borrower represents that performance of their obligations does not breach (a) any applicable regulation; (b) its constitutional documents or (c) any agreement it (or its Subsidiaries) has signed.

Borrowers may be restricted in their activities by law or regulation (e.g. if they belong to a regulated industry such as banking or insurance, or if they are public bodies), or by virtue of a general regulation affecting particular types of borrowing such as financial assistance. Subclause (a) is designed to address these issues.

8.031
Subclause (b) is intended to address the question of whether the borrower has power (capacity) to borrow the loan—some companies have limited borrowing powers in their constitutional documents.

8.032
Subclause (c) will confirm that this borrowing is not in breach of contractual provisions, such as a restriction on borrowing, or a negative pledge, given in a different loan agreement. The terms of these prior agreements (unlike the borrower's constitutional documents, which are often a matter of public record) are not generally available for inspection by the lenders on any public register, so there is little independent due diligence which the lenders can do to ensure that the representation in subclause (c) is correct. Including this

---

[10] That is, (a) if these events occurred the lenders should be entitled to accelerate and (b) commercial insignificance of this issue.

[11] Or at least to ensure that the Event of Default relating to misrepresentations is not an automatic Event of Default but allows a period for remedy as discussed in the context of Clause 25.4 (*EVENTS OF DEFAULT: Misrepresentation*).

Clause 21: Representations—Section 2—The LMA Representations

representation can assist in a good faith defence by the lenders to any claim by a third party, for example, that this loan agreement caused a breach of their existing contract and that the lenders were guilty of the tort of inducing a breach of contract.

Should Clause 21.3 *(Non conflict with other obligations)* repeat?

8.033

It is possible that regulations may be introduced after the date of the agreement which would be breached by continued performance of the borrower's obligations under the loan agreement or associated transaction. If this occurred, the lenders would want the right to accelerate the loan and therefore, given the commercial unlikelihood of such an event, this is a representation which can be repeated after drawdown in normal situations.

> In a more complex transaction, if the risk of change of law is not to fall simply on the borrower it might be appropriate to recast this[12] (at least in the case of subclause (a)) to give appropriate possibilities to the borrower to remedy the situation.

Clause 21.4 Power and authority

8.034

In this clause the borrower represents that it has power to perform its obligations under the documents and that they have been validly authorized.

This issue is a mixture of fact and law. The borrower may make the comment that they should not be required to give representations on matters of law (because that is not something on which they are competent to comment) to the extent that the representation is one of law. Nevertheless, as discussed from 8.004 onwards, lenders are likely to want to retain this representation to ensure that they have the right not to lend (or to accelerate) if the representation is untrue.

---

[12] Or at least to ensure that the Event of Default relating to misrepresentations is not an automatic Event of Default but allows a period for remedy.

Should Clause 21.4 *(Power and authority)* repeat?

8.035

It is not inconceivable that the continued performance of the borrower's obligations under the loan agreement could subsequently become subject to some additional authorization. The same comments apply as in relation to Clause 21.1 *(REPRESENTATIONS: Status)*.[13] Therefore, again, this is a representation which can be repeated after drawdown in normal situations.

> In a more complex transaction, if the risk of change of law is not to fall simply on the borrower it might be appropriate to recast this[14] to give appropriate possibilities to the borrower to remedy the situation.

Clause 21.5 Validity and admissibility in evidence

8.036

This clause is a representation that the borrowers have all necessary 'Authorizations' to enable them to comply with their obligations under the documents and to make the documents admissible in evidence. This representation refers not only to corporate authorizations but also consents (such as exchange control consent) licences, notarizations and registrations.[15]

This representation is one which the borrower might object to, on the basis that it is a matter of law on which they have no expertise.[16] Nevertheless, subject to the point in 8.067, it should normally be retained to ensure that, if untrue, the lenders have the right to accelerate and/or not lend if relevant authorizations are not in place. Of course, the lenders will also be taking advice from their lawyers on this issue and on the other matters of law referred to in the representations.

---

[13] That is, (a) if these events occurred the lenders should be entitled to accelerate and (b) commercial insignificance of this issue.

[14] Or at least to ensure that the Event of Default relating to misrepresentations is not an automatic Event of Default but allows a period for remedy.

[15] If any filings are required it may be appropriate to cross refer to Clause 21.8 *(REPRESENTATIONS: No filing or stamp taxes)* discussed in 8.042.

[16] See comments from 8.003 onwards.

Should Clause 21.5 *(Validity and admissibility in evidence)* repeat?

8.037

It is possible that further authorizations may become necessary for the loan agreement to continue to be performed and admissible in evidence in the borrower's country of incorporation. The same comments apply as in relation to Clause 21.1 *(REPRESENTATIONS: Status)*.[17] Therefore, again, this is a representation which can be repeated after drawdown in normal situations

> In a more complex transaction, if the risk of change of law is not to fall simply on the borrower it might be appropriate to recast this[18] to give appropriate possibilities to the borrower to remedy the situation.

Clause 21.6 Governing law and enforcement

8.038

In this clause the borrower confirms that the choice of law is valid and that an English judgement would be enforced in its place of incorporation.

Once again,[19] this representation should be retained, (subject to the point in 8.067) to ensure the lenders have the contractual rights they need if the statement is untrue. It is also a key point for the lenders' due diligence. These issues will be addressed by any legal opinion issued and borrowers ought to request that the representation is restricted with reference to any relevant qualification in the legal opinion.

Should Clause 21.6 *(Governing law and enforcement)* repeat?

8.039

It is possible that the borrower's jurisdiction of incorporation will cease to recognize judgements obtained in the law of the country chosen to have

---

[17] That is, (a) if these events occurred the lenders should be entitled to accelerate and (b) commercial insignificance of this issue.

[18] Or at least to ensure that the Event of Default relating to misrepresentations is not an automatic Event of Default but allows a period for remedy.

[19] See comments on Clause 21.5 *(REPRESENTATIONS: Validity and admissibility in evidence)* on 8.036.

246 Representations, Undertakings and Events of Default

jurisdiction. The same comments apply as in relation to Clause 21.1 *(REPRE-SENTATIONS: Status)*[20] Therefore, again, this is a representation which can be repeated after drawdown in normal situations

> In a more complex transaction, if the risk of change of law is not to fall simply on the borrower it might be appropriate to recast this to give appropriate possibilities to the borrower to remedy the situation.

Clause 21.7 Deduction of Tax

8.040

This clause confirms that the borrower is not required by law to make deductions on payments to Qualifying Lenders (once they have received any relevant approvals and, for non-bank lenders, as long as the tax authorities have not directed otherwise). Note that in an earlier version of the LMA Compounded/Term Rate Loan this clause read as follows '*It is not required to make any deduction for or on account of Tax from any payment it may make under the Finance Documents*'. This wording was changed because it resulted in an Event of Default in ANY circumstances where a tax deduction is required even if this is due to issues which are agreed commercially should not result in a gross-up (e.g. if the lender was not a Qualifying Lender in the first place).

If the borrower is not English this representation is likely to need to be amended to reflect the tax law in the borrower's country as to whom a payment can be made without deduction for Tax. If the borrower is English, it might be appropriate to delete the representation as discussed in 8.067.

Should Clause 21.7 *(Deduction of Tax)* repeat?

8.041

It is possible that a withholding tax will be imposed which did not exist on the day the loan agreement was signed. However, in this case, the lenders will not need the right to accelerate the loan. They have the protection of the

---

[20] That is, (a) if these events occurred the lenders should be entitled to accelerate and (b) commercial insignificance of this issue.

gross-up clause (Clause 15.2 *(TAX GROSS UP AND INDEMNITIES: Tax gross up)* subclause (c)). Therefore this representation should not be repeated.

Clause 21.8 No filing or stamp taxes

8.042

This clause confirms that no registrations or other filings are required and no stamp duty is payable in relation to the documents.

Clearly this clause needs to be amended (and corresponding conditions inserted to require the relevant filing, etc., to take place) if it is incorrect.

This clause is another area where the borrower may argue that it should not be required to make statements on matters of law,[21] but where, (subject to the point in 8.067), the lenders will usually want the representation in any event.

Should Clause 21.8 *(No filing or stamp taxes)* repeat?

8.043

It is possible that a filing requirement may arise or stamp duties may become payable in the future. It will be a question of judgement as to whether this is a real commercial risk in the context of the transaction or not. If the risk is thought not to be significant, this is a representation which could be repeated after drawdown. If the risk is thought to be significant, the representation should not be repeated but instead.

* lenders should rely on the stamp duty indemnity and
* the borrower should be given the opportunity to effect the relevant filing without its giving rise to an Event of Default—best done by recasting this as an undertaking.

Clause 21.9 No default

8.044

This clause reads.

---

[21] See comments from 8.003 onwards.

248 Representations, Undertakings and Events of Default

(a) *No Event of Default is continuing or might reasonably be expected to result from the making of any Utilization.*

(b) *No other event or circumstance is outstanding which constitutes a default under any other agreement or instrument which is binding on it...which might have a Material Adverse Effect.*

The impact of this representation depends on the definition of 'Material Adverse Effect' and in particular on whether that definition looks on the effect on the group as a whole, or on individual Obligors, or on individual group companies.

Assuming for the moment that the representation is not a 'Repeating Representation',[22] borrowers' comments on it will be made in light of the circumstances which exist at or about the time the representation is being negotiated. In these circumstances, the word 'might' in Clause 21.9 *(REPRESENTATIONS: No default)* subclause (b), even though it would be objectionable in the material adverse change Event of Default,[23] may well be a reasonable standard for the lenders to insist on—they want to be advised of all adverse possibilities before becoming obliged to lend.

Should Clause 21.9 *(No default)* repeat?

8.045

Clause 21.9 *(No default)* subclause (a) is a representation that there is no Event of Default and that none might reasonably be expected to result from the making of any Utilization. This is perhaps worth repeating in relation to new drawings so that, if a drawing is likely to result in an Event of Default (e.g. if it would result in a breach of a financial covenant) this representation would be incorrect, giving rise to an Event of Default and so enabling the lender not to advance the funds.

8.046

Clause 21.9 *(No default)* subclause (b) is different. This is a representation that there is no default (see Box 8.9) under any agreement which might have a material adverse effect.

---

[22] See discussion in 8.045 for issues which arise if this representation is repeated.

[23] See comments on Clause 25.12 *(EVENTS OF DEFAULT: Material adverse change)* in 8.279.

Clause 21: Representations—Section 2—The LMA Representations 249

> **Box 8.9**
>
> This representation relates to Events of Default and 'defaults' as opposed to 'Defaults'. The difference is significant. The borrower should not repeat a representation that no Default has occurred. The effect of this is that, if a Default has occurred (but it is not yet an Event of Default as, for example, the grace period is running) then the representation is untrue. Making an untrue representation is itself an Event of Default (without a grace period generally). The result of repeating a representation that no Default exists is therefore potentially to lose the benefit of the grace periods. Note this is different from having a condition precedent that there is no Default. In that case, if there is a Default, it is not a misrepresentation and therefore not an Event of Default. Instead, it simply relieves the lenders of the obligation to lend.

There is a hazard in repeating this representation, which is that there is a danger of a conflict between this and the cross default clause.[24] The cross default clause (Clause 25.5 (*EVENTS OF DEFAULT*: *Cross default*) of the LMA Compounded/Term Rate Loan) deals with the circumstances where, if the borrower is in breach of a contract with a third party, that should give rise to a right for these lenders to accelerate. If lenders wish to provide that default under an agreement which does not relate to Financial Indebtedness should be an Event of Default in certain circumstances[25] then the simplest way to deal with that clearly and without risking a conflict between Repeating Representations and the Events of Default is to deal with the issue directly as an Event of Default and not to repeat this representation (see Box 8.4).

Clause 21.10 No misleading information

8.047
This clause is a representation that the information provided to the lenders was accurate when given; that financial projections made were based on reasonable assumptions; and that nothing has happened since the information was provided and nothing has been omitted from the information provided, which makes it misleading.

---

[24] See the example referred to in Box 8.4.

[25] As to which, see the commentary on Clause 25.5 (*EVENTS OF DEFAULT*: *Cross default*) in 8.239.

250 Representations, Undertakings and Events of Default

8.048

Comment How contentious this representation is depends on the degree and type of information which has been provided to the lenders during the negotiation of the loan. For example, if the loan is to finance a new project, the borrower will not want there to be an Event of Default if the projections they made prove to have been optimistic. Rather than representing that the figures were based on reasonable assumptions, they will want to restrict the representation so that they are only saying that they believed the assumptions to be reasonable at the time the figures were provided.

It is common for borrowers to ask for the representation to be restricted to 'written' information provided by the management team. It is also sensible to keep a record of the information which has been provided.

Should Clause 21.10 (*No misleading information*) repeat?

8.049

This clause should not be repeated. It simply states that previous statements (in the **information memorandum**) were true when made and that nothing has happened which makes that document misleading. Once the lenders have signed the loan agreement they no longer rely on the information memorandum for their information (but rather on the updates from the borrower from time to time) nor do they expect that the facts stated in it will not change from time to time. Therefore, it is not intended that any changes from the position set out in the information memorandum which occurs after the date of the agreement should give rise to an Event of Default. Therefore, this representation should not be repeated.

Clause 21.11 Financial statements

8.050

This clause contains confirmation by the borrower that

- the Original Financial Statements were prepared in accordance with GAAP (in subclause (a)),
- they fairly present the financial position of the relevant company in relation to the period covered (in subclause (b)), and
- there has been no material adverse change in the position of the group or of the relevant company since those statements were prepared (in subclause (c)).

Should Clause 21.11 *(financial statements)* repeat?

8.051

The comments made on Clause 21.10 *(REPRESENTATIONS: No misleading information)* apply equally here. This representation simply updates the financial information provided up to the date of signing. Subclauses (a) and (b) are statements relating to the Original Financial Statements—which are a specified set of statements which never change—so, if those statements were true on the date the agreement was signed, they will always be true, so that repeating the representation is pointless. As for subclause (c)—if that were to be repeated, it would duplicate the function of the material adverse change Event of Default (and probably conflict with it). This representation should therefore not be repeated.

Clause 21.12 Pari passu ranking

8.052

This clause reads

Its payment obligations under the Finance Documents rank at least pari passu with the claims of all its other unsecured and unsubordinated creditors, except for obligations mandatorily preferred by law applying to companies generally.[26]

8.053

This clause is one of three clauses (with Clause 24.3 *(GENERAL UNDER-TAKINGS: Negative pledge)* and Clause 25.5 *(EVENTS OF DEFAULT: Cross default)*) which are important to an unsecured lender to ensure that they are equal with other lenders to the borrower outside of the syndicate. The intention is to ensure that the syndicate of lenders for this loan is at least equal with all other unsecured creditors, or, if not, that they know which creditors have priority.

The pari passu clause simply requires this loan to be of at least equal ranking with other unsecured debts (see Box 8.10).

> **Box 8.10**
>
> In other words, it requires the borrower to confirm that, on a winding up, to the extent that the lenders have an unsecured claim, they will share the assets

---

[26] The lenders might like to consider what obligations are mandatorily preferred by law.

252 Representations, Undertakings and Events of Default

> which are available to unsecured creditors, pro rata with such other creditors, subject to the exceptions set out in the clause.

8.054

It does not prevent the borrower from

- giving security for other debts—that is the purpose of the negative pledge;
- agreeing different, more favourable, terms in any loan agreements with other creditors—again, a specific covenant is needed to achieve this[27];
- paying other debts before making payment on the loan—if lenders want to achieve this, an undertaking not to prepay those other debts will be necessary (although in the context of sovereign debt two cases in the US involving Argentina cast some doubt on this proposition—see Box 8.11).

Box 8.11

During 2012/2013 the conventional understanding of the pari passu clause was successfully challenged by the US decision in the case of NML Capital v Argentina (26 Oct 2012). In that case, Argentina had issued bonds which contained a pari passu clause which stated that

1. *The Securities will constitute ... unsubordinated obligations of the Republic* and
2. *The payment obligations of the Republic under the Securities shall at all times rank at least equally with all its other ... [indebtedness]'.*

The court held that these two sentences addressed different issues, with the first being an agreement about the legal ranking of the debt (i.e. having the meaning which the pari passu clause in a loan agreement has conventionally been understood to mean). The second sentence (which is very similar to the LMA wording) was held to be an undertaking to make payment on its debts rateably—that is, not to give preference to some debts over others when choosing which to pay.

The court was influenced by a number of facts

- the fact that the clause appeared in a sovereign debt instrument—therefore the conventional interpretation of the clause as being a description of the

---

[27] Although, to an extent, the cross default clause has this effect, in relation to undertakings, if not in relation to fees and Margin. See discussion on Clause 25.5 (*EVENTS OF DEFAULT: Cross default*) subclause (d) in 8.250.

Clause 21: Representations—Section 2—The LMA Representations 253

> legal status of debts on a winding up cannot have been the purpose of the clause since sovereign states cannot be wound up;
> - the fact that Argentina passed a law (the 'Lock Law') prohibiting the Argentinian state from making payments on the **securities**; and
> - the existence of the two separate limbs of the clause noted earlier.
>
> The court was at pains to point out that it was not deciding on the meaning of the clause in general, but only on its application in the specific facts of the case.
> In a subsequent US case (White Hawthorne llc v Argentina) the same pari passu clause was given a different interpretation.[28]

8.055

In the context of sovereign debt, the function of the clause is debatable although the general opinion in the UK at least has been strongly opposed to the 'rateable payment' interpretation given to the clause in the case discussed in Box 8.11. Outside sovereign debt the rateable payment interpretation is even more suspect. It is hard to see how any borrower could comply with such an obligation unless it were limited to debts which originally fell due on the same day. In any event, outside sovereign debt, lenders have no need of the clause since they are protected by insolvency laws dealing with preferential payments.

Nevertheless, in view of the uncertainties created by the case quoted at Box 8.11, borrowers would be well advised to clarify the drafting, particularly in the (not uncommon) cases where there is not only a pari passu representation, but an undertaking as well.

8.056

The clause itself, on investigation, might look puzzling. It states that the obligations under the loan are at least pari passu with other creditors except for (a) secured creditors; (b) subordinated creditors; and (c) creditors preferred by laws applying to companies generally.

In most countries, these three specified circumstances are the main ways in which one claim may have a different priority to others and therefore it might be thought that the clause was unnecessary as it simply states the obvious truth. However, the clause is included because, although those are the three *main* ways in which two debts may have different priorities in insolvency, there are sometimes other, exceptional ways, which the lenders wish to be

---

[28] See the discussion at Wood, International Loans, Bonds, Guarantees, Legal opinions, 3rd ed from 11–027 onwards.

254 Representations, Undertakings and Events of Default

advised of (and not to be obliged to lend, if the position is that their loan will be junior to other, ordinary creditors without security).

For example, it may be that the law in the borrower's country,

8.057

- allows one claim to be preferred over another without giving security and without consent of the creditor who is effectively subordinated[29];

8.058

- provides that loans with certain attributes will be subordinate to others—as in the case of the English position on loans where the return to the lender varies with the profits of the borrower.[30]

The representation is helpful, therefore, in ensuring that the lawyers involved consider whether any such subordination may be applicable.

8.059

However, the pari passu clause gives the lenders little comfort unless they also know what claims may be preferred by operation of law applying to companies generally. Common examples are tax and employee payments as well as, sometimes, payments to certain companies such as public utility companies. This is an area for the lenders' due diligence. Having established what claims may have priority by operation of law, the lenders may want to include undertakings by the borrower not to allow indebtedness to those creditors to exceed a given amount.

Should Clause 21.12 *(Pari passu ranking)* repeat?

8.060

It is possible for the loan to cease to be pari passu with other creditors, for example, if there were a change in the law of the relevant jurisdiction. Therefore this representation can be repeated after the first drawdown in normal circumstances.

---

[29] As was the case in Spain until 2003, (and may still be the case in Spanish law-based jurisdictions) where **execution** of a debt instrument as an 'escritura publica' gave this priority.

[30] See discussion on the definition of 'Margin' at 1.041 onwards.

Clause 21: Representations—Section 2—The LMA Representations   255

> In a more complex transaction, if the risk of change of law is not to fall simply on the borrower it might be appropriate to recast this[31] to give appropriate possibilities to the borrower to remedy the situation.

Clause 21.13 No proceedings

8.061

This clause reads

(a) *No litigation, arbitration or administrative proceedings of or before any court, arbitral body or agency which, if adversely determined, might reasonably be expected to have a Material Adverse Effect has or have (to the best of its knowledge and belief) been started or threatened against it or any of its Subsidiaries.*

(b) *No judgement or order of a court, arbitral body or agency which might reasonably be expected to have a Material Adverse Effect has or ..... been made against it or any of its Subsidiaries.*

The reference to administrative proceedings is intended to pick up references to competition authorities and the like. Sometimes lenders extend this representation so as to also confirm that there is no litigation against the directors of any Obligor.

8.062

Comment The impact of this clause depends on whether the definition of 'Material Adverse Effect' relates to the effect on the group as a whole, or on any individual Obligor, or on any individual member of the group.

8.063

Assuming for the moment that this representation is not a 'Repeating Representation', borrowers' comments on it will be made in light of the circumstances which exist at or about the time the representation is being discussed.

---

[31] Or at least to ensure that the Event of Default relating to misrepresentations is not an automatic Event of Default but allows a period for remedy.

256 Representations, Undertakings and Events of Default

8.064

Comment In subclause (a), the borrower may wish to request the removal of the words 'if adversely determined' (or the addition of the words 'is reasonably likely to be adversely determined and which') particularly if the representation is to be repeated after the initial drawdown. These words have the effect that *any* proceedings taking place that could have a material adverse effect could trigger the clause and prevent drawing (or worse, result in acceleration if the representation is repeated) even though the proceedings in question are highly unlikely to have that result because the case in question is unlikely to succeed against the borrower.

8.065

Comment This representation has an important caveat—only litigation or judgements which might reasonably be expected to have a material adverse effect (in the case of litigation, if it were to be adversely determined) is relevant. The lenders may wish, in certain circumstances, to remove this carve-out at least for the initial representation, to ensure it has full details of all litigation at the time the loan agreement is signed. Both parties might prefer to use a monetary figure to gain more precision.

Should Clause 21.13 *(No proceedings)* repeat?

8.066

Subclause (a) of this representation should not repeat in its current form, since the effect is that the existence of major litigation would give lenders the right to accelerate, regardless of the merits of the case—see 8.064. Provided the words 'if adversely affected' are deleted then the representation may be repeated but there is a danger of a conflict arising between this Repeating Representation and any Events of Default dealing with litigation or judge-ments. There is no Event of Default relating to litigation in the LMA Compounded/Term Rate Loan. The nearest is Clause 25.8 *(EVENTS OF DEFAULT: Creditors' process)*, dealing with the execution of judgements. This may lead the borrower to assume that litigation against it will not give rise to an Event of Default unless the circumstances in Clause 25.8 *(EVENTS OF DEFAULT: Creditors' process)* occur. If lenders intend litigation to give rise to an Event of Default in circumstances which fall short of those referred to in Clause 25.8 *(EVENTS OF DEFAULT: Creditors' process)* then the clearest way to achieve this is to include an Event of Default to this effect and not to repeat this representation.

Clause 21: Representations—Section 2—The LMA Representations   257

Similarly, subclause (b) should not repeat—if lenders intend that judgements against the borrower should be an Event of Default in certain circumstances, the best way to achieve that would be to add an appropriate Event of Default rather than to repeat this representation.

Representations in different circumstances

8.067

The representations in Clause 21.5 *(REPRESENTATIONS: Validity and admissibility in evidence)* subclause (b), 21.6 *(REPRESENTATIONS: Governing law and enforcement),* Clause 21.7 *(REPRESENTATIONS: Deduction of Tax)* and Clause 21.8 *(REPRESENTATIONS: No filing or stamp taxes)* are not usually required of an English borrower in a straightforward unsecured loan, since, in those circumstances, these issues are a matter of English law on which the lenders, by common practice, are content to rely on their own lawyers.

The LMA Compounded/Term Rate Loan includes only very basic representations which will be applicable in all cases, covering issues such as power and authority. Additional representations will be necessary to reflect the specific transaction and the requirements of the lenders' credit decision.[32]

Clause 21.14 Repetition

8.068

This is the clause which deems certain representations to be repeated on certain dates during the life of the loan. It reads.

21.14 The Repeating Representations are deemed to be made by each Obligor by reference to the facts and circumstances then existing on

(a) the date of each Utilization Request and the first day of each Interest Period

...

8.069

For comments on Clause 21.14 *(REPRESENTATIONS: Repetition)* see 8.007 onwards and see also the commentary on each individual representation from 8.021 onwards.

---

[32] See Sect. 2 of the comments on Clause 24 *(General Undertakings)* from 8.199 onwards.

258 Representations, Undertakings and Events of Default

Possible Additional Representations

Sanctions

8.070
The scope of sanctions provisions varies considerably and needs to reflect the nature of the borrower's business. The core topics which are commonly included are.

- Policies and procedures—the borrower must have policies in place to ensure it complies with sanctions laws.
- Use of proceeds. Borrowers must not use the loan to finance an activity which breaches sanctions (e.g. purchase of goods from a country which is the subject of comprehensive sanctions).
- Sanctions targets and sanctioned countries. Borrowers must confirm that the group, its officers and employees are not on any sanctions list and that the group does not do business in a country which is the subject of comprehensive sanctions.

8.071
Other sanctions-related topics on which the lenders may want assurances include.

- Compliance—assurances that the group is not doing business in breach of any relevant sanctions.
- Clean funds—assurances that the loan will not be repaid from any source of income which breaches sanctions laws.
- Absence of investigations—assurances that no member of the group or its officers or employees is being investigated for sanctions breaches

8.072
Lenders are likely to want assurance on the relevant issues both at drawdown and also on an ongoing basis. As a result, representations on these issues may be Repeating Representations or alternatively, the ongoing assurances may be given by way of undertakings or Events of Default. As always, if there are both Repeating Representations and undertakings or Events of Default dealing with the same issue, it is important to ensure that the provisions are consistent and do not conflict.

8.073
Comment. Key issues for the borrower are

- Which countries' sanctions laws are relevant? The borrower will want this restricted to countries which are key to their business and the financing.
- Consequences of breach—compulsory prepayment not Event of Default.
- Limiting the extent to which the loan provisions impose additional sanctions risks on the borrower over and above the sanctions risks they have as a matter of law—see 0.188.
- Limiting the provisions with reference to materiality and knowledge.
- Dealing with the possibility of a lender being sanctioned.

Anti-corruption

8.074

Lenders commonly have policies and procedures designed to prevent bribery by those with whom they do business. The existence of such policies can be an effective defence to actions under legislation such as the UK Bribery Act 2010. Such policies may include a requirement for contractual protection, in the form of representations and undertakings, addressing the issue. As a result, although the LMA Compounded/Term Rate Loan does not include anti-corruption clauses, these are commonly added. They often follow the form of the core sanctions provisions and include assurances as to

- The borrower's compliance with relevant anti-corruption laws,
- The existence of policies and procedures designed to prevent bribery and
- No use of funds from the loan for bribery.

As with sanctions, lenders are likely to want assurance on the relevant issues both at drawdown and also on an ongoing basis. Again it is important to ensure any ongoing provisions are consistent, as discussed in 8.010.

Clauses 22–24: Undertakings—An Introduction

1. Purpose

8.075

The purposes of the undertakings are to ensure the lenders have the information they need; to ensure good housekeeping by the borrower; to give the lenders leverage; and to protect the borrower's assets.

The undertakings in the LMA Compounded/Term Rate Loan cover:

260 Representations, Undertakings and Events of Default

- Clause 22 (*Information Undertakings*);
- Clause 23 (*Financial Covenants*) and
- Clause 24 (*General Undertakings*) consisting of positive and negative undertakings relating to the protection of assets.

Other undertakings are likely to be required in any given case as discussed in Sect. 2 of the comments on Clause 24 *(General Undertakings)* from 8.199 onwards.

The undertakings are expressed to cease to be effective once there is no longer any loan outstanding.[33]

2. Shadow Directors

8.076

One issue which lenders should be aware of when exercising their rights under a loan agreement is the concept of '**shadow directors**'[34] A shadow director is a person in accordance with whose instructions the directors of a company are accustomed to act. There are similar concepts of de facto directors in many jurisdictions. The risk for the lenders is that, in times of financial difficulty, the lenders may step in and start to take an active role in the management of the borrower's business, thereby potentially becoming a shadow director and assuming the responsibilities of directors. The particular concern is that the lenders may then take on liability for issues like **wrongful trading** (under English law) or negligent mismanagement (under some other laws) under the local law in the place where the borrower is trading.[35] Whether a lender is a shadow director is a question of fact. See Box 8.12 for some examples of cases where the issue has been considered.

Box 8.12

- In Re PFTZM Ltd [1995] BCC 280, the lenders held weekly management meetings with a borrower in financial difficulties, monitoring the business. The court held that they were not a shadow director.
- In Ultraframe v Fielding [2005] EWHC 1638 (Ch) it was held that imposing conditions on the availability of financial support was not sufficient to make

---

[33] It is important to be clear that other provisions such as indemnities and undertakings to reimburse the lenders are not limited in this way. A claim under these other clauses may need to be made after the loan has been fully repaid, or before it is advanced.

[34] s251 Companies Act 2006.

[35] See comments on Clause 25.13 *(EVENTS OF DEFAULT: Acceleration)* in 8.290.

> the lenders shadow directors even if the circumstances resulted in the directors feeling that they had no practical choice other than to comply with those conditions.
> * In the Australian case *Buzzle Operations Pty Ltd (in liquidation) v Apple Computer Australia Pty Ltd*, ([2011] NSWCA 109) the court emphasized the difference between the situation where the directors take their own decisions, taking the lenders' views into account, and the situation where the directors are really ceding decision-making to the lenders.

3. Qualifications

8.077

Borrowers are likely to want to reduce the impact of the undertakings in a number of ways. The most common types of restrictions are:

* only prohibiting the relevant action if it is material or could have a material adverse effect;
* introduction of some reasonableness standard (e.g. 'reasonable' expenses, expenses 'reasonably incurred', 'reasonable' opinion, not to be 'unreasonably withheld', 'reasonably likely', etc.);
* requiring a greater degree of certainty or a closer link, for example, by replacing 'desirable' with 'necessary' or replacing 'could' with 'is likely to' or limiting indemnities to losses 'directly' caused by the relevant act;
* limiting the companies whose acts are restricted (see 0.142 onwards);
* baskets, allowing the prohibited act (such as the creation of security) in limited amounts (see Box 8.13).

Box 8.13

Issues to consider here are:

* whether the amount allowed is an annual figure or an absolute cap (or perhaps an annual figure plus a limit on the total allowed during the whole loan).
* if it is an annual figure, whether unused amounts can be carried forwards or backwards.
* whether the figure is a fixed amount or a formula (such as 5% of Tangible Net Worth).
* the size of the basket—generally lenders will want to impose very modest baskets on the negative pledge and on any prohibitions on incurring debt.

262   Representations, Undertakings and Events of Default

- whether each 'basket' is independent of the others (for example, if the borrower is permitted to dispose of fixed assets up to a value of $10 million, and is also allowed to give security up to an amount of $10 million, could an unused allowance on sale of assets be used to increase the amount of permitted security, so that the borrower could give security for $15 million provided its disposals of fixed assets were no higher than $5 million?).
- permissions for intra group transactions.
- permissions for transactions in the ordinary course of business (see Box 8.28).
- requiring only 'reasonable endeavours' to perform the undertaking (see Box 8.14).

Box 8.14

There is a difference between 'reasonable endeavours', 'all reasonable endeavours' and 'best endeavours', with 'reasonable endeavours' being at the lowest end of the scale and 'best endeavours' at the top end. Although the interpretation of a contract will always depend on the circumstances, there is case law which suggests that 'reasonable endeavours' might require the person to follow ONE reasonable course of action to achieve the result, while 'all reasonable endeavours' might require the party to explore ALL avenues reasonably available—that is, to leave no stone unturned. 'Best endeavours' has been described as an obligation to take steps 'which a prudent, determined and reasonable [person], acting in his own interests and designed to achieve that result would take'. But it does not include actions which would not be likely to succeed, and, depending on the context, it does not require the person to disregard its own financial interests entirely.[36] Too much should not be read into these observations however as each case will turn on its facts. Often in practice, when the issue has come before the courts, the question has been whether there have been any endeavours at all. Any Obligor would be well advised to keep records of all endeavours and to inform lenders of any difficulties.

Covenant Lite Loans

8.078

It is also worth mentioning that in the US leveraged syndicated loan market it is normal for there to be significant loosening of the undertakings which would be seen in other markets (see Box 8.15). According to the S&P/LSTA

---

[36] See Jet2.Com Limited v Blackpool Airport Limited [2012] EWCA Civ 417, where a number of cases were reviewed.

leverage loan index as of October 2021, 86% of outstanding US leveraged loans were covenant lite, despite research showing that recovery on covenant lite loans is lower than on other loans.

Box 8.15

Some of the features of these 'covenant lite' loans include:

- incurrence, rather than maintenance financial covenants (see 8.118)
- very loose financial ratios (so that breaches only occur if results are up to 50% off projections, as opposed to traditional cushions of 15% or so)
- **equity cure** rights (see 8.124)
- More unrestricted subsidiaries
- Ability to pay dividends and repay subordinated debt provided financial ratios are met (as opposed to, traditionally, only out of that part of excess **cashflow** not required to be used to prepay the loan)
- Long (say 60 day) grace periods on the Events of Default, misrepresentation not leading to Events of Default, and cross acceleration rather than cross default (see Box 8.39) and
- Ability to borrow money and make acquisitions provided certain financial ratios are met.

---

4. Cumulative Nature

8.079

Another issue which the borrower needs to consider is the fact that the provisions in the agreement are cumulative. The borrower may find that an act which is permitted under one provision may be prohibited under another provision. There are numerous examples:

- the borrower may have negotiated a provision which has the effect that material litigation is not an Event of Default if it is being contested and reserves have been made for it, but they may find that if they have to pay money into court in relation to the litigation—that causes a breach of the negative pledge;
- the borrower may be complying with its financial ratios but the lenders may still claim that there has been a material adverse change in its financial condition, triggering the material adverse change Event of Default;

264 Representations, Undertakings and Events of Default

- the borrower may have negotiated equity cure rights but it may find that they cannot exercise them because they have also undertaken not to issue new shares;
- the borrower may have negotiated the right to enter into certain types of derivatives in the undertaking relating to derivatives but may find that that is prohibited by the undertaking relating to Financial Indebtedness;
- the borrower may have the right to enter into cash pooling arrangements in certain circumstances under the negative pledge but may still find that cash pooling results in a breach of undertakings, for example, an undertaking not to lend money; or
- the borrower may believe they have the right to change the group structure; buy new companies and sell existing companies, but they may find that although this is not expressly prohibited, they have not negotiated appropriate carve-outs from any 'no disposals' or 'no acquisitions' undertakings to enable them to do this.

8.080

The list is endless.

Some borrowers try to deal with this by having a concept that if a transaction is specifically permitted by one clause, it is permitted for all purposes in the document. This causes two problems:

- First, it only works where transactions are specifically permitted, as opposed to falling outside the clause.
- Second, more importantly, the various prohibitions in the document are cumulative. So for example, lenders may be happy to agree that litigation is not an Event of Default if it is being contested and reserves have been made for it. However, quite separately from that, they have concerns about the provision of security, so that if the litigation in question requires the posting of security, that may well make a difference to the lenders' position.

In practice therefore, whenever borrowers negotiate carve-outs to one provision, they need to consider what other provisions are relevant and request corresponding changes to those provisions as well.

Clause 22: Information Undertakings   **265**

Clause 22: Information Undertakings

Clause 22.1 Financial statements

8.081

In this clause the company agrees to provide financial statements to the lenders.

There are a number of issues here.

8.082

- Which companies should the accounts relate to? This needs to reflect the credit decision and the basis on which financial ratios are tested.[37] The LMA Compounded/Term Rate Loan requires consolidated statements for the Company (the highest level in the group to which the lenders have recourse, which thus gives financial information for the whole of the group below the Company), and individual statements for each Obligor (thus ensuring that the lenders have financial information relating to those companies against which they have direct claims).

8.083

- How much time is allowed for preparation of the statements?

8.084

- Which types of financial statements are required? Normally, the lenders require annual audited statements plus half-yearly unaudited statements. This is what the LMA Compounded/Term Rate Loan provides for. In the case of sub-investment grade borrowers, lenders, not uncommonly, require additional financial statements such as monthly management accounts. In view of the possibility that some lenders may also be involved in trading in shares, there may be concerns that some information they receive under the loan agreement could constitute insider information which could restrict their ability to trade in the relevant shares. To protect against this risk the LMA added a provision (Clause 28.14 (*ROLE OF THE AGENT, THE ARRANGER AND THE ISSUING BANK: Relationship with the Lenders)* subclause (b)) allowing lenders who do not want to receive non-public

---

[37] See discussion of financial ratios in 8.117.

266 Representations, Undertakings and Events of Default

information to nominate a third party to receive information on their behalf. That third party can then filter the information as appropriate. Borrowers would be reluctant to take this role of filtering the information on themselves both because of the administrative burden and also due to fears of potential liability.

Clause 22.2 Compliance Certificate

8.085
This clause will be required where there are financial ratios. It requires the Company to deliver a Compliance Certificate (in the form attached as a schedule) signed by two directors of the company, with each set of financial statements, confirming that the ratios have been met and setting out their calculations of the figures. The Compliance Certificate also requires the directors to confirm that there is no Default (or, if there is a Default, to explain the facts).

The clause provides, as an option, for an auditor's certificate to be produced with the audited annual statements confirming compliance with the financial ratios. The auditor's willingness to do this needs their prior approval. They are only likely to agree to this if the form of report is agreed in advance and the lenders engage them directly to issue these reports.

8.086
If there are no financial ratios then lenders may decide to delete the requirement for Compliance Certificates. However, caution is needed here because the certificates also have the important function of requiring the borrower to consider the question of whether there is a Default on a regular basis.

Sometimes borrowers argue that regular confirmation of the position in relation to Defaults is unnecessary because the agreement contains an obligation to notify of a Default in any event. Lenders are likely to resist that because often it is not readily apparent that a Default exists, so it is useful to impose an obligation on the borrower, requiring them to pro-actively consider the question on a regular basis.

Clause 22.3 Requirements as to financial statements

8.087
This clause establishes certain requirements in relation to the financial statements. It

Clause 22: Information Undertakings   267

- requires a director to certify that each set of financial statements fairly reflects the financial position of the company; and
- requires each set of financial statements to be prepared using GAAP (which may or may not include IFRS as discussed in 1.035).

8.088

The clause gives the draftsperson two choices: either (i) the accounts are to be prepared in accordance with the relevant GAAP as it changes from time to time; or (ii) it gives the borrower the option to prepare the statements in accordance with the original GAAP, or to use changing GAAP with a reconciliation of what the figures would have looked like if the original GAAP had been used.

The second is known as a 'frozen GAAP' provision and is usually used to facilitate the working and testing of financial ratios.

As a practical matter, if the clause provides for a frozen GAAP provision then, if GAAP changes, there will be an additional administrative burden for the borrower in the production of ALL subsequent sets of accounts, during the whole life of the loan. For this reason, borrowers might like to require lenders to commit in advance to agree on appropriate changes to the financial ratios to reflect the change in GAAP going forward, and so remove the need to continue to provide these reconciliations to original GAAP. See Box 8.16 for appropriate wording to achieve this.

Box 8.16

The following wording, which was agreed between the Association of Corporate Treasurers and the LMA in the context of the move to IFRS in the UK, would also be suitable to deal with any other changes in GAAP:

If the Company notifies the Agent in accordance with [ ] (requirements as to financial statements) the Company and the Agent shall enter into negotiations in good faith with a view to agreeing any amendments to this Agreement which are necessary as a result of the change. To the extent practicable these amendments will be such as to ensure that the change does not result in any material alteration in the commercial effect of the obligations in this Agreement. If any amendments are agreed they shall take effect and be binding on each of the Parties in accordance with their terms.

268 Representations, Undertakings and Events of Default

Clause 22.4 Information: miscellaneous

8.089

Subclause (a) of this clause requires the borrower to give the lenders copies of all documents which the borrower sends to its shareholders.

8.090

Comment Subclause (a) is intended to ensure that those events that are significant enough to be notified to shareholders and/or creditors are, at the same time, notified to the lenders. However, in the case of private companies, it may be appropriate to limit the requirement to apply only to information which the borrower delivers to creditors or *is required by law* to deliver to its shareholders, since shareholders of private companies are often intimately involved in the day-to-day management and may receive more information than would be appropriate for a lender.

8.091

Clause 22.4 (*INFORMATION UNDERSTANDINGS: Information: miscellaneous*) at subclauses (b) and (c) require the borrower to give the lenders details of any significant litigation or judgements against them. They reflect the wording of the representations on litigation and judgements contained in Clause 21.13 (*REPRESENTATIONS: No proceedings*).

8.092

Comment This clause ought to reflect any changes agreed to in Clause 21.13 (*REPRESENTATIONS: No proceedings*) discussed from 8.061 onwards.[38]

8.093

Comment If (as suggested) Clause 21.13 (*REPRESENTATIONS: No proceedings*) is not repeated then, under the LMA Compounded/Term Rate Loan, the lenders will be entitled to be advised of litigation or judgements which fall within this clause but will not have any rights to take action as a result of such litigation or judgement unless the circumstances also constitute an Event of Default under, for example, the material adverse change Event of Default or the cross default clause. Lenders may wish to consider whether they want significant litigation or judgements to be an Event of Default[39] and, if not, whether they wish to be advised of it.

---

[38] Such as any removal of the presumption that litigation will be adversely determined, and any restriction of the scope of the clause, for example, to relate to Obligors only.

[39] See further commentary on Clause 21.13 (*REPRESENTATIONS: No proceedings*) in 8.061 and on Clause 25.8 (*EVENTS OF DEFAULT: Creditors' process*) in 8.266.

8.094

Clause 22.4 *(INFORMATION UNDERTAKINGS: Information miscellaneous)* subclause (d) requires the borrower to supply such further information about its business (or that of any group member) as any lender may reasonably request.

8.095

Comment The borrower may want to restrict Clause 22.4 *(INFORMATION UNDERTAKINGS: Information miscellaneous)* subclause (d) to exclude certain group members or to include only Obligors.[40] They may also want to restrict the generality of the clause[41] so as to discourage frequent unwarranted requests, particularly as the clause relates to the requirements of 'any Finance Party' so exposing the borrower to the requirements of every lender. Nevertheless, borrowers should bear in mind that the provision of information to lenders is often as much in the interests of the borrowers as the lenders, because it facilitates well-informed decisions by lenders.

Clause 22.5 Notification of default

8.096

This clause requires the borrower to notify the lenders of a Default, and, if requested, to confirm that there is no Default or, if there is a Default, to advise how it is being dealt with. One might query what incentive there is for the borrower to comply with this undertaking since, if there is a Default, then failure to notify the lenders of that fact will constitute another Default but will not make the borrower's legal position any worse.[42] See also the comments on Compliance Certificates in 8.086.

For this reason, it is important that the drafting ensures that failure to notify of a Default does indeed make the borrower's position worse. This is achieved by ensuring (in Clause 25.3 *(EVENTS OF DEFAULT: Other obligations))* that this undertaking either has no grace period or has only a very short grace period before it becomes an Event of Default. As a result, a breach of this undertaking results in an Event of Default (not just a Default) even though the grace period for the underlying Default may not have expired (see Box 8.17).

---

[40] See the discussion of the scope of the agreement from 0.142 onwards.

[41] Although they already have the benefit of the word 'reasonably'.

[42] Since the lenders have no more rights if there are two defaults than if there is only one.

270   Representations, Undertakings and Events of Default

Box 8.17

So, for example, the borrower may be in breach of the undertaking in Clause 24.1 *(GENERAL UNDERTAKINGS: Authorizations)* to maintain all necessary authorizations for performance of its obligations. Under Clause 25.3 *(EVENTS OF DEFAULT: Other obligations)* subclause (b), let us assume that a grace period of ten days has been given for this particular undertaking. Once the borrower realizes that a necessary authorization is missing, that is a Default but not an Event of Default. If the borrower fails to notify the lenders 'promptly' of the fact that an authorization is missing, that failure to notify is a breach of Clause 22.5 *(GENERAL UNDERTAKINGS: Notification of default)* and a Default in its own right. As long as no grace period has been given in relation to Clause 22.5 *GENERAL UNDERTAKINGS: (Notification of default)*, it is also an immediate Event of Default, so failure to notify has the result of depriving the borrower of the grace period they would otherwise have had in respect of the original Default.

8.097

Comment Lenders may prefer to replace the word 'promptly' with a specific time period.

Clause 22.6 Direct electronic delivery by company

8.098

This clause contains provisions which allow for communication by the Company electronically.

Clause 22.7 'Know Your Customer' checks

8.099

This clause contains provisions requiring delivery of information as necessary to allow the Agent and the lenders to comply with any applicable 'know your customer' regulations.[43]

These checks need to be carried out before signing. This clause requires additional information to be delivered in the event of a change of law, a change of status of an Obligor (e.g. de-listing), or a proposed secondary market purchase.

---

[43] Which, in England, arise under the Money Laundering, Terrorist Financing and Transfer of Funds (information on the Payer) (regulations 2017 (SI 2017/692) (as amended).

Clause 23: Financial Covenants

1. Purpose

8.100
Lenders use financial covenants for a number of reasons—

- Firstly they help to impose discipline on the borrower and to focus the attention of management on key financial goals.
- Secondly, they provide a mechanism by which the lenders can monitor the performance of the borrower's business and get early warning of any deterioration.
- Next, they can also be used to provide incentives for the borrower to achieve certain financial targets. For example, it is common to have provisions by which the Margin reduces or dividends are permitted, when targets are met.
- Lastly, at the end of the day, the financial covenants operate as a stop loss. That is, if the desired financial results cannot be met, the financial covenants give the lenders the right to accelerate the loan and exit the transaction.

8.101
The main questions which need to be considered in relation to the ratios are:

- which aspects of the borrower's financial condition should be tested?
- at which level of the group should the tests be run?
- in respect of what periods should the the tests be run?
- what should the consequences of breach of a ratio be?
- can a breach be cured? and
- how should the various words used in the tests be defined?

2. Which aspects of the borrower's financial condition should be tested?

8.102
A number of different ratios may be used, each of which is designed to highlight different types of financial difficulty, before these problems become entrenched. Precisely which ratios to test clearly depends on the identity of the borrower—with significantly fewer, and simpler, tests being used for

272   Representations, Undertakings and Events of Default

investment grade borrowers than in other situations. Ratios which may be tested include

- interest cover
- cashflow
- leverage
- liquidity
- gearing and
- tangible net worth.

8.103
In addition, financial tests may be used

- to restrict capital expenditure
- to give rise to a requirement for prepayment (a 'cash sweep') and
- sometimes, only to restrict taking on additional debt—that is, they are used on an 'incurrence' as opposed to a 'maintenance' basis (see 8.118)

8.104
And finally,

- it is because of certain limitations in the ratios that lenders will often include a 'clean down period' in a revolving credit.

We will look at these issues in turn, starting with interest cover.

Interest Cover

8.105
This ratio looks at the financial period just ended and compares income earned during that period (net of expenses) with the interest payable on loans during that period. The purpose of this ratio is to identify how easy it is for the borrower to service interest on its loans out of current income and without having recourse, for example, to sale of assets, past income, or currency exchange gains. The concept of EBITDA is used to define income earned. See Box 8.18.

Clause 23: Financial Covenants **273**

> **Box 8.18**
>
> EBITDA stands for Earnings before Interest, Tax, Depreciation and Amortization. It also excludes profits and losses from unusual items. It represents the total profit of the company for the period in question, disregarding the effect of
>
> - unusual items such as major asset sales, currency losses and currency profits—because what we are trying to get at is the core income of the company, to the extent that it can be earned again and again—it is **maintainable** earnings which are being measured,
> - tax and interest,—because these are not indicators of the health of the underlying business so they 'muddy the water',
> - depreciation and amortization—because these are notional figures reflecting the price paid for assets (in the case of depreciation) or goodwill (in the case of amortization) and the decision of the finance director about how long that asset would have value—again, nothing to do with the health of the company.

Cashflow

8.106

The second income-related ratio looks at cashflow. This ratio looks at actual cash received in a given period (net of cash paid out) and compares it with total scheduled loan payments during that period.

The point to focus on here is the distinction between earnings and cash. The difference is explained by the accruals concept, which is used in preparing a company's profit and loss accounts. That concept requires income and expenses to be allocated to the period in which they were earned or accrued even if payment is not made until some time later (or at all). So for example, if services are provided during December but not billed till January, the accounts will nevertheless show the price of those services in the December figures. So the accounts (and EBITDA) will recognize income before that income is actually received. Indeed, that income may never be received. So the cashflow ratio looks at cash actually received rather than money earned which may not be received. See Box 8.19.

> **Box 8.19**
>
> Ideally, Lenders would like to have both an interest cover ratio and a cashflow ratio because there are two ways in which a company may find that it doesn't have enough income to pay its debts—it either didn't earn enough in the first

274   Representations, Undertakings and Events of Default

place (the interest cover ratio will reveal this) or it earned the income but for some reason did not get paid (the cashflow test is designed to reveal this). An example may help. Assume a company has interest payments to make each month in the amount of $250,000.

In scenario 1 the company earns $1,000,000 in January but does not get paid until March, meaning that there is a potential problem paying the interest due in February. If the only test made in January was the interest cover ratio then there is no apparent cause for alarm—the company has earned plenty of money with which to pay the interest—but it has not received the cash yet. A cashflow cover test in January and February will reveal whether this is a problem building up or not.

Similarly in scenario 2 assume the company earns nothing in January but receives payment for work done in the previous year. The fact of having earned nothing in January may give rise to a problem paying the interest due in February and March. A cashflow test in January will not reveal any problem as the company has received plenty of cash with which to pay the January interest. An interest cover test in January would reveal the potential problem.

8.107

The cashflow ratio is different from the interest cover ratio in that

- it is concerned with all loan payments, not just interest, and
- it focuses on actual cash receipts and payments as opposed to income earned (but not received yet) and expenses accrued.

Hence it is useful to have tests based on cash actually received—that is, the cashflow test. But it is also useful to have a test (the interest cover ratio) based on income earned (EBITDA) in order to give advance warning of future cashflow problems.

Leverage (or Debt Cover)

8.108

This looks at the relationship between EBITDA for a period and the total amount of the borrower's debts. The purpose of the ratio is to look at the longer term—the whole life of the loan, and examine how easy it is for the borrower to pay off their total debts out of core maintainable earnings. It is similar to the income multiple used in consumer mortgages.

It is also worth noting that both the cashflow ratio and the interest cover ratio just look at payments of principal and interest which are scheduled to be made during the current period. They ignore future debt repayments and unscheduled repayments such as payments under a revolving credit. They also do not take into account debts on which no interest is due (such as PIK[44] notes—where interest may be capitalized). So, to take an extreme example, if the borrower's only financing was a loan which capitalized interest and had a **bullet repayment** after seven years, the company could earn practically nothing but neither the interest cover ratio nor the cashflow ratio would reveal a problem because those ratios are only looking at the ability to service the interest and principal which is scheduled to be paid in the period in question. So those tests would not highlight the issue ahead as to whether the company had enough to pay the final payments and capitalized interest.

This leverage ratio is therefore useful to address the total borrowing, regardless of maturities.

Liquidity

8.109

Another important ratio is the liquidity ratio, or 'quick' ratio. This is a test of solvency and compares current assets to current liabilities. It is somewhat unusual to see this ratio in a loan agreement, but, if it is included, the drafting will need to deal with how to value **contingent liabilities** such as guarantees (since those liabilities may never fall due) and how to value stock (since ultimately it may not be sold at the anticipated price).

This test is perhaps not as useful as the cashflow test or the interest cover test since it does not identify the time at which the assets were generated. So, for example, the company may be able to meet the liquidity ratio even if it earns no income for years, as long as it has cash in the bank generated by a single good piece of business sometime in the past.

However the liquidity cover ratio is a useful supplement to the other ratios because, at the end of the day, the issue is whether the borrower has liquid assets with which to pay its current debts. This ratio looks at ALL current debts so it will include payments to suppliers, employees, tax and the like. Liquidity was a key issue during the COVID pandemic, with some lenders suspending the operation of the usual earnings-related financial covenants on existing loans and replacing them with liquidity tests—the key question at that time was whether the company had enough cash to survive the crisis.

---

[44] Standing for 'payment in kind', see 0.036.

Gearing

8.110

The gearing ratio looks at the amount borrowed and compares it with the balance sheet value of the company to see if the company has over-borrowed against its assets. The relationship between the amount of borrowing and the amount invested in the company by shareholders will have a significant impact on the resilience of the company in times of financial stress. See Box 8.20.

Box 8.20

Gearing

Take the example of an investment trust. Investment trusts can borrow money to invest. This is called gearing. Gearing improves an investment trust's performance when its investments are doing well. On the other hand, if its investments do not do as well as expected, gearing lowers performance.

Example

If the investment trust is made up of £50 m of investors' money and £50 m of borrowing then the total fund available for investment is £100 m. Say the value of the fund goes down by 10% as a result of losses in the stockmarket— the value of the overall fund falls from £100 m to £90 m. However, bear in mind that the borrowing is still £50 m, therefore the remaining £40 m belongs to the investors.

So, although the overall fund went down by 10%, the investors' money has actually gone down by 20% (i.e. from £50m to £40m). Gearing boosts gains, but it also magnifies losses. Not all investment trusts are geared and deciding whether to borrow and when to borrow, is a judgement the investment manager makes. An investment trust that is geared is a higher-risk investment than one which is not geared (assuming the same underlying investments).

8.111

For this purpose, borrowings will include the various items (other than derivatives, and with liabilities under guarantees being a debatable item) included in the definition of Financial Indebtedness so as to catch transactions having the same commercial effect as borrowings. Subordinated debt will be an item for discussion with its treatment depending on the level of subordination.[45]

---

[45] See discussion of subordination in A1.034.

Tangible Net Worth

8.112
This test simply looks at the **book value** of the company's assets, less the amount of its liabilities. For this purpose, lenders generally exclude the value of **intangible** assets such as **goodwill**, looking instead at the value of tangible assets which can be sold. The company's assets are represented in its balance sheet by the figure shown in respect of 'shareholders funds', and therefore the starting point of the definition is the amount of shareholders' funds less items such as goodwill, which are intangible. Nevertheless, it is worth noting that the book value of the company's assets is no guide to their real value. The book value represents the price paid for assets and the assumed rate of depreciation, but that is not the same as the price at which they can be sold.

Summary

8.113
So, in summary, there are ratios which can test whether the company

* has earned enough recently to at least service interest on its debts (the interest cover ratio);
* has been paid enough recently to pay its debts (the cashflow ratio);
* has borrowed too much compared to its income (the leverage ratio);
* has borrowed too much compared with the amount invested by share-holders (the gearing ratio);
* can pay its debts as they fall due (the liquidity or quick ratio) and
* has enough assets (the Tangible Net Worth test).

In addition to these tests, lenders often impose restrictions on what the company can do with its profits. These are described next.

Restriction on Capex.

8.114
Lenders will often want to restrict the extent to which the borrower is allowed to make capital expenditures for two reasons. Firstly they want to prevent earnings, which are otherwise available for debt service, being used for other things. Secondly, they prefer the borrower to develop steadily rather than

278 Representations, Undertakings and Events of Default

in spurts. Heavy capital expenditure will usually result in increased operating costs, often with the return on the investment taking a little while to materialize. Firm and steady is therefore the preference.

Cash Sweeps

8.115
Lenders often want to ensure that if profits are high in a given period, those profits are used to prepay debt rather than being used for capital expenditure or being paid out to shareholders by way of dividends. This is particularly important in a cyclical industry.

Clean Down Period

8.116
As noted earlier, the cashflow ratio only measures the availability of cash to meet scheduled repayments. It does not address the ability to make repayments under a revolving credit. This is one reason why lenders often require a 'clean down period' in revolving credit. That is, they require the borrower to repay the revolving credit and leave it undrawn for a given period each year. This clean down is also intended to ensure that the borrower only uses the revolving credits to fund working capital needs, not as part of their permanent capital.

3. At which level of the Group should the tests be run?

8.117
This clearly needs to reflect the credit decision. Lenders may be concerned with the financial condition of the group as a whole and/or with the condition of specific companies (most likely the Obligors) within the group.[46] They may therefore wish to impose certain financial covenants on the Obligors in addition to any covenants for the group as a whole. If any specific companies (such as subsidiary undertakings or non-recourse companies)[47]

---

[46] See the discussion of the scope of the agreement from 0.146 onwards.
[47] See 0.146 onwards.

have been excluded from the definition of 'Group' then the lenders will probably want to have the ratios tested against the financial position of the group excluding those companies.[48]

4. In respect of what periods should the tests be run?

'Incurrence' tests

8.118
In covenant lite loans the financial covenants will apply on an 'incurrence' rather than a 'maintenance' basis. That is, instead of requiring the various ratios to be met in relation to successive financial periods throughout the life of the loan, they are only used on the occurrence of a specified event (for example, they may be used to prohibit the borrowing of further funds if they are not met, so that once additional funds have been borrowed, the tests will only become relevant again if the borrower wants to borrow further monies).

The rationale for this is that these lenders do not want to be consulted with requests for consent and the like, both because of manpower constraints and also because they do not wish to receive the non-public information which would go with such requests as this would hamper their freedom to invest. The size of the loan and its liquidity also enable them to take a less restrictive view than might be the case in smaller loans.

8.119
An incurrence basis for testing significantly devalues the financial ratios. Where they are tested on a 'maintenance' basis, they operate to give the lenders a steady stream of information about the business, and to forewarn the lenders if difficulties start to emerge. If the undertakings only apply on an 'incurrence' basis, this regular information flow will not occur.

'Maintenance' tests

8.120
Outside covenant lite loans, the financial ratios are drafted on a 'maintenance' basis. That is, the borrower is required to meet the ratio in each successive financial period. One drawback with these financial ratios is that there is often a mismatch between the timing of any problem and the occurrence of the

---

[48] With corresponding adjustment needed to the undertaking in Clause 22 *(Information Undertakings)* to provide financial information.

280   Representations, Undertakings and Events of Default

Event of Default. By the time a breach becomes apparent, the accounting period in which it occurred will have come to an end and the particular issue may have been resolved.[49] On the other hand, it may be evident that there is a problem and that once the accounts for the relevant period are produced, they will show a breach, but until the accounts are produced, there is nothing the lenders can do about it. It is for this reason that lenders often require to have an Event of Default relating to a material adverse change in financial condition notwithstanding the existence of financial ratios. See comments from 8.283 onwards on the interrelation of the material adverse change clause and the financial ratios.[50]

8.121
It is also worth noting here that the material adverse change Event of Default will, of necessity, be subjective—that is—it is always a question of opinion as to whether any given change is 'material' or not. So, if there is a deterioration in the financial condition of the borrower between test dates, unless the change is extreme, then lenders are likely to want to wait until there is a clearer Event of Default to rely on, rather than accelerate on the basis of the material adverse change Event of Default itself. This is in line with the general advice on the use of the material adverse change Event of Default. Nevertheless, the lenders will want the ability not to advance further funds and, if applicable, to freeze payment of dividends and the like. This is where the definition of 'Default' comes in. As long as the definition of Default is in the LMA standard form and the words 'the making of any determination' have not been excluded,[51] then the deterioration in financial condition should constitute a 'Default', enabling the lenders to freeze the loan until the situation becomes clearer.

5. What should the consequences of breach of a ratio be?

8.122
These ratios are particularly important because, unlike many of the other undertakings and Events of Default, breach of them does not necessarily

---

[49] Nevertheless, depending on the drafting of the financial ratios, the Event of Default may have occurred and, subject to anything agreed on equity cure rights, will not be capable of being cured (see 8.230).

[50] Lenders might also seek to make the tests predictive as well as historic, based on the predictions within the company's management accounts.

[51] See the discussion of 'Default' from 1.018 onwards.

mean there is a problem, simply that the credit risk has changed somewhat and that the financial assumptions made when putting the loan together are proving to have been too optimistic. They give advance warning of changes and are able to be graded subtly as opposed to the black or white nature of other provisions. For this reason, breach of a financial ratio need not be drafted to have the effect of an Event of Default. It is possible (and not uncommon) to provide that, within certain limits (breach of which will be an Event of Default) failure to meet a particular ratio simply affects the Margin.

8.123

Finance directors in established companies need to be sure that the numbers specified in the ratios are reasonable and will not give rise to an Event of Default too readily. The borrowers' argument is that, assuming the borrower is a reasonably well-established company, they need a robust loan agreement which will see them not only through good times but also through downturns. All companies have ups and downs, so setting ambitious ratios, or even ratios reflecting the current situation, if a breach of those ratios is an Event of Default, leads to a fragile position in which any deterioration in the borrower's condition will give the lenders the right to accelerate. This, in turn (through the cross default clauses), will result in its other lenders having the same right. The threat to their liquidity which this may cause (regardless of the overall financial stability of the company) could be sufficient to precipitate its collapse. If breach resulted in a change in Margin, this risk would disappear.

6. Can a breach be cured?

8.124

It is often agreed that if there is a breach of the financial covenants, this can be cured by an injection of equity. This is referred to as the 'equity cure right'. Lenders will usually put a limit on the number of times the equity cure rights can be exercised during the life of the loan.

8.125

A number of other issues arise here

- First, which ratios can be cured? A breach of the cashflow ratio is likely to be a temporary problem as long as EBITDA is on target, so lenders may well be happy to agree equity cure rights for this. Breach of the interest cover ratio is much more of a problem because that ratio is only measuring

282   Representations, Undertakings and Events of Default

the ability to service interest (not principal). If the ability to service interest is in doubt that is a serious problem.

* Second, how long does the borrower have to inject the equity? Often, borrowers will not know that there has been a breach of a ratio until after the end of the financial period in question, when the accounts are being prepared. In order to avoid triggering cross default clauses it is important that the cure period does not start until the borrower knows there is a breach—that is, until the date on which the Compliance Certificate is (or is required to be) delivered.
* Third, what should happen to the additional funds which are injected by way of equity? Lenders will probably want the moneys to be used to prepay debt to reduce the risk of the problem recurring. Borrowers may request that it be simply deposited in an account and released if the ratio is met the next time around. Regardless of what happens to the money in practice, a separate issue arises as to what its effect should be on the various ratios. Is it treated as

  – extra cash just for the cashflow covenant,
  – extra profit earned (i.e. an increase in EBITDA) for the interest cover and leverage ratios and/or as
  – a reduction in debt for the interest cover and leverage ratios?

* Also, given that other issues may be driven off these figures—such as the amount of the Margin and permitted capital expenditure, will the injection have any effect for these purposes or will it only be effective in relation to ensuring there is no Event of Default? These are issues for negotiation.

8.126
Another issue sometimes agreed is a **'Mulligan'** clause. This takes one of two forms. It may provide that there is only an Event of Default if the ratios are breached twice in a row. Alternatively, it may provide that the lender loses its right to accelerate for a breach of financial covenant if it does not exercise the right and, on a subsequent test date, the borrower meets the ratios.

7. How should the words used in the tests be defined?

8.127
This is an area where the financial team will need to be involved. There are a number of detailed issues to consider, which are beyond the scope of this book. A useful source of suggestions on this and on the financial ratios generally can be found in the Association of Corporate Treasurers' various guides to

the LMA facilities, (in particular their guides to the Investment Grade Facilities and to the Leveraged Facilities) which are available on the Association of Corporate Treasurers' website at www.treasurers.org.

Financial covenants in an asset finance transaction

8.128
An asset finance transaction will often include a security cover ratio (see Box 8.21).

Box 8.21

EXAMPLE SECURITY COVER RATIO
If at any time the Security Value is less than the Security Requirement then the Borrower shall, within 10 Business Days, either

(a) *prepay the Loan in such amount as shall be required to ensure that, after such prepayment, the Security Value is not less than the Security Requirement; or*
(b) *provide additional security for the Loan having a value, as determined by the Majority Lenders in their absolute discretion, equal to the difference between the Security Value and the Security Requirement.*

'Security Requirement' means, at any relevant time, an amount equal to one hundred and fifty per cent of the amount of the Loan[52] at that time;
'Security Value' means, at any relevant time, the value of the Security at such time as determined by the latest valuation delivered to the Lenders pursuant to Clause [].

---

[52] If the loan is a multicurrency loan, the ratio will generally be tested with reference to the Base Currency Amount of the loan (see definition of 'Base Currency Amount'). However, this exposes the lenders to an exchange rate risk in between the dates (usually the start of each Interest Period) when the loan needs to be readjusted to match the Base Currency Amount, as discussed in relation to Clause 8 *(Optional Currencies)*. So, if the loan may be outstanding in a currency which is not the same as the currency in which the security is likely to be sold (the 'Security Currency'), the lenders may require the ability to test the Security Requirement from time to time during Interest Periods, with reference to the amount of the loan at its then current exchange rate as against the Security Currency.

> This will specify that the value of the security must always equal at least a given percentage of the loan outstanding. The percentage varies between 120% and over 200%. The excess over 100% is designed to give the lenders a cushion for
>
> - interest which will accrue between commencement of proceedings and realization of proceeds of security;
> - expenses which will be incurred by the lenders in realizing the security;
> - the fact that values of assets tend to fall precisely when the lender requires access to them[53]; and
> - currency fluctuations, if the loan is a multicurrency loan or if the value of the security may be affected by the value of currencies other than the currency of the loan.

8.129

If the ratio is breached at any time, the borrower generally has the option of providing additional security or prepaying the loan to the extent necessary to bring the ratio back into line.

There are a number of issues that often arise in negotiation of this undertaking:

When and how is the security valued?

8.130

As to when, lenders frequently wish to have the ability to obtain valuations more often than annually. The issue often boils down to one of expense, with the borrower obtaining annual valuations but with a right for the Agent to obtain interim valuations at its own expense.

As to how, there are many options, including:

- each of the Agent and the borrower appoint a valuer, and the value is the average of the two;
- the borrower appoints a valuer but the Agent is able to challenge the valuation and, if it does so, the Agent's valuer's determination is the value;

---

[53] The reason for this is twofold. First, the borrower is more likely to have financial difficulties at a time of economic turmoil generally, when asset prices are also likely to have fallen; and second, the markets will often be aware that the sale is a distressed sale, which will always result in lower prices than a voluntary sale.

- each of the Agent and the borrower appoints a valuer and the valuation is the average of the two but the Agent has the ability to appoint a third if he disputes the borrower's valuation. The value will then be the average of the three (or of the Agent's two); and
- as above but the valuations can only be made by a valuer which is on a list of pre-agreed approved valuers.

The lenders may also want to include a fallback provision to deal with the (rare) eventuality that it proves impossible to obtain a valuation of the security. This happened in relation to ships after the credit crunch because certain types of ships were not being traded and therefore values could not be made.

Should there be any restriction on the types of assets that the lenders must accept?

8.131

Often the lenders will limit additional security to assets which have a public market, for example, stocks and bonds. If other assets may be permitted, lenders often require complete discretion as to how to value them, so as to protect themselves from

- being offered assets of a type which they would not have accepted at the commencement of the loan; and
- the possibility that there may be legal difficulties in relevant countries in creating valid security (such as security over moveable property[54]) or that any security created may be clawed back in an insolvency, for example, because it is a **preference.**

Should the value of additional security be determined by majority lenders?

8.132

Lenders may wish to consider whether the requirements as to the valuation of additional security should be determined by all the lenders or by a Majority. Individual lenders may not want to be required to accept security based on the views of the rest of the syndicate. However, the borrower will be likely to object to a requirement that the value should be agreed by all lenders as it exposes the borrower to the views of the most cautious lender.

---

[54] See A1.063.

How to value cash

8.133
If cash is part of the security (e.g. perhaps where moneys are blocked in an account where there is a restriction on the distribution of those moneys) then the borrower may request that the Security Requirement should be the relevant percentage of the loan minus the amount of cash cover. The effect of this request is to reduce the Security Requirement by more than the cash held, on the basis that the cash should count Dollar for Dollar against the loan. The argument is that, because cash is readily accessible, the justifications discussed above for requiring the Security Value to exceed the amount of the loan do not apply (see Box 8.22).

Box 8.22

For example, assume the loan is $10 million and the security cover ratio is 150%. If the security (excluding cash) is valued at $12 million, there is a shortfall of $3 million in the required Security Value. To cure this, the borrower would need to provide cash security of $3 million. If the borrower succeeds in its argument discussed here, however, then the cash security required will be only $2 million. This is because that $2 million will be counted against the $10 million loan on a dollar for dollar basis. That brings the amount of the loan which is not covered by cash security down from $10 million to $8 million. Security cover of 150% is required for that $8 million, resulting in a requirement that the value of non-cash security is at least $12 million and the existing non-cash security covers that requirement.

Release of Additional Security

8.134
The borrower often requests that if, after additional security has been given, the point comes when the ratio would be satisfied without taking into account the value of the additional security, the lenders should release that additional security.

Borrowers may also ask that the clause should not operate if, between the time of the shortfall and the date on which the clause would otherwise require prepayment or additional security, a repayment falls due which will have the effect of bringing the loan down to a figure such that there is no longer any shortfall.

Clause 24: General Undertakings—Section 1—The LMA Undertakings

8.135

The general positive undertakings in the LMA Compounded/Term Rate Loan are minimal—to maintain consents and comply with laws affecting the loan.

The negative undertakings in the LMA Compounded/Term Rate Loan consist of the negative pledge clause, a no disposals clause, and a clause prohibiting merger or change of business. See Box 8.23.

Box 8.23

It is interesting to compare the standard LMA Compounded/Term Rate Loan undertakings with those used by Moody's in their Assessment Framework,[55] used to assess the value of undertakings in leveraged loans. The framework highlights seven risk factors for leveraged loans and rates the protection which the loan undertakings give in relation to those risk factors from strong through weak to non-existent. Leveraged loans are, of course, far more restrictive than loans to investment grade borrowers and in the investment grade market restrictions on investments, prepayments of debt, payment of dividends and the like would be unacceptable. Nevertheless, the risk factors highlighted are instructive. In particular, it is worth noticing that the LMA Compounded/Term Rate Loan does not include any limitation on borrowings or on subsidiaries incurring debts (which is important because of the concept of structural subordination discussed in A1.036). Here is a very brief summary of the risk factors and covenants taken into account by the assessment framework.

Moody's assessment framework for leveraged loan covenants

Financial covenants and definitions

- Headroom
- Maintenance or incurrence
- Ebitda add backs

---

[55] See Moody's Investor Services Assessment Framework for Leveraged Loan Covenants, dated 4 February 2021 and available from Moody's website for a detailed discussion of the criteria for assessment.

288 Representations, Undertakings and Events of Default

Ranking and security including structural subordination

- Ability to dilute security by incurring pari passu debt against same security—e.g. incremental debt
- Ability to give security over other assets (or prior security over these assets) e.g. incurrence leverage ratio/permitted security
- Ability of non guarantor subsidiaries to borrow money

Cash leakage

- restricted payments and transactions with affiliates—looking at the carve outs and baskets for Permitted Payments

Leveraging risk

- ability to incur additional debt
- restrictions on ability to prepay other debt

Investing in risky assets

- restricted investments and acquisitions of companies—looking at the carve outs and baskets for Permitted Investments and Permitted Acquisitions

Asset sales and mandatory prepayments

- Restricted asset sales—looking at carve outs and baskets for Permitted Disposals
- Mandatory prepayments from asset sales and Excess cashflow

Voting rights, assignments, incremental facilities, etc.,

- Transfers to borrower affiliates permitted?
- Uncapped incremental facilities?

Clause 24.1 Authorizations

8.136

This clause requires each Obligor to obtain all necessary 'Authorizations' required in the place of their incorporation to enable them to perform their

Clause 24: General Undertakings—Section 1—The LMA Undertakings 289

obligations under the agreements and to ensure that the documents are admissible in evidence there.

8.137

Comment This undertaking relates to corporate authorities and other consents, licences, filings and registrations required under the laws in the place of incorporation of Obligors. It is somewhat less broad that the corresponding representation in Clause 21.5 *(REPRESENTATIONS: Validity and admissibility in evidence)* discussed in 8.036, which, unlike this Clause 24.1 *(GENERAL UNDERTAKINGS: Authorisations)*, is not limited to Authorizations from the Obligors' jurisdiction of incorporation. The two clauses should be reviewed together.

The clause not only requires the borrower to make sure they have all necessary 'Authorizations' but it also requires them to deliver copies to the Agent—borrowers might like to restrict this so that they are only required to deliver copies of the Authorizations 'on request'.

8.138

> Where this clause is restricted to the borrower's place of incorporation, (as it is in the LMA Compounded/Term Rate Loan), compliance ought not to be too onerous. However this is one of the clauses which, particularly in the context of secured transactions, may often be extended to apply to all 'Relevant Jurisdictions', which is likely to include the locations of secured assets and wherever the borrower conducts business. In this case the borrower may need to restrict the clause further, for example, by adding a materiality test.

Clause 24.2 Compliance with laws

8.139

This clause is a good housekeeping undertaking, requiring the Obligors to comply with all applicable laws if failure to do so would materially affect their ability to perform their obligations under the documents.

Clause 24.3 Negative pledge

8.140
The negative pledge clause prohibits the borrower from giving security unless that security falls within one of the exceptions to the clause. There are many different reasons for inclusion of a negative pledge and its significance varies from transaction to transaction.

Purpose

8.141
In an unsecured loan, it is one of the three clauses (pari passu, negative pledge and cross default) which the unsecured creditor will regard as particularly important as they ensure equality with other creditors. Its role here is

* to preserve equality—as a general requirement that lenders to the borrower (except, perhaps, in special cases such as asset or project financings), lend on the same (unsecured) basis;
* to provide advance warning of a change in financial condition—if the borrower needs to borrow significant amounts on a secured basis this may reflect a change in its condition;
* to protect the lenders' leverage in the event of the borrower's insolvency— the lenders may wish to ensure that there are no secured lenders for fear that a secured lender may be more prepared to take proceedings against a borrower than an unsecured lender and/or
* to protect the pool of assets which the borrower has at the start of the transaction, from being dissipated.

8.142

In a secured transaction lenders may be equally concerned as in an unsecured transaction to:
* protect their leverage in insolvency and hence prevent the existence of any other secured creditors; and
* protect the initial pool of assets from being dissipated.

In addition, if the lenders are taking security over substantially all the company's assets they will want the negative pledge so as to:

* facilitate the lenders' control of the company;

Clause 24: General Undertakings—Section 1—The LMA Undertakings   291

- enable the lenders to sell the company as a going concern should an Event of Default occur;
- reduce the likelihood of other creditors taking action against the company;
- bolster a floating charge[56] and
- simply as part of the range of undertakings designed to ensure the company does not undertake any other business, if the company is a single purpose company.

Consequences of breach

8.143

One problem with the negative pledge clause relates to the consequences of breach. The clause aims to ensure that if the lenders need to enforce their rights against the borrower, all its assets will be shared pro rata. However, if the borrower breaches the clause, the lenders' remedy is to accelerate. If they do accelerate, they will then be in the situation which the clause was intended to avoid—that is, of having to enforce but not having equal access to the borrower's assets. In other words, the clause does not in fact protect the lenders against a borrower which breaches the clause. The position may be different if the person taking security knew, or should have known, that that security was given in breach of the negative pledge.[57]

One variation on the negative pledge permits security to be given but only if the lenders are equally and rateably secured. This may be difficult to give effect to, given the fluctuating value of security and of the debt concerned, unless there were a formal security sharing agreement.

Content

8.144

Generally, it is in all parties' interests to ensure that the clause permits the borrower's day-to-day activities and that it does not have the result of forcing the borrower to regularly request consent under it. The scope of the clause

---

[56] See Box A1.12.

[57] This is one reason for the representation at Clause 21.3 (*REPRESENTATIONS: Non conflict with other obligations*)—to help ensure that if anything done under this loan arrangement is a breach of prior agreements, the lenders can point to the representation and show that they were unaware of the breach.

292   Representations, Undertakings and Events of Default

(e.g. does it prohibit title financing?)[58] and of any exceptions (e.g. does the operation of law exception depend on the relevant security also arising in the ordinary course of trading?)[59] needs to be reviewed in the context of the borrower's business and country of operations.

8.145

The negative pledge clause in the LMA Compounded/Term Rate Loan falls into three sections:

- First the clause prevents the creation or existence of 'Security'[60] (at subclause (a));
- Second the clause outlaws quasi security (at subclause (b)) if that takes the form of one of the items specified in the clause and if its primary purpose is to raise Financial Indebtedness;
- Third the clause sets out the exceptions (at subclause (c)).

Clause 24.3 (*Negative pledge*) Subclause (a) Prohibition on Security

8.146

This subclause prevents the creation or existence of 'Security' (see Box 8.24). The clause does not only prohibit the borrower from creating Security but also says the borrower must not '*permit [Security] to subsist*'. This outlaws those security interests which arise at law such as liens[61] It also has an impact on Security created by companies which initially were not restricted but become restricted at a later stage.[62]

8.24

In this subclause (a) (unlike subclause (b) relating to certain forms of quasi security) all manner of Security is prohibited, whether or not it is created as security

---

[58] See comments below on Clause 24.3 (*GENERAL UNDERTAKINGS*: *Negative pledge*) subclause (c) from 8.165 onwards.

[59] See comments on Clause 24.3 (*GENERAL UNDERTAKINGS*: *Negative pledge*) subclause (c)(iv) in 8.158.

[60] 'Security' is defined to mean '*a mortgage, charge, pledge, lien or other security interest securing any obligation of any person or any other agreement or arrangement having a similar effect*'.

[61] See the discussion on Clause 24.3 (*GENERAL UNDERTAKINGS Negative pledge*) subclause (c)(iv) in 8.158.

[62] See Box 0.23.

Clause 24: General Undertakings—Section 1—The LMA Undertakings   293

> for Financial Indebtedness.[63] For example, security arising in the context of litigation, such as judgement liens, will be prohibited under subclause (a)—subject to any relevant exceptions in subclause (c).

8.147

Comment The prohibition in this clause relates to all members of the group. The borrower may want to limit the prohibition to Obligors on the basis that lenders have no recourse against members of the group which are not Obligors and therefore should be unconcerned with their assets.[64]

Clause 24.3 (*Negative pledge*) Subclause (b) Prohibition on Quasi Security

8.148

(b) *no Obligor shall (and the Company shall ensure that no other member of the Group will):*

   (i) *sell, transfer or otherwise dispose of any of its assets on terms whereby they are or may be leased to or re-acquired by an Obligor [or any other member of the Group];*

  (ii) *sell, transfer or otherwise dispose of any of its receivables on recourse terms;*

 (iii) *enter into any arrangement under which money or the benefit of a bank or other account may be applied, set off or made subject to a combination of accounts or*

 (iv) *enter into any other preferential arrangement having a similar effect,*

in circumstances where the arrangement or transaction is entered into primarily as a method of raising Financial Indebtedness or of financing the acquisition of an asset.

8.149

This subclause outlaws quasi security if that takes the form of one of the items specified in the clause. This prohibition on quasi security only applies

---

[63] See commentary on Clause 24.3 (*GENERAL UNDERTAKINGS Negative pledge*) subclause (b) from 8.148 onwards.

[64] See 0.164.

294   Representations, Undertakings and Events of Default

where it occurs primarily for the purpose of raising Financial Indebtedness. The purpose, of course, is to ensure that, no matter the legal structure, if the commercial effect is equivalent to security, it is prohibited. The qualification relating to Financial Indebtedness is intended to distinguish between quasi security and arrangements which do not amount to raising finance.

8.150
The specific forms of quasi security prohibited by this clause are:

* sale and repurchase or leaseback;
* selling receivables but keeping the risk and
* set off or similar arrangements with cash.

There is also a provision (in subclause (b)(iv)) stating that similar arrangements are also prohibited.

One area which lenders might like to consider is cash pooling because it may result in funds being used for the benefit of non-Obligors and thereby removed from the grasp of the lenders. See Box 8.25.

Box 8.25

Cash pooling is an arrangement which many corporate groups have, which is designed to minimize fees and interest payments and to ensure that all group members, wherever situated, have the benefit of funds held in the pool by other group members. In effect, these arrangements have the commercial effect of treating the group as a single entity, paying interest only on any net debit amount.

There are two principal mechanisms for the operation of the pool: one is real and the other notional. Under the 'real' system, cash in the accounts of any individual group member are regularly swept into a 'central' account on which all group members who are members of the cash pool can draw. The transfers have the effect of intercompany loans between group members.

In the notional system, no transfers are made but lenders effectively charge interest on a 'net' basis. However, in order to do this, lenders will usually require all pool members to guarantee each others' debts in relation to the pooled accounts so as to enable the bank to use surpluses in one account to offset against debits in another account in the event of insolvency of a pool member.

Therefore, whichever route is used, a lender could find that funds which are earned by its borrower may be on-lent to a different entity (in the case of a 'real' pool) or set off against debts of a different entity (in the case of a notional pool) and thereby removed from the grasp of the lender.

Clause 24: General Undertakings—Section 1—The LMA Undertakings 295

8.151

Cash pooling falls within the scope of subclause (b)(iii)—as being '*an arrangement under which money or the benefit of a bank account may be applied, set off or subject to a combination of accounts*' but this is only prohibited if '*the arrangement ... is entered into primarily as a method of raising Financial Indebtedness*' (see the last two lines of subclause (b)). Raising Financial Indebtedness may arguably be one of the purposes of the arrangement, but is rarely the primary purpose, so that cash pooling is unlikely to be prohibited by this clause in most circumstances.[65]

Even if it were, subclause (c)(ii) (discussed in 8.154) expressly allows netting and set off in the ordinary course of banking arrangements so that cash pooling would probably be allowed (although some borrowers ask for clarification of this as noted in 8.154).

Lenders may want to consider whether they want to protect themselves against money leaking from the borrower to other group members via a cash **pool**. One option could be at least to require guarantees of the loan from all members of the cash pool. Another would be to take security on important bank accounts and prevent those accounts from being used as part of the pool.

Borrowers needing to have cash pool arrangements need to consider whether they breach any other provision of the loan agreement such as perhaps restrictions on lending or giving guarantees or on dealings with affiliates.

Clause 24.3 (*Negative pledge*) Subclause (c) Exceptions to the negative pledge

The exceptions are as follows.

Clause 24.3 (Negative pledge) Subclause (c) (i) Existing Security

8.152

Subclause (c)(i) allows security already in place but only to the extent of the principal amount specified in the schedule.

---

[65] But of course it may breach some other clause, for example, there may be restrictions on lending or borrowing money or giving guarantees or it may even breach the no disposals undertaking.

296   Representations, Undertakings and Events of Default

8.153

Clause 24.3 (c) (ii) Netting or Set off in the Course of Ordinary Banking Arrangements.

This subclause reads:

(ii) any netting or set off arrangement entered into by any member of the Group in the ordinary course of its banking arrangements for the purpose of netting debit and credit balances.

8.154

Sometimes borrowers ask for additional exceptions to this clause to expressly permit set off arrangements under such things as cash pooling, bank standard terms and arrangements with suppliers and customers. These arrangements would not normally be entered into 'primarily for the purpose of raising Financial Indebtedness' and so would not be prohibited by subclause (b). However subclause (a) prohibits 'Security' which is defined to include things with the same commercial effect as security. Then the concern arises that cash pooling may not be considered to be merely 'banking arrangements' but something more than that. Similarly, standard terms of banking arrangements may give rise to other security in addition to the right to set off debit and credit balances. Expressly permitting netting and setoff as part of the borrower's financing or cash management arrangements or pursuant to a bank's standard terms of business may therefore be helpful.

Clause 24.3 (c) (iii)

This subclause reads:

any payment or close out netting or set off arrangement pursuant to any hedging transaction entered into by a member of the Group for the purpose of:

A. *hedging any risk to which any member of the Group is exposed in its ordinary course of trading or*
B. *its interest rate or currency management operations which are carried out in the ordinary course of business and for non-speculative purposes only*

excluding, in each case, any Security or Quasi Security under a credit support arrangement in relation to a hedging transaction.

Clause 24: General Undertakings—Section 1—The LMA Undertakings   297

8.155

This subclause is designed to allow netting and set off for derivatives as long as those derivatives were not speculative in nature. However it specifically excludes credit support arrangements. These are arrangements which are designed to protect the parties to a derivative from the credit risk of their counterparty. See Box 8.26.

Box 8.26

Take for example an interest rate **swap**. The parties to the swap will have agreed that one party will make payments to the other calculated on one basis (for example, they may have agreed to make monthly payments at a fixed rate of say 5% on a notional sum of $100 million, over the next five years, in exchange for the counterparty making payment at a floating rate of interest on the same notional sum on the same dates over the same period). Each party has a credit risk on the other for the payments due under the swap. Additionally, as interest rates move, one party will become 'out of the money'. If it wanted to terminate the swap at a time when it was out of the money, it would need to compensate the counterparty for the whole future stream of income. This termination payment can get quite high.

To protect against this credit risk, parties to a derivative commonly require credit support arrangements to be put in place. Indeed some market participants are required to provide credit support for derivatives under various regulatory regimes.

Credit support under **ISDA** documentation either operates by way of a security arrangement (in which case it is prohibited by the negative pledge) or it operates by way of title transfer—the collateral giver passes the title to cash or another asset to the recipient and has a contractual right to receive 'equivalent assets' back once the relevant obligations under the derivative are discharged. The precise documentation for the arrangement will depend on whether the posting of collateral is a regulatory requirement or not, whether the collateral relates to an initial margin or a variable ongoing margin, whether the collateral is given to a custodian or to the derivative counterparty, whether the derivatives in question are cleared through central counterparties or not and also on the appropriate governing law (for example the New York law Annex has different consequences to the English law Annex).[66]

8.156

If the definition of Financial Indebtedness used in the loan agreement includes derivatives then those arrangements which do not create security may nonetheless be prohibited by the restrictions on Quasi Security on the basis that they are a 'preferential arrangement having a similar effect' as prohibited by Clause 24.3 (*Negative pledge*) subclause (b)(iv).

---

[66] See Goode and Gulifer "Legal Prooblems of Credit and Security", 7th ed at 6.43 onwards.

298   Representations, Undertakings and Events of Default

8.157

*Comment B*orrowers will want to ensure that the negative pledge does not restrict them from entering into derivatives in order to hedge against risks (such as energy prices or interest rates) faced by the business and so may want to amend the exception so as to allow Security and Quasi Security for derivatives or under ISDA standard terms.

Clause 24.3 (c) (iv) Operation of Law

8.158

Many security interests arise without being deliberately created by the borrower and, subject to the exceptions in this Clause 24.3 *(Negative pledge)* subclause (c), the existence of these forms of security is prohibited, regardless of the fact that they were not created on purpose and they do not secure borrowings. They will be permitted under subclause (iv) if they are 'liens' which arise both by operation of law and in the ordinary course of trading. See Box 8.27.

Box 8.27

Examples of security which arises by operation of law *or* in the ordinary course of trading may include

- security over an asset as security for a debt arising from a transaction relating to that asset—for example, in England, if equipment is delivered to a repairer the repairer will be entitled to hold onto the equipment (and will have security over it) until paid;
- security arising by statute—for example, in some countries, the tax authorities have security over a company's property for any tax owing; or environmental agencies have security over a company's property for clean-up costs of environmental incidents caused by the company;
- security arising under standard terms of banking arrangements—for example, under such arrangements, banks may have security over property deposited with them for safe keeping;
- security in favour of unpaid sellers (in some countries, unpaid sellers automatically have security in the assets sold until they have been paid for them);
- security given or arising automatically in the context of litigation, while proceedings are pursued.

Clause 24: General Undertakings—Section 1—The LMA Undertakings

8.159

The exception is cumulative. It requires the security to arise *both* by operation of law *and* in the ordinary course of trading. Box 8.27 lists examples of situations where security might arise automatically by operation of law OR in the ordinary course of trading. However, they will not all be permitted by this exception which requires the security to satisfy BOTH limbs of the test. For example, security for clean-up costs in some circumstances would not be permitted because, although the security arises by operation of law, the environmental incident may well not have occurred 'in the ordinary course of trading'. Security under standard banking terms does not normally arise by operation of law, even though it is in the ordinary course of trading. To the extent that the relevant security is not permitted under this clause, it would be counted towards the threshold amount in Clause 24.3 *(Negative pledge)* subclause (c)(x).

8.160

Comment Sometimes borrowers ask for the exceptions in subclause (iv) to be independent, not cumulative, so that liens arising by operation of law are permitted (e.g. in respect of taxes) and liens arising in the ordinary course of trading are also permitted. Lenders prefer the cumulative requirement as, without it, the borrower's ability to deliberately create security in the ordinary course of trading is unlimited (see Box 8.28).

Box 8.28

Despite the frequency of the use of the expressions 'ordinary course of trading' and 'ordinary course of business' in contracts and in legislation, these expressions have no precise, clear meaning.

What is the ordinary course of trading?

It is clear that the 'ordinary course of trading' is a more restrictive expression than the 'ordinary course of business'. It will include activities which the business does, and expects to do, as part of its trading (meaning buying and selling), such as disposals of stock and acquisitions of raw materials. It is unlikely to include acquisitions of fixed assets or businesses.

What is the ordinary course of business?

This expression has a number of possible meanings. For example, if a company commonly enters into a particular type of transaction, that is probably in the ordinary course of business. Less clear would be the case where a company had never entered into a particular type of transaction, but that type of transaction was common in the industry. In one instance,[67] the courts held

---

[67] This case was Ashborder BV v Green Gas Power Ltd (2004) EWHC 1517, which looked at the expression in the context of floating charges. See also 'Defining the "Ordinary Course of Business"', *Journal of International Banking Law and Regulation*, 2004, Volume 19, Issue 12, p 513.

300   Representations, Undertakings and Events of Default

> that even an unprecedented or exceptional transaction could be in the ordinary
> course of business (although that case involved the interpretation of a statute,
> not a contract, so that the purpose of the expression was quite different to its
> purpose in a loan agreement). Given the uncertainty, this expression should be
> used with caution.

8.161

Another point to note here is that the expression 'lien' is a technical term
under English law. See A1.044. This is unnecessarily restrictive. For example,
if the borrower operates in a country where unpaid sellers automatically have
a security interest until paid, that ought not to cause a breach of the negative
pledge even if the characteristics of the security interest do not amount to a
'lien'.

Lenders may require that any security permitted under this subclause must
be discharged within a specified period.

Clause 24.3 (Negative pledge) Subclause (c) (v) and (vi) After Acquired Property/Companies

8.162

These clauses allow the borrower to purchase assets or companies which
already have security on them provided that the security is discharged within
a specified period after the acquisition.

8.163

Comment The requirement in subclauses (c)(v) and (vi) that the security must
be discharged within a period after the acquisition is one which a borrower
might seek to resist. Existence of that security does not contain any adverse
implications as to the borrower's financial position and retention of these
restrictions may make acquisitions more difficult. If the lenders view the
purpose of the negative pledge as being to protect the borrower's existing
pool of assets, this requirement is unnecessary. If, on the other hand, lenders
are concerned simply to ensure equality and leverage on a winding up,[68] they
will require these provisions to remain as drafted.

---

[68] See 8.140 onwards.

Clause 24: General Undertakings—Section 1—The LMA Undertakings

Clause 24.3 (Negative pledge) Subclause (c) (vii) Under the Finance Documents

8.164

This allows the security created by the documents.

Clause 24.3 (Negative pledge) Subclause (c) (viii) Under Certain Title Finance Arrangements

8.165

This subclause permits title financing arrangements such as hire purchase arrangements if they are in the ordinary course of trading. This would permit such things as hire purchase of company cars or computers. The permission is important since, without it, it is unclear whether title financing arrangements are prohibited by the negative pledge in the first place.

They are clearly not prohibited by Clause 24.3(a) [the prohibition on Security] since the key characteristic of title financing is that the financed asset belongs to the financier, not the user. Clause 24.3(a) prohibits the borrower from giving Security on its assets but in title financing the borrower's asset would be its contractual rights under the title financing arrangement rather than the asset itself.

Clause 24.3 (Negative pledge) (b) [the prohibition on Quasi Security] is unclear, particularly because it prohibits only a sub-category of finance leasing—sale and leaseback.

By permitting title financing in certain circumstances it becomes reasonably clear that it is prohibited in all other circumstances.

Clause 24.3 (Negative pledge) Subclause (c) (ix) Other

Other common exceptions are,

8.166

- Security created by non-recourse subsidiaries (unless non-recourse subsidiaries have been excluded from the ambit of the loan altogether).[69] The argument is that this cannot harm the group except to the extent of the

---

[69] See 0.161.

302 Representations, Undertakings and Events of Default

assets to which recourse is available for the limited recourse finance. As long as those assets are disregarded for the purpose of this loan (e.g. excluded in calculations of financial ratios) then existence of security created by non-recourse subsidiaries should not concern the lenders.

8.167

- Security over property acquired after the loan agreement is signed, where the security is given to secure financing for purchase of that property. Some lenders may agree to this exception on the basis that giving security in these circumstances is not to the detriment of the existing pool of assets, provided the property being acquired does not replace an asset from the existing pool. On the other hand, lenders may not agree to this exception if they are concerned that the fact that the borrower is raising money on a secured basis might indicate some change in its financial status, or if they want to ensure equality with other lenders.

8.168

- Liens in the context of litigation.[70] Even where those liens arise by operation of law (and many, such as payments into court, are not created by operation of law), the litigation may well not be in the ordinary course of trading and therefore these security interests, if permitted at all, would only be permitted if they fell within the threshold set in Clause 24.3 (*Negative pledge*) subclause (c) (x). This could result in a large difference between the negotiated position in relation to litigation[71] and the position in practice. Nevertheless, lenders may justifiably argue that the circumstances in which they are content to see litigation occur will differ depending on whether that litigation involves the creation of security or not.

8.169

- Security which is given in order to access a particular (advantageous) source of funds only available on secured terms, such as export credit.

---

[70] Examples are payments into court or security for costs in a contested matter. Also see Goode, *Commercial Law*, 22.73 onwards for details of other security interests which may arise in the course of litigation in England.

[71] See Clause 25.8 (*EVENTS OF DEFAULT*: *Creditors' process*) in 8.266.

Clause 24: General Undertakings—Section 1—The LMA Undertakings   303

8.170

* Security for trade finance such as pledges of goods for the provision of letters of credit.

8.171

* Intra Obligor security.

8.172

* Rent deposits for leasehold property.

8.173
The lenders should note that there is no cap on the amount of security which can be given under these various exceptions. The only cap is in subclause (x) and it relates only to security created under subclause (x). Lenders may prefer to agree a higher cap in subclause (x) rather than extending the categories of security which can be created without a cap.

Clause 24.3 (c) (x) Threshold

8.174
This exception reads.
(x) any Security or Quasi-Security securing indebtedness the principal amount of which (when aggregated with the principal amount of any other indebtedness which has the benefit of Security given by any member of the Group other than any permitted under paragraphs (i) to (ix) above) does not exceed [] (or its equivalent in another currency or currencies).

8.175
Comment Some borrowers ask for an annual figure to be allowed with carry forward of unused amounts.

8.176
Comment Another option is to set an aggregate figure at a percentage of Tangible Net Worth.

304   Representations, Undertakings and Events of Default

8.177

In negotiating the threshold amount, the parties need to ensure that it is flexible enough to protect the lenders' interest as well as accommodating the likely commercial needs of the borrower. As with financial ratios,[72] the borrower needs to ensure that the agreement will be robust enough to see it through downturns, up to a point. If on the downturn only minimal secured lending is permitted, the effect of this clause may be to accelerate the downturn which might otherwise have been avoided.

8.178

Lenders often argue that a lower threshold is appropriate because they will give consent under it whenever withholding consent would be detrimental to the borrower's interest. This argument should be treated with caution.[73]

8.179

The amount of the threshold also needs to be set with the other terms of the clause in mind. If title retention is prohibited, the amount of the threshold needs to be higher. Similarly, if there were two separate exceptions: one for security arising by operation of law and a second for security arising in the ordinary course of trading, the threshold could be lower.

Clause 24.4 *Disposals*

Clause 24.4 (*Disposals*) reads

8.180

(a) No Obligor shall [(and the Company shall ensure that no other member of the Group will)], enter into a single transaction or a series of transactions (whether related or not) and whether voluntary or involuntary to sell, lease, transfer or otherwise dispose of any asset.

The lenders may wish to restrict major disposals (even if they are at market value)[74] as they may affect the ability of the borrower to earn income to service the debt; or they may indicate a cashflow problem; or a change in business strategy. In the LMA Compounded/Term Rate Loan, the clause is not only designed to ensure that value is maintained in the company (that would be the role of any Tangible Net Worth covenant and/or restriction on

---

[72] See discussion on financial ratios from 8.123 onwards.

[73] See Box 0.5.

[74] If so, no exception should be made allowing disposal on arm's length terms nor should the clause be replaced by a Tangible Net Worth covenant.

Clause 24: General Undertakings—Section 1—The LMA Undertakings 305

distributions to shareholders), but also to prevent changes in the composition of the company's major assets ('asset stripping'). For the purpose of this clause, note that the construction clause in the LMA gives 'assets' a very wide definition. It is not limited to fixed assets and things like cash and future income fall within the definition.

8.181

This clause is very wide, given the broad definition of 'assets'. Borrowers commonly ask to introduce some concept of materiality eg by limiting it to fixed assets, material assets, a material part of their assets, or disposals which have a 'Material Adverse Effect'.

8.182

In the interests of clarity borrowers might want to ask for an exception to allow disposals of cash and cash equivalents. Some argue that this is unnecessary as payment of a dividend, or purchase of an asset for cash, for example, are clearly not intended to be prohibited by the clause, falling outside the ordinary understanding of the idea of disposal of assets.

8.183

In sub-investment grade loans it is common to allow disposals of capital assets, provided the net proceeds (or a proportion of the proceeds) are used to prepay the loan or are reinvested within a given period of time. In the Leveraged LMA, this is achieved by having a definition of 'Permitted Disposals' and then requiring the net proceeds from the disposal to be used to make a compulsory prepayment of the loan, unless those proceeds are 'Excluded Disposal Proceeds'. Some issues here are

* What deductions to make from proceeds in arriving at the figure for net proceeds—for example, expenses and tax?
* If the proceeds are not to be used to make a prepayment, for example, because they are to be reinvested—how soon must the reinvestment occur?
* Whether all the net proceeds of all assets are required to be used to make a prepayment or whether to restrict the required prepayment so that it only applies to major assets or only requires prepayment if a given leverage ratio is breached and
* When the prepayment must be made

8.184

Comment The clause may apply only to Obligors or to all members of the group. Borrowers may wish to restrict it to Obligors as lenders have no claims against other group members.[75]

Clause 24.4 (*Disposals*) subclause (b) exceptions to no disposal clause

8.185

The first exception in subclause (b) allows disposals in the ordinary course of trading. This allows such day-to-day activities as disposal of stock in trade.

Note the difference between the 'ordinary course of business' and the 'ordinary course of trading' discussed in Box 8.28.

8.186

This exception also needs to be considered in the context of any security given to the lenders. The extent to which Obligors which have provided security are able to sell the assets which are the subject of that security in the ordinary course of their business may be a determining factor in the characterization of the security as a fixed charge or as a floating charge.[76] Assets which are intended to be subject to a fixed charge must not be able to be sold without the consent of the lenders and, if necessary, this clause should be adjusted to reflect that.

8.187

The second exception in subclause (b) reads

(ii) *of assets in exchange for other assets comparable or superior as to type, value and quality (other than an exchange of a Non—Cash Asset for Cash).*

8.188

Comment Borrowers may want to adjust this to allow disposals for cash if the cash is reinvested within a reasonable period in assets which would otherwise have qualified under this subclause.

---

[75] See 0.164.

[76] Ashborder BV v Green Gas Power Ltd (2004) EWHC 1517 (Ch D).

Clause 24: General Undertakings—Section 1—The LMA Undertakings 307

8.189

Borrowers commonly request a broad exception allowing disposals for fair value on arms' length terms. If this is achieved then many of the more detailed issues relating to the clause as discussed here will become irrelevant. However lenders should be cautious in agreeing such a broad exception, as it would enable the borrower to transform income producing assets into cash—which is one of the things the clause is trying to prevent.

Other exceptions commonly allowed here include:

* disposal of obsolete assets;
* intra group disposals (although lenders will need to consider whether disposals to companies which are not Obligors are permissible);
* disposal of cash or cash equivalents;
* disposals of shares in other group members;
* disposals where the proceeds are used to prepay a part of the loan.

Subclause (iv) allows disposals up to a maximum threshold amount in any financial year.

8.190

The threshold needs to be set at a level which does not confound the normal activities of the borrower and which allows for some flexibility in changing financial circumstances. The borrower may need to sell some significant assets in a downturn and some ability to do this may be necessary.

8.191

Lenders may also want to consider whether there are any assets (such as intellectual property rights) which may have low value on their own, but disposal of which would have a disproportionate effect on the borrower's business, and to include a different threshold in relation to those assets. See the discussion of collateral stripping at Box 0.21.

8.192

Comment Some borrowers ask for an annual figure to be allowed with carry forward of unused amounts.

8.193

Comment Another option is to set an aggregate figure at a percentage of Tangible Net Worth.

308   Representations, Undertakings and Events of Default

Clause 24.5 Merger

8.194

This clause prohibits mergers and 'corporate reconstruction'.[77] This clause addresses the lenders' concerns that:

* the resultant entity may not take on the liabilities of the borrower;
* it may not benefit from all the rights which the borrower had (e.g. licences) which may be necessary for the conduct of the business and
* the merger may cause a conflict of interest for the lenders or result in the new borrower being an entity which the lenders do not want to do business with—the decision to do business with a company involves other considerations—not just credit risk.

8.195

Comment This clause applies to every individual member of the group. Borrowers may wish to restrict this to Obligors.[78]

8.196

In view of the lack of clarity around the expression 'corporate reconstruction' borrowers may want to specifically permit solvent liquidations and reorganizations or limit the clause so that it only applies if there is a Material Adverse Effect.

Clause 24.6 Change of business

8.197

This clause prohibits change of business. This undertaking relates to the general nature of business of (a) the Company (being the top company in the group to which the lenders have access) and (b) the group as a whole. It does not[79] restrict the Company or the group from selling or stopping carrying on any part of its business nor from acquiring new businesses, provided the general nature of the Company's and group's businesses remain the same.

---

[77] There is no clear legal or business meaning for the expression 'corporate reconstruction'. There is some case law (Re Mytravel Group [2004] EWCA Civ 1734) which emphasizes that the key characteristic is that the identity of the shareholders before and after the event is substantially the same.

[78] See 0.164.

[79] But the no disposals covenant probably does restrict this.

Clause 24: General Undertakings—Section 1—The LMA Undertakings **309**

8.198

Comment Lenders may wish to make this undertaking more restrictive in certain cases, for example, they may want to extend it to also prohibit ceasing to carry on a material part of its business.

Clause 24: General Undertakings—Section 2—Other Common Undertakings

8.199

Each transaction is likely to require additional conditions precedent, representations, undertakings and/or Events of Default to reflect the credit decision taken by the lenders. The following are the areas which are often the subject of additional provisions. The headings below are largely taken from the Leveraged LMA (commonly used as a resource in drafting restrictions in loan agreements for sub-investment grade borrowers)[80] with a few additional categories—

* Authorizations and compliance with laws
* Restrictions on business focus.
* Restrictions on dealing with assets and security.
* Restrictions on movement of cash—cash out.
* Restrictions on movement of cash—cash in.
* Information.
* Granting powers to others.
* Reflecting regulatory or legal risks.
* Undertakings relating to assets given as security.
* Miscellaneous.

For the purpose of simplicity, this book deals with these additional issues of concern to lenders altogether in relation to the undertakings. Nevertheless, for each additional provision which the lenders include in the undertakings, they are likely to also require a representation and/or a condition precedent addressing that issue. They need also to consider whether the issue is best addressed by an undertaking or by an Event of Default.[81]

---

[80] By their nature, the areas which these additional provisions may need to deal with are endless and no summary of them can be complete. This selection should therefore be viewed as being by way of example only, of some of the more common issues.

[81] See Box 0.4.

1. Authorizations and Compliance with Laws

8.200

Some examples are

- environmental undertakings such as:

  - an environmental report as a condition precedent to the loan and
  - undertakings to comply with environmental regulations (possibly complemented by insurance[82]) (see Box 8.29).

- paying tax and other claims which have priority in insolvency or which give rise to liens[83] (see Box 8.30).
- undertakings in relation to sanctions, anti-bribery and similar regulations.

Box 8.29

Environmental liabilities may have a significant impact on the borrower's financial position; on the value of its assets (including assets it may have given to the lenders as security); on the priority of the lenders' security, or on the lenders' exposure if it were to take control of the assets over which it has security. It may simply be a matter of lender policy only to lend to companies or projects which can demonstrate compliance with high environmental standards.

Box 8.30

For example, in the US under **ERISA** (Employee Retirement Income Security Act) liens may arise on a company's assets if it fails to comply with the requirements of the Act. For a US borrower, it is therefore common to include undertakings and Events of Default related to compliance with the requirements of ERISA.

---

[82] Where there are no specific environmental concerns, borrowers might argue that specific undertakings are unnecessary as they are covered by the general undertakings to comply with the law. Where undertakings are included borrowers will want to include materiality restrictions.

[83] The borrower may wish to ensure they have the right to contest these claims as long as they make appropriate reserves.

Clause 24: General Undertakings—Section 1—The LMA Undertakings

2. Restrictions on business focus

8.201

Some examples (additional to the ones already looked at) are

- No acquisitions of companies or shares in companies and no joint ventures.[84]
- No acquisitions of other assets. Clearly the degree of restriction which is workable will depend on the transaction. It is worth noting that, like the 'no disposals clause', this prohibition relates to a very broad category of 'assets'. So if a restriction along these lines is included, it will need careful consideration of appropriate exemptions.[85]
- No new contracts. A similar point arises here as in relation to the acquisition of assets.[86]

3. Restrictions on dealing with assets and security

8.202

Some examples are

- An undertaking to maintain the ranking of the loan as at least pari passu with the borrowers' other unsecured debt except for those debts preferred by law. See the discussion on Clause 21.12 *(REPRESENTATIONS: Pari passu ranking)* from 8.052 onwards. Borrowers might request the deletion of this clause since in most cases the ranking of the debt is an insolvency law issue, outside the control of the borrower. Also, in view of the uncertainties created by the Argentine case discussed in Box 8.11, if the undertaking is included, borrowers will want it to be clear that the undertaking relates only to the priority of debts and not the order in which they are paid.
- Undertakings to conduct all transactions on an arm's length basis (including perhaps restrictions on transactions with affiliates and on payments to directors and employees).[87]

---

[84] Issues commonly discussed in this context are (i) acquisition of shares in listed companies (sometimes, only if security is given on those shares to the lenders) and (ii) acquisition of businesses similar to that already conducted by the borrower, in countries approved by the lenders and provided certain financial ratios are met.

[85] Borrowers are likely to need the clause to permit acquisition of trading assets and services in the ordinary course of business.

[86] Exclusions for the ordinary course of trading and materiality carve-outs are likely to be needed.

[87] Borrowers will need to consider whether any arrangements they have such as incentive schemes for employees, or cash pooling arrangements, breach this undertaking.

- Undertakings to maintain adequate insurance
  - in accordance with industry standards;
  - against key risks identified by the lenders such as key man insurance, business interruption insurance, pollution or other liability insurance, political risk insurance or insurance against physical damage to assets;
  - with approved insurers (in an asset finance, the lenders are effectively taking a credit risk on the insurers if there is an insured incident) and to
    - provide a regular expert opinion as to the acceptability of the insurance—both as to risks covered and as to the identity of the insurers;
    - provide regular evidence that the insurance is up to date;
    - make a mandatory prepayment of the loan (or repair of asset) out of insurance proceeds;
    - ensure the lenders have some protection (insurance?) against the risks of the insurance not paying out, for example, because it is cancelled for non-payment of premiums or because there was a breach of warranty by the insured;
- Undertakings to maintain their assets in good condition[88];
- Requirements to maintain appropriate hedging arrangements.

4. Restrictions on movements of cash—cash out

8.203
Some examples are

- No lending money or giving credit[89];
- No giving guarantees[90];
- No payment of dividends. Clearly the shareholders want to make a profit so if this restriction is included it will need to reflect the commercial agreement. Often dividends are permitted if certain financial tests are met after the dividend is paid and provided there is no Default and

---

[88] Borrowers are likely to want some materiality concept here.

[89] Issues to consider here include trade credit to customers, intra group lending, advance payments on capital expenditure, deferred consideration for disposals, cash pooling arrangements and cash deposited at banks.

[90] Borrowers are likely to need an exception for the ordinary course of business to cover things like performance bonds, letters of credit and cash pooling, as well as for indemnities included in standard term documents. Materiality thresholds or a basket allowing guarantees up to a specified amount are also commonly requested.

Clause 24: General Undertakings—Section 1—The LMA Undertakings   313

• No prepayment of debt. There are often transaction-specific issues to consider here. If there are shareholder loans, exceptions may be negotiated similar to those for the payment of dividends.

5. Restrictions on movement of cash—cash in

8.204

Some examples are

• No issuing new shares (with an exception for equity cure rights if these are agreed);
• No new borrowing.[91] In this context borrowers may request exceptions for

   – refinancing existing debt
   – intra group borrowings
   – debts in the context of cash pooling
   – derivatives (if the definition of Financial Indebtedness from the LMA Compounded/Term Rate Loan is used) and
   – subordinated debt, particularly if the shareholder may wish to inject moneys in that way for tax reasons. Lenders' response to this request may depend on the degree of subordination.[92] Subordination which allows payment prior to a winding up may not be acceptable.

6. Information

8.205

Some examples are requirements to

• provide access to books and accounts[93];
• provide management reports;
• give access to auditors[94] and
• copy the Agent in on major communications (and advise of defaults or disputes) under specific contracts/insurance.

---

[91] The lenders may be particularly concerned about new borrowing or other indebtedness by a subsidiary which is not an Obligor but whose assets are relevant for the purpose of financial ratios, since the lenders are structurally subordinate to such claims—see A1.036.

[92] See A1.033.

[93] See comments on Clause 22.1 *(INFORMATION UNDERTAKINGS: Financial statements)* in 8.084 in relation to insider trading.

[94] Note that in the UK, any contractual clause which restricts an audited person's choice of auditor is ineffective by virtue of Regulation 12 Statutory Auditors and Third Country Auditors Regulation 2016 (SI 2016/649), implementing a European Directive on the subject.

7. Granting powers to others.

8.206

* undertakings not to give a negative pledge to a third party (as that would restrict the lenders' ability to negotiate further security) and
* undertakings not to agree more favourable loan terms with others (sometimes referred to as a 'most favoured nations' clause).

8. Reflecting regulatory or legal risks

8.207

Where a particular risk is identified in legal due diligence, the lenders may want to include provisions reflecting that risk. An example is the undertaking not to use the loan in contravention of financial assistance regulations. Another would be an undertaking not to establish a place of business in a particular jurisdiction.[95]

Sometimes the loan agreement contains a representation from the borrower as to the location of its 'Centre of Main Interests' (commonly referred to as its 'COMI') and an undertaking not to change its COMI. This reflects the EU regulation on insolvency—which states that a company will be made insolvent in the state where the company has its 'COMI'.[96] See Box 8.31.

Box 8.31

Where is the COMI?

Article 3(1) of the EU Insolvency Regulation 2015/848 (the 'Recast Insolvency Regulation') states that the COMI 'shall be the place where the debtor conducts the administration of his interests on a regular basis and is ascertainable by third parties'. There is a rebuttable presumption that the COMI is in the country of the company's registered office. There is some case law predating the Recast Insolvency Regulation[97] which held that that presumption that the COMI was the place of incorporation could only be rebutted if factors to the contrary exist which are both 'objective and ascertainable by third parties' and that importance must be given to the place where the company has its core

---

[95] Such an undertaking is often included to lessen the risk of the need to effect registrations in those jurisdictions.

[96] This is also reflected in the *UNCITRAL* Model Law on Cross-Border Insolvency (Model Law).

[97] Re Eurofood IFSC Ltd [2006] EUECJ C-341/04 (Eurofood) and Interedil Srl (in liquidation) v Fallimento Interedil Srl and another [2011] EUECJ C-396/09.

Clause 24: General Undertakings—Section 1—The LMA Undertakings

> administration. These factors are reflected in the preamble to the Recast Insolvency Regulation. The location of the COMI is not always clear-cut and it may therefore be difficult for a borrower to make a representation confirming the location of its COMI. An undertaking not to 'knowingly' or 'deliberately' change the COMI would be preferable for the borrowers.
>
> The lenders' main concern is of course that they will have conducted their insolvency due diligence in the place of incorporation of the borrowers and they want to be sure that that is in fact the place where insolvency may occur. Where a lender is secured, they have substantial protection from the effects of insolvency law as a result of article 8 of the regulation which effectively allows enforcement of security in one jurisdiction in the EU unaffected by insolvency proceedings taking place in a different jurisdiction within the EU.

9. Undertakings relating to assets given as security[98]

8.208

Asset-related undertakings are often contained in the relevant security document. Some borrowers ask for a 'stripped out' security document (which contains no commercial terms, but simply creates the security) with all commercial provisions being contained in the loan agreement. This can assist with compliance and with ensuring the documents are consistent. The following undertakings may be included (either in the security documents or in the loan agreement):

- to repair the asset;
- not to allow anyone to have a lien (e.g. for repair) on the asset or to limit the amount of any such lien to an agreed figure;
- not to make any major changes to the asset;
- not to install equipment belonging to third parties onto the asset;
- to allow inspection of the asset;
- to use the asset responsibly—that is, in accordance with applicable regulations including environmental rules and not to use it for illegal trades;
- to operate the asset itself (not through a third party);
- to notify the Agent of major issues relating to the asset for example, damage or claims and
- to insure the asset.

---

[98] See also 0.250.

8.209

Commonly, the following provisions will also be included:

- a condition precedent as to evidence of value and condition of the asset and constitution of the security;
- an Event of Default if:

  - any other security over the asset becomes enforceable,
  - the asset is confiscated or nationalized or.
  - a major insurance incident or environmental claim arises in relation to the asset and[99]

- if the asset which is taken as security is a particular contract or a particular contract is key to the credit decision, the lenders may want

  - a condition precedent that the contract has become unconditional and the security on it has been constituted;
  - a representation that the copy delivered is the complete agreement;
  - an undertaking not to amend it and to comply with the obligations under it;
  - an Event of Default if it comes to an end[100];
  - agreement (confirmed by the counterparty) that the income from the contract will be paid directly to a specified account;
  - restrictions on the use of money in the account;
  - a 'waterfall' providing for a series of accounts with different purposes and regular payment into these accounts from income generated;[101]
  - no sharing of the income;
  - no alteration to the contract (confirmed by the counterparty);
  - agreement to perform its obligations under the contract;
  - ability (confirmed by counterparty) for the Agent to terminate the contract and/or to step in and perform it;
  - confirmation from the counterparty that it will not exercise rights of set off or counterclaim in relation to payments under the contract and
  - if the contract assigned, a notice of assignment acknowledged by the counterparty to the contract (see Box 8.32).

---

[99] May be included as a compulsory prepayment event—see commentary on Clause 10.3 (*PREPAYMENT AND CANCELLATION*: *Change of control*) at 4.011.

[100] But the borrower will want an opportunity to find an acceptable replacement contract and, by doing so, to avoid occurrence of the Event of Default.

[101] See Box 0.32.

Clause 24: General Undertakings—Section 1—The LMA Undertakings 317

> **Box 8.32**
>
> Notice of assignment is frequently given to the counterparty, who is often required to acknowledge the notice and give certain direct confirmations to the lender in that acknowledgement. Additionally, the counterparty may be asked to
>
> - confirm that they have not received any other notice of assignment (because priority of competing assignments depends on the order in which notice of assignment was given to the counterparty) and/or
> - undertake to the lender to perform their obligations under the contract.
>
> In many cases, unless the counterparty is related to the borrower or has some incentive for assisting with the financing, they will be unwilling to give all (or any) of the confirmations requested in the acknowledgement, some of which (particularly the waivers of rights of set off and counterclaim) would be detrimental to the counterparty's own interests.

10. Miscellaneous

8.210

Other miscellaneous undertakings could include:

- Undertakings in relation to pensions. Many companies have operated 'defined benefit' pension schemes over the years, under which employees, on retirement, were entitled to receive a set income during their retirement. Most have now moved to schemes based on income earned by contributions made by their employees. The defined benefit schemes have put great pressure on the finances of those companies which ran such schemes, and, in the EU, numerous steps have been taken to try to ensure that those companies will be able to meet their pension obligations over the years. In the UK these steps include the power (under the Pension Schemes Act 2021) of the pensions regulator to deter and penalize wrongdoing in relation to such schemes. Lenders will want to do due diligence in relation to such schemes and may want the borrower to confirm that it is in compliance with its obligations in relation to pensions and to undertake to continue to be so.

8.211

- Undertakings to give the lenders and their advisers access to the borrowers' premises and records. Borrowers often want this restricted so that access is only available while there is a Default outstanding, access must be with notice and at reasonable times, and perhaps limiting the frequency of access (e.g. to once per year).

8.212

- Undertakings to retain appropriate senior management of the company and not to amend their service contracts in a way which would be prejudicial to the lenders. These undertakings are highly subjective and therefore difficult both to comply with and to enforce. Borrowers are likely to want to remove the undertaking or to add a 'reasonable endeavours' qualification.

8.213

- Undertakings to assert and protect their rights in relation to intellectual property. These undertakings are usually only required if intellectual property is of particular importance to the borrower. Borrowers are likely to want to add materiality carve-outs.

8.214

- Undertakings to keep all bank accounts and do all their derivative transactions with a lender. The acceptability of this depends on the service available from lenders. Borrowers commonly want freedom to enter into derivatives with third parties to enable them to get the best price.

8.215

- Undertakings to restrict the amount of cash balances which group members have—and transfer those funds by way of intercompany loan to the parent company borrower.

8.216

- A further assurance clause—that is, an undertaking to do whatever may be necessary to keep the security in effect.

8.217

- Undertakings not to make any change in the group structure (or identity of group members). For example, the issue of new shares in a subsidiary to a third party will affect the impact of what has been agreed in the undertakings, for example, as to intra group transactions.

8.218

- Undertakings not to make any change in the constitution of the borrowers (and ensure the constitution only allows the existing business). This can bolster the effectiveness of the undertakings relating to change in business.

8.219

- Limits on short-term borrowings and undertakings to pay off all short-term debt for a minimum period each year. The intention is to ensure the borrower is not using short-term debt for long-term needs.

8.220

- Undertakings to pay its debts as they fall due (unless contested in good faith).

8.221

- Sometimes, separateness undertakings, designed to reduce the risk of 'substantive consolidation' in relation to special purpose vehicles if there is a US connection. See Box 8.33.

Box 8.33

'Substantive consolidation' is a principle which applies in the US, which allows a number of companies to be wound up as a single entity, if those companies have been managed as a single entity. In other words, the separate corporate status of the companies will be ineffective if this principle applies. Clearly, lenders who have transacted with one company will not want its assets to be used to settle liabilities of other companies and therefore they will want to try to ensure that their borrower is managed independently of any other companies, so that substantive consolidation will not arise. This is the role of the 'separateness undertakings'. The borrower undertakes to manage its business separately from that of its affiliates—for example, by keeping separate bank accounts, separate headed paper, and only transacting business with affiliates on arm's length terms.

Clause 25: Events of Default—Section 1—Introduction

1. Purpose

8.222

The purpose of the Events of Default is to give the lenders the contractual right to require early repayment (and not to lend any new money) if

320   Representations, Undertakings and Events of Default

certain specified events happen. The existence of these rights gives the lenders leverage to negotiate adjustments to the transaction (such as a change in security or Margin) if any of the specified events occurs. The Events of Default are not[102] concerned with fault, but only with risk—they set out the circumstances in which it is accepted that the level of risk has changed and the lenders should be entitled to renegotiate.

2. Objective versus subjective

8.223

The Events of Default should be objective, and subjective tests and words (such as 'reasonable' and 'material') should be avoided as far as possible. Objective wording makes it easier for lenders to exercise their rights and gives the borrower more certainty as to the circumstances in which the loan may cease to be available.[103] Nevertheless, complete objectivity is not always possible and where recourse to subjective words is necessary, the lenders will want to add 'in the opinion of the Majority Lenders', (see Box 8.34) to make recourse to the Event of Default more predictable in its results, while the borrower will wish to omit those words and thereby impose some more objective standard of reasonableness or materiality. Under English law, if a dispute arose, the courts would not look into the question of whether the Majority Lenders were correct in their opinion, as long as the lenders exercised their discretion honestly and in good faith and for the purposes for which the discretion was given.[104]

Box 8.34

In this context it is interesting to note that the lenders are likely to prefer that it should be the opinion of the Majority Lenders which counts rather than the opinion of the Agent. As discussed from 10.002 onwards, Agents want to ensure that, as far as possible, their role under the document is purely 'mechanical and administrative'.

---

[102] Subject to the comments made on Clause 25.5 (*EVENTS OF DEFAULT: Cross default*) in 8.256.

[103] Although some borrowers prefer to see subjective words because it makes it harder for lenders to exercise their rights.

[104] See Wood, International Loans, Bonds, Guarantees Legal Opinions, 3rd ed at 14–028 et seq.

Clause 25: Events of Default—Section 1—Introduction   321

3. Control over the relevant events

8.224

Borrowers are also concerned to ensure that they have the ability to avoid the occurrence of an Event of Default and so to avoid the acceleration of the loan. So they will want to ensure, as far as possible, that Events of Default do not occur automatically, but only after they have had an opportunity to rectify the situation (see Box 8.36) and that the acts of others over which they have no control cannot result in an Event of Default (see Box 8.35).

Box 8.35

For example, the borrower will not want termination of an important contract to be an Event of Default. If that contract was key to the lenders' credit decision, the borrower will want to negotiate the possibility of finding a replacement contract and so avoiding an Event of Default.

For similar reasons, borrowers want to restrict the Events of Default to circumstances affecting Obligors (not any group member).[105] They will be particularly keen to avoid Events of Default relating to their **joint venture** partners or other contracting parties.

8.225

Comment In some circumstances where Events of Default are included relating to parties over which the borrower has no control, such as a joint venture partner, the lenders may agree that no Event of Default will occur with reference to events relating solely to that person if either

- that person is replaced in the relevant contract or other relationship by an acceptable substitute;
- the borrower can show that its ability to service the debt has not suffered and/or perhaps
- additional security is provided.

4. From Default to acceleration

See Box 8.36 for an explanation of the steps from Default to acceleration.

---

[105] See 0.164.

322 Representations, Undertakings and Events of Default

Box 8.36

Stages of a default flow chart

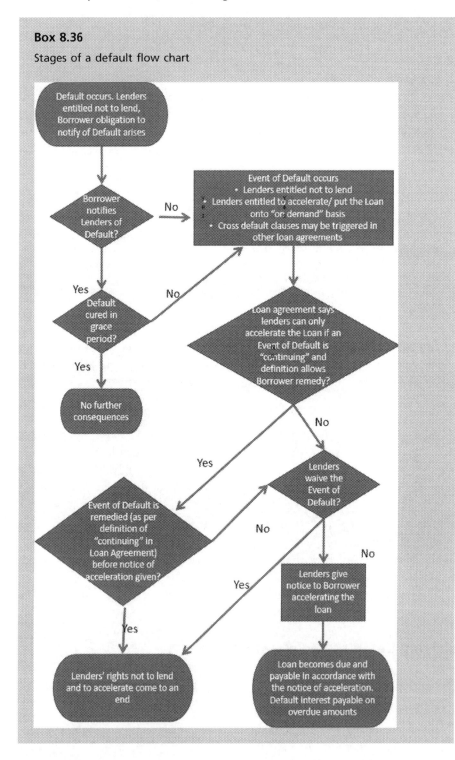

Clause 25: Events of Default—Section 1—Introduction   **323**

8.226

A Default (as discussed in the context of the definitions in Clause 1 *(Definitions and interpretation)* at 1.014) is something which may or may not mature into an Event of Default, such as breach of an undertaking.[106] It automatically results in the release of the lenders from their obligation to lend new money unless the Majority Lenders waive the Default. See the discussion on Clause 4.2 (*CONDITIONS OF UTILIZATION*: *Further conditions precedent*) subclause (a)(i) from 2.024 onwards.

Some Defaults are automatically also Events of Default. An example is the misrepresentation Event of Default, discussed in 8.232. There is no grace period or any other requirement (e.g. to give notice) applicable to this particular Event of Default. Many Defaults only become Events of Default after a period of time and/or the giving of notice (e.g. Clause 25.3 (*EVENTS OF DEFAULT*: *Other obligations*) subclause (b)), see Box 8.37.

Box 8.37

This distinction between automatic Events of Default (such as misrepresentation) and others is important for both the borrower and the lenders. The borrower is keen to have the opportunity to remedy problems before they become Events of Default. Both borrowers and lenders will be keen to ensure that Events of Default do not arise too readily because of the rights that they will give to other lenders under their cross default clauses. Hence, only certain events are automatic Events of Default. Automatic Events of Default usually include non-payment (unless there is a good reason for the non-payment); breach of financial ratio (unless equity cure rights have been granted); breach of the obligation to notify of a Default; cross default; insurance undertakings; deliberate or particularly serious wrongdoings such as the breach of the negative pledge and insolvency-related Events of Default. Other events give the borrower an opportunity to remedy.

8.227

Once a Default occurs, the borrower is obliged to notify the lenders. Failure to do so results in a separate (usually automatic) Event of Default.[107]

---

[106] It must not be confused with a 'default' (as opposed to a 'Default'), as that expression is used in Clause 21.9 *(REPRESENTATIONS: No default)* subclause (b) as discussed in Box 8.9. In Clause 21.9 *(REPRESENTATIONS: No default)* subclause (b) the word is being used without a capital letter, and is therefore given its natural meaning as opposed to the meaning given by the definitions in Clause 1 *(Definitions and Interpretation)*. The natural meaning of 'default' is simply 'failure' or 'breach'.

[107] See commentary on Clause 22.5 *(INFORMATION UNDERTAKINGS: Notification of default)* in 8.096.

324   Representations, Undertakings and Events of Default

Once an Event of Default has occurred, the lenders have the right to accelerate the loan. Acceleration does not happen automatically. The lenders can elect whether or not to exercise that right and the loan will only become repayable early if the lenders make a demand for such payment in accordance with Clause 25.13 *(EVENTS OF DEFAULT: Acceleration)*.

The lenders' right to accelerate the loan, or not to lend additional moneys, will cease to be exercisable in certain circumstances if the document (Clause 25.13 *(EVENTS OF DEFAULT: Acceleration)*) states that those rights are only exercisable while the Event of Default is 'continuing'.[108]

Clause 25: Events of Default—Section 2—The LMA Events of Default

The events which constitute Events of Default in the LMA Compounded/Term Rate Loan are as follows:

Clause 25.1 Non-payment

8.228
It is an Event of Default under Clause 25.1 if the borrower fails to make a payment when due. A grace period is only normally allowed in respect of administrative or technical error or a 'Disruption Event' (defined to mean disruption to the payment system or financial markets or an unavoidable systems error). There are options to allow different grace periods for different reasons for delay. Default interest will nevertheless accrue from the due date.

8.229
Comment Sometimes borrowers ask for a grace period for payments (such as reimbursement of expenses) which are payable on demand, as opposed to payments of principal and interest, which have a due date for payment. Lenders should be aware that, in the LMA Compounded/Term Rate Loan, some of the indemnities are expressed to be payable on demand (e.g. the costs and expenses clause at 19.1 *(COSTS AND EXPENSES: Transaction expenses)*), and others state they are payable within a specified period (usually within three business days) of demand. (e.g. the tax indemnity in 15.3(a) *(TAX GROSS UP AND INDEMNITIES: Tax indemnity)*), so that any grace

---

[108] See commentary on Clause 1.2 *(DEFINITIONS AND INTERPRETATION: Construction)* subclause (e) in 1.065 for a discussion of 'continuing'.

Clause 25: Events of Default—Section 2—The LMA Events of Default **325**

period agreed in this clause will be cumulative with the period specified in the relevant indemnity clause.

Clause 25.2 Financial covenants

8.230
It is an Event of Default under Clause 25.2 (*EVENTS OF DEFAULT: Financial covenants*) if there is a breach of a financial covenant. This is set out separately since no grace period is appropriate as, in general, the breach cannot be remedied except as discussed in the context of equity cure rights in the discussion on Clause 23 (*Financial covenants*). If equity cure rights are given then it is important to ensure that the drafting, either in this Clause 25.2 or in the financial ratio itself, provides that the breach only occurs (and the grace period starts) when the Compliance Certificate is required to be delivered, as opposed to the end of the financial period to which the ratios relate. Otherwise the cure rights may be illusory because the cure period may expire before the Event of Default is discovered—see 8.124.

Another reason for its separate treatment is that financial ratios are not promises which may be broken, in the same way as other undertakings, but, instead, they are tests which may be met or not.

Clause 25.3 Other obligations

8.231
Under Clause 25.3, a breach of any other undertaking is an Event of Default. The clause divides the various undertakings into different types, giving some (but not all) undertakings grace periods so that they are not automatic; and then allowing for those non-automatic Events of Default to have different grace periods.

Some lenders prefer the grace to run from the Default (rather than following the LMA Compounded/Term Rate Loan, which is to allow it to run from the date the borrower[109] is aware of, or is notified by the lenders of, the Default). However, this approach may make the Event of Default automatic in practice (as the grace period may expire before any party is aware of

---

[109] Or rather, in the LMA Compounded/Term Rate Loan, the 'Company'. This gives rise to the possibility that if a borrower is aware of the Default but the Company is not, the grace period will only run from the date the Company is aware of it.

the Default). As a result, it may prevent the possibility of avoiding the occurrence of an Event of Default (and thus avoiding triggering the rights of other lenders under their cross default clauses).

Breaches which are often included as automatic Events of Default (i.e. with no grace period) include failure to maintain insurance, failure to notify of a Default and breach of undertakings which themselves include a grace period.

Clause 25.4 Misrepresentation

8.232
Clause 25.4 provides that it is an Event of Default if a representation is incorrect in a material respect when made or when deemed repeated.

8.233
Comment The LMA Compounded/Term Rate Loan formulation requires the representation to be incorrect in a 'material respect'. Some lenders may object to this in that it introduces a concept of materiality to each representation, which would be better negotiated in the representations themselves. Nonetheless it is preferable to the position sometimes requested that the misrepresentation should only constitute an Event of Default if it materially affects the borrower's ability to pay.

8.234
Comment This Event of Default is not only triggered if any of the representations made in the loan agreement are incorrect but also if any representation in *'any other document delivered by or on behalf of an Obligor under or in connection with any Finance Document'* is incorrect. Borrowers may want to restrict the clause to written representations.

8.235
It is worth noting that default under this clause is automatic. There is no grace period as a misrepresentation cannot be undone. However, this leads to the result that the opportunity to remedy will be different if, for example,

- the borrower repeats a representation to the effect that there have been no changes to a particular contract, at a time when changes have been made, or if
- the borrower undertakes not to amend a particular contract, but enters into an amendment nevertheless.

Clause 25: Events of Default—Section 2—The LMA Events of Default 327

The borrower will have no grace period for the misrepresentation but would have one for the breach of undertaking.

8.236
Comment If representations are repeated, borrowers should consider requesting an opportunity to remedy the underlying situation and thus prevent a misrepresentation from automatically being an Event of Default.

8.237
Comment Beware. Even if the representations are not deemed repeated, the same effect may be achieved if the Event of Default says something along the following lines: '*if any representation was untrue when made or would have been untrue if repeated at any time*'. This has the same effect as Clause 21.14 *(REPRESENTATIONS: Repetition)* of the LMA Compounded/Term Rate Loan.

> Occasionally the same effect is achieved by adding a requirement to a Utilization Request, Selection Notice (choice of Interest Periods) or Compliance Certificate to the effect that the Repeating Representations are true.

Clause 25.5 Cross default

8.238
The existence of an Event of Default under a loan facility clearly gives the lenders significant leverage to renegotiate, for example, new Margins and/ or security and/or greater control over the borrower's affairs, perhaps even to require some changes in business, such as sale of assets, as a condition to their maintaining the availability of the loan. The purpose of the cross default clause is to ensure that, if any other lenders have this degree of leverage over the borrower, then so does this syndicate. The intention is to ensure that this syndicate is not left out of any such renegotiation and to ensure that their interests are not marginalized. Nevertheless, the effect of the clause, for the borrower, is to change a localized problem, with an individual lender, which may be relatively easy to solve, into a wider problem, affecting all its lenders, which will be more difficult to solve. A borrower will want to restrict the circumstances in which this clause may operate.

328 Representations, Undertakings and Events of Default

Clause 25.5 (*EVENTS OF DEFAULT: Cross default*) Subclause a

The first part of this clause reads.

[it is an Event of Default if] .....any Financial Indebtedness of any member of the Group is not paid when due nor within any originally applicable grace period.

Two definitions are key to the clause: 'Financial Indebtedness' and 'Group'.

Financial Indebtedness

8.239
Under the LMA Compounded/Term Rate Loan, the clause is only triggered by non-payment of, or rights to accelerate in respect of, 'Financial Indebtedness' and not by non-payment of, or other events relating to, ordinary commercial debts (e.g. payment for supplies). This is because,

- failure to pay Financial Indebtedness has far more serious consequences (potential for the relevant creditor to accelerate their debt, causing, at the very least, a liquidity crisis) than failure to pay ordinary commercial debts (probably resulting in court action) and
- the loan agreement deals with court action and the like under separate provisions (representation as to proceedings at Clause 21.13 *(REPRESENTATIONS: No proceedings)* and Event of Default as to creditors' process at Clause 25.8 *(EVENTS OF DEFAULT: Creditors' process)*).

8.240
The definition of Financial Indebtedness includes derivatives (in subclause (g) of the definition). These are treated in the same way as borrowed money (not ordinary commercial debts) for the purpose of the cross default clause because a failure to pay when due in respect of a derivative can (just as non-payment of a loan can) trigger a large unanticipated payment, resulting in a liquidity problem for the borrower.

8.241
Comment Borrowers may want to make adjustments to the cross default clause to ensure that it is not triggered by a default by the counterparty to the derivative (see the discussion on the definition of Financial Indebtedness from 1.033 onwards). In particular they may want to limit the cross default clause so that, in relation to derivatives, only a non-payment by the borrower

Clause 25: Events of Default—Section 2—The LMA Events of Default   329

will be relevant (i.e. to exclude derivatives from all but subclause (a) of the clause).

Group

8.242
The second issue is the definition of 'Group'. Exclusions for non-material subsidiaries and/or non-recourse companies may also be appropriate.[110]

The borrower may ask that the cross default clause should relate only to Obligors, as the lenders have no direct claim against other group members. However this is an instance where, in many cases, the lenders will resist on the basis that problems with other group members may indicate wider problems; could result in reputational problems for the group and may result in the Obligors needing to provide support for their group members.

8.243
It is also worth noticing (see 8.238) that the clause applies if payment is not made within any 'originally applicable' grace period. This is intended to prevent the clause from being circumvented by other lenders simply extending their grace periods while negotiations proceed.

Clause 23.5 (*EVENTS OF DEFAULT: Cross default*) Subclause (b)

8.244
This clause reads as follows

(b) *Any Financial Indebtedness of any member of the Group is declared to be or otherwise becomes due and payable prior to its specified maturity as a result of an event of default (however described).*

Subclause (a) deals with the non-payment of a financial debt and subclause (b) deals with its acceleration. Where another lender exercises a right to require early payment of a debt, provided that right results from a default, this clause will apply.

---

[110] See the discussion in 0.158.

330   Representations, Undertakings and Events of Default

The words '*event of default (however described)*' are intended to indicate that simply describing an Event of Default as something else (such as a 'Termination Event' in a finance lease) will not circumvent the clause. See also Box 8.38.

8.245
Comment Some borrowers may ask for an exception to this clause if the acceleration does not result from a payment obligation and the ability of the borrower to make payment and perform its other obligations under this loan is unaffected. The argument is that where the default is not in payment, it should not concern the lenders unless the acceleration of the loan by the other lender also impacts on the ability of the borrower to service this loan.

8.246
Lenders will be reluctant to agree such an exception because the actual acceleration of a loan (unless within the threshold amount allowed in Clause 25.5(e) (*EVENTS OF DEFAULT: Cross default)* subclause e, will change the borrower's financial position, regardless of the reason for the acceleration. Even if the change does not affect the borrower's ability to service this debt, the lenders will want the right (which having the Event of Default gives it) to review the risk involved in the loan and to renegotiate terms appropriate for the altered risk.

8.247
Comment Borrowers often ask for an exception to this clause if the declaration that the debt is due is being contested in good faith. As currently worded, the cross default will be triggered even if there has not actually been an Event of Default under another loan agreement if the lender under that loan agreement demands payment early. In other words, all that is required to trigger this clause is for another lender to demand payment early, regardless of whether they are entitled to do that or not. Nevertheless lenders are likely to resist this change as it is not uncommon for borrowers to negotiate and to challenge the existence of the Event of Default at the same time. If the lender had conceded this point they would be frozen out of the negotiations.

Clause 23.5 (*EVENTS OF DEFAULT: Cross default*) Subclause (c)

8.248
This clause reads as follows.

Clause 25: Events of Default—Section 2—The LMA Events of Default 331

Any commitment for any Financial Indebtedness of any member of the Group is cancelled or suspended .... as a result of an event of default (however described).

This clause deals with the situation which might arise, for example, in the case of a revolving credit, where the lenders may not accelerate the loan, but simply refuse to re-advance it on a rollover as a result of an Event of Default. (see also Box 8.38).

> **Box 8.38**
>
> It is not clear whether suspension of a facility after a 'Default' and before an 'Event of Default' will trigger this clause. The question is, will the fact that a lender is not obliged to advance a loan because of a 'Default' (as opposed to an 'Event of Default') amount to a *'[suspension of the loan] as a result of an Event of Default (however described)'*? Does the fact that we called it a 'Default' prevent it from being an *'Event of Default (however described)'*? There is no definite answer but, given the common practice of making a very important distinction between a 'Default' and an 'Event of Default', it is probable that the suspension of a facility during a 'Default' will not trigger this clause (unless there is also an Event of Default).
>
> A similar point arises in relation to compulsory prepayment events—are they not merely Events of Default by another name? Again there is no clear answer but as long as the concept of compulsory prepayment events is limited to events which happen to a borrower but which do not involve any breach on their part, it is at least arguable that they are different in nature to Events of Default.

8.249

Comment A borrower may suggest that if the commitment in question has never been drawn, such as in a backstop facility, the clause should not apply, since the cancellation will not result in the same sort of liquidity crisis (and hence leverage for the provider of the facility) as the requirement for early repayment of a loan.

Clause 23.5 (*EVENTS OF DEFAULT: Cross default*) Subclause (d)

8.250

This clause reads as follows.

Any creditor of any member of the Group becomes entitled to declare any Financial Indebtedness of any member of the Group due and payable prior to its specified maturity as a result of an event of default (however described).

332   Representations, Undertakings and Events of Default

This clause applies if another lender becomes entitled to declare its debt due early as a result of an Event of Default. In other words, the other lender does not actually accelerate, (which would be caught by Clause 25.5(b) (*EVENTS OF DEFAULT: Cross default*) subclause (b)) but simply has the right to do so.

Some borrowers request deletion of subclause (d), (see Box 8.39).

Box 8.39

If (d) is deleted; the clause is referred to as a cross acceleration clause rather than a cross default clause; as it is triggered by acceleration rather than default.

The borrower's argument for this is that if the other lender does not actually exercise its right to accelerate, for example, because the borrower persuaded the lender that the default in question was technical and unimportant, then the other syndicates should not be entitled to accelerate. They also argue that giving this right would be to give this syndicate derivative rights which they had not actually required in their own loan agreements (see Box 8.40).

Box 8.40

For example, assume a borrower has two loan agreements. One is for $10 million and is with Bank A and includes an undertaking that the borrower will maintain its Minimum Tangible Net Worth at not less than $30 million. The second agreement is for $5 million and is with Bank B and includes an undertaking that the borrower will maintain its Minimum Tangible Net Worth at not less than $20 million. The borrower's Minimum Tangible Net Worth falls to $25 million and Bank A is entitled to accelerate. The borrower's argument is that Bank B should not also be able to accelerate as otherwise, effectively, he is being given the benefit of A's (more stringent) financial covenant.

8.251

The borrower may also argue that Clause 25.5(d) (*EVENTS OF DEFAULT: Cross default*) subclause (d) is unnecessary, since, provided the borrower is paying this debt, there is no need for concern.

The difficulty with agreeing to a cross acceleration clause as opposed to a cross default clause is that, in many instances, particularly in unsecured corporate loans, it defeats the main purpose of the clause (which is

Clause 25: Events of Default—Section 2—The LMA Events of Default   333

to ensure that the syndicate's interests are not marginalized in any renegotiation between the borrower and another lender). If the clause is drafted as a cross acceleration clause it does not achieve this objective since the syndicate will have to wait for the results of the negotiation with the lender in question before it has any rights for itself.

8.252
Nevertheless, as in everything, much depends on the credit decision. In the case of a standalone asset or project finance, if the structure of the loan is such that there is little that any other lender could do which would have an adverse impact on this loan, a cross acceleration clause may be more appropriate than a cross default clause.

Similarly, in an unsecured corporate transaction with a borrower which is financially very strong, a cross acceleration clause may be acceptable if the lenders can be satisfied that all lenders are being (and will be) treated equally in this respect. A consistent policy of agreeing only cross acceleration clauses (if achievable) helps avoid Events of Default having a 'spiralling' effect—that is, turning problems which could be overcome relatively easily into much more intractable problems. Cross acceleration clauses allow the problem to be isolated to the particular creditor.

Clause 23.5 (*EVENTS OF DEFAULT: Cross default*) subclause (e)

8.253
Subclause (e) provides a threshold amount so that defaults on debts which are below the threshold will not trigger cross default. This threshold is a cumulative figure applied to all the companies restricted by the clause. Sometimes a threshold is applied separately to different companies in the group—so, for example, there may be a different, and separate, threshold for the parent company or for an Obligor than the amount which applies to other group companies.

8.254
Comment The borrower should try to maintain a consistent position on its cross default clauses, and have, for example, the same thresholds in each of them. This makes compliance easier and prevents weak cross default clauses in one agreement indirectly benefiting other lenders (see Box 8.41).

334 Representations, Undertakings and Events of Default

> **Box 8.41**
>
> An example clarifies this. Assume a borrower has two loan agreements, both for $10 million. In one (Loan A) they have negotiated a cross default clause triggered by financial debts over $1 million. The other (Loan B) has a cross default clause triggered by ordinary debts over $250,000. The borrower fails to pay a creditor $300,000 due to a temporary liquidity problem. This would not be a problem under Loan A alone, but becomes so because of its effect under the cross default clause in Loan B. Loan B is capable of being accelerated because its cross default clause is triggered by the non-payment of the debt of $300,000. Loan A is therefore also capable of being accelerated because Loan B (which is a financial debt in excess of $1 million and is therefore relevant for the cross default clause in Loan A) is capable of being accelerated. The weakest cross default clause has, in effect, benefited both syndicates.

Reducing the impact of the cross default clause

8.255
A borrower should bear in mind that careful drafting of a loan agreement (by including compulsory prepayment events and grace periods, in particular) will reduce the negative impact of cross default clauses in other agreements.

Compulsory Prepayment Events

8.256
Borrowers should ensure that issues which do not imply any form of failure by the borrower or any of its group members (e.g. change of shareholding, imposition of sanctions or total loss of a secured asset) are not dealt with as Events of Default, but rather as compulsory prepayment events.[111] For this to achieve its objective, the cross default clauses need to distinguish between early repayment of the loan caused by an Event of Default (which will trigger the cross default clause) and early repayment for other reasons (which will not). See Box 8.38.

---

[111] For example, change of control, dealt with in Clause 10.3 (*PREPAYMENT AND CANCELLA-TION: Change of Control*) in 4.011.

Clause 25: Events of Default—Section 2—The LMA Events of Default

Grace Periods

8.257

The borrower should be negotiating grace periods into its Events of Default. The cross default clause will only be triggered when another lender actually has the right to accelerate (or cancel) the facility. This will not happen until any relevant grace period has expired. In practice therefore, as long as there is, for any given event, a period between its being a Default and its becoming an Event of Default, the borrower will have an opportunity to have negotiations with an individual lender so as to avoid the occurrence of an Event of Default (so long as those negotiations do not include discussion of rescheduling[112] or extension of any original grace period for non-payment[113]) and therefore avoid the triggering of the cross default clauses.

Consents

8.258

It is also worth bearing the cross default clause in mind when requesting or giving consent under the loan agreement. Borrowers will want to ensure that any consent given is comprehensive and does not only relate to the original issue, but also to any consequential breaches of the cross default clause. Lenders on the other hand will not want to waive their rights under the cross default clause until they are sure that no other lenders plan to use their rights under their cross default clauses.

The simplest way to deal with this is to make consents comprehensive but conditional on all other affected lenders waiving their rights under their cross default clauses arising as a result of the original issue.

Clause 25.6 Insolvency

Clause 25.6 (a)

The first part of the insolvency Event of Default reads as follows
25.6 Insolvency

(a) *a member of the Group*

---

[112] See Clause 25.6 (*EVENTS OF DEFAULT: Insolvency*) subclause (a) in 8.260.
[113] See comments on Clause 25.5 (*EVENTS OF DEFAULT: Cross default*) subclause (a) in 8.243.

336 Representations, Undertakings and Events of Default

    (i) *is unable or admits inability to pay its debts as they fall due,*

   (ii) *suspends making payments on any of its debts or*

 (iii) *by reason of actual or anticipated financial difficulties, commences negotiations with one or more of its creditors (excluding any Finance Party in its capacity as such) with a view to rescheduling any of its indebtedness.*

8.259

Clause 25.6 (a)(i) covers the cashflow test of insolvency—inablity to pay debts as they fall due. It also applies if a group company commences rescheduling negotiations with a creditor.

8.260

Comment The borrower may want to restrict this so that it applies only to Obligors.[114] They also want to restrict it so that it only applies if the negotiations are with creditors generally rather than with one or more of its creditors. Although case law gives borrowers some comfort (see Box 8.42), borrowers would be better placed to clarify in the clause itself that it is only intended to catch 'substantial' problems, not, for example short-term cashflow problems which result in it needing to negotiate extra time for payment say of an individual supplier.

Box 8.42

In one case[115] the court distinguished between rescheduling discussions in the ordinary course of business and the rescheduling referred to in this clause which must result from 'actual or anticipated financial difficulties' and, because the general thrust of the clause is to deal with insolvency issues, the court's view was that the level of those difficulties would need to be substantial. The court went on to emphasize that the question was one of interpretation of the contract which would always depend on the facts of the case.

Clause 25.6 (b)

8.261

(b) The value of the assets of any member of the Group is less than its liabilities (taking into account contingent and prospective liabilities) (see Box 8.43).

---

[114] See 0.164.

[115] Grupo Hotelero Urvasco SA v Carey Value Added SL [2013]EWHC 1039.

Clause 25: Events of Default—Section 2—The LMA Events of Default   337

> **Box 8.43**
>
> The reference to contingent and prospective debts in this clause reflects the test of insolvency contained in s123 Insolvency Act 1986.
>
> A 'contingent' debt is a debt (such as that under a guarantee) which may or may not become due depending on the occurrence of an event outside the parties' control. A 'prospective' debt is one which has not yet fallen due. Its precise ambit is unclear.

8.262

Clause 25.6(b) is rather similar to the balance sheet test of insolvency. It provides for there to be an Event of Default if assets are less than liabilities. The wording of the clause reflects part of the wording of s123 Insolvency Act 1986, which deems a company unable to pay its debts if the court is satisfied that the value of its assets is less than the value of its liabilities. However, it differs from the Insolvency Act test in that it purports to be a simple, objective, test, which, as explained in Box 8.44, is actually open to many different interpretations. The difficulty is that it is not clear on what basis assets and liabilities are to be valued for the purpose of this clause. It might be better to reword the clause to clarify that it is subjective, for example, to provide that it is an Event of Default if

"*The Company cannot reasonably be expected to meet all its liabilities, looking at the Company's assets and making proper allowance for the nature of prospective and contingent liabilities*"

This reflects case law on this issue. See Box 8.44.

> **Box 8.44**
>
> The value of the company's assets will be significantly different depending on whether they are valued on a going concern basis or a breakup basis. This issue received considerable attention during the credit crunch of 2007–2008, and again during the COVID pandemic. In preparing their accounts, management is required to assess the company's ability to continue as a going concern, taking into account a wide range of factors, including all available information about the future, looking forward at least 12 months. Thus it is often a question of judgement as to whether accounts should be prepared on a going concern basis or not. The decision will impact the value of the company's assets.
>
> In relation to contingent liabilities, the question again arises as to how these should be valued depending on the likelihood of a claim in respect of those liabilities. The amount of the liability to be taken into account under a contingent liability is not clear-cut.

> In BNY Corporate Trustee Services Ltd v Eurosail-UK 2007-3BL Plc [2013] UKSC 28 the court considered an Event of Default in a contract which stated that it was an Event of Default in the event of the borrower
> *within the meaning of Section 123(1) or (2) ... of the Insolvency Act 1986 being deemed unable to pay its debts.*
> The court held that the company would not be deemed unable to pay its debts simply because its assets were less than its liabilities. It was not a simple mathematical exercise but instead required an assessment of whether the company could reasonably be expected to meet all its liabilities, looking at the company's assets and making proper allowance for the nature of prospective and contingent liabilities. (In that case, many of the liabilities were denominated in a different currency from the assets and fell due sometime in the future).

Limited recourse provisions

8.263

It is worth noting the decision of the High Court in a case in 2013[116] which held that even if the debts of a company were limited recourse in nature, that did not prevent those debts from being taken into account for the purpose of the two insolvency tests. The case in question related to a limitation on recourse provision which stated that the creditor could only take legal action for an amount up to the value of the assets of the company. Its purpose was to try to limit the risk of the company becoming insolvent. The case did not relate to the type of non-recourse company discussed in 0.161 but is a good reminder of the need to exclude such companies from the scope of the agreement entirely if there are any such companies in the group.

Clause 25.7 Insolvency proceedings[117]

8.264

This clause makes it an Event of Default if steps are taken for suspension of debt, arrangements with creditors, appointment of a liquidator, enforcement of security or the like, unless the relevant action is frivolous or vexatious and is discharged within a specified period of time.

---

[116] ARM Asset Backed Securities SA (2013) EWHC 3351 Ch.

[117] This Event of Default is intended to allow the lenders to take action before an administration or similar is agreed.

Clause 25: Events of Default—Section 2—The LMA Events of Default **339**

Some may wonder whether an insolvency Event of Default is necessary because, even if the loan is not accelerated on insolvency, the lenders would be able to claim in the insolvency for the whole debt so, arguably, the ability to accelerate has achieved no advantage.

The purpose of this Event of Default is to enable the lenders to accelerate, and claim payment of the whole debt, at an earlier stage of the insolvency process than would otherwise be possible. This may, for example, enable them to exercise rights of set off or enforcement of security prior to a formal winding up.

The clause applies to all companies in the group (but does allow solvent winding up of group members which are not Obligors). Borrowers may seek to restrict the clause to Obligors.[118]

8.265

Comment The clause is triggered at an early stage when 'any step is taken'. Borrowers will want to ensure that minor problems do not cause an Event of Default so they may request some carve-outs such as

- Exceptions for disputed items as long as the proceedings are dismissed within a set period of time;
- restricting the clause (which currently catches arrangements with 'any' creditor, and appointment of a receiver to 'any' asset) so that instead it refers to arrangements with 'its creditors generally' or appointments relating to a 'substantial part' of its assets or
- limiting the clause so that it only operates if an administrator, etc., is **actually** appointed.

Clause 25.8 Creditors' process

Clause 25.8 reads.

Any expropriation, attachment, sequestration, distress or execution affects any asset or assets of a member of the Group ………

8.266

Clause 25.8 deals with distress or execution (i.e. enforcement of court judgements or **arbitration** awards) as well as expropriation (e.g. nationalization).

The clause allows a number of options. It may be drafted so that,

---

[118] See 0.164.

340   Representations, Undertakings and Events of Default

- any enforcement (without any regard to the amount in question) is an Event of Default;
- it is only an Event of Default if the value of the assets concerned exceeds a threshold amount or
- it is only an Event of Default if, in addition to the above, the relevant enforcement order remains in place for a given period of time.

8.267

Borrowers will normally ask for all these exceptions to apply so as to allow them time to appeal the enforcement or other action.

8.268

The clause also relates to every group member. The borrower may want to restrict it to Obligors.[119]

There is no other specific Event of Default dealing with litigation or with administrative proceedings in the LMA Compounded/Term Rate Loan.

8.269

Comment In cases other than unsecured corporate loans to investment grade borrowers, lenders may want an additional Event of Default relating to litigation or unpaid judgements. This can be achieved by repetition of the representation as to no litigation in Clause 21.13 (*REPRESENTATIONS: No proceedings*), but a better option (not least because it would be more easily understood) would be to include a specific Event of Default.[120] See also Box 8.45.

Box 8.45

Litigation, Judgement and Enforcement

If a provision is included to the effect that litigation or other proceedings will be an Event of Default as referred to in 8.269, borrowers will normally ask for exceptions relating to litigation which is being contested in good faith by appropriate proceedings, diligently pursued and with reasonable prospects of success, and for which a reserve has been established.

---

[119] See 0.164.

[120] See commentary on Clause 21.13 (*REPRESENTATIONS: No proceedings*) in 8.066.

Clause 25: Events of Default—Section 2—The LMA Events of Default   **341**

Clause 25.9 Ownership of the Obligors

8.270
Clause 25.9 *(Ownership of Obligors)* makes it an Event of Default if an Obligor ceases to be a group member. This ought not to happen as if the borrower wants to sell an Obligor, it can use the mechanism in Clause 27 *(Changes to the Obligors),* to allow the Obligor to stop being an Obligor in order to allow the sale to proceed, provided, of course, that the sale does not breach the no disposals undertaking.

Other Events of Default

8.271
Lenders will usually need to add specific Events of Default relating to the transaction and credit risk in question. These will follow from the additional undertakings discussed in Clause 24 *(General Undertakings)* in 8.199.

Clause 25.12 Material adverse change

8.272
The loan agreement will often include some form of material adverse change clause. This clause can be highly contentious. Lenders argue that they cannot be expected to list in advance every circumstance which may arise which could give them cause for concern. This clause is needed as a risk allocation issue to ensure that everything is covered. Borrowers object to the clause principally because of its uncertainty and subjectivity. As with other likely contentious issues, it is sensible to address the issue in the term sheet.

The arguments around the clause fall into two categories: whether to include the clause and, if included, what it should say.

Should there be a material adverse change Event of Default?

8.273
The borrower's objections to including the clause are:

* The *uncertainty* of the circumstances in which it may be used;
* The fact that lenders *don't use it* (so why have it?);
* The *fragility* it imposes on the borrower's overall business and.
* The fact that it gives *excessive power* and discretion to the lenders.

342 Representations, Undertakings and Events of Default

Uncertainty

8.274

From the borrower's perspective, one of the main issues of concern in the loan agreement is certainty as to the continued availability of funds. If the finance is unexpectedly withdrawn, the consequences are likely to be very difficult for the borrower. For this reason, the borrower wants all Events of Default to be clear and objective, including no element of subjectivity. It is argued that the material adverse change clause, because it is not clear what events can trigger it, causes too much uncertainty as to the continued availability of funds.

Lenders may counter this with the reassurance that the very uncertainty of the clause should give the borrower comfort that it is unlikely to be used except in the most extreme circumstances. Lenders who wish to accelerate the loan would always be advised to rely on the objective Events of Default (e.g. non-payment or breach of undertaking) rather than the subjective ones, since, were the court to disagree with the lenders as to whether or not a particular set of facts fell within the clause, the lenders would be liable in damages for breach of contract if, for example, they failed to advance funds when not entitled to do so.[121] The amounts involved could be significant. In other words, the uncertainty works both ways.[122]

Lack of Use

8.275

Borrowers often comment that the clause is rarely used and so must be pointless.[123]

The lenders' response is that the existence of the clause is likely to trigger discussions in circumstances where there is cause for concern. Lack of use of the clause as a trigger for acceleration does not make it pointless in its role as prompting discussions and negotiations. Moreover, even though in

---

[121] This must be contrasted with merely serving notice of acceleration incorrectly, when no Event of Default has in fact occurred. Serving such notice may, in some circumstances, of itself, not be a breach of contract and may be simply ineffective. See Concord Trust v The Law Debenture Corp (2005) 1 WLR 1591. The borrower may therefore want the lenders to agree not to serve notice of acceleration unless an Event of Default has occurred.

[122] In fact, some borrowers like to scatter the Events of Default clause with subjective words such as 'material' and 'reasonable', sometimes preferring those over absolute numbers because of the uncertainty this creates and the corresponding caution the lenders will have in enforcing their rights.

[123] Nevertheless, it is used. See BNP Paribas SA v Yukos Oil Co (2005) EWHC 1321 (Ch) and Cukurova Finance International Ltd & Anor v Alfa Telecom Turkey Ltd (British Virgin Islands) [2013] UKPC 2.

Clause 25: Events of Default—Section 2—The LMA Events of Default

many cases the clause will not be used to accelerate the loan, either because of uncertainty of application or because of publicity concerns or concerns to avoid precipitating an industry-wide crisis, that does not mean that there will never be cases where those concerns will not apply. See also Box 8.46.

Box 8.46

There are concerns in many jurisdictions as to whether the clause is enforceable or not in any event. These concerns are founded on a number of different legal principles including

- Uncertainty. Is the clause sufficiently clear as to the circumstances in which it will operate or will it be void for uncertainty?
- Unilateral nature of the clause—some jurisdictions have a legal principle that one party cannot reserve to itself unilateral and exclusive control over the implementation of an agreement.
- Might it be contrary to principles of good faith and fair dealing?

In English courts, the clause is not of itself unenforceable, but there may be difficulties in establishing whether any given set of circumstances falls within the circumstances envisaged by the clause. This will be determined with reference to the supposed intention of the parties at the date of the agreement.

Fragility

8.276

Borrowers then argue that including this provision makes the provision of the finance fragile, in that the occurrence of events which could pose a threat to the business can itself cause the loan to be withdrawn. Businesses face new threats regularly. They surmount some and not others and should be given the opportunity to do so. Many businesses are cyclical, making the clause particularly unpalatable if the loan is agreed at the top of the cycle.

344   Representations, Undertakings and Events of Default

Excessive Power to the Lenders

8.277

There are those who argue[124] that the clause (in some of its varieties) may give so much discretion to the lenders that it, in effect, makes the facility a demand facility and not a long-term commitment at all. The ultimate decision is being given to the lenders as to what threats are acceptable. Lenders counter that the clause contains its own checks and balances against abuse of that power since the consequences to the lenders of using this clause as a justification for failure to advance further funds in circumstances when a court ultimately decides that the circumstances did not entitle the lenders to do so, are likely to be significant.[125]

Nevertheless, lenders will argue strongly for the inclusion of the clause, drafted appropriately to address some of the borrower's concerns, so as to ensure that the risk of unforeseen problems would fall on the borrowers, not the lenders and to give the lenders some opportunity to negotiate in such circumstances. The clause is particularly important in relation to the financial ratios, as discussed from 8.121 onwards.

If included, what should the clause say?

See Box 8.47.

Box 8.47

Commonly an Event of Default specifies clearly what is meant by a material adverse effect, as in this specimen:
  'Material Adverse Effect' means [in the reasonable opinion of the Majority Lenders] a material adverse effect on:

(a) *the business, operations, property, condition (financial or otherwise) or prospects of the Group taken as a whole;*
(b) *[the ability of an Obligor to perform [its obligations under the Finance Documents]/[its payment obligations under the Finance Documents and/ or its obligations under [Clause [20.2] (Financial condition)] of this Agreement]]/[the ability of the Obligors (taken as a whole) to perform [their*

---

[124] This argument is sometimes made by ratings agencies, particularly in relation to loans needed for liquidity purposes.

[125] However the decision in Concord Trust referred to in the footnote to 8.274 devalues this argument as it appears that in certain circumstances lenders would not have liability to borrowers if they sent notice of acceleration at a time when no Event of Default had actually happened even though that notice may have a significant effect on the borrower as a result of the impact of cross default clauses.

Clause 25: Events of Default—Section 2—The LMA Events of Default 345

> *obligations under the Finance Documents]/[their payment obligations under the Finance Documents and/or their obligations under [Clause [20.2] (Financial condition)] of this Agreement]] or*
>
> *(c) the validity or enforceability of the Finance Documents or the rights or remedies of any Finance Party under the Finance Documents.*

8.278

The drafting points to be addressed are

* How likely must the material adverse effect be?
* In whose opinion is this to be decided? and.
* Material adverse effect on what?

How Likely Must the Material Adverse Effect Be?

8.279

The first question is, how likely must the adverse effect be? The options range from: '', at one end of the spectrum to, '*an event occurs which will have*' [or 'has had'] '*a Material Adverse Effect*'; at the other end of the spectrum. Borrowers can be expected to object to words such as 'may', 'might' and 'could', as giving too much of a hair trigger, while lenders are unlikely to agree words such as 'will have' or 'has had' except in very strong credits, as being insufficiently flexible.

Options in between include '… *which could have a Material Adverse Effect*' or '*which could reasonably be expected to*'. This last op*the Lenders believe that a Material Adverse Effect may occur*tion provides for a fair degree of objectivity and preserves the clause as one of last resort for the lenders.

In Whose Opinion is this to be Decided?

8.280

If anyone's opinion is to be specified, the lenders would clearly prefer the clause to be tested with reference to their opinion, for example, '*an event occurs which the Lenders reasonably expect to have a Material Adverse Effect*'. Borrowers will want to resist this strongly. Where the Event of Default is subjective (i.e. tested with reference to the lender's opinion) all that is necessary is for the lender, honestly and rationally to have the opinion at the time when they served notice of the Event of Default. The question of whether

346   **Representations, Undertakings and Events of Default**

a material adverse effect actually occurred is not relevant (see e.g. <u>Lombard North Central Plc v European Skyjets Ltd [2022] EWHC 728</u>).

What Does There Need to be a Material Adverse Effect On?

8.281
It is helpful, in the definition of 'Material Adverse Effect' to specify what must be affected. Common options include:

- prospects (of the company, or the industry it is operating in, or other);
- financial condition;
- ability to perform its [payment] obligations under the loan agreement;
- validity and enforceability of the documents.

Prospects

8.282
Borrowers are particularly concerned about clauses which look forward and look at a change in 'prospects' either of the borrower or the industry it is involved in, because

- prospects change regularly, often adversely;
- a change in prospects often does not result in a change in fortunes;
- it is at such times they most need the certainty of finance;
- a clause which is triggered by a change in prospects is too uncertain and
- all companies face threats to their prospects all the time—there is rarely a situation in which any company can say that there are no circumstances which exist which might cause a material adverse effect on their prospects (see Box 8.48).

Box 8.48

For example, assume a loan is made to a company which runs hotels in Madrid. The Spanish government decides to encourage the tourist industry and introduces a tax credit for the construction of new hotels in Madrid. This new tax credit could amount to a material adverse change in the company's *prospects* as it will presumably result in a greater supply of hotel rooms and a possible need for the company to drop its prices or have more empty rooms.

Clause 25: Events of Default—Section 2—The LMA Events of Default   347

Financial Condition

8.283

A second option is to provide that the material adverse effect must be on the financial condition of the borrower, see Box 8.51. However, the borrower may argue that this would be inappropriate if the agreement also contains financial covenants, because if the borrower is meeting the objective tests which have been set in the financial covenants, the lenders should not be able to accelerate on the basis of a subjective test.

The lenders' response would be that they need the material adverse change clause to deal with a change in financial condition which has not yet been picked up by the ratios. In other words, the material adverse change clause will supplement the ratios and help deal with the timing problem discussed in the commentary on financial ratios, see 8.120. It will permit the lenders to take action immediately when a financial problem becomes apparent, without having to wait until the date on which ratios are next due to be tested (see Box 8.49).

> **Box 8.49**
>
> So, for example, assume ratios are tested every six months, and there is a requirement that the Tangible Net Worth should not fall below $30 million. Assume also that the Tangible Net Worth figure drops to $10 million, one month after the last test date. If the material adverse change Event of Default is triggered by a change in financial condition, the lenders will be able to accelerate (or at least, not advance additional funds) without having to wait until the next date on which the ratios are tested.

8.284

Comment Where there are financial ratios, any material adverse change clause which looks at a change in the borrower's financial condition should reflect the agreement on the ratios (see Box 8.50). The simplest way to achieve this would be to provide that a material adverse change in financial condition is only an Event of Default if the lenders have reason to believe that the change is likely to result in a failure to meet a financial ratio when next tested and that such failure would, if not cured (e.g. by the exercise of any applicable equity cure rights) be an Event of Default (rather than simply result in a change in Margin).

348 Representations, Undertakings and Events of Default

> **Box 8.50**
>
> An example may clarify. Assume the financial ratios require the Tangible Net Worth to be tested six monthly and, if below $30 million, to be an Event of Default. A drop below $35 million simply changes the Margin. Assume that the Tangible Net Worth on one test date was $40 million, but it falls to $35 million over the next month. This is a material adverse change in financial condition, but should not give the lenders the right to accelerate, because that is contrary to the intention agreed in the financial ratios. The right to accelerate should only apply if the figure drops below £30 million.

Ability to Perform Obligations Under the Loan Agreement

8.285

A third option is to provide that the material adverse effect must be on the ability of the borrower to perform its obligations under the agreement. Many borrowers prefer this to the formulation which talks of a material adverse effect on financial condition, because, for many borrowers, there is plenty of scope for a change in financial condition before ability to service the debt or perform other obligations are seriously prejudiced. This formulation preserves this clause as one of the last resort for the lenders.

Validity and Enforceability of the Documents

8.286

Many material adverse change clauses will be expressed to be triggered by any material adverse change in the validity or enforceability of the documents, as well as by changes in the various other factors described earlier.

8.287

Comment Other suggestions sometimes made by borrowers to ameliorate the material adverse change clause are

- in a syndicated loan, to require a higher proportion of the lenders than normal (not just Majority Lenders, but introduce a concept of 'Supermajority') to have to agree before this clause can be used;
- require notice to be given to the borrower, and an extended grace period, before the clause can be used—so as to allow an opportunity for discussion and to avoid triggering cross defaults.

Clause 25: Events of Default—Section 2—The LMA Events of Default 349

> **Box 8.51**
>
> It is interesting to notice the facts of a case[126] which considered the interpretation of a representation (not an Event of Default) that there had been no material adverse effect in the financial position of the company since a specified date. The lenders argued that the expression 'financial condition' included factors such as changes in market or economic conditions which would affect the financial condition of the borrower, and in particular, a funding shortfall for a planned project. The argument failed with Blair J decided that
>
> - the first port of call in determining whether there had been a change in financial condition was the financial statements although other facts were relevant. Nevertheless an expected funding gap was not relevant— as that related only to the ability to fund obligations which were as yet uncommitted;
> - in looking at whether a change in financial condition is 'material' it would only be so if it materially affected the borrower's ability to repay the loan.[127]
> - the change must not be temporary and
> - if the lender knew when signing the agreement that a given set of facts was likely (e.g. a funding shortfall for a planned project) they could not then call an Event of Default under the material adverse change clause if that set of facts materialized.

Clause 25.13 Acceleration

8.288

This clause reads.

On and at any time after the occurrence of an Event of Default [which is continuing] the Agent may, and shall if so directed by the Majority Lenders, by notice to the Company:

(a) *cancel each Available Commitment of each Lender whereupon each such Available Commitment shall immediately be cancelled and each Facility shall immediately cease to be available for further utilization;*

---

[126] Grupo Hotelero Urvasco SA v Carey Value Added SL [2013] Bus. L.R. D45.

[127] The judge quoted the following texts with approval. The Encyclopaedia of Banking, where it states: '*if the change would have caused the bank not to lend at all or to lend on significantly more onerous terms, for example, as to margin, maturity or security*'; and Zakrzewski, Law and Financial Markets Review, which considers a change to be material that: '*substantially affects the borrowers' ability to repay, or, more generally, significantly increases the risks assumed by the lender*'.

350   Representations, Undertakings and Events of Default

(b) *declare that all or part of the Utilizations, together with accrued interest, and all other amounts accrued or outstanding under the Finance Documents be immediately due and payable, whereupon they shall become immediately due and payable and/or*

(c) *declare that all or part of the Utilizations be payable on demand, whereupon they shall immediately become payable on demand by the Agent on the instructions of the Majority Lenders.*

(d) ....

8.289

This clause sets out the contractual remedies for an Event of Default. These remedies are to cancel the commitment and/or to accelerate the loan and/or to put it on an on demand basis. The wording requires the Agent to exercise the relevant right on behalf of the syndicate and provides that the Agent may act on its own initiative.[128] It also provides that the Agent will exercise the rights if the Majority Lenders so require (subject always to the provisions of Clause 28 (*Role of the Agent, the Arranger and the Issuing Bank*).

8.290

It is worth noting subclause (c). This gives the lenders the right to declare that they have the right to demand immediate repayment of the loan (without actually doing so). This can be useful as it avoids the debt actually becoming immediately due. In many jurisdictions, directors must stop trading within a set period of time after the date on which the company is unable to pay its debts (or fails some similar financial test of solvency). See Box 8.52.

Box 8.52

Wrongful trading

Directors' duties on insolvency are an important issue to bear in mind if the lenders start to consider their enforcement/restructuring options following an Event of Default. In some countries, directors can be held personally liable if they are found guilty of 'negligent mismanagement' of a company, and the threshold they are required to comply with may be very high. In such countries, directors are likely to want to stop trading at a very early stage, making it difficult to arrange a restructuring. In England the issue is wrongful trading[129]—that is, carrying on trading after the point at which 'that person knew or ought to have concluded that there was no reasonable prospect that

---

[128] See Clause 28 (*Role of the Agent, the Arranger and the Issuing Bank*) from 10.001 onwards as to the Agent's liabilities to syndicate members.

[129] Insolvency Act 1986 Sect. 214.

Clause 25: Events of Default—Section 2—The LMA Events of Default

> the company would avoid going into insolvent liquidation'. However the directors have a defence to any action if they 'took every step with a view to minimizing the potential loss to the company's creditors as ... [they] ought to have taken'. The availability of this defence gives directors more scope for having discussions around restructuring than in many countries.

Accelerating the loan will make it immediately due and so can trigger the start of this period. This can make it impossible in practice to negotiate a rescheduling outside the insolvency procedures of the relevant country.

The option of using subclause (c) instead can be a useful right for the lenders in these circumstances. The Ideal Standard case[130] considered the effect of this right and concluded that it did not suspend the underlying repayment schedule which continued in effect until demand was made.

8.291

An issue which the LMA Compounded/Term Rate Loan leaves open is whether the contractual remedies disappear at any point after an Event of Default occurs. Borrowers frequently ask for the words 'which is continuing' to be included in the first sentence of 25.13 (*EVENTS OF DEFAULT: Acceleration*), quoted in 8.288, so that the remedies cannot be exercised after the Event of Default has been remedied. If these words are included, Clause 1.2 (*DEFINITIONS AND INTERPRETATION: Construction*) subclause (e) of the LMA Compounded/Term Rate Loan defines what is meant by 'continuing'.[131]

---

[130] Strategic Value Master Fund Ltd v Ideal Standard International Acquisition S.A.R.L. & Ors [2011] EWHC 171 (Ch).

[131] See comment on Clause 1.2 (*DEFINITIONS AND INTERPRETATION: Construction*) subclause (d) in 1.065.

Boilerplate and Schedules

This Part deals with the remainder of the loan agreement (clauses 26 (*Changes to the Lenders*)—end in the LMA Compounded/Term Rate Loan[1]) and with the schedules. These provisions are often referred to as 'boilerplate'. The boilerplate contains important clauses relating to issues such as loan transfers, the agency role, notices and jurisdiction. The schedules are used to attach additional documents and lists, such as the drawdown notice, confidentiality letter and list of conditions precedent, as well as currency specific provisions (such as the Reference Rate Terms for Optional Currencies) in a multicurrency loan.

---

[1] References in this book to the LMA Compounded/Term Rate Loan are to the LMA Multicurrency Term and Revolving Facilities Agreement incorporating Term SOFR for use in Investment Grade transactions, available to LMA members via www.lma.eu.com.

Changes to Parties

Clause 26: Changes to the Lenders—Section 1—Methods of Transfer

9.001

This clause deals with loan transfers. Before looking at the wording of the clause itself, this introduction looks at the methods of transfer available and at issues which arise in relation to transfers of secured loans.

In summary, the methods by which a new lender can derive an interest in the loan under English law are:

* transfer (see Box 9.1) of rights and obligations (classically, by **novation**);
* assignment of rights;
* **sub-participation** (which is a contract between selling and buying lender) and
* credit derivatives.

© The Author(s), under exclusive license to Springer Nature   **355**
Switzerland AG 2024
S. Wright, *The International Loan Documentation Handbook*, Global Financial Markets,
https://doi.org/10.1007/978-3-031-38489-9_10

356 Changes to Parties

> **Box 9.1**
>
> The word 'transfers' may be used:
>
> - to indicate a complete transfer of the entire legal relationship (or a specified percentage of it) from one lender to another, for example, by novation, rather than a transfer of some aspects of the legal relationship— for example, rights only but not obligations, as would be achieved by an assignment or
> - in a less technical sense, to include all the different methods by which a party other than one of the original lenders can either come to be a lender of record or to have an interest in the loan.

Clause 26.2 (*CHANGES TO THE LENDERS: Company consent*) of the LMA Compounded/Term Rate Loan uses the word 'transfer' in its sense of a transfer of the whole legal relationship.[1] Often the word 'transfer' is used in this sense when making a distinction between the legal effect of a novation and an assignment.

9.002

Within each of these categories, there are numerous options available and each has a different regulatory and accounting impact as well as a different impact on the credit risk of the parties and on their rights and obligations. The first two options (novation and assignment) result in the new lender becoming a lender of record with direct claims against the borrower. Under the last two options (sub-participation and credit derivatives) the original lender remains the lender of record and the new lender's rights are against the original lender, not the borrower.[2] Generally the loan agreement seeks only to regulate the first two options, since the other options do not involve the borrower, save for the need to obtain the borrower's consent to disclosure of confidential information, which is dealt with in Clause 38 (*Confidential Information*). However see also the discussion on 'behind the scenes' transfers in Clause 26 (*Changes to the Lenders*) in 9.035–6.

9.003

Whichever of the four methods outlined earlier is used, a lender planning to transfer an interest in a loan must ensure that it complies with any relevant **prospectus legislation** in the country in which it is operating and in the

---

[1] ie the LMA Multicurrency term and Revolving facilities Agreement incorporating Term SOFR for use in investment Grade Transactions, available to LMA members via www.lma.eu.com

[2] At least, that is the case initially. The new lender may gain rights against the borrower at a later stage under a risk sub-participation or a credit derivative which is settled by physical settlement.

Clause 26: Changes to the Lenders—Section 1—Methods of Transfer 357

countries in which it is inviting participants to consider taking an interest in the loan. It must also ensure that it has authority from the borrower to disclose any confidential information which it may be planning to disclose to potential participants and that the wording of such authority from the borrower covers the circumstances in hand.[3]

The four methods of giving a new party an interest under the loan agreement are discussed here.

1. Novation

9.004

This is a commonly used transfer method in syndicated loans. Novation involves the discharge of the original contract and its replacement by a new contract between the new parties (see Box 9.2).

There are two key issues to be considered in relation to a novation, which are:

- mechanics of the novation—what documents need to be signed? and
- effect of novation—what issues does the fact that it creates a new contract give rise to?

Box 9.2

Clause 26.6 (*CHANGES TO THE LENDERS: Procedure for transfer*) subclause (c) of the LMA Compounded/Term Rate Loan creates a novation by the following words:
  '*On the Transfer Date:*

(i) *to the extent that in the Transfer Certificate the Existing Lender seeks to transfer by novation its rights and obligations under the Finance Documents each of the Obligors and the Existing Lender shall be released from further obligations towards one another under the Finance Documents and their respective rights against one another shall be cancelled (being the 'Discharged Rights and Obligations');*

(ii) *each of the Obligors and the New Lender shall assume obligations towards one another and/or acquire rights against one another which differ from the Discharged Rights and Obligations only insofar as that Obligor and the New Lender have assumed and/or acquired the same in place of that Obligor and the Existing Lender'.*

---

[3] See discussion of Clause 38 (*Confidential Information*) of the LMA Compounded/Term Rate Loan in 11.034.

358   Changes to Parties

Mechanics

9.005

Originally, novation was thought to be a cumbersome method for transfer of syndicated loans as it required all parties to the loan agreement to be party to the novation. The mechanism now included in most syndicated loan documentation avoids this difficulty by providing for the novation to be effected by the selling and buying lender signing a 'Transfer Certificate' which is countersigned by the Agent (and sometimes the borrower), with the result being specified in the agreement to have the effect of novation. This operates on the principle that the lenders which are not party to the transfer certificate make an offer at the time of signing the loan agreement,[4] to accept any person as a lender under the agreement if that person follows the mechanism for novation provided for.[5]

Effect

9.006

The effect of novation is to create a new contract. This may have tax consequences. For example, because novation does not involve a transfer it is unlikely to result in a stamp duty whereas assignment potentially does give rise to a stamp duty subject to applicable exceptions. Secondly the withholding tax treatment of a loan may depend on the identity of the person who made the advance. Novation will involve the making of a new advance, whereas assignment will not. The fact that novation creates a new contract may also cause difficulty with such things as security, consents and hardening periods, as discussed in the following paragraphs.

---

[4] Which offer is made to the public at large and may be accepted by a person completing the mechanism specified in the offer—being, in this case, the execution of a Transfer Certificate. This idea of an offer to the public at large being established by Carlill v Carbolic Smoke Ball Company (1892) 2QB 484.

[5] The effectiveness of this mechanism was confirmed in Habibsons Bank Ltd v Standard Chartered Bank (Hong Kong) Limited [2010] EWCA Civ 1335, distinguishing an Australian case (Goodridge v Macquarie Bank Limited [2010] FCA 67) which had held that a similar mechanism was simply an agreement to agree.

Security

9.007
The effect of a novation on any security requires consideration of the law which governs the security as well as the law which applies to the loan agreement.

In many countries, security can only be given for a debt which exists at the time the security is given. So, in such countries, security cannot be given at the time the loan agreement is signed as security for a debt which will or may come into existence (by the novation) at a future date.

In other countries, security can be given for future debts but priorities issues may arise (does a creditor who had second priority security and who advanced funds against that security before the new loan was created gain priority over the new loan?) Security problems with a novation can be avoided if the security secures a different debt, such as the covenant to pay in favour of a security trustee contained in the security document, or a parallel debt. This issue is dealt with in this commentary on Clause 26 (*Changes to the Lenders*) from 9.022 onwards.

Consents

9.008
Any consent given (e.g. exchange control consents) for the loans made by the original lenders will not necessarily also apply to the new loans made by new lenders as a result of novation. If using novation, parties should ensure that, as a matter of construction, all relevant consents apply not only to the original loans made by original lenders, but also to new loans which spring up from novations effected under the loan agreement.

Hardening periods

9.009
In most countries, if a company is wound up, certain transactions that it has entered into within a certain period prior to the winding up (the 'hardening period') may be challenged in certain circumstances. Because novation results in a new contract, any new loans that arise may fall within a relevant hardening period and they, or any security for them, may be open to challenge

360   **Changes to Parties**

where the original loans (or loans transferred in a different way) would not. Precisely what transactions may be successfully challenged will depend on the law in the place in which the insolvency of the company concerned occurs.

2. Assignment[6]

9.010

Assignment is an alternative method of transfer which avoids many of the problems of novation as it does not create a new contract. Assignment keeps the existing contract in place but has the effect that rights once owned by one lender (principally the right to be repaid and receive interest) will, after the assignment, belong to a different lender (see Box 9.3).

Box 9.3

So the key differences between this and a novation are that

- obligations are not transferred and
- it is the *original lender's rights* which now belong to the new lender, rather than the new lender owning a *new set of rights.*

Unless the loan agreement says otherwise (which it often does) consent of the borrower is not required.

9.011

The principal issues with assignment related to:

- effect on indemnities;
- effect on security and
- effect on obligations.

---

[6] Often words are not used accurately, and a document may be referred to as an 'assignment' which in fact has the effect of an assignment and assumption agreement discussed in 9.016.

Clause 26: Changes to the Lenders—Section 1—Methods of Transfer   **361**

Effect on indemnities

9.012

Personal rights (where one party is only willing to perform in favour of a particular counterparty and it would be unjust to enforce performance in favour of a different party) cannot be assigned[7] (see Box 9.4).

> **Box 9.4**
>
> For example, an employer may not assign an employment contract so as to require the employee to work for a different company. A publisher cannot assign the benefit of an author's contract to write a book if the author relied on the publisher's skill as a publisher.[8]

This may not be the case where the contracting party expressly or impliedly contracted with the original counterparty or its assigns.[9]

Arguably, indemnities could be personal rights because it is likely that attributes of the person holding the indemnity will affect the likelihood of a claim being made under it. For this reason any new lender who takes an interest through an assignment ought to ensure that the contractual provisions of the loan agreement (and in particular any indemnities such as the indemnity for taxes) are expressed to benefit not only the original lenders, but also assignees, so reinforcing the argument that the indemnities are not personal in the first place.

English law assignments come in many forms (see A1.051 onwards). Usually a lender will be transferring only part of its interest in the agreement and therefore the assignment will be equitable, not statutory. The lenders will usually give notice to the borrower through the Agent. The effect is that, unless the assignor disputes the payment, the borrower must pay the new lender (through the Agent) in order to be discharged from the debt.[10]

---

[7] British Waggon Co v Lea & Co (1879–80) LR 5 QBD 149.

[8] Griffith v Tower Publishing (1897) 1 Ch 21.

[9] Tolhurst v Associated Portland Cement Manufacturers (1900) Ltd (1903) AC 414.

[10] If the lenders did not give notice, the assignment would, as a matter of English law, still be effective in a liquidation of the existing lender, but the new lender would not be able to receive payment direct, only through the existing lender.

362 Changes to Parties

Effect on security

9.013

The assignment does not cause the security problems which novation causes because the debt which is secured does not change. That debt still exists but simply belongs to a new party.

n many jurisdictions, an assignment of a debt automatically carries with it (and allows an assignee to benefit from) any security for the debt without the need for that security to be specifically transferred. However, there may be requirements which need to be complied with in the jurisdiction where the security is, for example, for the new lender to be registered on the security register. Such requirements would be fatal to the liquidity of the loan in the secondary market. In such cases, therefore, the use of a structure which avoids these additional requirements may be necessary, for example, trustee/parallel debt/guarantee structure. See further 9.022 onwards in relation to transfers of secured loans

Effect on obligations

9.014

It is not possible to assign obligations under English law (see Box 9.5).

Box 9.5

There is a difference here between assigning and delegating. A person may delegate their obligations to another and the person to whom the obligations are owed may have to accept the performance of those obligations by another if the identity of the person performing the obligation is not critical to the person to whom the obligation is owed. For example, a company which has agreed to deliver cement to a specified place can delegate that obligation, while an architect who has a contract to design a new building for housing the national opera company cannot delegate that obligation because the skills of the person performing the obligation are important to the other party to the contract.

9.015

Lenders under a syndicated loan have obligations (principally to advance funds) as well as rights. The obligation to advance funds to the borrower

Clause 26: Changes to the Lenders—Section 1—Methods of Transfer **363**

cannot be delegated, since the identity of the person performing that obligation is relevant for the borrower. So the assignment is inappropriate for loans where there are significant ongoing personal obligations on the lenders. This would be the case in a revolving credit, a multicurrency loan and a term loan which has not yet been fully drawn, for example.

9.016

Nevertheless, a hybrid can be, and often is, used in these situations. This is referred to as an 'Assignment and Assumption Agreement'. The commercial effect of such an agreement is similar to the novation but without its disadvantages. The assignment and assumption agreement involves three parts:

* the existing lender assigns its rights to the new lender;
* the new lender agrees with the borrower to perform the obligations owed by the existing lender (to the extent of the amount transferred) and the borrower agrees to accept that performance and
* the borrower agrees with the existing lender not to pursue it for the performance of its obligations (to the extent of the amount being transferred).

The effect is that the new lender has assumed the obligations but there is no discharge of a contract and replacement with a new contract, as in a novation. The security, consents and hardening period issues which novation gives rise to are therefore avoided. The document has the effect of an assignment coupled with an assumption of obligations by the new lender. Of course, this document is similar to a novation in that it will be necessary for all parties to the loan agreement to be a party to it. Therefore, it is usually effected using a transfer certificate mechanism as used for a novation and discussed in 9.005.

3. Sub-participation

9.017

A sub-participation is very different from an assignment and a novation because it does not involve the new lender in acquiring a relationship with the borrower. The new lender acquires rights against the existing lender, but not against the borrower. It is sometimes referred to as a 'silent' participation. This can be achieved either by:

* a risk sub-participation or

364   Changes to Parties

- a funded sub-participation.

Risk sub-participation

9.018
For a fee, the sub-participant gives a guarantee to the existing lender in relation to the portion of the loan the risk of which is being transferred. The effect for the existing lender is to change its credit risk from a risk on the borrower to a risk on the sub-participant. For the sub-participant, if it is required to make payment, it will be subrogated to the rights of the existing lender in relation to the borrower.

Funded sub-participation

9.019
This is usually achieved through a sub-loan. Here the new lender advances funds to the existing lender on the basis that the obligations of the existing lender to repay those sums are limited to amounts received by the existing lender from the borrower. The effect for the existing lender is to reduce the amount of its total credit risk by the amount of the sub-loan. The effect for the new lender is that it takes two credit risks: does the borrower repay the existing lender and does the existing lender repay the new lender? It may also involve additional tax risk in relation to possible withholding taxes on interest payable under the sub-loan.

4. Credit derivatives

9.020
An alternative method of transferring credit risk is by using credit derivatives. These are highly flexible instruments which can be used to create investments which differ from the underlying debt in many significant ways, such as credit risk and pricing. The documents are in standard form International Swaps and Derivatives Association (ISDA) agreements. Because there is no change in the legal relationship between the lender and borrower, there is no effect on the underlying loan or its security.

Clause 26: Changes to the Lenders—Section 1—Methods of Transfer 365

There may be issues in some jurisdictions as to whether these derivatives amount to gambling or insurance. ISDA maintains a wealth of legal opinions on these issues in various jurisdictions which are available to ISDA members on their website. Credit derivatives can be very complex although the basic underlying concepts are simple. We focus here on the credit default swap only.

Credit default swap

9.021

Under a credit default swap, the original lender makes periodic payments to the counterparty of a small percentage of the principal amount due to the original lender from the borrower. These payments are similar in amount to the fee which would be paid in relation to a risk sub-participation. If a Credit Event occurs, the swap will become due for settlement. The swap may provide for cash settlement or for physical settlement. In the case of cash settlement, the counterparty will pay the difference between the face value of the debt (the amount due from the borrower) and its current market value (see Box 9.6). In other words, they will compensate the original lender for the loss in value of the debt. In the case of physical settlement, the counterparty will pay (usually) the full amount of the face value of the loan and the loan will be transferred to it.

Box 9.6

The credit default swap is very flexible. It may relate to a single payment instalment, or to a single loan agreement, but more commonly it relates to a group of borrowers, a group of loan agreements, a portfolio of debt and so on. The credit protection being purchased may also be limited to particular tranches of risk such as the first 5% of loss suffered. Participants in the CDS market do not even need to hold any of the underlying debt. As discussed in the Introduction in 0.243, these instruments have led to an active market in credit risk, quite separate from the market in the underlying debt.

366 Changes to Parties

Clause 26: Changes to the Lenders—Section 2—Transfers of Secured Loans

9.022
It will be clear from the previous paragraphs that transferring secured loans gives rise to particular problems. This section looks at the different structures which have been developed to allow the syndication of secured loans. The first point to make is that the issues discussed in this section relate to syndications, not sub-participation or credit derivatives. Because sub-participation and credit derivatives do not affect the legal relationship between the borrower and its lenders, they also do not affect the security for the loan. The problems addressed in this section arise only when there is a change in the members of the syndicate, that is, under English law, when there is an assignment or novation.

As well as the legal issues discussed in Section 1, syndicating secured loans gives rise to the administrative question of how to avoid the need for signatures from all lenders when security needs to be released or amended. Any requirement (as in some jurisdictions) that any change in identity of a secured party needs to be registered in the registry where the security is registered, can be fatal to the liquidity of the underlying debt. So it is common in secured syndicated loans for security to be given to one of the lenders (often the Agent, or a special Security Agent or Security Trustee) on behalf of all the lenders.

9.023
Two questions therefore need to be addressed in considering the structuring for transferable secured loans:

- who should the security be given to? and
- what debt should it secure?

There are three common options, with the choice depending on the jurisdictions of the parties and of any security:

- security given to a trustee for the lenders, as security for the covenant to pay the trustee contained in the security documents;

Clause 26: Changes to the Lenders—Section 2—Transfers of Secured Loans 367

- security given to an agent for the syndicate as security for the underlying debts to syndicate members[11] or
- security given to an agent for the syndicate as security for a parallel debt or joint creditorship.

1. Security to a trustee for the covenant to pay

9.024

In jurisdictions which recognize the concept of trusts,[12] the security is given to a Security Trustee (normally one of the lenders) as trustee for the lenders from time to time.[13] It will be given to the trustee as security for the covenant, in the security documents, to pay the trustee the amounts due to the lenders from time to time. It is important to take care, in drafting the security, to ensure that it does indeed secure the covenant in favour of the trustee.

The trust route has a number of advantages over the other structures described below, notably in that

- changing a trustee is simple and
- the lenders do not take a credit risk on a trustee.

2. Security to an Agent

9.025

In jurisdictions which do not recognize the concept of trust, the security will be held by the Agent as agent for the syndicate members from time to time. In such cases, due diligence will be necessary on the question of what will happen to the security and its proceeds in the event that the Security Agent becomes insolvent when holding proceeds but before they have been distributed.[14] This may also be relevant for regulatory purposes—such as the

---

[11] Or for the obligation to pay the underlying debts to the Agent on behalf of the syndicate members.

[12] Recognition of trusts in relation to syndicated loans is not limited to common law jurisdictions and countries which have ratified the 1985 Hague Convention on recognition of trusts. Japan, South Africa and Luxembourg have adopted their own versions of trust law.

[13] It is not necessary to identify all beneficiaries of a trust at the time the trust is created as long as it is clear enough to be able to identify who the beneficiaries are at any given time.

[14] See discussion on trustees versus agents in A1.039.

368   **Changes to Parties**

Basel regulations—where the question arises as to whether the lenders are in fact simply unsecured creditors of the Agent, particularly if the parallel debt structure is used as described below.

A second disadvantage of an Agent is what happens to the security if the Agent needs to be replaced? Under English law the trust property automatically vests in a new trustee without the need for any transfer. With an Agent, the security may need to be reconstituted in favour of the new Agent.

Thirdly, of course, the lenders' lawyer will need to consider how such security would be enforced in practice—for example, will the Agent be able to claim as secured creditor for the whole debt?

Security to an Agent as security for the underlying debts[15]

9.026

This structure is only available if, in the jurisdiction where the security is located, it is possible for security to be given to (and to be enforceable by) one person as security for debts owed to different persons (although payable to the security holder on behalf of those persons) and without the need to make any changes to the registration when there is a change in the members of the syndicate.

If this structure is to be used, it will be necessary to ensure that the security secures the debts owed to lenders who take an interest in the loan after the date of creation of the security.[16] This involves consideration of the method of transfer.

9.027

If interests in the loan are transferred by assignment or by assignment and assumption, the original debts made by the original lenders, which are secured by the security, remain in place throughout, despite any transfers, but are owed to new lenders. Security can be given for the debts existing at the time the security is created, and that security should remain effective to secure those debts as assigned to new syndicate members (subject to any registration requirements).

---

[15] Or for the obligation to pay the underlying debts to the Agent on behalf of the syndicate members.

[16] Unless under the law which governs the security, and taking account of its conflict of law rules, the obligation to pay the Agent will be regarded as a different debt, independent of the underlying debts, in which case the security may be given for the obligation to pay the Agent and the method of transfer may be disregarded.

Clause 26: Changes to the Lenders—Section 2—Transfers of Secured Loans 369

9.028

If, on the other hand, interests in the loan are transferred by novation, it is important to ensure that the security secures any new debts made by new lenders as a result of the novation as well as the original loans made by the original lenders. It is not sufficient for the security to be given to an agent (or trustee) on behalf of the syndicate from time to time. It must also secure the debts created from time to time. This is an area for due diligence in the country of security. In most countries it is not possible to create security for future debts which may or may not be advanced by persons unknown. In others, such security may be possible but there may be priority issues if second priority security has been created on the secured assets after the date of the original loan but before the date on which the novation occurred. See Appendix 1 in A1.069.

The same point arises in a multicurrency loan if the original loan is repaid and then re-advanced on a change of currency. Does the security secure the new advance, and might there be a loss of priority to other lenders?

Security to an Agent as security for a parallel debt

9.029

This route is often used in those countries in which trusts are not recognized but it is also not possible for security to be given to an agent on behalf of the syndicate because security can only be given in favour of the secured creditors themselves and not to an agent on their behalf. In these countries, syndicates must either accept the administrative inconvenience of registering a change in security holder whenever there is a change in the syndicate (which would severely hamper the liquidity of the loan and therefore the amount of money which could be raised) or use an alternative route.

9.030

The alternative route often used is the so-called 'parallel debt'. Here, security is given to the Agent as security for a 'parallel debt' expressed to be owed to the Agent. This debt is equal to the total amount outstanding under the loan agreement. It is specified that the amount of the parallel debt reduces pro rata with all payments of the underlying debt. It is also specified that any recoveries under the parallel debt must be shared pro rata with the lenders. While this structure has become market standard in some countries, it may be vulnerable to challenge as being a fiction in other jurisdictions. It may also be open to challenge as being a preference in some countries, as the security

370   Changes to Parties

is granted to an entity which has not advanced all the funds. Nevertheless, the structure is gaining increased acceptance, as evidenced by the fact that it has been held to be effective in France (in the Belvedere case in 2011) and in Poland (file no IV CSK 145/09).

Security to Agent as security for joint creditorship

9.031

A similar solution to the parallel debt in some countries involves the concept of 'joint creditorship' in certain circumstances. A joint creditorship is rather similar to the more common idea of joint and several debtors. Where there is a group of joint and several debtors owing a sum of money, they must ensure that the sum is paid, on the basis that the person who is owed the debt has the right to sue any one of the debtors for the whole debt

9.032

Under a joint creditorship—in those countries which have the concept—the sum of money is owed to a group of creditors. It may also be that the local law permits any one of those creditors to sue, (alone) for the whole amount of the debt on behalf of the group. In this way, the security can be given to the person to whom the debt is owed (if, under local law it can be given to just one of the creditors), and (crucially) that creditor is entitled to sue in its own name for payment of the whole debt.

An alternative to a parallel debt

9.033

An alternative which avoids the fictional element of a parallel debt is for a company (an **spc** subsidiary of a lender) to guarantee the loan on a limited recourse basis, with recourse limited to its recoveries under security. The security would then be given to the spc as security for the borrower's obligation to indemnify (or cash collateralize) the spc for payments made under the guarantee (see Box 9.7). In this way security is given in favour of the person to whom the debt is owed without the need to create a 'parallel debt'. The method of transfer of the underlying debt then becomes irrelevant as far as the security is concerned. The main disadvantages of this route are the added structural complexity and the need to establish and maintain a special purpose company. Given the increased tendency to recognize both trusts and parallel debts, and the extra expense and complexity of this route, this alternative mechanism is uncommon.

> **Box 9.7**
>
> An alternative structure to a parallel debt
>
>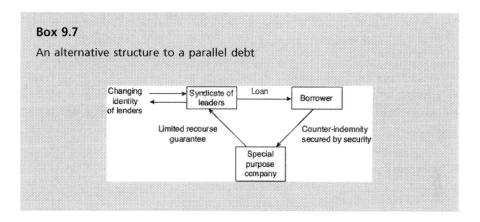

Clause 26: Changes to the Lenders—Section 3—The LMA Clause

Consent to transfers

9.034
Clause 26 (*Changes to the Lenders*) deals with transfer of the loan. An important question which needs to be addressed is the extent to which the borrower's consent is required for a transfer. There are two separate aspects to this, being

- consent to transfers 'behind the scenes' such as sub-participations and credit derivatives and
- consent to transfers which result in a change in the lender of record.

Consent to transfers 'behind the scenes'

9.035
Traditionally there has been no restriction on the lenders' ability to enter into sub-participations, credit derivatives or other arrangements which do

372   **Changes to Parties**

not affect the lender of record. This is the position in the standard LMA Compounded/Term Rate Loan. The reasoning is that these arrangements do not involve the borrower but are private arrangements entered into by the lender.

However as noted in the Introduction in 0.240, the evolution of active markets for credit risk through the credit default swap market and the distressed debt market can cause significant difficulties for borrowers in trying to negotiate reschedulings because of the lack of transparency as to who is holding the ultimate risk, and the different motivations of different players. For example a lender holding a credit default swap may prefer a Credit Event to occur so as to trigger payment under the swap. A party which has bought into the loan at a discount may also have less motivation than other lenders to try to arrange a turnaround for the company.

9.036

Borrowers may therefore be concerned to try to restrict 'single name' credit derivatives[17] and sub-participations or at least to have the right in certain circumstances to be informed about them. However, lenders would generally be very reluctant, as a matter of policy, to permit any such restrictions as they could have a significant impact on the lenders' strategic options in running their own business. Many lenders have strict transfer criteria with which all their loans must comply

Occasionally a borrower may succeed in including a provision to the effect that lenders cannot enter into arrangements which result in their losing their control over the exercise of their voting rights. Another possibility is to ask lenders to agree to inform them of such arrangements in certain circumstances (e.g. in the event of a refusal of a consent or following an Event of Default).

Consent to transfers which change the lender of record

9.037

Changing the lender of record has a much greater impact on the borrower than the 'behind the scenes' arrangements just discussed. For example:

---

[17] A 'single name' credit derivative is one which relates to the credit risk of a single entity, as opposed to one which relates to a pool of debts.

Clause 26: Changes to the Lenders—Section 3—The LMA Clause 373

- The credit standing of the lender may be an issue, particularly in a revolving credit, a term loan with a long drawdown period or a multicurrency loan, in all of which the borrower is exposed to the risk that the lender may be unable to advance funds as agreed;
- The credit standing of the lender may also be an issue as a result of the market disruption clause, if there is one (see 5.024): depending on what has been agreed on in that clause, certain lenders may be more likely than others to have a funding problem which could help to trigger the clause;
- The identity and location of the lender can impact the borrower's withholding tax obligations;
- Lenders who have purchased debt at a discount may have different motivations towards rescue than other lenders;
- Certain types of lenders, such as hedge funds may not have the manpower to deal with requests for consent and their motivation may not be transparent;
- Lenders with small amounts of exposure to the borrower may have less motivation to support a turnaround in the event that the company gets into difficulties;
- The lender of record will have access to confidential information about the borrower's business, which could be abused.

9.038

For all these reasons, the borrower would like to ensure that their consent is required for a change in the lender of record. This is the default position in the LMA Compounded/Term Rate Loan, subject to three provisos—

- first, such consent must not be unreasonably withheld,
- second, the consent is not required if an Event of Default has occurred and
- third, consent is not required in the case of a transfer to an Affiliate of a lender.

In many of the other LMA documents, the consent of the borrower is not required for a transfer.

9.039

Comment The reason the borrower's consent is not required following an Event of Default is to facilitate a sale in the distressed market as well as to allow for physical settlement of derivatives. However as discussed earlier, transfers at such time can cause problems for restructurings so that borrowers may want to restrict this if possible.

374   Changes to Parties

9.040

Comment The question of whether or not it is unreasonable to withhold consent is of course subjective. It might be helpful to specify some circumstances in which the parties agreed that it would be reasonable to withhold consent.

9.041

Comment If the borrower's consent is not needed for transfer, it should consider specifying certain parameters within which the right to transfer must be exercised (see Box 9.8). However, borrowers need to bear in mind that the more restrictive the transfer provisions, the smaller the pool of money will be for funding the loan. Restrictions on transfer may come at a cost.

Box 9.8

Examples of limits on transfers which a borrower may wish to specify include:

- no transfers such that the amount of the participation of any lender of record is less than a given figure. This will have the effect of limiting the number of lenders of record with whom the borrower needs to deal and also ensuring each of them has a reasonable level of commitment to the borrower;
- no transfers to be made to a competitor (either specified by name or by industry sector) or to a lender to a competitor;
- no transfers to a lender with lower than a certain credit rating (particularly for revolvers or term loans with long drawdown periods);
- no transfers to a lender which is a counterparty to [significant] transactions with the borrower because it will give rise to rights of set off[18];
- no transfers by the Agent if it would reduce the Agent's participation below a certain figure;
- loan only to be transferred to 'Qualifying Lenders' [see discussions on Clause 15 (*Tax Gross up and Indemnities*)];
- no transfers to specific named entities listed in a schedule;
- transfer only allowed to specific named entities listed in a schedule;
- transfers only within the existing syndicate;
- no transfers to lenders which have previously been in a minority refusing consent to a request and
- transfers only permitted to entities which can provide banking services including fixed term overdraft facilities.

---

[18] For example, problems may arise if the borrower's debt is being traded at a discount. Assume that a debt of $100 is bought for $70 by a purchaser which owes $100 to the borrower. The purchaser may now, in some jurisdictions, offset its debt to the borrower against the borrower's debt to it. The result is that, for an outlay of $70, the purchaser can avoid a payment of $100. The effect may be to make it more difficult for a company whose loan is being traded at a discount to collect their

9.042

Sometimes lenders might also like the right to withhold consent to proposed transferees if they are taking significant credit risks on the other lenders. For example, this might be appropriate in a project finance transaction, where there is a long drawdown period, and insufficiency of funds during the construction would be fatal to the viability of the project.

Clause 26.1 Assignments and transfers by the lenders

9.043

This clause allows a lender to assign its rights or to transfer its rights and obligations (by novation). The clause states that assignment or transfer may only be made to '*an entity regularly engaged in purchasing or investing in loans, securities, or other financial assets*'.[19] Even if it were restricted to 'financial institutions' the court has interpreted this phrase very broadly as discussed earlier in Box 0.27.

9.044

The wording can also allow transfers to the borrower or its Affiliates. The LMA has included a note in the LMA Compounded/Term Rate Loan, cross referring to the Leveraged LMA, which contains optional additional wording in two different versions to deal with this. In one version, such transfers are prohibited. In the alternative version they are allowed but the transferee has no voting power and cannot pick and choose which lender to take out—the offer to take a transfer must be made to all lenders pro rata.

---

debts from customers. In the event of liquidation of the company, it will be the company's creditors who will lose out. In some countries, set off exercised shortly before liquidation may be unwound, so the advantage which the customer obtained may not be permanent. (In the UK, under Rule 4.90(2) of the Insolvency Rules 1986, set off is not available against a debt acquired a time when the party knew that insolvency proceedings of the debtor were imminent). Nevertheless, avoiding such sales in the first place would be preferable.

[19] This does not, of course, restrict the nature of sub-participants, or of those to whom risk may be sold in a cash settled credit derivative.

376   Changes to Parties

Clause 26.2 Company consent

9.045

This clause requires the borrower's consent to be obtained for an assignment (i.e. of rights only) or transfer (i.e. of rights and obligations) other than to an Affiliate of an existing lender or following an Event of Default. This consent is not to be unreasonably withheld or delayed and is deemed given if not refused within five Business Days[20] of a request.

Clause 26.3 Other conditions of assignment or transfer

9.046

Subclause (b) of this clause provides that an assignment will only be effective if the new lender confirms it accepts the obligations in the loan towards the rest of the syndicate members and when all applicable 'know your customer' checks are completed.

Subclause (c) provides that the documentation to achieve a transfer (which, under Clause 26.1 (*CHANGES TO THE LENDERS: Assignments and transfers by the Lenders*) subclause (b), must take the form of a novation) must follow the requirements of Clause 26.6 (*CHANGES TO THE LENDERS: Procedure for transfer*). Due diligence is necessary to ensure that novation is a satisfactory method of transfer for the loan in question and that a different method (e.g. assignment and assumption) may not be more suitable.[21] If the parties want to use assignment, Clause 26.7 (*CHANGES TO THE LENDERS: Procedure for assignment*) sets out a procedure for that option.

9.047

Clause 26.3 (*CHANGES TO THE LENDERS: Other conditions of assignment*) subclause (d) ensures that no additional withholding tax or increased cost expense will be borne by the borrower as a result of any transfer or change

---

[20] This period of time is designed to fit with the LMA's standard forms for trading of debts in the secondary market so lenders are reluctant to change it.

[21] See Sections 1 and 2 of the commentary on this Clause 26 (*Changes to the Lenders*) from 9.001 onwards.

Clause 26: Changes to the Lenders—Section 3—The LMA Clause

in Facility Office if that extra cost would arise in the circumstances existing at the time of the transfer.

However there are two exceptions to this principle.

9.048

Firstly, this provision only applies after the primary syndication has been completed. It is in relation to Treaty Lenders that this exception is most relevant. If a lender is only eligible to receive payment gross as a result of a double tax treaty, the effect of this exception is that the borrower will have to gross up payments to that lender until they receive a direction from the tax authorities enabling them to pay without a tax deduction. That would have been the case if the Treaty Lender had been a signatory to the loan agreement in the first place and the rationale for this exception is that the question of whether primary syndication predates or post dates loan signature should have no impact on the withholding tax position. Nevertheless where primary syndication post dates loan signature there is clearly less scope for the borrower to avoid the problem by delaying the due date for the first interest payment as discussed in Box 6.7.

9.049

The second exception relates to the 'DTTP Scheme' discussed in 6.012. Under that scheme, in the UK, if a Treaty Lender has a 'passport' confirming its eligibility for relief, and if the borrower submits the necessary forms to the UK tax authorities within 30 days of the lender becoming a lender then the borrower will benefit from a speedy process for obtaining approval from the UK tax authorities to make payment to the lender without deducting tax. This second exception therefore provides that if the lender has provided the necessary information to the borrower to enable them to use the scheme, then the borrower's protection against gross-up is removed. The idea is that it is now within the control of the borrower to submit the forms within 30 days

9.050

Comment However the risk remains for the borrower that the Agent may take some time to notify them of the transfer, so the borrower may want to adjust the clause to ensure that they must receive the lender's details in sufficient time to enable it to comply with the 30-day requirement for eligibility for the faster processing.

9.051

Comment Some lenders require an adjustment to this clause to allow transferees or other lending offices to have the benefit of the tax and increased

378 Changes to Parties

cost indemnity clauses if the change was made for the benefit of the borrower pursuant to Clause 18 (*Mitigation by the Lenders*).

Clause 26.4 Assignment or transfer fee

9.052
This clause provides for the buyer to pay a **transfer fee** to the Agent.

Clause 26.5 Limitation of responsibility of existing lenders

9.053
This clause is an **exclusion clause** limiting the sellers' responsibility to buyers in relation to the borrower.

Clause 26.6 Procedure for transfer

9.054
This clause of the LMA Compounded/Term Rate Loan uses a Transfer Certificate mechanism. This involves seller and buyer of a portion of the loan signing a transfer certificate,[22] with details of the transfer completed, and delivering that to the Agent. The aim of this mechanism is to simplify the trading of interests in the loan and avoid the need for a lengthy new document to be prepared, agreed and signed by all lenders each time there is a loan transfer.

Clause 26.6 (*CHANGES TO THE LENDERS: Procedure for transfer*) specifies that the effect of this certificate is to discharge the rights and obligations of the existing lender vis-a-vis the borrower (to the extent they are being transferred) and to substitute the same rights and obligations as between the borrower and the new lender. This is a novation—discharging one contract and replacing it with another contract which is identical except for the parties. The agreement provides for a transfer to be effective on the later of the date proposed in the transfer certificate and the date on which the Agent

---

[22] See Section 1 of the commentary on this Clause 26 (*Changes to the Lenders*) in 9.005.

Clause 26: Changes to the Lenders—Section 3—The LMA Clause

completes the certificate. There is an obligation on the Agent to complete the certificate as soon as practicable, subject to completion of necessary 'know your customer' checks.

9.055

The certificate does not deal with commercial issues which are of no concern to the Agent such as apportionment of interest (if the sale is part way through an Interest Period and Clause 26.10 (*CHANGES TO THE LENDERS: Pro rata interest settlement*) does not apply). Such matters will already have been dealt with in the document[23] signed by the seller and buyer at the time the trade was agreed and which set out the commercial terms of the trade such as its effective date.

Clause 26.7 Procedure for assignment

9.056

This clause provides an optional procedure to follow if lenders wish to transfer the loan by assignment.

Clause 26.8 Copy of Transfer Certificate, Assignment Agreement or Increase Confirmation to Company

9.057

This clause requires the Agent to deliver a copy of any transfer certificate or assignment agreement to the Company.

Clause 26.9 Security over lenders' rights

9.058

This optional clause allows lenders to provide this loan to their own financiers in order to secure borrowings by the lenders. Including this type of provision may be necessary in order to enable the lenders to access certain sources of finance such as funding from central banks.

---

[23] See, for example, the LMA forms of documentation for loan transfers.

380 Changes to Parties

The provision states that the borrower cannot be required to pay anyone other than the lender, nor to pay more than would be due to the lender. They also provide that it will be the lender who remains liable to perform the obligations under the agreement.

Clause 26.10 Pro rata interest settlement

9.059
This optional clause provides a mechanism which may be used if the Agent is prepared to arrange for the apportionment of interest and fees between sellers and buyers when the transfer date occurs in the middle of an Interest Period. It provides that, at the end of the Interest Period, the interest due from the borrower will be apportioned between seller and buyer so that the seller receives the interest accrued up to the sale date and the buyer will receive the balance.

Clause 27: Changes to the Obligors

Clause 27.1 Assignments and transfers by Obligors

9.060
This clause prohibits the borrowers and guarantors from transferring their rights or obligations under the agreement.

Clause 27.2 Additional Borrowers

9.061
This clause allows additional group members to become entitled to make drawings under the facility if there is no Default and

- the new party is approved by the lenders (with an option for the draftsperson to require only Majority Lender approval);
- the new party signs an Accession Letter and

Clause 27: Changes to the Obligors **381**

- the new party delivers certain conditions precedent (notably, legal opinions satisfactory to the Agent relating to the relevant country and compliance with any 'know your customer' checks).

In addition, Clauses 21.14 (*REPRESENTATIONS: Repetition*) subclause (b) and 27.5 (*CHANGES TO THE OBLIGORS: Repetition of representations*) provide for the Repeating Representations to be repeated by a new borrower on the date it becomes a new borrower, and therefore accession of a new borrower is also conditional on those Repeating Representations being true.

9.062

Comment The Company (the top company in the group to which the lenders have recourse) needs to ensure that, when the document is being negotiated, they identify the companies which may be wishing to rely on the availability of funds from the facility and specify them as borrowers in the first instance. They will also want to minimize the requirements which need to be satisfied for other group companies to draw the facility. For this reason, the Company may request:

- that where the new borrower is from the same country as one of the existing Obligors, they should be entitled to draw the loan without consent of the lenders (because that consent is imposed largely to enable lenders to consider any legal issues which may be highlighted by a legal opinion) and there should be no need for a new legal opinion[24];
- that addition of borrowers from other jurisdictions should require Majority Lender (not all lender) approval. Nevertheless, lenders may resist this and require unanimous consent for the addition of such borrowers, so as to enable them to review any relevant legal opinion as a condition of their consent, rather than rely on the Agent (in accordance with Clause 27.2 (*CHANGES TO THE BORROWER: Additional Borrowers*) subclause (a)(iv)) to determine its acceptability.

---

[24] Lenders may resist this point, particularly if the facility has a long drawdown period, so as to protect against change in law in the intervening period.

382   Changes to Parties

Clause 27.3 Resignation of a Borrower

9.063

This clause allows a borrower to cease to be an Obligor once it has repaid its loans and other moneys due from it under the agreement, provided there is no Default at that time. The Company, if it is a borrower, may not resign.

Clause 27.4 Additional Guarantors

9.064

This clause provides a mechanism for a new group company to become an additional guarantor. This is likely to be used when other guarantors are resigning. The only prerequisites to addition of guarantors are the same conditions precedent as for an additional borrower (including a legal opinion satisfactory to the Agent) and Repeating Representations.

Clause 27.5 Repetition of representations

9.065

This clause states that the Repeating Representations are repeated on a new Obligor becoming a party to the agreement.

Clause 27.6 Resignation of a Guarantor

9.066

This clause provides a mechanism for guarantors to resign. The Company, if a guarantor originally, may not resign. Other guarantors may resign but only if all lenders agree and there is no Default.

The Finance Parties

Clause 28: Role of the Agent, the Arranger and the Issuing Bank

10.001

This clause is the only clause in the agreement where the **Arranger** appears. At the time the loan agreement is signed, the Arranger's task is completed and the main purpose of referring to the Arranger in this clause is to give them the benefit of the exclusion clause. However, given that the exclusion clause is effectively retrospective insofar as the Arranger is concerned[1] this clause is no substitute for including an exclusion clause in appropriate pre-loan agreement documentation.

Clause 28 (*Role of the Agent, the Arranger and the Issuing Bank*) of the LMA Compounded/Term Rate Loan[2] is concerned with defining the role of the Agent and the Arranger as being that of facilitators of the transaction but not standing in for the lenders nor looking after their interests, nor assuming the fiduciary duties which attach to persons who represent others in a legal matter (see Box 10.1).

---

[1] See <u>Sumitomo Bank v Banque Bruxelles Lambert (1997) 1 Lloyds Law Reports 487</u> for a case where an exclusion clause in the loan agreement did not protect the Arranger from liability in respect of its duty of care as Arranger.

[2] Reference in this book to the LMA Compounded/Term Rate Loan are to the LMA Multicurrency Term and Revolving Facilities Agreement incorporating Term SOFR for use in Investment Grade transactions, available to LMA members via www.lma.eu.com.

© The Author(s), under exclusive license to Springer Nature Switzerland AG 2024
S. Wright, *The International Loan Documentation Handbook*, Global Financial Markets, https://doi.org/10.1007/978-3-031-38489-9_11

384   The Finance Parties

> **Box 10.1**
>
> The general English law position is that, where someone represents another in a legal matter, that person has duties (known as 'fiduciary duties') to look after the interests of the person he is representing. However, a fiduciary relationship cannot be superimposed on a contract in such a way as to alter the operation which that contract was intended to have in accordance with its true construction.
>
> Fiduciary duties generally include:[3]
>
> - a duty to act carefully;
> - a duty to avoid conflicts of interest and subordinate his own interests to that of his principals;
> - a duty not to make a secret profit and
> - a duty not to sub-delegate.

10.002

The intention in a syndicated loan is that the Agent should have an administrative role only and should not be obliged to look after the interests of syndicate members nor (as far as practical) to exercise any discretions on their behalf and that therefore, a fiduciary relationship should not arise. Instead, it is intended that it should simply act as a conduit for receipt of money and information with limited ability to take decisions on behalf of lenders. The extent to which other lenders are relying on the Agent is limited as far as possible. In Torre Asset Funding[4] the court considered the agency clause (which was in LMA 'standard' terms) and gave effect to the terms of the documents, without implying wider duties.

10.003

The loan agreement does, in certain cases, allow the Agent to take decisions on behalf of the syndicate. Notably, Clause 25.13 (*EVENTS OF DEFAULT: Acceleration*) permits the Agent to exercise the right of acceleration without being directed to do so by the syndicate. Clause 4.1 (*CONDITIONS OF UTILIZATION: Initial conditions precedent*) permits the Agent to decide whether conditions precedent have been met satisfactorily.[5] In Torre Asset Funding, the court highlighted the fact that, where the Agent had discretions such as these, there was an implied term (known as the 'Socimer implied term'

---

[3] See Philip Wood, International Loans, Bonds, Guarantees, Legal Opinions, 3rd ed 2019 in 17-08.
[4] Torre Asset Funding Ltd v Royal Bank of Scotland Plc [2013] EWHC 2670 (Ch) in paras 142–8.
[5] See Box 2.4.

or the 'Braganza duty' after a subsequent case[6]) that these discretions would not be exercised capriciously or arbitrarily.[7] Therefore in exercising these rights, and in the relationship with the borrower generally, the Agent should be aware that, where in practice it takes decisions on behalf of the syndicate (such as the decisions to approve conditions precedent, or to approve a legal opinion for the purpose of accepting a new Obligor), it must not abuse the power it has been given.

Clause 28 (*Role of the Agent, the Arranger and the Issuing Bank*) clarifies the administrative function of the Agent. The clause was substantially restructured during 2014, principally in order to clarify that the Agent was not to be liable where it acted on instructions from the lenders or on the advice of professional advisers.

Clause 28.1 Appointment of the Agent

10.004
This clause is the appointment of the Agent by the lenders.

Clause 28.2 Instructions

10.005
This clause gives control of the loan to the Majority Lenders; provides for all lenders to be bound by the instructions of the Majority Lenders to the Agent; allows the Agent to require security for liabilities before taking action at the direction of the Majority Lenders and gives the Agent discretion to act on its own initiative. It also permits them to act as they think best in the interests of the lenders and absolves them of liability where they take action with the authority of the lenders or under the advice of professional advisers. See Box 10.2.

---

[6] Braganza v BP Shipping Ltd [2015] UKSC 17.

[7] See paras 35–37 of the judgement. This is referred to as the 'Socimer' or 'Braganza' implied term.

386 The Finance Parties

> ### Box 10.2
>
> Note here the 'Socimer implied term' or 'Braganza duty' referred to in 10.003. That is an implied term to the effect that discretions may not be exercised perversely. In Torre Asset Funding[8] the judge gave an example, saying it may be a breach of the implied term if the Agent failed to notify lenders of an Event of Default which it was aware of, if the only rational action was to notify them. Following that case the LMA made substantial revisions to the text of Clause 28 (*Role of the Agent, the Arranger and the Issuing Bank*), as well as to other provisions of the Agreement, designed to limit the potential liability of the Agent. The prime example is Clause 4.1 (*CONDITIONS OF UTILIZATION: Initial conditions precedent*) subclause (b) discussed in Box 2.4, relating to satisfaction of conditions precedent. Another example is Clause 28.3 (*ROLE OF THE AGENT, THE ARRANGER AND THE ISSUING BANK: Duties of the Agent*) subclause (g), which states that the Agent only has the duties expressly imposed on it by the documents and 'no others shall be implied'.

Clause 28.3 Duties of the Agent

10.006

The duties of the Agent are specified in this clause. These are to pass on documents received, pass on information received as to existence of a Default, and, if it is aware of a non-payment, to advise the lenders. The duties are stated (in subclause (a)) to be 'purely mechanical and administrative'. See Box 10.3.

> ### Box 10.3
>
> These duties were considered in the Torre Asset Funding case referred to in 10.002 where the Agent (in its separate capacity as agent for junior lenders) was involved in discussions with the borrower for rescheduling of the junior debt. These discussions constituted an Event of Default under the loan agreement, although the Agent had not realized that. The question arose as to whether the Agent should have notified the lenders of the Event of Default. The court held that because:
>
> - the Agent's duties were specified to be 'mechanical and administrative', and
> - the clause stated that the Agent was entitled to assume that no Default had occurred unless it had actual knowledge of a non-payment and was

---

[8] See Box 10.3.

> entitled to rely on statements made to it (so that it was entitled to rely on the borrower's statement that no Default had occurred), and
> - the clause provides that the Agent 'may' (not 'shall') notify lenders of information which it receives;
>
> the general scheme was clear and clearly meant that when the Agent received information, it was not obliged to evaluate whether that information constituted an Event of Default or not. The agreement clearly limits the Agent's notification obligations to those specifically set out in the clause.

These are in addition to other duties specifically set out in the agreement, such as the duty to distribute moneys received.

Clause 28.4 Role of Arranger

This clause specifies that the Arranger has no obligations except those specifically set out in the documents.

Clause 28.5 No fiduciary duties

This clause states that none of the Agent, the Arranger nor the Issuing Bank has any fiduciary duties. See Box 10.1. Much of the clause specifically allows the Agent, Arranger and Issuing Bank to do things which would be in breach of their fiduciary duty if they had such a duty—for example, Clause 28.6 (*ROLE OF THE AGENT, THE ARRANGER AND THE ISSUING BANK: Business with the Group*) allowing the Agent, Arranger and Issuing Bank to conduct other business with the borrower (even though this may give rise to a conflict).

Clause 28.6 Business with the Group

This clause allows the Agent, Arranger and Issuing Bank to conduct other business with the borrower group.

388 The Finance Parties

Clause 28.7 Rights and discretions

10.007
This is the clause referred to in Box 10.3, which

- allows the Agent to rely on certificates which it receives as being accurate,
- allows the Agent to assume that no Default has occurred unless it has received notice to the contrary or has actual knowledge of non-payment,
- allows the Agent to assume that requests from the Company are authorized by the borrowers,
- allows the Agent to instruct professional advisers and rely on their advice (specifically stating that they will not have any liability as a result),
- allows lenders to communicate direct with the borrower and not through an Impaired Agent,
- allows the Agent to act through its employees and
- allows (but does not require) the Agent to pass on information which it reasonably believes it has received in its capacity as Agent.

Clause 28.8 Responsibility for documentation

10.008
This clause provides that none of the Agent, Arranger or Issuing Bank is liable for the accuracy of information supplied in connection with the transaction, or for the effectiveness of the documents. The intention is that the Agent, Arranger and Issuing Bank should simply be facilitators but should not assume any responsibility in relation to information circulated to the syndicate or for the effectiveness of the loan documentation. They are simply acting as co-coordinators, not inviting the syndicate to rely on them. The Agent instructs the lawyers and leads the negotiation but

- the syndicate members are not bound by that negotiation—they are given their own opportunity to review the documents and make comments; and
- the Agent is not underwriting the effectiveness of their lawyers—if a mistake is made which impacts on the transaction, the intention is that that risk should be borne equally by all the syndicate members.

Clause 28.9 No duty to monitor

10.009

This clause clarifies that the Agent has no duty to monitor whether an Event of Default has occurred, or whether any party is in breach of any of its obligations under the documents.

Clause 28.10 Exclusion of liability

10.010

This clause states that neither the Agent nor the Issuing Bank is liable for anything it does or fails to do except in the case of 'gross negligence or wilful misconduct'—that is, liability for negligence is excluded. The gross negligence standard is generally accepted market practice. It supplements the general principle that the Agent is simply an **administrator** and all risks (including the risk of negligence by lender's employees) are shared equally among the syndicate. Nevertheless, it is difficult to specify in advance what circumstances a court might hold to fall within the definition of 'gross negligence',[9] particularly given the general approach which courts take to exclusion clauses.[10] The main protection for the Agent is to exercise its rights with care and to involve the syndicate members in any potentially contentious decisions which have to be taken.

Clause 28.11 Lenders' indemnity to the Agent

10.011

This clause requires the lenders to indemnify the Agent for any losses and expenses incurred in its role as Agent.

---

[9] The meaning of any phrase depends on the facts of the case but in one case, for example, it was interpreted to mean a serious disregard of or indifference to an obvious risk—see Red Sea Tankers v Papachristidis [1997] 2 Lloyd's Rep. 547.

[10] See A1.027.

Clause 28.12 Resignation of the Agent

10.012
This clause allows the Agent to substitute a different group member as Agent without consent of any other party. It also allows the Agent to resign and (in subclause (h)) allows the Majority Lenders to require the Agent to resign. (See also the discussion from 0.217 onwards). If the Agent wants to resign and have its position assumed by a third party, the syndicate (not the borrower) has the right to appoint a substitute, but if they fail to do so within 20 days, the Agent may do so. This right can be useful for an Agent as it may be the only way to resolve a conflict of interest. It is therefore important that the Agent's ability to resign cannot be restricted by other parties (although it may be frustrated if it cannot find a third party willing to take on the role).

10.013
Comment Note the clause allows the Agent to impose revised terms unilaterally on the other parties in relation to the agency fees, duties and responsibilities of the Agent in order to induce the replacement Agent to take up its role. The only restrictions are that the Agent must be acting reasonably; the rights and obligations must be 'consistent with then current market practice for the appointment and protection of corporate trustees' and the revised fees must be 'consistent with the successor Agent's normal fee rates'. Borrowers may want to object to the unilateral nature of this clause, particularly where no Default has occurred. Agents, on the other hand, may feel that it is a necessary protection, without which their ability to resign and remove themselves from, for example, situations where they have a conflict of interest, may be unworkable.

Clause 28.13 Confidentiality

10.014
This clause provides that the agency department of the Agent will be treated as a separate entity from the rest of the Agent bank so that information received by the agency department will not be deemed to be known to personnel in other divisions of the Agent bank. This clause is particularly important in the context of the Agent's duties set out in Clause 28.3 (*ROLE OF THE AGENT, THE ARRANGER AND THE ISSUING BANK: Duties of the Agent*) discussed in 10.006

Clause 28: Role of the Agent, the Arranger and the Issuing Bank 391

Clause 28.14 Relationship with the Lenders

10.015

This clause requires the lenders to give the Agent five Business Days' notice of a change in Facility Office or lender.

10.016

This clause also allows lenders to appoint a third party to receive information on their behalf. This is to deal with the issue of public and private information as discussed in 0.235.

Clause 28.15 Credit appraisal by Lenders and Issuing Bank

10.017

This clause contains confirmation by the syndicate members that they have not relied on any representations by the Agent or the Arranger or the Issuing Bank but have undertaken their own financial due diligence and will continue to do so. This is designed to protect the Agent and Arranger from liability for misrepresentation and from the argument by syndicate members that they were led to join the syndicate in reliance on the superior expertise of the Arranger and/or the Agent in relation to the proposed transaction.

Clause 28.16 Agent's management time

10.018

This is an optional clause allowing the Agent to charge for their management time in addition to their fees.

Borrowers may expect management time to be included in the Agency fee except perhaps after a Default. They may prefer to refer to Agent's management time in the clauses dealing with costs and expenses of amendments and enforcement so as to limit the circumstances in which the Agent can charge management time.

392   The Finance Parties

Optional provisions dealing with amounts paid in error

10.019

Following an unusual case in the US (where an Agent mistakenly made substantial overpayments to the syndicate and initially found itself unable to recover those payments from syndicate members), the LMA published an optional slot in clause giving the Agent a contractual right to be reimbursed for any payments made in error. There was much discussion of whether such a clause was necessary or appropriate and also on the precise wording of the clause put forward by the LMA. Meanwhile, the case was reversed on appeal,[11] thus allowing the Agent to recover the erroneous payments even without the express contractual right to do so. Commentary on the LMA wording can be seen in the 6th edition of the ACT Borrower's Guide to the LMA Investment Grade Agreements.

Lehman Provisions and the Agent

10.020

There are also optional provisions which are part of the Lehman provisions discussed in the Introduction and which.

* require the Agent to disclose the identity of Defaulting Lenders on request either by the borrower or by the Majority Lenders
* allow the Majority Lenders to replace an Impaired Agent
* allow payments to be made through a different party—not the Agent (if it is an Impaired Agent), and
* require the Agent to provide the borrower with a list of the lenders, either monthly or on request.

---

[11] In re Citibank August 11, 2020 Wire Transfers, 2nd U.S. Circuit Court of Appeals, No. 21-487.

Clause 29: Conduct of Business by the Finance Parties

10.021

This clause provides that the lenders can organize their affairs (particularly their tax affairs) as they think fit, and that they are not required to claim any particular tax credit or tax relief which might be available to them. This clause is discussed in the context of Clause 15.4 (*TAX GROSS UP AND INDEMNITIES: Tax credit*) in 6.035.

Clause 30: Sharing among the Finance Parties

Clause 30.1 Payments to Finance Parties and Clause 30.2 Redistribution of payments

10.022

Clause 30 (*Sharing among the Finance Parties*) is the pro rata sharing clause. Its function is to ensure that each lender recovers the same proportion of its debt as each of the other lenders. The clause provides that if any lender recovers a greater proportion than any other, then it will share the excess with the others, reflecting the basic concept of a syndicated loan that, if there is a loss, the lenders should suffer equally.

This clause does not however oblige any lender to exercise its set off rights against the syndicated loan (see Box 10.4).

Box 10.4

For example, assume lender A,

(a) has a bilateral facility of $10 million to borrower B; and
(b) is a member of a syndicate of ten lenders which have provided a loan of $100 million to B with each lender lending $10 million.

Assume that B fails to repay either loan but has a bank account with A with $5 million in it and that the law in the country where the bank account is held allows set off rights as against either of the facilities. Lender A has two choices (absent any special relationship as discussed below):

---

394 The Finance Parties

> - It may use the $5 million deposit to set off against its $10 million bilateral facility. In this case, after the set off, it will be owed $10 million on the syndicated loan and $5 million on its bilateral facility;
> - Alternatively, it may use the $5 million deposit to set off against its interest in the syndicated loan. It would then need to share the $5 million with all other nine members of the syndicate—leaving A retaining a benefit of only $0.5 million from the set off. The result would be a continued debt to B of $10 million on its bilateral facility and of $9.5 million in respect of the syndicated loan.
>
> Clearly A would prefer to use the set off for the purpose of the bilateral facility. This is not prohibited by the clause.

It may be, however, that exercising a set off for the benefit of a different debt could be challenged if the lender in question had some special relationship[12] with lenders who would have benefited from the sharing clause had the set off been applied to this loan; those other lenders may be able to claim that the lender's action was in breach of a fiduciary duty (if they can show that such a duty exists).

Clause 30.3 Recovering Finance Party's rights

10.023
If a lender makes a payment of a surplus under this clause then this clause provides that the borrower still owes them the amount they have paid over. This clause is necessary since the exercise of the right of set off will have extinguished the debt owed to the recovering lender (see Box 10.5).

> **Box 10.5**
>
> In the example in Box 10.4, if the set off were exercised against the syndicated loan, after the set off the borrower would only owe A $5 million, as the other $5 million has been extinguished by the set off. However, after the sharing, A has a shortfall of $9.5 million. This clause provides that B now owes A the amount (i.e. $4.5 million) which A has paid over to the other lenders.

Nevertheless, it is possible that this provision may not be effective in the insolvency of the borrower since it may contravene the pari passu principle

---

[12] For example, if it were the Agent.

Clause 30: Sharing among the Finance Parties 395

which is applicable in insolvency (because the debt, having been paid to the lender, is then treated as not having been paid).[13]

The intention of course is that the lenders who have received payment under this clause should have their claim against the borrower reduced by the amount received, so that the total amount due by the borrower is unaffected by the clause.

10.024

Comment Borrowers might want an adjustment to the clause to state this expressly.

10.025

It is also worth noting that, as a matter of English law, the recovering lender is unlikely to be able to exercise set off rights in insolvency in relation to the amounts newly due to it as a result of the operation of the clause.[14]

Clause 30.4 Reversal of redistribution

10.026

This clause provides for the payments to be reversed if, after the sharing has occurred, the lender that had recovered more than the others is required to refund that excess recovery to the borrower or other Obligor.

Given that some countries require rights of set off which have been exercised shortly before an insolvency to be reversed this is an important provision for the lender which originally had the extra recovery.

Clause 30.5 Exceptions

10.027

This clause provides that the obligation to share additional recoveries does not apply if the result would be that the lender which had the additional recovery would not have a valid claim against the borrower (e.g. pursuant to Clause 30.3 (*SHARING AMONG THE FINANCE PARTIES: Recovering Finance*

---

[13] This is one reason for the exception in Clause 30.5 (*SHARING AMONG THE FINANCE PARTIES: Exceptions*), relieving the lender of the obligation to share if as a result they would no longer have a valid claim against the borrower.

[14] See *International Loans, Bonds, Guarantees, Legal Opinions*, 3rd edn by Philip Wood in 17-016.

396   The Finance Parties

Party's rights)) after the sharing. It also does not apply if a lender recovered a greater percentage of its loan than other lenders as a result of taking legal action (including amounts paid in settlement of that action) which others could have joined in but declined to do so. This exception is important if the right of individual action referred to in Clause 2.3 (*THE FACILITIES: Finance Parties' rights and obligations*) subclause (c) (discussed in 2.006) is to have any real value.

Administration

Clause 31: Payment Mechanics

Clause 31.1 Payments to the Agent

11.001

This clause in the LMA Compounded/Term Rate Loan[1] sets out the payment mechanics. Payments are to be made to the Agent in the principal financial centre for the currency concerned (or in the case of Euro, in one of the principal financial centres or in London '*as specified by the Agent*'[2]). This effectively passes exchange control risk and risk of insolvency of intermediaries[3] to the borrower.

The Clause requires payment to be made in '*such funds specified by the Agent as being customary ... for settlement of transactions in the relevant currency in the place of payment*'. This refers to the practices in different markets from

---

[1] References in this book to the LMA Compounded/Term Rate Loan are to the LMA Multicurrency Term and Revolving Facilities Agreement incorporating Term SOFR for use in Investment Grade transactions, available to LMA members via www.lma.eu.com.

[2] The ability of the Agent to specify the place of payment is intended to assist in the event of a Euro breakup, as it would allow the Agent to require payment outside the Eurozone.

[3] Other than the Agent's correspondent bank in the relevant country.

© The Author(s), under exclusive license to Springer Nature
Switzerland AG 2024
S. Wright, *The International Loan Documentation Handbook*, Global Financial Markets,
https://doi.org/10.1007/978-3-031-38489-9_12

398   Administration

time to time, for example, payments may required to be made in **CHIPS**[4] in some markets.

Clause 31.2 Distributions by the Agent

11.002
This clause provides for the Agent to distribute moneys received to the bank accounts specified by the various parties, with at least five Business Days' notice of the bank account details being required.

Clause 31.3 Distribution to an Obligor

11.003
This clause allows the Agent to use moneys which are owed to an Obligor under the agreement in settlement of any moneys due from that Obligor as long as it has that right under the set off clause (Clause 32 *(Set Off)* discussed in 11.014) or the borrower consents.

Clause 31.4 Clawback and pre-funding

11.004
This clause provides protection for the Agent if it disburses sums (e.g. to the borrower) on the assumption that all others will contribute when due and any party (e.g. a lender) fails to do so. In these circumstances the party which received the payment must repay it to the Agent up to the amount of the missing contribution plus interest. This clause operates in both directions, that is, both for payments to the borrower which are to be funded by the syndicate, and for payments to the syndicate which are to be funded by the borrower. In relation to payments to the borrower, the clause provides that if the lender which failed to make its contribution also fails to compensate the Agent for its funding costs, then the borrower must do so.

The clause clarifies that the Agent is not obliged to make payments before they have received the corresponding sum.

---

[4] See Goode *Commercial Law*, 6th edn, Chapter 18 for a discussion of payment systems.

Clause 31: Payment Mechanics **399**

Clause 31.5 Partial payments

11.005

This clause deals with partial payments. It provides that where the borrower pays less than the full amount due, that payment will first pay sums due to the Agent in its capacity as such (such as its fees, costs and expenses) or to the Issuing Bank (excluding reimbursement of payments made under letters of credit); then interest, other fees and commission; then principal; then any other sums. This clause prevents the borrower specifying how such a payment is to be allocated (see Box 11.1).

> **Box 11.1**
>
> For example, lenders would not want a partial payment to be applied against principal (and therefore reduce the amount on which interest was chargeable) when interest remained outstanding, particularly in countries where there are restrictions on the ability to charge interest on interest.

11.006

Comment Other lenders (e.g. a security trustee) who receive fees or incur expenses may wish to have their fees and expenses in the first level, pro rata with the Agent.

11.007

The clause provides that the order of application (excluding subclause (i) providing for the Agent's fees and expenses to be paid first) may be amended by the Majority Lenders.

11.008

Comment The Majority Lender override may require adjustment in a combined facility where the lenders may be different for the different facilities, so as to ensure the order cannot be changed to the detriment of the lenders of one of the facilities.[5]

---

[5] See discussion of 'Majority Lenders' in 1.040 and see also 11.027.

400   Administration

Clause 31.6 No set off by Obligors

11.009
This clause provides for payment to be made by the borrowers, free of set off or counterclaim. If the borrowers have a claim or debt due from any lender, they must pursue their other remedies for that and not simply withhold payment under the loan agreement (which would cause the lender to incur additional costs in funding the amount withheld).

11.010
Comment Borrowers sometimes request amendment allowing them to exercise set off rights in relation to Defaulting Lenders. Lenders are likely to resist this as the lenders' ability to use the loan as collateral may depend on absence of set off rights.

Clause 31.8 Currency of account

11.011
This clause requires all payments to be made in the currency in which the relevant sum is denominated 'pursuant to this Agreement'. with the aim of the reducing the risk of a redenomination in the event of a Euro breakup.

Clause 31.9 Change of currency

11.012
This clause deals with the situation where a country might be changing to a new currency (such as if it adopts the Euro) and there is a transition period in which there is more than one lawful currency in that country.

Clause 31.10 Disruption to payment systems, etc.

11.013
This clause provides an optional mechanism to deal with disruption to payment systems (defined to mean disruption to the payment system or

financial markets or unavoidable systems error) and allows the Agent to bind the syndicate in relation to any payment arrangements which it agrees with the borrower to deal with such an eventuality.

Clause 32: Set Off

11.014
This clause gives the lenders a contractual right of set off. This is more extensive than the right of set off they would have in the absence of express provision if the bank account were in England. For example, it allows amounts due in different currencies to be converted into the same currency to allow a set off.

11.015
Comment Borrowers need to ensure that giving this right of set off does not breach any negative pledges they have signed.

11.016
Comment Borrowers also sometimes request that the right can only be exercised while an Event of Default is continuing.

Clause 33: Notices

11.017
This clause deals with notices. Any two parties to the agreement may agree between themselves that e-mail is an acceptable form of communication. Particular care should be taken with any notices of default or acceleration to ensure they are delivered in accordance with this clause.

It is also sensible to ensure that if other documents are involved in the transaction (e.g. security documents) the notices clauses in those documents conform to this.

402 Administration

Clause 34: Calculations and Certificates

Clause 34.1 Accounts

11.018

This clause provides that the lenders' accounts will be prima facie evidence of the existence of the debt. As far as English law is concerned, there is no need to have a promissory note to evidence the debt and market practice is not to require notes (see Box 11.2).

Box 11.2

Promissory notes are often found in loans with US lenders. One of the main reasons for this (but see the LSTA's Complete Credit Agreement Guide, 2nd ed in 5.1.8 for a fuller discussion) is that notes may give a procedural advantage in terms of enforcement since they are contracts quite distinct from the underlying arrangement and courts are reluctant to allow the debtor to raise a defence based on the underlying arrangement.[6]

Clause 34.2 Certificates and determinations

11.019

This clause states that the lenders' certificates as to amounts due under the documents are conclusive except in the case of manifest error. Nevertheless, evidence which is stated to be conclusive under the agreement may not be accepted as such in court.

---

[6] Questions may arise under English law as to whether a promissory note which relates to a floating rate of interest would benefit from this advantage because of the requirement that a promissory note should contain a certain and unconditional payment obligation. Nevertheless, it is thought that, even if the promissory note relates to a floating rate of interest, it will benefit from the advantages of negotiable instruments as a result of commercial usage—see Goode *Commercial Law*, 6th ed in 19.21.

Clause 34.3 Day count convention and interest calculation

11.020
This clause provides that calculations of fees, interest, etc., will be based on a 360-day year except for currencies where that is not the market practice. The 360-day year convention matches the currency markets for most currencies (see Box 11.3). Some currencies (e.g. Sterling) work on a 365-day year. Regulations in some countries require the annual (i.e. on the basis of a 365-day year) interest rate to be specified. In this case the interest would still be calculated in accordance with the convention in the relevant currency market but there would need to be further description in the agreement converting the interest rate to a 365-day basis.

> **Box 11.3**
>
> The effect of the convention is to marginally change the interest calculation by assuming that there are only 360 days in a year. So, to calculate 30 days' interest on $3 million, the calculation is $3 million X 30/360 X interest rate (not $3 million X 30/365 X interest rate as one might expect).

11.021
This clause also deals with rounding conventions for calculation of interest. The convention recommended for compounded risk free rates is ONLY to round interest which falls due for payment, not the individual daily rates used in calculating the interest due. (This is necessary to ensure that the daily amounts add up to the accrued amount).

Clause 35: Partial Invalidity[7]

11.022
This clause states that if any part of the agreement is illegal or unenforceable, that will have no effect on the rest of the document.

---

[7] A provision may only be severed under English law if it passes the 'blue pencil test' set out in Goldsoll v Goldman (1915) 1 Ch 292, which requires that the rest of the contract must be able to stand if the offending part is simply deleted.

404 **Administration**

Clause 36: Remedies and Waivers

11.023

This clause addresses the issues of waiver by election and by **estoppel**.[8] In the principal case[9] on waiver by estoppel, Lord Cairns said that if one party leads another 'to suppose that the strict rights arising under the contract will not be enforced, or will be kept in suspense or held in abeyance, the person who otherwise might have enforced those rights will not be allowed to enforce them where it would be inequitable having regard to the dealings which have thus taken place between the parties'.

11.024

The main concern in relation to a loan is that, following a default, the lenders may lead the borrower to believe that they do not intend to exercise their rights and, ultimately, they may be held to have waived the rights or be estopped from exercising them. This clause provides that that will not happen.

There is also a concern that if lenders continue to perform the loan agreement following an Event of Default, they will be held to have affirmed the contract and will therefore lose their right to terminate it.[10] The clause therefore also provides that no election by a lender to affirm the agreement will be effective unless in writing.

Nevertheless, the clause will be read **contra proferentem** and should not be relied on to be effective in the circumstances of any given case. If the borrower defaults and the lenders do not plan to exercise their rights immediately, they should write to the borrower advising that they are reserving their rights to be exercised as they see fit in the future. These letters are referred to as 'Reservation of rights letters'. Lenders should also be aware that the effectiveness of reservation of rights letters will be decided by the court in the light of all the circumstances. A case in 2022 (see Box 11.4) provides interesting insights into the effectiveness of the no waivers clause and reservation of rights letters where time passes between the occurrence of the Event of Default and the enforcement.

---

[8] For further detail see Treitel, *The Law of Contract*, 15th edn from 3-114 onwards.

[9] Hughes v Metropolitan Ry (1877) 2 App Cas 439.

[10] See Tele2 International Card Co SA v Post Office (2009) EWCA Civ 9.

Clause 37: Amendments and Waivers   **405**

> **Box 11.4**
>
> In Lombard North Central Plc v European Skyjets Ltd [2022] EWHC 728 (QB) a borrower had regularly been late in making loan repayments over the course of three years. The loan agreement contained a no waiver clause and reservation of rights letters had been sent. During the course of the three years various proposals were discussed, although it was unclear at the time whether these were proposals or agreements. The lender's faith in the borrower deteriorated and eventually the lender accelerated the loan on the basis of the delayed payments, even though at the time of acceleration, those payments had been made (but there were other Events of Default).
>
> On the facts of the case the court decided that the lender had waived its rights to accelerate on the basis of the earlier non-payments. Neither the no waiver clause nor the reservation of rights letter prevented positive statements and actions by the lender (such as acceptance of late payment and asserting that they would not enforce as a result of the non-payment, subject to various conditions) from having their objective effect.
>
> The case illustrates that reservation of rights letters are just part of the picture when deciding on whether lenders have waived their right to accelerate.

Clause 37: Amendments and Waivers

11.025

Clause 37 *(Amendments and waivers)* regulates the level of consent between lenders required for amendment or waiver of provisions of the documents. The general provision is that Majority Lender[11] consent is required to amend or waive. However, consent of all lenders is needed for certain issues—generally the key issues which will have been subject to credit committee approval. These are set out in Clause 37.2 *(AMENDMENTS AND WAIVERS: All Lender matters)*. They include the Margin, interest, fees, commission and so on; the loan amount; the drawdown period; the due dates for payment; the definition of Majority Lenders; the pro rata sharing clause, the change of control clause, the governing law and jurisdiction clause (particularly important in the context of issues such as a potential Euro break up, as well as for the general assessment of the credit risk involved in the transaction) and Clause 37.2 *(AMENDMENTS AND WAIVERS: All Lender matters)* itself. Clause 37.3 *(AMENDMENTS AND WAIVERS: Other exceptions)* also

---

[11] See discussion of 'Majority Lenders' in 1.040.

406   Administration

provides that changes relating to the rights or obligations of the Agent or Arranger or Issuing Bank can only be made with their consent.

11.026

It is important that alterations to the due dates for payment cannot be made without the consent of all lenders as otherwise the rights of individual lenders provided for in Clause 2.3 (*THE FACILITIES: Finance Parties' rights and obligations*) (see 2.006) would be illusory. Similarly, a clause saying that due dates can only be changed with the consent of all lenders will be of little comfort if individual lenders can only take action to recover their debt with the approval of Majority Lenders.

11.027

Comment Lenders need to consider whether any other issues should require unanimous approval to change. This may include:

- release of security;
- any particular conditions precedent which are key such as any relating to security;
- any provisions which one lender requires as a matter of policy, but which other lenders may not be concerned about (such as environmental and social policies) and
- any provisions designed to protect one group of lenders in a facility which has different lenders participating in different parts of the facility. See Box 11.5.

Box 11.5

If a loan agreement consists of Tranches which can be syndicated separately, care is needed in dealing with amendments to clauses dealing with the relationship between the Tranches. One approach is to include a clause along the following lines.

Any amendment or waiver which relates to the rights or obligations applicable to a particular Utilization, Facility or class of Lenders and which does not materially and adversely affect the rights or interests of Lenders in respect of other Utilizations, Facilities or another class of Lender shall only require the consent of the Majority Lenders, all Lenders or all Lenders forming part of that affected class (as applicable) as if references in this paragraph to "Majority Lenders", or "Lenders" were only to Lenders participating in that Utilization, Facility or forming part of that affected class.

Clause 37: Amendments and Waivers 407

> Another approach is to specify the situations in which the normal Majority Lender rule is not to apply and to set out specific voting requirements for those situations. Areas which are likely to need consideration include:
>
> - provisions which are specific to the relevant Tranche such as the purpose or pricing of the tranche, or the waiver of any conditions precedent to its use (such as waiver of a Default);
> - prepayments and cancellations (do these need to be made pro rata between Tranches or must one be prepaid first?);
> - pro rata sharing (should the Tranches be treated separately or should any surplus recoveries by one lender be shared among lenders to all Tranches?);
> - the partial payments clause (Clause 31.5 (*PAYMENT MECHANICS: Partial Payments*)), which allows the order of payments to be varied by the Majority Lenders. Should this require a majority in relation to each Tranche?
> - Changes to any of these clauses

11.028

Comment The borrower may also consider requesting that a provision be included to deal with lenders not responding to requests for consent. A nonresponse has the same effect as a no vote, since generally, where consent is sought, the requirement is to obtain consent from whatever constitutes 'Majority Lenders'. See Box 11.6.

> **Box 11.6**
>
> There are two common alternatives for dealing with this. In one version ('delay and it's OK') a lender is treated as giving consent if it does not respond to the request within a specified time. In the second (preferable) version, a lender who fails to respond is ignored for the purpose of calculating the level of consent obtained—this is referred to as a 'snooze you lose' clause.

11.029

This is also where you might see a 'yank the bank' clause discussed in 4.023.

11.030

Clause 37.4 (*AMENDMENTS AND WAIVERS: Changes to reference rates*) is an optional clause dealing with permanent unavailability or inappropriateness of a relevant rate used in the calculations of interest (such as Sonia) and allowing for a lesser number of lenders to be required to approve any consequential changes to the interest rate terms than would otherwise have been required—as discussed in 0.140.

408   Administration

There is also an optional provision here which is part of the Lehman provisions referred to in the Introduction from 0.204 onwards. This provides that

11.031

* the voting rights of any Defaulting Lender will be calculated on the basis of moneys actually advanced—ignoring the undrawn Commitment of the Defaulting Lender

11.032

* the Defaulting Lender will not be taken into account for the purpose of consents if it fails to respond to a request within a specified period; and

11.033

* the borrower may require a Defaulting Lender to transfer its entire participation in the loan to a company nominated by the borrower.

Clause 38: Confidential Information

11.034

This Clause is an express confidentiality undertaking by the lenders. It was inserted as a result of increased participation of non-bank lenders in syndicates (see 0.233).

11.035

The Clause imposes duties of confidentiality on the lenders. It allows disclosure of confidential information in specified circumstances. For different categories of information recipients, there are different conditions on which disclosure may be made. Broadly speaking, if the recipient does not have duties of confidentiality, then in some cases (such as secondary market purchasers) the recipient must sign a Confidentiality Undertaking in the form set out in the Loan Agreement (the "Undertaking" condition) and in others (such as where disclosure is required by law) the lender may disclose information as long as they advise the recipient that the information is confidential and may include price sensitive information (the "Information" condition). In other cases (eg disclosure to **rating agencies**) there are no conditions.

Clause 38: Confidential Information   409

11.036

Comment Note that in most cases, if the recipient has duties of confidentiality, there are no conditions to disclosure. Borrowers might prefer to require explicit confidentiality undertakings rather than relying on general duties of confidentiality so as to restrict the uses to which confidential information may be put.

Borrowers should review the conditions for each category of lender.

11.037

The categories of persons who may be given confidential information are

- Affiliates of lenders and their professional advisers (subject, where appropriate, to the Information condition);
- actual or potential secondary market purchasers and investors including sub-participants and parties to credit derivatives (and anyone financing such purchasers and investors), (subject, where appropriate, to the Undertaking condition);
- representatives for a lender (this is designed to avoid difficulties with any lenders who do not want to receive non-public price sensitive information as discussed in 0.235) (subject, where appropriate, to the Undertaking condition);
- anyone to whom disclosure is required by law, regulation or the rules of a relevant authority or stock exchange or in litigation or similar proceedings (subject, where appropriate, to the Information condition);
- anyone who provides services to the lenders in connection with the administration of the loan (subject to the Undertaking condition, and there is a different form of confidentiality undertaking applicable to this case);
- anyone to whom a lender has given security over this loan (subject to the Information condition where practical in the lender's opinion);
- rating agencies and
- numbering service providers[12]—of very limited information which is not (and which the borrower represents is not) price sensitive information.

11.038

Comment A lender's duties of confidentiality are expressed to expire 12 months after it has ceased to be a lender. Borrowers may want to consider

---

[12] Securities which are traded such as bonds and debt instruments, are given a Securities Identification Number, which is unique to that instrument, to allow them to be readily identified and traded efficiently. The agency responsible for issuing this number needs details of the security—hence the need to allow certain information to be provided for this purpose.

410 Administration

whether 12 months is a sufficiently long period. They may also want to consider whether there should be overriding prohibitions on giving confidential information to certain categories of persons such as competitors.

11.039

Comment Sometimes borrowers ask to be kept informed of the people to whom confidential information has been passed, but in many cases this will be impractical for lenders.

11.040

Finally, it is worth noting that these confidentiality undertakings can be hard for the borrower to police. If confidential information is leaked, the borrower may not discover the fact; if it does it will be hard to identify the source of the leak and it is hard to identify the loss caused by the leak.

Clause 39: Confidentiality of Funding Rates

11.041

The need for this clause arises if cost of funds is relevant as a fallback to the contractually agreed interest rates (see 0.136 and 0.138), or in calculation of a market disruption (see 5.023) In these circumstances, the relevant clauses may require lenders to disclose their cost of funding their participation in the loan. Lenders prefer to keep funding costs (and hence market perception of their creditworthiness) confidential.

Clause 40: Bail-In

11.042

The rationale behind this clause is described in 0.196. The clause requires parties to accept that their rights against lenders may be restricted by the application of special resolution procedures for systemically important lenders. As it reflects statutory requirements it is not generally the subject of negotiation.

Clause 41: Counterparts

11.043

This clause allows the agreement to be executed in counterparts. In this case, the Agent's lawyer will produce a **conformed copy** which indicates the signatories.

Governing Law and Enforcement

Clause 42: Governing Law

12.001

This clause in the LMA Compounded/Term Rate Loan[1] provides that the Agreement will be governed by English[2] law. Choosing English or New York law for loan agreements makes syndication of very large loans easier than many other **governing laws** because of the loan market's familiarity with English and New York law. Another factor is the predictability of these laws. They respect freedom of contract to a large extent and are reluctant to interfere in negotiated agreements, making for a fair degree of certainty in relation to the effect of the agreement.

The ability of a party to choose the law which applies to a contract may be limited and this is an issue for due diligence. Many countries disallow a choice of law if it is made in order to avoid a mandatory provision of the law which would otherwise apply. Others require there to be some connection between the transaction and the law chosen.[3]

---

[1] References in this book to the LMA Compounded/Term Rate Loan are to the LMA Multicurrency Term and Revolving Facilities Agreement incorporating Term SOFR for use in Investment Grade transactions, available to LMA members via www.lma.eu.com.

[2] Incidentally there is no such thing as UK or British contract law. Technically it is the law of England and Wales.

[3] See discussions on Schedule 17 (*Legal Opinion*) in 13.110.

© The Author(s), under exclusive license to Springer Nature
Switzerland AG 2024
S. Wright, *The International Loan Documentation Handbook*, Global Financial Markets,
https://doi.org/10.1007/978-3-031-38489-9_13

414   Governing Law and Enforcement

12.002

The LMA Compounded/Term Rate Loan also contains optional wording choosing English law to apply to non-contractual obligations (such as claims in negligence or other torts or delicts[4]) arising in relation to the agreement. This wording stems from Rome II[5] which allows parties who are pursuing a commercial activity to agree in advance on the law which will apply to non-contractual obligations. Where the loan is unsecured and the loan agreement is the only document governing the relationship, choosing English law for non-contractual obligations may be sensible so as to have all issues dealt with by a single legal system. However where there are security documents which will be governed by different laws, choosing English law for non-contractual obligations arising out of those documents would probably be inappropriate since issues may arise in relation to the assets over which security is taken, which would be best dealt with under the law of the location of the asset.

Clause 43: Enforcement

Clause 43.1: Jurisdiction

12.003

This clause gives the English courts 'exclusive' jurisdiction (subject to the points discussed in 12.004) to deal with disputes relating to the Agreement. Lenders commonly require borrowers to submit to the jurisdiction of the courts of the country of the chosen governing law. Clearly it makes sense, if English law has been chosen as the governing law, to choose the English courts to settle disputes so that they will be applying a law they are familiar with. English and New York courts are also popular because of their expertise in dealing with this nature of transaction and because of the predictability of the results.

Note that it is usual to submit to the jurisdiction of courts rather than submitting disputes to arbitration because, for claims in debt (as opposed to claims in damages) courts are usually faster and cheaper than arbitration. See also Box 12.1.

---

[4] See A1.012.

[5] *Regulation 864/2007 adopted into UK law after Brexit by the EU (Withdrawal Act) 2018.*

Clause 43: Enforcement   **415**

> **Box 12.1**
>
> Would arbitration be better?
>
> **Arbitration** is unusual for loan agreements. It may be considered in cases where the alternative is to use courts which are known to be slow, expensive and/or unpredictable. It may also be considered if the due diligence unearths the fact that the country where the borrower's assets are located will not necessarily enforce a judgement given by the chosen court. In this event, it may be that an arbitration award would be more effective than a court judgement, at least in relation to an unsecured loan.[6] Whenever arbitration is considered as an alternative to the courts however, it will be necessary to consider whether it will be necessary to have recourse to the courts in any event in order to enforce any security. In many jurisdictions, security can only be enforced with the assistance of the courts and/ or the assistance of the courts may be necessary to enable the lenders to give good title to the property which is the subject of the security.
>
> One option which is increasingly popular is to include 'optional' arbitration provisions—that is, to submit to the jurisdiction of the courts but also to give the lenders the option of arbitration. This may be helpful if the borrower is expected to have some assets in countries which will enforce judgements of the chosen courts and some in countries which may not do so. Such clauses are permissible in England but may not be so in other countries.[7]

12.004

The LMA provides two options for the jurisdiction clause—a 'one way' clause and a 'symmetrical' clause. In the 'one way' clause, the submission to the jurisdiction of the English courts is expressed in Clause 43.1 (*ENFORCEMENT: Jurisdiction*) subclause (c) to leave the lenders (but not the borrowers) with the continued right to take action in other countries. Lenders generally want the right to take action in other countries as well as the courts specified as they may find, in practice, that it is simpler to start proceedings directly in the country of the borrower or guarantor rather than obtaining an English judgement which they will then need to enforce locally. This is often referred to as a 'one way' jurisdiction clause. Under a 'symmetrical' jurisdiction clause, on the other hand, all parties agree that they will only take legal action in the specified courts.

---

[6] This may be the case if the relevant country is party to international treaties as to reciprocal enforcement of arbitration awards (the 1958 United Nations Convention on the Recognition and Enforcement of Foreign Arbitral Awards—the 'New York Convention').

[7] In 2012 a Russian case Telefonnaya Kompaniya (RTK) v Sony Ericsson Mobile Communication Rus held that a clause submitting to arbitration but giving the lenders the sole right to litigate contravened the rights of equal access to courts.

416   Governing Law and Enforcement

12.005

However, if, under a 'one way' jurisdiction clause, the lenders seek to take action in a country other than England, or the borrower were to seek to take action elsewhere, that country will apply its own law in interpreting the effectiveness of Clause 43.1 (*ENFORCEMENT: Jurisdiction*) subclause (c) and in deciding whether to accept jurisdiction. Post Brexit, it can no longer be assumed that an EU member state will give effect to the parties' agreement as to which courts will have jurisdiction, nor that they will enforce an English judgement. That will be a matter for the local law in the relevant EU country. As a result of the Hague convention[8] courts in an EU member state (and in other countries party to the Convention) will recognize 'symmetrical' jurisdiction clause but the convention does not protect 'one way' jurisdiction clauses.

12.006

One way jurisdiction clauses came under scrutiny in 2012 and 2013, when a French case[9] found that, as a matter of French law, they were invalid and that the effect was as though no jurisdiction had been agreed upon. Subsequently, the English court[10] held that as a matter of English law, one way jurisdiction clauses were effective.

Which type of jurisdiction clause to use will therefore need consideration based on the location of the borrower and its assets. While lenders like to keep the flexibility of 'one way' clauses, if the borrower has a close connection with, or assets in, a country where under local law, the 'one way' clause might be ineffective, lenders may prefer to use the option of a symmetrical clause.

Clause 43.2: Service of process

12.007

The lenders will require non-English borrowers irrevocably[11] to appoint someone in England to accept service of any proceedings on their behalf

---

[8] The 2015 Hague Convention on Choice of Court Agreements.

[9] The decision of the Cour de cassation in Mme X v Rothschild Civil Division 1, 26 September 2012, 11–26022.

[10] In Mauritius Commercial Bank Ltd v Hestia Holdings [2013] EWHC 1328 (Comm).

[11] In a series of cases it has been held that service on a **process agent** is valid, even if the appointment has been terminated, if the principal had agreed with their counterparty that the appointment was irrevocable. See e.g. The Bank of New York Mellon, London Branch v Essar Steel India Ltd [2018] EWHC 3177 (Ch).

under Clause 43.2 (*ENFORCEMENT: Service of process*). This will be a condition precedent to advance of the loan. This avoids the need to serve proceedings abroad, which can be a time-consuming process.

Some lenders do not like borrowers to appoint group members because of the risk of sale or dissolution, and prefer that the borrower use a third party which specializes in providing agents for service of proceedings as a commercial service. Using embassies or consulates is not a good idea as they are immune from legal proceedings.

Schedules

Schedule 1: The Original Parties

13.001

Schedule 1 of the LMA Compounded/Term Rate Loan[1] specifies the original parties.

Schedule 2: Conditions Precedent

Part I   Conditions precedent to initial utilization

13.002

For the original borrowers, the conditions precedent set out in the LMA Compounded/Term Rate Loan consist of

- corporate documents;
- legal opinions and
- other.

---

[1] References in this book to the LMA Compounded/Term Rate Loan are to the LMA Multicurrency Term and Revolving Facilities Agreement incorporating Term Sofr for use in Investment Grade transactions, available to LMA members via www.lma.eu.com.

© The Author(s), under exclusive license to Springer Nature Switzerland AG 2024
S. Wright, *The International Loan Documentation Handbook*, Global Financial Markets, https://doi.org/10.1007/978-3-031-38489-9_14

420   Schedules

Corporate documents

Conditions (a) and (b) require constitutional documents and board resolutions.

13.003

It is normal to require copies of the constitutional documents and of board resolutions of the Obligors despite the provisions of section 40(1) Companies Act 2006,[2] as lenders do not want to be involved in unauthorized transactions. The resolutions will, of course, need to have been made in accordance with the company's constitution, including such matters as quorum, notice of meeting and declaration of directors' interests.

13.004

Condition (c) requires specimen signatures of the people who are authorized to sign the documents.

13.005

Condition (d) optionally requires a shareholders' resolution from the shareholders in the guarantors. This will be required if there are concerns as to breach of directors' duties; see Box A1.23. Such a resolution will not assist if the company was insolvent at the time of, or as a result of, the guarantee (not least because the question of **transaction at an undervalue** will be relevant in those circumstances).

13.006

Condition (e) requires a certificate confirming that the borrowing will not exceed any applicable borrowing limits. This is because it is not unusual for the powers of the directors to authorize borrowings or guarantees to be limited by the company's constitution, sometimes with reference to matters which are not a matter of public record. This condition precedent addresses this issue.

---

[2] Which reads 'In favour of a person dealing with a company in good faith, the power of the board of directors to bind the company or to authorize others to do so shall be deemed to be free of any limitation under the company's constitution'.

Legal Opinions

13.007
Condition 2 requires two legal opinions:

* An opinion in the country of incorporation of any Obligor—this opinion will cover capacity, tax, choice of law and enforceability of judgements. The LMA envisages a possibility that this opinion need not be issued by the Agent's lawyer as it is not uncommon for lenders to accept that this 'capacity opinion' can be given by the borrower's lawyer. This is because the legal issues addressed by the capacity opinion are usually relatively straightforward; and
* An opinion in the country whose law was chosen to govern the agreement—this will cover enforceability and will be issued by the Agent's lawyer.

Lenders will also need to consider asking for opinions in other jurisdictions—principally, in a secured transaction—in the location of the asset over which security is taken.

In some cases lenders should also consider taking advice in relation to insolvency and enforcement of judgements in any places where the Obligors have any significant presence if that is not the same as the place of incorporation. See further 13.088 onwards.

Other conditions precedent

13.008
The other conditions precedent required by the LMA Compounded/Term Rate Loan are

* an acceptance by the person appointed to accept service of legal proceedings in the English courts (see Clause 43.2 *(ENFORCEMENT: Service of process)* in 12.007);
* delivery of the Original Financial Statements;
* payment of fees and expenses and
* such other assurances as the Agent thinks necessary

422   **Schedules**

Comment Borrowers may object to the last item in the above list in the interests of certainty, particularly in a revolving credit facility or a term loan with a long availability period.

13.009
Conditions precedent relating to any other items which were important to the credit decision need to be added as discussed in the comments on Clause 24 (*General Undertakings*) in 8.199. These might include conditions precedent as to execution and registration of security and guarantees, and conditions precedent as to key assets and contracts.[3]

Part II   Conditions precedent to additional Obligors

13.010
The key conditions precedent to future Obligors are substantially the same as for the initial drawdown but relating to the new Obligor and with the addition of an accession letter[4];

Conditions precedent in other commercial circumstances

Conditions Precedent in Asset Finance

13.011
In an asset finance transaction, because some conditions, such as those relating to security over the asset being acquired, cannot be satisfied before the loan is advanced there will be two sets of conditions precedent–
- those which are to be satisfied on or before the time of the drawdown notice (as with a corporate transaction); and
- those (e.g. the mortgage) which are to be satisfied on drawdown.

---

[3] See the commentary on Clause 24 (*General Undertakings*) from 8.199 onwards.
[4] See Schedule 6 (*Form of Accession Letter*) in 13.022.

The first set will generally include approval of insurances and delivery of a copy of the purchase contract in addition to the conditions precedent normally required for a corporate loan. For the sake of practicalities, the legal opinions will often be delayed and will form part of the second set of conditions (to enable the opinions to cover the mortgage issues). However, the lender's lawyer will usually agree the form of legal opinion with the relevant lawyers before the loan agreement is signed.

13.012

The additional conditions precedent applicable on drawdown will include

- experts' reports (e.g. environmental and/or safety issues and reports on the insurances);
- evidence of ownership and registration of the asset;
- delivery (and registration as needed) of the security documents;
- evidence of the state of repair of the asset and
- evidence of all consents, etc., needed for operation of the asset.

13.013

The moneys will be advanced direct to the seller and/or the seller's mortgagee. The agreement should provide for the conditions precedent to be satisfied by a specific time of day on the drawdown date, to ensure that they are satisfied in sufficient time to enable the lenders to authorize payment. See also Box 13.1.

Box 13.1

In asset finance, given that some conditions precedent to drawdown (e.g. the mortgage) cannot be satisfied until after the moneys have been drawn, and the lenders will not want to advance until the conditions are satisfied, the parties will need to agree how this issue is to be resolved. One solution is to use a 'payment letter'. The lender tables a letter irrevocably undertaking to pay the relevant amount, for value on that day to the seller's account. The seller will exchange the title document for this payment letter. Of course the lender will not proffer the payment letter for exchange until it is satisfied that:

- all conditions precedent to the loan (other than the title document and the mortgage) are in order; and
- the original title document and mortgage are acceptable (and, if applicable, are acceptable for registration in any relevant registry).

This solution relies on the seller (and its banker) accepting the credit risk of the lending bank.

Conditions Precedent in Project Finance

13.014

In a project finance transaction there will be at least two different circumstances in which conditions precedent will be required: the first drawdown, and subsequent drawdowns. There may be an additional requirement for conditions precedent (e.g. to the release of certain guarantees or security which apply during the construction period only) to be satisfied once construction is complete and the project moves into the operational phase.

Conditions Precedent to First Drawing

13.015

These will include similar documents and facts to those required in a corporate transaction (corporate authorities, process agent's letter, legal opinions, specimen signatures plus a requirement that there is no Default and that Repeating Representations are true).

In addition there will be other conditions precedent, such as:

- All contracts necessary for the project (such as a construction agreement, offtake agreement, concession agreement, shareholders' agreement and any supply contract) must have been signed and become effective.
- All financing documents (such as funding commitments from other lenders and shareholders, intercreditor arrangements and security sharing arrangements) must have become effective.
- All security must have been constituted and perfected.
- All necessary consents and licences must have been obtained.
- The insurance must be in place and have been approved by the lenders.
- Auditors must have been authorized to communicate directly with the lenders.
- The financial model (containing budgets and assumptions of income) must have been agreed.

> ### *Conditions Precedent to Subsequent Drawings*
>
> **13.016**
> These may include (as well as a requirement that there is no Default) such issues as
>
> - confirmation of completion of a particular stage of construction of the project;
> - updating of the assumptions in the financing plan and compliance with financial ratios (possibly more strict than those which justify acceleration);
> - injection by other lenders and shareholders of a specified amount of funds and
> - evidence that the relevant funds are required for the project.
>
> The funds will be paid to a Disbursement Account and only available for drawing from that account on production of invoices or other evidence of their utilization.
>
> ### *Conditions Precedent to Release of Security on Completion of Construction*
>
> **13.017**
> This will include confirmation from an expert that the project is in all respects ready for operation, and, in many cases, confirmation that it has been operating in accordance with the plans for a given period of time.

Schedule 3: Requests

Schedule 3
   Schedule 3 sets out the form of various notices to be given by the borrower.

426   Schedules

Part 1—Utilization Request

13.018

This specifies the date, currency, amount and Interest Period for the drawing as well as the account to be credited. It also confirms the factual conditions precedent set out in Clause 4.2 (*CONDITIONS OF UTILIZATION*: *Further conditions precedent*) (no Default and all Repeating Representations are true). The main purpose of this is to ensure that the borrower considers these issues at the time of drawing so that it does not issue a drawdown request if these statements are untrue.

Part 2—Selection Notice

13.019

This selects the Interest Period for a loan (after its initial advance) and specifies any required change of currency. As with the utilization request, if there is to be a change of currency, the form requires the borrower to confirm the factual conditions precedent (no Default and Repeating Representations true). This is because a change of currency can result in the lender advancing additional funds to the borrower.[5]

Schedule 4: Form of Transfer Certificate

13.020

Schedule 4 sets out the form of transfer certificate.

This document is used to transfer interests in the loan to new lenders. It confirms

- relevant contact details;
- tax status for the purpose of withholding tax (if applicable);
- the limitation on the seller's responsibility to the purchaser in respect of the loan interest purchased and
- details of the amount transferred and the effective date of the transfer.

---

[5] See Clause 8 (*Optional Currencies*) from 3.019 onwards.

It is signed by the seller, buyer and Agent and, under the LMA Compounded/Term Rate Loan, takes effect as a novation.

Schedule 5: Form of Assignment Agreement

13.021

This sets out the form of document to be used if a new lender chooses to purchase a participation by assignment rather than by a transfer using the transfer certificate mechanism in Schedule 4 (*Form of Transfer Certificate*).[6]

Schedule 6: Form of Accession Letter

13.022

Schedule 6 sets out the form to be signed to add a borrower or guarantor. The letter simply has the new party:

* agree to be bound by the agreement;
* confirm its country of incorporation and
* provide contact details.

There is an option to effect the document by a deed, which may be useful, for example, in the case of the addition of a guarantor, to avoid **consideration** issues.[7]

Schedule 7: Form of Resignation Letter

13.023

Schedule 7 sets out the form to be signed by a borrower or guarantor which is ceasing to be an Obligor under the agreement. As well as requesting release from the agreement, the Obligor confirms that no Default exists.

---

[6] See 9.001 onwards for a discussion of assignments and transfers.

[7] See A1.024 for an explanation of deeds and consideration.

428 Schedules

Schedule 8: Form of Compliance Certificate

13.024
Schedule 8 sets out the form of certificate to be signed to confirm compliance with specified undertakings in the agreement (such as the financial covenants, and confirmation that no Default has occurred).

Schedule 9: Existing Security

13.025
Schedule 9 is to list existing security for the purpose of the negative pledge.

Schedule 10: LMA Form of Confidentiality Undertaking

13.026
Schedule 10 is the form of confidentiality undertaking required under the confidentiality clause, for example, if confidential information is to be given to proposed sub-participants.

The LMA form of this letter contains the undertaking to keep 'Confidential Information' confidential. These provisions largely mirror the terms of Clause 38 (*Confidential Information*), discussed in 11.034.

13.027
For the letter to be enforceable there needs to be consideration for its issue. The consideration is usually the provision of the information. It is important that the letter is signed before the information is delivered, both for practical reasons and because otherwise, the consideration would be past, and therefore ineffective. See A1.024.

Schedule 11: Timetables

13.028
Schedule 11 sets out timings for notifications for requests for different currencies and in different markets.

Schedule 12: Form of Increase Confirmation

13.029
This is the form of letter to be signed by any lender who agrees (pursuant to Clause 2.2 (*THE FACILITIES: Increase*)) to take over the Commitment of a lender whose participation is being cancelled or prepaid as a result of issues such as illegality or prepayment following additional costs such as grossing-up costs.

Schedule 13: Form of Letter of Credit

13.030
This sets out the form of any letter of credit to be issued under the agreement.

Schedule 14: Reference Rate Terms

13.031
This schedule sets out the currency specific terms relating to the charging of interest. The LMA Compounded/Term Rate Loan includes schedules for Dollars, Sterling, Swiss Francs and Euros. For Dollars and Euros, schedules are provided for both term rate and compounded rate options.

For each currency and interest rate option, the schedule lists

- specific definitions (such as 'Central Bank Rate') and specifies what that definition means in the context of the currency in question; and
- specific topics (such as 'cost of funds as a fallback'—see 13.032) and specifies whether the clauses in the body of the loan agreement which relate to that topic apply to the relevant currency and interest rate option or not.

430   Schedules

The definitions and topics addressed by the schedule for Compounded Rate Loans are different from those for Term Rate Loans. The details for Term Rate Loans are different depending on how the relevant term rate is calculated (eg is it an IBOR-based rate or something different such as CME Term Sofr). The details for Compounded Rate Loans will depend on why the compounded rate is relevant: was that the original rate chosen or does it apply because of a Rate Switch or Term Fallback Option?[8] We will therefore look at the Schedules for term rates and compounded rates separately, using the headings from the LMA Compounded/Term Rate Loan.

1. Schedule for Compounded Rate Loans

13.032

Cost of Funds as a Fallback

This refers to the mechanism which is to apply if the data necessary for the calculation of interest as intended is unavailable, as discussed in 0.134–5 in the context of Term Rate Loans and in 0.137 in the context of Compounded Rate Loans.

13.033

Additional Business Day

As discussed in 0.131 and 1.010, different places need to be open for business for different purposes, and this is reflected in the definition of 'Business Day' which has different requirements as to what constitutes a Business Day depending on the action which is required to happen on that day. This concept of Additional Business Day is designed to ensure that any action which requires a rate fixing to be made can only happen when the market for the relevant interest rate is open. So, an 'Additional Business Day' in respect of any given currency and interest rate, is defined to mean a day when the underlying market is open for business. In the context of Compounded Rate

---

[8] So, for example in the Reference Rate Terms for Euros with a compounded interest rate in, the LMA Compounded/Term Rate Loan, there is provision for a Rate Switch CAS, but not for either a Fallback CAS or a Baseline CAS.

Loans, the underlying market is open on an RFR Banking Day; in the context of Term Rate Loans based on Euribor, the underlying market is open on Target Days,[9] and in the context of CME Term Sofr, an Additional Business Day needs to be a day on which trading is happening in US Government Securities.

13.034

Baseline CAS

If the currency and interest rate concerned apply from the outset, then the schedule will specify whether there is a Baseline CAS for this currency or not, and if so, how it is calculated. See 0.128.

13.035

Break Costs

The schedule will specify whether Break Costs apply to this currency and interest methodology or not, and if so, how it is calculated. See Box 0.13.

13.036

Business Day Conventions

This will specify the conventions applied in the relevant market to deal with such things as monthly periods which end on non-business days—do they get extended or shortened so as to end on a business day?

13.037

Central Bank Rate

The Schedule will identify the relevant Central Bank (usually used as a fallback if the relevant Daily Rate (Sofr etc.) is unavailable as discussed in 0.137) and if it issues more than one rate—explain which rate this refers to.

---

[9] Hence an Additional Business Day for Euros is a Target Day and for Sterling and Swiss Franks it is an RFR Banking Day.

432 Schedules

13.038

Central Bank Rate Adjustment

This is the credit adjustment spread (if any) which will be applied if the Central Bank Rate is used as a fallback to the relevant risk free rate. The amount of the adjustment will need to be negotiated.

13.039

Daily Rate

The Schedule will identify the relevant Daily Rate (Sofr etc.). The LMA formulation also allows for a historic[10] Central Bank Rate (plus applicable credit adjustment spread) to be used if necessary as well as an optional zero floor on the Daily Rate.

13.040

Comment Note that, historically, for loans based on Libor, the zero floor commonly applied to Libor/Euribor. To achieve the same economic effect, the zero floor would need to apply to the aggregate of the Daily Rate and any Baseline CAS.[11]

13.041

Fallback CAS

This is the credit adjustment spread which will apply if the relevant currency started off as a Term Rate Loan but became a Compounded Rate Loan as a result of the operation of the various fallback mechanisms as discussed in 0.134 and 0.135. Although the LMA Compounded/Term Rate Loan does not provide for compounded rates to be used as a fallback to Euribor (see footnotes in 0.135) it does envisage that users might decide to include such a fallback. In that case users should note that the spread would have a different function for Term Rate Loans based on an IBOR (such as Euribor) and for other Term Rate Loans. See Box 13.2.

---

[10] Up to a specified number of days old.
[11] Or, if there is none, a similar adjustment.

Box 13.2

Note that the economics of the relevant credit adjustment spread will differ, depending on the currency and the economics of the applicable term rate. So, for Euros, if the interest rate started on the basis of Euribor and moved to compounded €str, the spread would compensate for the different pricing of those two interest rate products. If a loan moved from CME Term Sofr to compounded Sofr, on the other hand, the economics of the pricing for the two are comparable as both are based on risk free rates. There should be no significant credit adjustment spread arising from the switch. So for Euribor, if a Fallback CAS were to be included in the Reference Rate Terms, this figure would need to be agreed. For CME Term Sofr, on the other hand, the Reference Rate Terms would define the Fallback CAS to equal the Term Reference Rate CAS (if any).

13.042

Lookback Period

The Schedule will specify the duration of the Lookback Period discussed in 0.121.

13.043

Margin and L/C Margin

The Schedule will specify the Margin (and L/C Margin for letters of credit if applicable) for the currency.

13.044

Market Disruption Rate

This is the rate to be used for comparison purposes to determine whether lenders are entitled to charge a different interest rate as a result of 'market disruption' as discussed from 5.020 onwards. It may be that the market disruption clauses in the body of the agreement do not apply at all, or it may be agreed that they apply to all currencies and rates or that they only apply to Euribor but not to other interest rates.

434 **Schedules**

13.045

One of the complexities here is that, to make this comparison, you need an interest rate for an Interest Period, not for a particular day. So this is where Schedule 16 and the Cumulative Compounded RFR Rate come in. This is the rate for an Interest Period. It does not include any credit adjustment spread. The Market Disruption Rate is the Cumulative Compounded RFR Rate for the Interest Period plus any Baseline CAS.[12]

13.046

Rate Switch CAS

If the currency and interest rate concerned apply following a Rate Switch then the schedule will specify whether there is a Rate Switch CAS for this currency or not, and if so, how it is calculated.

Reporting Day

This concept is only necessary if the market disruption provisions are included or cost of funds applies as a fallback. In these cases, it is the date by which lenders need to advise the Agent of their cost of funds.

13.047

RFR

The Schedule will identify the relevant risk free rate (Sonia, Sofr, etc.).

13.048

RFR Banking Day

As discussed in 0.131 this is defined as a day when the relevant market is open for business.

---

[12] Where the compounded rate is only relevant as a result of a rate switch or fallback mechanism there may be a Rate Switch CAS or Fallback CAS in place of the Baseline CAS.

Schedule 14: Reference Rate Terms **435**

13.049

Published Rate Contingency Period

This concept may be used in the context of Clause 11A *(Rate Switch)* allowing for a change in the method of calculation of interest if the official methodology for publication of the relevant benchmark rate is changed on anything other than a very short-term basis.

13.050

Interest Periods

The Schedule will set out the available Interest Periods for the relevant currency and what period will apply in the absence of a selection by the borrower.

2. Schedule for Term Rate Loans

13.051
In addition to the issues relevant for Compounded Rate Loans, the Schedule for Term Rate Loans will deal with the following.

13.052

Rate Switch Currency

The Schedule will specify whether the currency is a Rate Switch Currency or not—in other words, whether provisions for converting the interest rate for the currency onto a different basis are hardwired into the agreement or not, as discussed in 0.115.

436　　Schedules

13.053

Choice of 'Term Fallback Option'

This reflects the temporary fallback options for Term Rate Loans which do not bear interest at Euribor, discussed in 0.134. That waterfall of fallback options may or may not include the concept of a Term Fallback Option, such as use of a fixed Central Bank Rate or Compounded Reference Rate as a fallback to CME Term Sofr[13] if other options such as ICE Benchmarks Term Sofr are unavailable or not included in the waterfall.

13.054

Alternative Term Rate

This also reflects the temporary fallback options for Term Rate Loans discussed in 0.134. That waterfall of fallback options may or may not include the concept of an Alternative Term Rate such as ICE Benchmarks Term Sofr if the original Term Rate (such as CME Term Sofr) is temporarily unavailable.

13.055

Alternative Term Rate Adjustment

If the waterfall of options for dealing with temporary unavailability of the intended term rate includes the concept of an Alternative Term Rate then this definition will be used to define any appropriate difference in pricing between the Primary Term Rate (being the rate intended to be used) and the Alternative Term Rate.

13.056

Backstop Rate Switch Date

If the relevant currency is a Rate Switch Currency then this definition will be used if the plan is to have a backstop date by which the switch must happen.

---

[13] Note that the LMA note that they do not envisage compounded reference rates as a fallback to Euribor in the event of temporary unavailability.

Schedule 14: Reference Rate Terms

13.057

Central Bank Rate and Central Bank Rate Adjustment

These definitions will be included in this schedule if a fixed Central Bank Rate is chosen as the Term Fallback Option for the relevant currency in place of the Compounded Reference Rate.

Fallback Interest Period

Another definition which is used in the context of the waterfall of options dealing with temporary unavailability of the Primary Term Rate.

13.058

Market Disruption Rate

This is the rate to be used for comparison purposes to determine whether lenders are entitled to charge a different interest rate as a result of 'market disruption' as discussed in 5.020.

13.059

For a Term Rate Loan based on Euribor, the Market Disruption Rate is the same as the Term Reference Rate because no credit adjustment spread is appropriate in these circumstances.

13.060

For a Term Rate Loan Based on CME Term Sofr, the loan agreement may or may not include a separate Term Reference Rate CAS[14] as discussed in Box 0.17. If there is a separate Term Reference Rate CAS it will be included in the definition of the Market Disruption Rate for CME Term Sofr.

13.061

Overnight Rate and Overnight Reference Day

Again these definitions relate to the waterfall of fallback provisions dealing with temporary unavailability of the Primary Term Rate as discussed in 0.134.

---

[14] Being the equivalent of the Baseline CAS in a Compounded Rate Loan.

438   Schedules

This definition is used in the context of an 'Interpolated Primary Term Rate' where rates are needed for different periods of time in order to calculate the Interpolated Primary Term Rate. In the context of CME Term Sofr the Overnight Rate is Sofr on the relevant Overnight Reference Rate.

13.062

Primary Term Rate

The term rate which is intended to apply (e.g. CME Term Sofr or Euribor).

13.063

Quotation Day and Quotation Time

The day and time at which rate fixing occurs in the relevant market.

13.064

Term Reference Rate CAS

This is the equivalent, in relation to a Term Rate Loan, of the Baseline CAS in relation to a Compounded Rate Loan. It may or may not appear as a separate element in the pricing. See Box 0.17.

Schedule 15: Daily Non-Cumulative Compounded RFR Rate

13.065

This Schedule sets out the calculation of the rate of interest (excluding Margin and any credit adjustment spread) attributable to any given day. The detailed calculation will depend on whether the parties have decided to use observation shift (i.e. to make the calculation based on the number of banking days in the observation period) or not to use it (i.e. to make the calculation based on the number of banking days in the Interest Period).

Schedule 15: Daily Non-Cumulative Compounded RFR Rate **439**

This commentary on the Schedule is divided into three parts

* First, we explain the principles of the calculation of the interest rate attributable to a given day
* Second, we set out the formula used to calculate the Annualised Cumulative Compounded Rate on any given day—which is a key input to the calculation of the interest rate attributable to any given day
* Third, we break down the formula and explain its constituent parts.

13.066

1. Principles of the calculation of the interest rate attributable to a given day

As discussed earlier, (see 0.123) this rate is calculated by looking at the amount by which a given sum will have grown over a period of time[15] ending on one day and comparing it with the amount by which it will have grown over the same period but ending on the following day.

The expression "$UCCDR_i$"[16] is used to describe this rate of interest inherent in the amount by which any given sum will have grown from the start of the Interest Period up until that day if you had reinvested the original sum plus accrued interest daily at the relevant risk free rate every day during that period of time.

13.067

So, for example, if we had invested 1000 at Sonia on day 1 and reinvested it (plus accrued interest) daily at Sonia for 3 months, it might have grown to 1010 and to 1009 at the end of the previous day. That is 1% in 3 months which is an annual rate of 4%. So the Annualised Cumulative Compounded RFR rate for that 3 months is 4% and the unannualized rate is 1%. The unannualized rate one day before the end of the three months was 0.9%. So the increase in the unannualized rate over the last day was 0.1%. On the basis of a 360-day year that equates to an annual rate of 3.6%. So the Daily Non-Cumulative Compounded RFR Rate for that day is 3.6%.

The steps needed to make the calculation of the annual rate of interest attributable to a particular day (the Daily Non-Cumulative Compounded RFR Rate) are

---

[15] The 'Cumulation Period'.

[16] **The Unannualised Cumulative Compounded Daily Rate.**

440 Schedules

13.068

- Identify the amount by which the given sum will have increased over the relevant period (In the example we saw that principal of $1000 mil would have increased by $10 mil over a 3 month period)
- Express that as a rate of interest (in our example, 1%)
- Compare that with the amount to which it had grown one day earlier, also expressed as a rate of interest (in our example 0.9%)
- Convert the difference (currently an unannualized rate and in our example 0.1%) to an annualized rate (in our example 3.6%).

13.069

So setting out the steps required to turn the raw data inputs of the Daily Rate into the final compounded rate turns out to be more complicated than just describing the general idea! Turning those steps into a formula is more complicated still.

13.070

At the heart of the LMA calculation of the rate of interest attributable to any given day is a formula, which is used to calculate the Annualised Cumulative Compounded RFR Rate for a period of time (the Cumulation Period) starting at the beginning of the Interest Period and ending on that day (4% in the above example). The formula is explained from 13.073 onwards.

13.071

There is then a definition of the unannualized rate (UCCDR or the Unannualised Cumulative Compounded Daily Rate—1% in our example) and of the UCCDR from the previous day (0.9% in our example).

13.072

The Schedule then has a calculation of the Daily Non-Cumulative Compounded RFR Rate, which compares the UCCDR for one day with that from the previous day and converts the difference (0.1% in our example) to an annualized rate (3.6% in our example). See Box 13.3 for the formula used to make this calculation.

This is the Daily Non-Cumulative Compounded RFR Rate which is the attributable to that day and the basis of charging interest for that day.

> **Box 13.3**
>
> $$(UCCDR_i - UCCDR_i - 1) \times dcc/n$$

2. The formula for calculating the Annualised Cumulative Compounded Daily Rate

13.073

So it all starts with the formula for calculating the Annualised Cumulative Compounded Daily Rate—which looks like this (assuming you are not using Observation Shift)

$$\left[\prod_{i=1}^{d_0}\left(1 + \frac{\text{DailyRate}_{i-\text{LP}} \times n_i}{dcc}\right) - 1\right] \times \frac{dcc}{tn_i}$$

We also need to know what the various letters in the formula refer to. Here are some explanations

'd_0' means the number of RFR Banking Days during the Cumulation Period;
'i' means a series of whole numbers from one to d_0, each representing the relevant RFR Banking Day in chronological order during the Cumulation Period;
'$\textbf{DailyRate}_{i-LP}$' means for any RFR Banking Day 'i' during the Cumulation Period, the Daily Rate for the RFR Banking Day which is the applicable Lookback Period prior to that RFR Banking Day 'i';
'n_i' means, for any RFR Banking Day 'i', the number of calendar days from, and including, that RFR Banking Day 'i' up to, but excluding, the following RFR Banking Day;
'dcc' means 360 or, in any case where market practice in the Relevant Market is to use a different number for quoting the number of days in a year, that number and
'tn_i' means the number of calendar days during that Cumulation Period.

442 Schedules

3. Deconstructing the formula and explaining its constituent parts

13.074
If you would like to try to understand this formula (and the similar one in Schedule 16 (*Cumulative Compounded RFR Rate*)) here is an explanation.

13.075

Step 1 Calculate the amount to which a given sum will have grown on a given day if invested at the risk free rate

At the heart of the formula for calculation of the Annualised Cumulative Compounded RFR Rate is the expression

$$`1 + \frac{\text{Daily Rate}_{i-\text{lp}}}{\text{dcc}}`,$$

This calculates the amount to which a given sum (the 1 in the formula) will grow on any given day as a result of accruing interest at the Daily Rate (or rather, at the Daily Rate for a few days earlier as discussed in 0.121). Because the Daily Rate is expressed as an annual rate of interest, to calculate this amount you need to divide the rate by 360 or 365 (depending on the currency and what day count convention is used for that currency) to find out what the growth would be in a single day. That explains the presence of the 'dcc' in the formula—referring to the day count convention.

13.076

Step 2 Adjust for non banking days

Then another adjustment needs to be made to deal with non banking days. So if we are doing the calculation on a Monday, and the last Banking Day was the preceding Friday, we will take the Friday rate and apply it to the Saturday and Sunday in order to calculate the amount to which the initial sum has grown since the last Banking Day. That explains the n_i in the formula—defined as follows

Schedule 15: Daily Non-Cumulative Compounded RFR Rate 443

ni means, for any RFR Banking Day 'i' during the Cumulation Period, the number of calendar days from, and including, that RFR Banking Day 'i' up to, but excluding, the following RFR BankingDay;

So this is the formula so far and it tells us the amount which a given sum (1) will have grown to on any given Banking Day since the last Banking Day

$$\left(1 + \frac{\text{Daily Rate}_{i-\text{LP}} \times n_i}{\text{dcc}}\right)$$

13.077

Step 3   Calculate how much the initial investment will have grown to if compounded over a period of days

So let's say on day 1 our initial 1 grew to 1.1—we now have 1.1 to invest on day 2. To calculate what that 1.1 will grow to on day 2 we multiply the 1.1 by the Daily Rate for day 2. Whatever the result of that is, we multiply by the Daily Rate for day 3 and so on.

So, to calculate the total growth of a given sum over a period of time you multiply the result of the above calculation for day 1 by the results for day 2 and so on, for however many RFR Banking Days there are in the period which you are trying to calculate.

The formula used to describe this uses a mathematical expression which may be unfamiliar. It is known as capital Pi and looks like this

$$\prod.$$

It means you take a series of numbers and multiply them together. In our case the series of numbers is the result of the formula on each day. The numbers above and below the capital pi symbol (do) tell you how many numbers are in the series—that being the number of RFR Banking Days for which you are making the calculation

$$\prod_{i=1}^{d_0}\left(1 + \frac{\text{Daily Rate}_{i-\text{LP}} \times n_i}{\text{dcc}}\right)$$

where

444   Schedules

d_0 *means the number of RFR Banking Days in the Cumulation Period; and*

i means a series of whole numbers from one to d0, each representing the relevant RFR Banking Day in chronological order in the Cumulation Period;

This now tells you how much your initial investment (1) will have grown to during the period of the calculation.

13.078

Step 4   Calculate how much the initial investment will have grown BY (as opposed to how much it has grown TO)

To do this you need to take away the original investment of 1—so now you know how much it has grown by as opposed to how much it has grown to. That explains the -1 in the formula

13.079

Step 5   Turn that into an annual figure

If the initial investment has grown by this amount over this period of time—what rate of growth is that on an annual basis? That explains the expression dcc/tn in the formula

13.080
So the final formula looks like this

$$\left[\prod_{i=1}^{d_0} \left(1 + \frac{\text{DailyRate}_{i-\text{LP}} \times n_i}{\text{dcc}} \right) - 1 \right] \times \frac{\text{dcc}}{tn_i}$$

It is very similar to the formula used in Schedule 16 (*Cumulative Compounded RFR Rate*) and explained in Box 13.6. The difference is that this formula is intended to measure growth over any given period of time (the 'Cumulation Period') while the one in Schedule 16 (*Cumulative Compounded RFR Rate*) is measuring the rate for an Interest Period. See Box 13.4.

Schedule 16: Cumulative Compounded RFR Rate 445

> **Box 13.4**
>
> In Schedule 15 (*Daily Non-Cumulative Compounded RFR Rate*), this formula
> is used to calculate the growth of an initial investment on one day, and to
> compare it with the growth the following day, so as to calculate the increase
> in growth on that last day (the 'Daily Non -Cumulative Compounded RFR Rate'
> for that day). In Schedule 16 (*Cumulative Compounded RFR Rate*) it is used
> to calculate the rate of growth of an initial investment over a whole Interest
> Period, so as to calculate the interest rate for the Interest Period (the 'Cumu-
> lative Compounded RFR Rate' for the Interest Period), if a rate is needed for
> that for the purpose of the market disruption clause as discussed in 13.045.

Schedule 16: Cumulative Compounded RFR Rate

13.081

This Schedule sets out the calculation for the rate of interest payable on
a Compounded Rate Loan for an Interest Period (which the LMA calls
the Cumulative Compounded RFR Rate) for the purpose of the market
disruption clause (if any). See Box 13.5.

> **Box 13.5**
>
> The rate for an Interest Period (and hence this Schedule) will only be needed
> if a market disruption clause is included in the agreement, in which case it
> will be needed in order to decide whether the lenders' funding costs exceed
> this rate or not. Apart from for the purpose of the market disruption clause,
> the rate of interest is expressed to be the rate for each day (the 'Daily Non-
> Cumulative Compounded RFR Rate' for that day) plus any applicable Margin
> and/or credit adjustment spread.

13.082

Here is the formula for the calculation

$$\left[\prod_{i=1}^{d_0} \left(1 + \frac{\mathrm{DailyRate}_{i-\mathrm{LP}} \times n_i}{\mathrm{dcc}} \right) - 1 \right] \times \frac{\mathrm{dcc}}{d}$$

where

446 Schedules

'd_0' means the number of RFR Banking Days during the Interest Period;

'i' means a series of whole numbers from one to d_0, each representing the relevant RFR Banking Day in chronological order during the Interest Period;

'$DailyRate_{i-LP}$' means for any RFR Banking Day 'i' during the Interest Period, the Daily Rate for the RFR Banking Day which is the applicable Lookback Period prior to that RFR Banking Day 'i';

'n_i' means, for any RFR Banking Day 'i', the number of calendar days from, and including, that RFR Banking Day 'i' up to, but excluding, the following RFR Banking Day;

'dcc' means 360 or, in any case where market practice in the Relevant Market is to use a different number for quoting the number of days in a year, that number and

'd' means the number of calendar days during that Interest Period.

> **Box 13.6**
>
> As discussed in 13.080, the difference between this formula and the one in Schedule 15 (*Daily Non-Cumulative Compounded RFR Rate*) is that Schedule 15 (*Daily Non-Cumulative Compounded RFR Rate*) makes the calculation in relation to the 'Cumulation Period'—being the period of time from the start of the Interest Period to the date of the calculation; while the formula in Schedule 16 (*Cumulative Compounded RFR Rate*) makes the calculation for the whole Interest Period. So the 'd' in the formula in Schedule 16 (*Cumulative Compounded RFR Rate*) means the number of calendar days in the Interest Period, and is replaced by 'tn_i' in the formula in Schedule 16 (*Cumulative Compounded RFR Rate*), where tn_i means the number of calendar days in the Cumulation Period.

Schedule 17: Legal Opinions

For the sake of convenience, the form of a legal opinion is discussed here as though it was attached to the LMA Compounded/Term Rate Loan as Schedule 17 (*Legal Opinions*).

This commentary on legal opinions is not intended to be a comprehensive review of the subject,[17] but rather an overview of the process and of the

---

[17] For which, see Philip Wood: International Loans, Bonds, Guarantees, Legal opinions, *3rd* edn, 2019 in Part 5.

expectations of the parties involved. In particular, suggestions as to qualifications which may be necessary for certain opinions, and issues which need to be considered before an opinion can be given, are intended as examples only.

Schedule 17: Legal Opinions—Section 1—Introduction

1. Types of opinion

13.083

In financial transactions, legal opinions usually address some or all of the following:

- capacity and authority (the power of the company to enter into the transaction and the fact that it has been properly authorized). This opinion is sought in the jurisdiction of incorporation of the relevant borrower or guarantor;
- enforceability. This opinion is sought in the jurisdiction of the governing law of the documents (and sometimes, to a limited extent, in the jurisdiction of incorporation—see 13.103);
- tax consequences and/or
- choice of law and enforceability of judgements. This opinion is sought in the jurisdiction of incorporation of the borrower.

2. Limits on scope of opinion

13.084

The legal opinion does not cover insolvency issues, questions of fact or priority and enforcement of security.

448   Schedules

Insolvency issues

13.085

The types of insolvency law issues on which the lenders may need advice but which are not covered by the opinion include

- the circumstances in which a liquidator will be able to avoid certain aspects of the transaction;
- priority of the lenders' claims in an insolvency;
- the circumstances in which lenders may find that they have to agree to a rescheduling of their debt, or might find themselves unable to enforce any security, as a result of some compulsory rehabilitation of the company under insolvency procedures or
- directors' duties in insolvency such as the point at which they must stop trading—these may have a significant impact on the ability to organize a rescheduling of the debt if difficulties arise.

These issues are not covered because they are too complex to be summarized usefully and they often involve a lot of discretion for the liquidator.

Factual issues

13.086

The opinion also does not usually cover issues of fact such as the location of a company's 'centre of main interests' (see 8.207) or whether performing obligations under the documents breaches any other contract signed by the borrower. The lawyer issuing the opinion is unlikely to have personal knowledge of such factual issues.

Often the legal conclusion (such as the conclusion that the documents are binding) depends on factual issues (such as the fact that certain specified persons attended the board meeting which approved the transaction). In this case the lawyer will state those factual assumptions which they have made in order to come to the legal conclusion stated in the opinion. This is the role of the 'assumptions' in the opinion discussed in 13.096. It may be sensible to request the borrower/guarantor to give representations in the loan documents to the effect that those factual assumptions are correct.

Priority and enforcement of security

13.087

The opinion does not generally deal with issues such as

- priority of the security;
- how long enforcement might take;
- what it might cost;
- whether self-help is available;
- the predictability of the courts;
- any restrictions which may be imposed on the sale of the asset concerned in the event of enforcement (e.g. restrictions on the identity of any purchaser or any requirement for consent, such as an export licence, before such sale can proceed) or
- duties of the security holder such as duties to give the security provider an opportunity to pay before enforcing, duties to other mortgagees or other duties such as interference with contracts.

3. Locations of opinions

13.088

In an international transaction, the laws of many countries may impact the legal effect of the transaction, as discussed in the analysis of the opinion which follows from 13.093 onwards. The usual practice is to require legal opinions only from the place of incorporation of the relevant borrowers/guarantors; the country of the law chosen to govern the agreement and the location of any asset taken as security. Sometimes advice (which may or may not include a requirement for a legal opinion) is also sought in other jurisdictions (e.g. perhaps if a borrower has significant assets in a given location or the place where its centre of main interests may be—see 8.207).

450   Schedules

4. Which lawyers?

13.089

A legal opinion is only an opinion. Its value depends on the expertise of the lawyer giving it. The choice of lawyer is of course very important. It is also important that the lawyer is adequately insured.

Advice from the borrower's in-house counsel is helpful in relation to factual issues which external lawyers would be unable to confirm (e.g. as to no breach of other contracts). However, generally, lenders will require an opinion of external lawyers, rather than in-house counsel.

Practice differs in different countries as to which lawyers should be asked to issue opinions. In the US, borrowers' external lawyers are asked to issue enforceability opinions to the lenders. In England, the normal practice is to require the enforceability opinion from the Agent's lawyer and not from the borrower's lawyer. Sometimes the borrower's lawyer may be asked for a capacity opinion, particularly if the lenders do not have lawyers in the borrower's place of incorporation. For more detail on precisely what an English lawyer will cover see the Guide issued by the City of London Law Society.[18] That guide also highlights the professional conduct and other issues which an English lawyer needs to consider before issuing an opinion in favour of a person who is not their client (referred to as a 'third party opinion').

The lawyers' roles

13.090

The purpose of a legal opinion in a loan transaction is to ensure that the lenders are aware of the legal risks involved in that transaction and that those risks are kept to a minimum. It is the responsibility of the Agent's lawyer to arrange the issue of appropriate legal opinions.

The legal opinion is not an insurance policy, but rather it is an expression of a professional opinion as at the date of the opinion. Ultimately, precisely what the opinion says is up to the issuer. There is no obligation on the lawyer to advise recipients if the law changes after the opinion is issued.

---

[18] Practice of English lawyers in giving opinions on financial transactions is explained in some detail in 'A guide to the questions to be addressed when providing opinion letters on English law in financial transactions', issued by the City of London Law Society and available at www.citysolicitors. org.uk under the financial law committee section.

13.091

The Agent's lawyer's role is not simply to request the correspondent lawyers to issue an opinion, but also to try to ensure that those lawyers address the issues and advise of all potential problems. This can be a difficult task if the relevant country has laws which are completely different to those in the country of the Agent's lawyer. For example, the concept of overcollateralization[19] (relevant, e.g. under German law) is unknown to lawyers in many other countries. As a result, unless the coordinating lawyer happens to be aware of the overcollateralization concept, they are unlikely to ask for advice on that topic.

13.092

To minimize the risk that the Agent's lawyers will only raise queries on legal issues with which they are already familiar under their own law, the usual opinion obtained in the context of a loan financing addresses very broad principles which should, together, cover all potential issues.[20]

The risk remains that the coordinating lawyer and local lawyer may have different understandings of the meaning of the opinions requested (e.g. did they both appreciate that the opinion on power—referred to in 13.099— required confirmation that the transaction was within the company's express power rather than a confirmation given in reliance on protections given by law?), or that the breadth of the opinions requested will result in the local lawyer failing to give specific advice.[21] If those involved in agreeing legal opinions are aware of these hazards, they are more easily avoided.

Schedule 17: Legal Opinions—Section 2: Form of Opinion

13.093

The advice obtained will often be encapsulated in a legal opinion. The usual form of opinion is divided into

---

[19] The idea that security may be open to challenge if the value of the asset taken as security is substantially greater than the amount secured.

[20] These general principles are: due incorporation and continued existence, power, authority, due execution, no contravention of law or constitution, valid and enforceable obligations, effectiveness of security, no consents or filings needed, no unexpected tax consequences, choice of law and jurisdiction and enforcement of judgements. Each of these topics is discussed in more detail from 13.097 onwards.

[21] See, for example, the comments in 13.105.

452 Schedules

- the introduction
- the assumptions
- the opinions
- the qualifications.

1. Introduction

13.094

The introduction sets out the lawyer's role in the transaction and specifies the documents reviewed.

> *We have acted as solicitors to the Agent in connection with a credit agreement dated [] (the Credit Agreement) made between [] (the 'Borrower'), the lenders party to the Credit Agreement and [] (the 'Agent'). Terms defined in the Credit Agreement have the same meaning in this letter.*
>
> *We have examined the following documents.* [This section will list the documents reviewed which will usually be the Credit Agreement itself plus the appropriate corporate authorities and any consents reviewed and searches of public records which have been conducted.]
>
> *and such other documents as we have deemed necessary as a basis for the opinions set out in this letter.*

13.095

This section may also identify who is entitled to rely on the opinion. In a syndicated loan, the opinion must be able to be relied on not only by the lawyer's client (that is the Agent), but also by all other syndicate members. It would be unusual for the opinion to allow reliance by any party which is not a direct lender at the stage of primary syndication.

2. Assumptions

We have made the following assumptions

13.096

The assumptions will cover issues which are outside the opinion of the lawyers such as:

- that copies of documents supplied are complete and accurate;

Schedule 17: Legal Opinions—Section 2: Form of Opinion **453**

- that signatures are genuine;
- that information provided by searches is up to date;
- that certain statements of corporate officers (e.g. as to the persons attending board meetings and the issue of notice of meeting and the like) are true.

The assumptions will also include relevant assumptions as to the effect of laws of other countries.

3. Opinions

13.097

The opinions give the legal confirmations required. The opinions themselves mirror, to a large extent, the representations in the loan agreement. Adjustments to one often need also to be made to the other.

The legal opinions will cover some or all of the points discussed here, and those points will be addressed by the lawyer in the relevant jurisdiction, as identified by the conflict of law analysis conducted by the Agent's lawyer. For example, the due incorporation opinion may be required from a different lawyer than the lawyer who issues the opinion on the effectiveness of the security.

For each opinion discussed in the following paragraphs, it is discussed in relation to the principal jurisdiction(s) from which that opinion is usually required.

Due incorporation and continued existence

13.098

We are of the opinion that the Borrower is a limited liability company, duly incorporated and validly existing [in goodstanding] under [English] law.

Giving this opinion involves not only ensuring that the company is indeed a limited liability company, but also ensuring that no resolution for winding up (or similar in the relevant jurisdiction) has been passed nor has an administrator or similar officer been appointed. This opinion will be required in the place of incorporation.[22] In countries such as the US, which have a concept

---

[22] A company may also be the subject of an insolvency process (such as an English administration) in its place of business. For example, a company may be made the subject of a winding up procedure in the EC in the country where it has its 'centre of main interests', regardless of the place of

454   **Schedules**

of goodstanding (where, for example, failure to pay an annual registration tax may result in the company being struck off or its licence to conduct business removed) the opinion will include confirmation of goodstanding.

Power

13.099

The execution, delivery and performance by the Borrower of the Credit Agreement are within the Borrower's corporate powers.

This opinion will be required in the place of incorporation.[23] Lenders want to be sure that the transaction is specifically within the company's power. They do not generally want to rely on protections (such as those in s40 (1) Companies Act 2006 in England) for those dealing with companies where there is a problem with the company's capacity (power) to enter into particular transactions. Hence, this opinion requires the lawyer to confirm that the transaction is within the company's power.

Authority

13.100

The execution, delivery and performance by the Borrower of the Credit Agreement have been duly authorized by all necessary corporate action (if any).

This opinion will be sought in the place of incorporation.[24] The requirement is for the lawyer to confirm that the company has complied with whatever procedures (such as holding a board meeting and associated issues, e.g. notice of meeting, quorum, voting at the meeting and disclosure of interests, and, if a **power of attorney** has been used, due authorization of issue of the power of attorney) as are necessary to authorize the entering into of the transaction and that the directors are not exceeding their powers in authorizing the transaction. In some cases there may be internal, non-public limits on the directors' authority which do not affect third parties. Nevertheless,

---

incorporation of the company. Advice on insolvency may therefore sometimes also be sought in those places although this is unusual due to the difficulty in identifying the location of the centre of main interests—see Box 8.31.

[23] In some cases the 'seat' of the company is the place which determines these issues.

[24] Also relevant may be the place of the seat.

Schedule 17: Legal Opinions—Section 2: Form of Opinion **455**

lenders will not wish to become involved in a transaction which was not properly authorized, so will usually require specific confirmation that the directors were authorized.[25]

Due execution

13.101
The documents have been duly executed by the Borrower.

This opinion covers both the form of the execution (e.g. deed, notarization, witnessing, etc.), and the question of whether in fact the correct people actually signed the document. The opinion will be required in the place of incorporation at the minimum (because that will determine who has been authorized to sign documents on behalf of the company). The confirmation may also be required in the place of the law chosen to govern the agreement, which may impose requirements as to formalities (such as a requirement that the document be executed as a deed). The law of the place of execution may also be relevant as it also may impose requirements as to formalities such as the need for a witness or for notarization.

This opinion is a mix of fact and law and, as noted, may involve legal issues in a number of places. Assumptions will therefore be needed in relation to the impact of those other laws and also as to relevant factual issues, such as that the person who signed the document is the person he claimed to be.[26]

No contravention of law or constitution

13.102
The execution, delivery and performance by the Borrower of the Credit Agreement do not contravene any provision of [the Borrower's constitutional documents] or any law rule or regulation applicable to the Borrower in [England].

This opinion is usually required in all places from which an opinion is sought, but with the reference to constitutional documents being limited to the place of incorporation. This opinion is required because some breaches of law may result in fines or other sanctions but not invalidity of the documents.

---

[25] This opinion usually involves a mix of fact and law and the opining lawyer may have to rely on certificates from directors (such as a certificate confirming who attended at a board meeting or a certificate as to compliance with any non-public restrictions on the directors' authority) and include an assumption that those certificates are accurate.

[26] The lenders may obtain comfort on this by requiring notarization of the documents.

456   Schedules

This opinion therefore supplements the enforceability opinion. There is some doubt about its scope e.g. it probably only extends to laws prohibiting the relevant action, not imposing adverse consequences.[27] It will be necessary for the lawyer giving this opinion to ascertain what regulatory authorities (e.g. authorities regulating the banking and insurance businesses, or the offering of investments, etc.) the borrower's business, and the transactions contemplated by the loan agreement are subject to.[28]

Valid and enforceable obligations

13.103

The agreement constitutes the legal, valid, binding and enforceable obligations of the Borrower under [English] law.

This is the essence of the enforceability opinion (sometimes also referred to as the validity or remedies opinion). It is generally accepted[29] that it does not mean that the loan is enforceable in the sense that the borrower can be forced to do what it has promised or in the sense that if the lender obtained a judgement it would be able to enforce that judgement. Rather, the opinion is only that the local court will give a remedy.[30] The opinion confirms that the lenders are not unable to pursue a claim in court for any reason, such as **sovereign immunity**, failure to pay stamp duty, breach of exchange control requirements or lack of regulatory approvals by the borrower. The opinion will usually be required in the place of the law chosen to govern the agreement and, in the event that it is different, the law of the country chosen to have jurisdiction. The lenders often also require confirmation from lawyers in the place of incorporation and/or business that the agreement is valid against the borrower in those places.[31]

---

[27] See Wood: International Loans, Bonds, Guarantees, Legal Opinions, 3rd ed at 44-038 onwards.

[28] For example, might any aspect of the transaction, such as a swap, be regarded as insurance, or gambling, in the relevant jurisdiction, and therefore be subject to regulatory approval?

[29] See Wood: International Loans, Bonds, Guarantees, Legal Opinions, 3rd ed in 44–034.

[30] This is why an English lawyer would not state that the agreement 'is enforceable in accordance with its terms' because an English court will not necessarily actually require the borrower to do what they have promised, by ordering specific performance. The court may order specific performance, but that is at the discretion of the court. A simple statement that the agreement is 'enforceable' rather than 'enforceable in accordance with its terms' is generally accepted to mean that it is actionable in court.

[31] This opinion from any place other than that of the law chosen to govern the agreement requires careful consideration of the conflict of law issues—see paragraphs 59–60 of the commentary on legal opinions at the City of London Law Society website quoted in 13.089. See also *Legal Opinions in International Transactions*, 44-033–44-035.

13.104

It is expected that the lawyer providing the opinion will consider all circumstances in which the agreement or any clause of the agreement may not be enforceable as expected. So if, for example, there is a risk of recharacterization[32] or there may be a problem enforcing the grossing-up clause, this should be stated (usually in the qualifications).

Further advice as to costs, procedures, priorities and the likely time involved in any enforcement may also be needed. These issues are normally addressed in advice but not included in the legal opinion itself.

Most of the qualifications discussed in 13.113 are qualifications to this opinion.

Effectiveness of security[33]

13.105

The form of the opinion statement in relation to security interest varies. Philip Wood states, in 'International Loans, Bonds, Guarantees and Legal Opinions' 3rd ed. that the opinion should say no more than

> *"The security agreement creates a security interest over the assets stated to be covered by the security interest to the extent that the company has title to those assets and to the extent that those assets are alienable by a security interest. The security interest has been duly perfected by filing/registration at the relevant debtor indexed filing/registration office in [country] for those assets over which a security interest may be perfected by filing/registration. No opinion is expressed on....."*

13.106

There follows a long list of topics excluded from the opinion e.g. security on future assets—see 44-085 Wood. In particular, Wood points out that key issues in relation to security are priority; title to the assets; enforceability and effect of insolvency all of which are too complex to be covered by a legal opinion and that therefore the security issues would be better dealt with by advice, rather than legal opinions.

---

[32] See Appendix 2.

[33] An opinion may be required as to the priority of the security as well as its effectiveness. Given the different regimes affecting priority of security, the formulation of the opinion and appropriate assumptions will be made on a case-by-case basis.

458   **Schedules**

To the extent that a legal opinion is issued in relation security, Wood suggests it should be limited to issues of due execution, proper form (eg deed), documentary taxes and registration requirements.

This opinion will be sought in the place of the **proper law**[34] of the security (not necessarily the same as the law chosen to govern the loan agreement) from the lawyers responsible for drafting and if applicable, registering the security.

13.107

Issues which commonly arise in relation to security (and on which lenders should seek advice, if not a legal opinion) include:

- Whether it is possible under the proper law to create security over the assets in question (e.g. property which does not yet exist, intangible property, movable property or property which has been mixed with, and cannot be separated from, other property such as oil in a pipeline).
- Whether it is possible under the proper law to create security for the type of liability in question (e.g. as security for a future debt, such as might be constituted if the loan is transferred by novation, or is repaid and redrawn, as in a revolving credit or a multicurrency loan, or for a debt which is uncertain or fluctuates in amount).
- Whether the security can be created in favour of that security holder (e.g. are there restrictions on the identity of the security holder or are there problems with a charge back?[35]).
- Whether the security over the asset in question has been correctly established in accordance with the requirements for creating security over that asset (e.g. are there notification requirements, registration requirements or formal requirements, for example, as to delivery or as to the form in which such security must be created?) (see Box 13.7).

Box 13.7

Where the security needs to be registered, that will be referred to here. There may be a timing issue if the security is to be registered after the opinion is to be given. In that case the Agent will usually rely on the lawyer (acting for the Agent, not the borrower) who is responsible for the registration to confirm

---

[34] Other laws may be relevant depending on the type of asset over which security is being taken as discussed below.

[35] Creating security in favour of A over a debt owed by A.

Schedule 17: Legal Opinions—Section 2: Form of Opinion   **459**

> that will be done and that lawyer will need to ensure they are in possession of everything which is necessary to ensure that the registration will be effected.

- Whether the security has been correctly constituted so as to create security for the debt in question (e.g. can the security be given to an Agent on behalf of the lenders or must it be given to the person to whom the debt is owed? If the secured debt is repaid and redrawn, as in a revolving credit or, often, a multicurrency agreement, or if it is novated, as in a loan transferred by novation, will the security be discharged by the intermediate repayment or by the novation?).
- Whether there are any restrictions on the enforceability of the security, such as overcollateralization issues.
- in what circumstances[36] might the lenders need court approval to enforce their rights against the borrower or the assets which are the subject of the security?
- In what circumstances an insolvency of any person could have an impact. For example,
  - If the borrower becomes insolvent, in what circumstances might the security be set aside (e.g. transactions at an undervalue if the borrower is English)?
  - If security is taken over rights under a contract, will that security be recognized in an insolvency of the parties to the contract?

No consents or filings needed

13.108

No authorization or approval (including exchange control approval) or other action by, and no notice to or filing with, any government, administrative authority or court is required for the due execution, delivery and performance by the Borrower of its obligations under the Credit Agreement except for [] [which has been effected].

This opinion is usually required in all places from which an opinion is sought. This opinion is required because some absences of approval may result in fines or other sanctions but do not make the documents invalid. This

---

[36] See 'Administration' in Appendix 2.

460 Schedules

opinion therefore supplements the enforceability opinion. It will be necessary for the lawyer giving this opinion to determine whether any aspects of the transaction may require approvals or filings and also to ascertain what regulatory authorities the borrower's business is subject to that may result in a need for approvals. The lawyer will also be expected to consider the effect on any necessary consents, etc., of any intermediate payment of the loan, as in a revolving credit or multicurrency loan, or any transfer of the loan by novation. Will the relevant consent apply to all future advances and all novated loans or will it fall away as a result of the intermediate payment or novation? It is also worth noticing that sometimes consents such as exchange control consents are limited to payments of principal and interest but do not cover e.g. payment of indemnities or payment of the loan on acceleration, in which case this opinion would need to be qualified accordingly.

Note also that the opinion only relates to consents required by the borrower, not those required by the lender.

No unexpected tax consequences

13.109
There is no tax imposed by [the Borrower's country] or any taxing authority thereof either (i) on or by virtue of the execution of the documents or (ii) on any payments to be made by the Borrower pursuant to the documents and neither the Agent nor any of the Lenders is or will be resident or subject to taxation in [the Borrower's country] by reason only of the execution, delivery performance or enforcement of the documents.

There may be tax consequences (in addition to the normal corporation tax issues of the lender and the borrower) in the place of execution (e.g. stamp tax), any place from which payment is to be made (e.g. withholding tax), or from which payment *may* be made, for example, under a guarantee (e.g. deemed tax residence of lender), as well as in any other country with which the loan, or the borrower, is connected. This opinion is therefore usually required in all places from which an opinion is sought.

Schedule 17: Legal Opinions—Section 2: Form of Opinion **461**

Choice of law and jurisdiction

13.110

The choice of [English] law to govern the documents and the submission to the jurisdiction of the [English] courts are valid under the law of [the country chosen to have jurisdiction] [the Borrower's country].

This opinion is usually sought in the place of the courts chosen to have jurisdiction (probably the same as the law chosen to govern the agreement) as well as in the country of incorporation. The lenders will wish to be satisfied that (all else being equal[37]) the country chosen to have jurisdiction will accept jurisdiction and will apply the chosen law.

The lenders may also want lawyers in the country of incorporation to confirm that the choice of law and jurisdiction is valid from their perspective. For example, they want to be sure that there is no prohibition on citizens of that country submitting to the jurisdiction of other courts.

Enforcement of judgements

13.111

Final and conclusive judgements issued by the courts of [England] are recognized and enforceable in [the Borrower's country of incorporation/ business] without re-examination of the merits of the case.

This opinion is usually required in the place of incorporation.[38] This opinion will, of course, need to be qualified by whatever matters as are relevant to the enforceability in the relevant country of foreign judgements. For example, these might include qualifications that the original proceedings did not contravene natural justice and that enforcement will not contravene public policy.

---

[37] The opinion does not require confirmation that the courts will actually accept jurisdiction and apply the chosen law, since that depends on the facts at the time—for example, whether proceedings have started elsewhere. The opinion, instead, requires confirmation that the submission, and choice of law are 'valid'.

[38] Other places which may be relevant include any place of business or location of the borrower's assets.

462   Schedules

Pari passu

13.112
The obligations of the Borrower under the Credit Agreement rank at least pari passu with all other obligations of the Borrower which are not secured and which are not mandatorily preferred by law applying to companies generally.

This opinion will usually be sought in the place of incorporation and/ or potential insolvency. The lawyer giving the opinion will need to consider whether there are, or may be, any obligations of the borrower which may be preferred over other obligations, or whether this particular debt may be subordinated to other debts, other than as a result of security, or as a result of law affecting companies generally. Examples are the subordination that affects loans to English borrowers[39] where the lenders' return varies with the profitability of the borrower,[40] and the priority that may be obtained in certain jurisdictions[41] by executing a loan agreement as an escrita publica.

4. Qualifications

13.113
Finally come the *qualifications*. These list the legal issues that may result in difficulties for the lenders. Given that the purpose of the opinion is to ensure the lenders are aware of the risks inherent in the transaction before they advance funds, it is important for lenders (with assistance from the co-coordinating lawyers) to ensure that they understand the implications of the qualifications for the transaction in hand.

Insolvency qualification

13.114
The enforceability of the rights and remedies provided for in the documents may be limited by insolvency, bankruptcy, reorganization, moratorium or other similar laws affecting generally the enforceability of creditors' rights from time to time in effect.

---

[39] And borrowers in other jurisdictions whose law is based on English law.
[40] See s3 Partnership Act 1890 discussed in 1.042.
[41] Whose law is based on Spanish law, for example, the Philippines.

Schedule 17: Legal Opinions—Section 2: Form of Opinion 463

This qualification is necessary in relation to the opinion as to validity and enforceability discussed from 13.103 onwards. However, acceptance of the qualification without further investigation may result in the lenders failing to be made aware of issues which are important in the assessment of the transaction. After all, it is in the event of insolvency that the documents are most likely to be tested and the lender is most likely to need to rely on the rights granted to them. It is therefore often necessary for the co-coordinating lawyer to investigate the details behind this opinion to determine how insolvency of an Obligor might affect the lenders. In particular they will be concerned to investigate

- whether any transactions are vulnerable to be set aside if the company is insolvent or wound up[42]
- whether there are compulsory rehabilitation procedures which might prevent the lender from enforcing its security or force it to accept restructurings or reschedulings approved by a majority of creditors and
- the ranking of debts on insolvency

Equitable principles qualification

13.115
The enforceability of the rights and remedies provided for in the documents is subject to general principles of equity including application by a court of competent jurisdiction of principles of good faith, fair dealing, commercial reasonableness, materiality, unconscionability and conflict with public policy and other similar principles.

13.116
This qualification is often included in relation to the opinion as to enforceability discussed in 13.103 (see Box 13.8).

---

[42] For example, transactions at an undervalue or preferences under English law. Set off under some laws.

464   **Schedules**

> **Box 13.8**
>
> Some countries have general principles requiring lenders to act reasonably in exercising their rights. This may (e.g.) prevent them from relying on an Event of Default if the event is minor in nature but the lenders' remedy (acceleration) is disastrous for the borrower. In England, outside of consumer areas, there is no general principle of fair dealing but there are a number of principles which apply in specific instances, such as estoppel, the contra proferentem rule, relief against forfeiture, **restitution** for unjust enrichment, the law on exclusion clauses and equitable principles which apply to equitable remedies. There is also a rule of interpretation that the more unreasonable an item in an agreement seems to be, the more unlikely it is that that is the true intention of the parties.[43] There is also an implied duty of rationality (often referred to as the 'Braganza duty' after the leading case). This is an implied obligation, in the absence of clear language to the contrary, to exercise a contractual discretion in good faith and not capriciously or arbitrarily. See Braganza *v BP Shipping Ltd & anr [2015] UKSC 17.*. Because of these various principles and rules, this qualification is included in an English legal opinion.

Other qualifications

13.117

The opinion will then list the other qualifications which the lawyer giving the opinion considers necessary, such as

- qualifications in relation to any individual clause which may be unenforceable for any reason not already covered by the other qualifications. So, for example, an English opinion will probably include qualifications as to the enforceability of the default interest clause,[44] the severability clause,[45] any clauses requiring the borrower to pay the lenders' costs of enforcement,[46] any clause stating that certificates are conclusive,[47] and the effectiveness of exclusion clauses.[48] and

---

[43] See L Schuler AG v Wickman Machine Tool Sales Ltd [1974] AC 235.

[44] Is it a penalty? See Goode Commercial Law 6th ed in 3.141 for a discussion on the law on penalties.

[45] For example, Clause 31.5 (*PAYMENT MECHANICS: Partial payments*) of the LMA Compounded/Term Rate Loan—on the basis that such a clause may not affect the basis (outlined in Goldsoll v Goldman (1915) 1 Ch 292) on which a court will disregard (or 'sever') provisions of a contract.

[46] Since, in any legal proceedings, the court will make its own award on payment of costs.

[47] Such a clause will not necessarily make such certificates admissible in evidence.

[48] For example, liability for fraud cannot be excluded, and exclusion clauses will be read contra proferentem—see further Goode *Commercial Law* from 3.77 onwards.

Schedule 17: Legal Opinions—Section 2: Form of Opinion 465

- qualifications and/or assumptions as to defences which may be available to the borrower, such as commercial benefit or lapse of time.

13.118

The lenders and the co-coordinating lawyer need to examine each qualification (and assumption) and decide:

- if the risk it discloses is acceptable (e.g. in relation to the issue on the risk that default interest may be unenforceable as a penalty, are the lenders happy to proceed nevertheless);
- if the risk is likely to be a real risk in the circumstances of the case (e.g. if the lawyer has included an assumption or qualification as to mistake, is there a possibility of mistake being an issue in this transaction) and
- if anything can be done to reduce the risk (e.g. if the opinion shows that judgements may not be enforced, would submission to arbitration be a better arrangement).

Appendix 1: Some English Law Concepts

This Appendix seeks to give those readers who do not have an English legal background a very basic road map to some of the areas of English law which are important for the purpose of international lending and which are not covered in other parts of this book. It is intended to be a brief introduction to the topics covered and where to look for further information on those subjects. It is not intended to be a comprehensive list of the relevant topics nor a comprehensive treatment of any of those subjects.

Section 1: Some Basic Concepts

1. English law

A1.001

English law is more strictly known as the law of England and Wales. England is part of the UK, which comprises three different legal jurisdictions.

Scotland has its own laws. Northern Ireland has similar but not the same law as England and Wales.

English law comprises statutes and common law[1]

---

[1] See A1.002.

© The Editor(s) (if applicable) and The Author(s), under exclusive license to Springer Nature Switzerland AG 2024
S. Wright, *The International Loan Documentation Handbook*, Global Financial Markets,
https://doi.org/10.1007/978-3-031-38489-9

468   Appendix 1: Some English Law Concepts

2. Sources of law[2]

A1.002

Common versus civil law

To a certain extent, the distinction between common and **civil law** is historical (see Box A1.1).

Box A1.1

Civil law systems developed from Roman law, which was the earliest significant example of a legal system. It influenced most of the legal systems of the world. In the fifth century BC, the Twelve Tables of Rome were engraved on bronze tablets. They were largely a declaration of existing customs concerning such matters as property, payment of debts and appropriate compensation or other remedies for damage to persons. These Tables and their Roman successors, including the Justinian Code, led to civil law codes that provide the main source of law in much of modern Europe, South America and elsewhere.

The common law system of England developed in a different manner. Before the Norman Conquest (1066), England was a loose confederation of societies, the laws of which were largely tribal and local. The Anglo-Norman rulers created a system of centralized courts that operated under a single set of laws that superseded the rules laid down by earlier societies. This legal system, known as the common law of England, began with common customs, but over time it involved the courts in lawmaking that was responsive to changes in society.

A1.003

The most significant distinction between civil law systems and common law systems is that civil law systems are based on a codified set of rules, while common law systems develop through cases which come to court, and with decisions in those cases binding in (or creating 'precedents' for) future cases unless they can be distinguished from the earlier cases.[3] Judges in a common law system help to create the law.

To an increasing extent this distinction is becoming blurred as, in common law jurisdictions, the case law is supplemented by an ever-increasing volume of formal rules and regulations (statutes or legislation) created by modern

---

[2] See Goode, *Commercial Law*, 6th edn, 1.01–1.63.

[3] That is, if a difference can be identified which justifies a different decision being reached.

Section 1: Some Basic Concepts   **469**

governments. Similarly, in civil law countries, the subtleties of judicial interpretation and the weight of judicial precedents are recognized as involving
the courts in significant aspects of lawmaking.

Case law versus statute

A1.004

Case law is another expression for common law—that is, the law which
emerges from cases which come before the courts. Statute (or legislation)
is the expression used for the formal rules and regulations issued by the
government of the relevant jurisdiction.

Common law versus equity[4]

A1.005

The distinction here is based on the origin of the law (or the right or remedy)
in question. Equity was the system of rules which were applied in one system
of courts (the Courts of Chancery), while the common law was applied in
other courts (Box A1.2).

Box A1.2

Until 1854 there were two sets of courts in England which gave two different
types of remedy and recognized different rights and obligations. One court
applied the common law and the other (the Chancery Court) applied 'equity'.
The historical reason for this was that, before the establishment of the courts
of equity in the fourteenth century, the remedies available in courts were
limited to damages and delivery of property and there was no relief available
for breach of faith. Claims for other relief were to the King, who delegated
these issues to the Lord Chancellor who decided these issues in the Courts of
Chancery. So the Courts of Chancery arose in order to mitigate the harshness of
the common law courts. The Courts of Chancery applied 'equitable' principles
and remedies.

---

[4] See Hanbury and Martin, *Modern Equity*, 22nd edn, 2021, Chapter 1.

470   Appendix 1: Some English Law Concepts

A1.006
Now all English courts apply all law, whether it derives from common law, equity or statute. However, the concept of equity is still important, for example, because certain principles (some of which are discussed in the following paragraphs by way of example) apply to equitable remedies and equitable interests which do not apply in other circumstances.

A1.007
Equitable remedies which are available include (among an array of other equitable remedies)[5]:

- Specific performance (requiring a party to perform their obligations, as opposed to requiring them to pay damages instead). Specific performance will not be granted where damages is an adequate remedy (e.g. in the case of a breach of a contract for sale of generic goods) or for breach of a contract for personal services.
- Injunctions (usually requiring a party not to do something).
- Restitution (requiring a party to refund assets if he has been unjustly enriched at another's expense).

A1.008
Equitable concepts developed by the courts include (again, by way of example, and among an array of other equitable concepts):

- the distinction between legal and beneficial ownership,[6] giving rise to the development of trusts[7]; and
- mistake and misrepresentation.

A1.009
Some equitable principles are that

- Equity treats as done that which should have been done. So, for example, an agreement to create a mortgage of an asset will, subject to certain conditions, be given effect to in equity as if the mortgage has been effected and so will create an immediate equitable interest[8] in the asset for the transferee.[9]

---

[5] See Hanbury and Martin, *Modern Equity*, 22nd edn, 2021, Part V.

[6] See A1.019.

[7] See Appendix 2.

[8] See A1.019.

[9] See Goode, *Commercial Law*, 2.33.

Section 1: Some Basic Concepts   **471**

- Parties must come to equity with clean hands. So an equitable remedy will not be available to a party which has not acted in good faith.
- An equitable interest can be defeated by a **bona fide** purchaser for value without notice.[10]

3. Types of claims and rights

A1.010

Action in rem versus action in personam[11]

This is the distinction between the method of enforcement of a 'real' right (or right in property, otherwise known as a 'proprietary interest') and the method of enforcement of 'personal' rights (which is simply a right to sue a legal entity). 'Real' rights are rights in property, for example, ownership is a real right. Security is also a real right—someone with security has a right, in certain circumstances, to take the property over which he has security and use proceeds of that property to pay the secured debt. That is a right in property as opposed to the personal right to require the borrower to pay the debt.[12]

A1.011

Chose in action

This is the name given to an asset which is not a physical asset but which is simply a right which must be enforced by taking legal action. For example, money in a bank account is not a physical asset. It is a claim against the bank with whom the account is held. If the bank does not pay the moneys over on request, the only right which the person who deposited the money has is to take legal action against the bank. Hence the name chose (French for thing) 'in action', that is, enforceable only by taking legal action.[13]

---

[10] See A1.022.

[11] See further, Goode, *Commercial Law*, 2.06 – 2.09.

[12] Or, more accurately, it is a right enforceable against all the world (a right in rem) as opposed to a right which is enforceable only against specific person(s)—(a right in personam).

[13] See further, Goode, *Commercial Law* 2.16.

472   Appendix 1: Some English Law Concepts

A1.012

Contract versus tort

Contracts are agreements or promises which are enforced by the courts. Tort is the word given to the law relating to the circumstances in which a person will be liable for the consequences of their actions in circumstances where there is no contract. (It is similar to the continental concept of 'delict').

Damages for breach of contract are broadly based on the loss which arises as a result of the breaking of the arrangement, and so will generally cover lost profit.

Tort is based on liability for the foreseeable consequences of your actions for others (e.g. negligence). Damages in tort are therefore based on the extent to which the harm caused by the tort was foreseeable.

A1.013

Damages versus debt[14]

A claim for a debt is a claim to be paid a sum of money which is outstanding (e.g. the purchase price of goods delivered, or a claim under a guarantee). A claim in damages is a claim for monetary compensation for some action or inaction by another party, which has resulted in loss. So, for example, if one party does not perform its obligations under a contract, the other will have a claim in damages. See Box A1.3.

Box A1.3

This distinction is particularly important in those structures (such as are common in structured, project and asset finance and also in secured corporate-based lending) where loans are made to a company, relying in part on the security of contracts (such as an offtake agreement in project finance, or a **residual value guarantee** in asset finance) which that company has with a third party. The lender is taking security over a particular payment, or series of payments, which will be used to service the debt in certain circumstances. In the event that there is a default by the third party under the contract, however, the claim on which the lender is relying is usually a claim for damages for breach of the contract.

---

[14] See Goode, *Commercial Law*, in 3.116.

Section 1: Some Basic Concepts 473

A1.014

The main disadvantages of a claim in damages, as opposed to a claim for a debt which is due, are

- the claimant will have to prove that the loss he suffered was caused by the other's action or inaction;
- the amount which will be recovered will be calculated on the basis of the loss which would have been suffered had the claimant taken reasonable steps to mitigate its loss[15] and
- the amount which will be recovered under a claim in damages is uncertain.[16]

A1.015

A provision in a contract for payment of **liquidated damages** avoids these difficulties, although the issue may arise as to whether such a provision is a penalty.[17]

A1.016

Joint versus several

A joint obligation is one which a number of parties owe jointly, as in the situation where two parties borrow a sum of $10 million and undertake to repay it jointly. The lender must join both borrowers in any claim on the debt. The borrowers must, together, pay the full debt and if either one is unable to pay, the other is liable to pay the full amount.

A1.017

A **several obligation** is an independent obligation of one party which is not affected by the obligations of other parties. So if two parties each had a several liability to pay $10 million, the total due would be $20 million. Each debt is entirely independent of the other. The lender may pursue each party on its

---

[15] Often (misleadingly) referred to as the 'duty to mitigate', as this is a rule of the measure of damages—there is no 'duty' involved.

[16] Of course, there is also the commercial disadvantage that, if the contract is onerous on the counterparty, they may seek to renegotiate for lower payments, and, in practice, acceptance of that lower rate may be better for the borrower than the alternative, of insisting on maintaining the original terms and, in the event that the counterparty is unable to pay, claiming in damages against the counterparty, potentially making it insolvent, and receiving only a small proportion of the damages awarded.

[17] See Appendix 2.

474   Appendix 1: Some English Law Concepts

debt without involving the other party, and non-payment by one party of its debt does not give the lender a claim on the other party.

A1.018

A joint and several obligation is a combination of the above. So if two parties borrow $10 million and undertake, jointly and severally, to repay it, the lender may sue both parties together on their joint undertaking or it may sue either individual borrower on its several undertaking (which, under English law at least, is to repay the whole loan of $10 million).

Obligations of borrowers and guarantors are usually made joint and several so as to allow lenders the option of choosing which parties to pursue and not involving parties where there may be procedural or cross border difficulties or where it would be uneconomic to do so. Obligations of lenders are usually several since lenders are not prepared to take responsibility for the actions of other lenders.

Legal versus beneficial interest[18]

A1.019

The legal owner of an asset is the person who has title to it. The beneficial owner may be different—it is the person who is *entitled in fairness* to the benefit of having that asset. He is also described as having an 'equitable interest' in the asset (see Box A1.4).

Where legal ownership is with someone who is not also the beneficial owner, the legal owner holds as trustee[19] for the beneficial owner (or **beneficiary**). A trust may be created by a document, or it may arise simply as a result of the circumstances, as in the example referred to in Box A1.4.

Box A1.4

For example, if two people (A and B) pay for something, but one only (A) gets title, that one may be both the legal and the beneficial owner if it is clear that the other (B) intended to make a gift. If B did not intend to make a gift, then A will be the legal owner and both A and B will be beneficial owners (those entitled to the benefits of ownership) with beneficial interests (also known as 'equitable interests') proportionate to their contribution to the price.

---

[18] See further Goode, *Commercial Law*, 2.20–2.40.
[19] See A1.039.

A1.020

Ownership versus possession[20]

Ownership involves having title. This gives the person having it the right to deal freely with the thing, for example, to sell it.

Possession is a much more limited concept. The person with possession may or may not have the consent of the owner. They do not have the right to dispose of the thing, and their continued right to possession depends on the terms agreed with the owner (e.g. a lease or licence) or on the law (e.g. a lien created by operation of law).

A1.021

The difference can be illustrated by the situation in which a company sells its warehouse to a purchaser (the purchaser has ownership), and where it temporarily lets the warehouse to another company (the lessee has possession).

4. Miscellaneous Legal Concepts

A1.022

Bona fide purchaser for value without notice

Otherwise sometimes called 'equity's darling', because an equitable interest can be defeated by such a purchaser (see Box A1.5).

Box A1.5

This concept is relevant where two entities have conflicting interests, for example where one party has security over an asset but another person has bought the asset without knowing of the security. The buyer will take free of the security if the security was an equitable interest only (such as a **charge**,[21] but not a legal mortgage) and the buyer is a **bona fide purchaser for value without notice**.

---

[20] See Goode, *Commercial Law*, 2.20–2.47.
[21] See A1.045.

476   Appendix 1: Some English Law Concepts

A1.023

The expression means a party

* acting in good faith ('bona fide');
* which acquired a legal interest, either a security interest, such as a mortgage, or an ownership interest (a 'purchaser');
* which gave value for that interest ('for value') and
* which had no notice of the prior equitable interest.

A1.024

Consideration[22]

Some benefits given in exchange for a promise (but see Box A1.6. Gratuitous promises (e.g. gifts) may be enforceable if the agreement to make them is made by a **deed**.[23] Otherwise, English contract law requires some form of exchange, or benefit, or 'something of value in the eye of the law'[24] in order for a promise to be enforceable. There are numerous rules relating to consideration (such as the rule that past consideration is no consideration) that are outside the scope of this book.[25]

Box A1.6

One aspect of consideration which many non-English lawyers find strange is that the courts will not enquire into the value of the consideration, and that, for example, a contract under which a company disposes of an asset for a price which is only a very small percentage of the value of the asset, will nevertheless not be open to challenge on the basis of absence of consideration.

Nevertheless, shareholders and creditors of companies which enter into uncommercial bargains are not without redress. In relation to shareholders, the directors have a duty to promote the success of the company—see Box A1.23. Creditors are protected by the provisions relating to transactions at an undervalue—see A1.081.

---

[22] See Treitel, *The Law of Contract*, Chapter 3.

[23] See A1.025.

[24] Thomas v Thomas (1842) 2 QB 851 in p. 859.

[25] And for which see Treitel, *The Law of Contract*, Chapter 3.

Section 1: Some Basic Concepts **477**

A1.025

Deed

An agreement will only be enforced by a court if either

* there is consideration for it; or
* the agreement is executed as a deed.

So, executing a document as a deed will have the effect of making the agreement enforceable by a court even though there is no consideration for it, and the agreement is gratuitous (e.g. an agreement to give a gift).

A1.026

Originally deeds were formal documents which the person signing had to seal with their personal wax seal. This formality helped to ensure that those agreeing to make gifts were prompted to consider their action before proceeding. With the disappearance of personal wax seals (and their substitution by red stickers) much of the extra formality involved in executing a deed fell away. In 1989, legislation was introduced in England[26] which abolished the need for a seal at all[27] and stated that a document would be a deed if it made clear on its face that it was intended to be a deed[28]; and if it was executed as a deed (and, in relation to execution as a deed, set out requirements for witnessing without the need for sealing); and if it had been delivered.[29]

Deeds are required for certain types of transactions, such as powers of attorney.[30]

---

[26] s1(2) Law of Property (Miscellaneous Provisions) Act 1989.

[27] At least, in relation to execution of deeds by individuals and by companies incorporated under the Companies Acts.

[28] Of course, countries with laws based on those of England and Wales may still require deeds to be sealed and sealing is still required in England for bodies in relation to which the common law requirements have not been modified by statute.

[29] See Treitel, *Law of Contract* in 3–174 for further discussion of the requirement for delivery.

[30] s1 Powers of Attorney Act 1971.

478 Appendix 1: Some English Law Concepts

A1.027

Exclusion (or Exemption) clauses[31]

Exclusion clauses are included in a wide variety of transactions. This explanation focuses on exclusion clauses in the types of documents which are common in international finance—therefore, it does not look at exclusion clauses contained in transactions with consumers.

An exclusion clause is a clause which seeks to reduce the circumstances in which one party will have liability to another, or to reduce the amount of that liability (see Box A1.7).

> **Box A1.7**
>
> Clauses will be subject to the same restrictions as exclusion clauses if they have the effect of restricting liability even if that is done indirectly (e.g. by an 'entire agreement' clause,[32] which seeks to exclude the possibility of reliance on representations made outside the written agreement).

A1.028

Exclusion clauses may be challenged under the common law on a variety of grounds.[33] In particular, they are read contra proferentem.[34] They are also subject to a statutory test of reasonableness if they attempt to exclude liability for statutory misrepresentation[35] or negligence, or if they are included in a transaction which is conducted on one party's standard terms.[36] Exclusion clauses in standard form documents and any attempt to exclude liability for statutory **misrepresentation** or negligence will only be effective in circumstances where the court considers it reasonable for this to be effective on the facts in question (but see Box A1.8).

---

[31] See Goode, *Commercial Law*, in 3.77.

[32] A clause which states that the written document constitutes the entire agreement between the parties—the intention of which is to prevent parties from asserting that representations made prior to the agreement being signed had any contractual force and therefore, indirectly, of limiting liability in relation to any such representations.

[33] See Goode, *Commercial Law*, from 3.77 onwards.

[34] See Appendix 2.

[35] s3 Misrepresentation Act 1967.

[36] s2(2) Unfair Contract Terms Act 1977. The reasonableness test will also apply to clauses excluding liability for breach of contract (i.e. not only to clauses excluding liability for negligence) in certain cases involving consumers and standard form documents—s3 Unfair Contract Terms Act 1977.

Section 1: Some Basic Concepts **479**

> **Box A1.8**
>
> This reasonableness requirement is subject to a rather unusual qualification.[37] That is, in most cases,[38] the reasonableness test will only apply to exclusion clauses in contracts which are governed by English law and would have been governed by English law had there been no express choice of law. Many international loan agreements are only governed by English law by choice and therefore the exclusion clause will not be subject to the reasonableness test.[39]

A1.029

Misrepresentation[40]

There are numerous types of misrepresentation under English law, each of which has different consequences. This explanation relates only to liability for negligent misrepresentation, which is (hopefully) the most likely category in the context of international finance.

A1.030

Liability for negligent misrepresentation may arise either at common law[41] or under the Misrepresentation Act 1967 (statutory misrepresentation). In each case, liability arises if a person is induced to enter into a contract by a statement which was misleading. Broadly speaking liability will only arise if

- a person gives information negligently;
- the other person relied on it;
- the person giving the information entered into a contract with the other (in the case of establishing liability under the statute) or owed a duty of care to the other (in the case of establishing liability under the common law) and
- the other suffered loss as a result and that loss was foreseeable at the time the misrepresentation was made.

---

[37] Contained in s27 Unfair Contract Terms Act 1977.

[38] Excluding, that is, exclusion clauses relating to statutory misrepresentation and certain other issues such as personal injury which are not relevant for our purposes.

[39] Except to the extent it attempts to exclude liability for statutory misrepresentation.

[40] See Treitel, *The Law of Contract*, Chapter 9.

[41] See Hedley Byrne & Co Ltd v Heller & B Partners Ltd (1964) AC 465.

480   Appendix 1: Some English Law Concepts

An exclusion clause in relation to liability for misrepresentation[42] will be effective only if the courts hold that it is fair and reasonable for it to be effective (which will depend, among other things, on how much opportunity there was for the recipient to verify the information).

Statements of opinions and forecasts are capable of being representations, particularly if those relying on the statements reasonably perceive that the person making the statement (e.g. an Arranger in an information memorandum) is in a position, for example, because of its special expertise, such that its opinions carry weight.[43]

A1.031

Under English law (apart from any specific legislation which may apply in particular circumstances, such as prospectus legislation) there is no duty to disclose information but information disclosed must not be misleading. There is a duty to disclose if subsequent facts make a statement untrue before it has been acted on.[44]

A1.032

Pari passu

Pari passu means having an equal level of priority. If two pari passu debts owed to A and B respectively are due on the same day and there are not enough funds to pay both—neither of them has priority over the other.[45]

Debts are pari passu even if due on different dates. Therefore it is quite feasible for A to recover in full while B faces a shortfall simply because A's debt falls due first. Moreover, the general view is that voluntarily paying one debt while leaving another unpaid is perfectly permissible even for pari passu debts,[46] unless such payment constitutes a preference (see 'preferences' in Appendix 2).

---

[42] Including clauses which will have a similar effect, such as an 'entire agreement' clause—see Box A1.7.

[43] See further Treitel, *The Law of Contract*, in 9-015.

[44] See further Treitel, *The Law of Contract*, in 9-159.

[45] See Appendix 2.

[46] See commentary on Clause 21.12 (*REPRESENTATIONS: Pari passu ranking*) of the LMA Compounded/Term Rate Loan in 8.052.

Section 1: Some Basic Concepts **481**

A1.033

Subordination[47]

Giving one debt a lower ranking in terms of its priority of payment than another debt. The expression encompasses a wide variety of arrangements.

A1.034

Subordinate Security

This does not necessarily involve subordinated debt (see Box A1.9).

Box A1.9

For example, assume Company A borrows $10 million from B and gives B a mortgage on land as security. It then borrows $10 million from C and gives a second (subordinate) mortgage to C. Assume A is wound up and the land sold at a price of $5 million. A has other assets worth $3 million and no other creditors. B will recover $5 million from the security. A's remaining assets ($3 million) will be shared pro rata between B and C, with B recovering $1 million and C recovering $2 million.[48]

If the loan to C had been subordinate to B's loan (as well as the security being subordinate) then B would have recovered all of the surplus $3 million and C would have recovered nothing.

A1.035

Different Levels of Subordination of the Debt

The 'subordinate' debt may be subordinate

* as to principal only—that is, interest may be paid on the subordinated debt but not principal;

---

[47] See Philip Wood, *Project Finance, Securitisations and Subordinated Debt*, 3rd edn, Chapters 10–14.

[48] The assets of $3 million are shared in the ratio of the outstanding claims which, after B has taken the security, are $5 million to B and $10 million to C, which is 1:2.

482   Appendix 1: Some English Law Concepts

- as to both principal and interest—that is, no payments, whether of principal or interest, may be made on the subordinated debt[49];
- in a winding up (or on the occurrence of some other condition such as an Event of Default) only—that is, unless the condition occurs, payments may be made on the subordinated debt or
- at all times—that is, the prohibition on payments under the subordinated debt commences immediately.

A1.036

Structural Subordination

It is not necessary to have a contractual subordination agreement in order for a debt to be subordinate. This can also be achieved through the corporate structure by lending to a shareholder without taking any rights against its subsidiary through which income is generated. By doing this, the lender is structurally subordinate to all creditors of the subsidiary, since it has no claim against the subsidiary and can only access the subsidiary's assets via any dividend which the subsidiary pays to its parent. That dividend can only be made after retention of sums to pay the subsidiary's creditors—(see Box A1.10).

Box A1.10

Assume a lender lends $10 million to a holding company (Company A), whose only assets are its shares in its subsidiary, Company B. The lender takes security, in the form of a mortgage on the shares in Company B. Company A has no business of its own, and is simply a holding company.

Assume both Companies A and B become insolvent and are wound up at a time when Company B has assets worth $20 million and debts of $20 million. Company A's only debt is the loan.

The assets of Company B will be used to pay its debts. There will be no surplus and the shares in Company B (and therefore the mortgage on those shares) will be worthless. The lender to Company A will therefore recover nothing as Company A has no assets. If, on the other hand, the lender had a guarantee from Company B, it would have been entitled to make a claim in the insolvency of Company B. Without such a claim, it is structurally subordinate to the creditors of Company B.

---

[49] This might be expected for a shareholder's loan, but not for a loan made by a commercial lender.

Section 1: Some Basic Concepts   483

A1.037

For this reason, many lenders will normally only lend to operating companies and not their shareholders. Alternatively they will require guarantees from the operating companies of loans to their shareholders (subject to any legal difficulties involved in giving upstream guarantees[50]) or will take assignments of intercompany loans made by the shareholder to its subsidiary.[51] This is also one reason why lenders may want to impose restrictions on borrowings by subsidiaries of their borrowers.

A1.038

Miscellaneous Categories of Subordination

There are miscellaneous other circumstances in which a loan may be subordinated to other debts including

* Automatic subordination of shareholder loans in insolvency in Germany
* Equitable subordination in the US—which applies if a US court considers that a creditor which is also a shareholder has engaged in inequitable conduct to the detriment of other creditors in an insolvency; and
* Subordination resulting from the provisions of the Partnership Act in the UK or from the form of execution of the document in some other countries as discussed in 8.057.

A1.039

Trustees versus agents

A trustee is the legal owner of property (the trust property) which it holds on behalf of others—who have beneficial ownership of that property as discussed in A1.019. The trust property, although belonging to the trustee, will not form part of its estate, so that in a liquidation of the trustee the trust property will not be available to the trustee's liquidator. Agency, on the other hand, also involves one person representing another, but, in the case of agency, the agent does not own property on behalf of another, they simply owe contractual duties to the persons they represent. Those persons have rights in personam, not the rights in rem which **beneficiaries** of a trust have.

---

[50] See A1.081-2.

[51] However, in some countries shareholder loans are automatically subordinated to creditors so that an assignment of such a loan would not have the desired effect.

484   Appendix 1: Some English Law Concepts

Section 2: Security[52]

1. Introduction

A1.040

Under English common law there are a number of ways to create security, each of which has a technical description (mortgage, charge, lien, **pledge**). These words are often not used in their technical sense. Moreover, statutes have added to the common law and created statutory mortgages and liens which have different characteristics to their **common law** equivalents. These factors make a focus on the common law meanings of the words used to describe different concepts of security of limited value. Nevertheless, we summarize those meanings in this section in the interests of clarity.

A1.041

'Security' means a proprietary right (i.e. an interest in property) to secure a liability. In other words, security requires the secured party to have an ownership interest in an asset which it can use to secure a liability. See Box A1.11.

Box A1.11

Security is the right to take an asset and use its proceeds to pay the secured debt. It follows that when reviewing the security document there are two key clauses—the clause creating the security on the asset and the clause which identifies when and how the proceeds of the security will be applied to the debt.[53]

A quick review of the clause which creates the security will establish

- the identity of the asset on which the security is given,
- the debt it secures and
- the identity of the holder of the security.

The second key clause to review is the application of funds clause (sometimes referred to as a '**waterfall**') which establishes what is to happen to the income and sale proceeds from the secured asset. It is particularly important in relation to the proceeds of the security prior to an Event of Default.

---

[52] See Ross Cranston et al, Principles of Banking Law, 3rd edn, 2017, chapter 18.

[53] Of course there will also be undertakings relating to the secured asset as discussed in 8.208, as well as contractual powers in favour of the mortgagee supplementing the powers which they have as a matter of general law.

Guarantees do not fall within the definition of security given in A1.041—they do not give an ownership interest.[54] Rights of set off also do not fall within the definition as they are procedural rights which do not amount to an ownership interest.

2. Types of security[55]

The types of security which can be created at common law[56] in England are:

A1.042

Mortgages

These[57] involve the borrower giving legal title (i.e. ownership) of the asset to the lender. The lender will own the asset subject to the borrower's '**equity of redemption**'—its right to redeem, or pay off, the debt and have title passed back to it. The most common example is a statutory assignment of a chose in action—see A1.053.

A1.043

Pledges

These involve the borrower physically handing an asset (or something, such as a key or a document of title, which gives control of an asset) over to the lender (or other party), in order to persuade the lender to advance funds. Pledges can only be used with physical assets or documents of title representing assets, such as bearer shares or bills of lading. The lender can retain the asset till the debt has been repaid or, in default of payment, the lender can sell the asset and apply the proceeds to the secured debt.

---

[54] They are referred to as personal security as opposed to real security.

[55] See Goode, *Commercial Law*, from 22.15 onwards.

[56] Excluding those which arise by operation of law, which are discussed at Goode, *Commercial Law*, from 22.64 onwards.

[57] Other than in relation to land, where the common law position has been supplemented by statute.

486   Appendix 1: Some English Law Concepts

A1.044

Liens

A common law lien[58] is a right to retain goods to secure payment of a contract debt. As with a pledge, a lien involves one party having possession of an asset owned by another but, in the case of the lien, possession was given for some other contractual purpose and not for the purpose of raising funds. A common example in international finance is the repairer's lien—an item of machinery may be delivered to a third party for repair. The repairer can keep the equipment, and has a security interest in it, until he is paid for his services. The distinction between this and the pledge is the fact that, in the case of the lien, the security is not deliberately created for the purpose of raising money. Another difference is that the lien holder (unlike a pledgee) has no implied right of sale.

A1.045

Charges

Charges do not depend on title, or on possession. A charge gives its holder the right to take the charged asset in certain circumstances and apply its proceeds against the debt. A charge may be a **floating charge** or a **fixed charge**.

A1.046

Floating Charge[59]

A floating charge is a security which gives the chargor the freedom to deal with the subject matter of the security until the charge '**crystallizes**'. A floating charge is generally expressed to crystallize on the occurrence of an Event of Default in accordance with the terms of the loan agreement (usually, whether or not the lender has delivered a notice accelerating the loan). The

---

[58] Note there are numerous other types of liens, such as maritime liens and statutory liens—see Goode, *Commercial Law*, in 22.65–22.69.

[59] The expression 'floating charge' is a bit of a misnomer—'floating security' would be a better name since the security interest in question does not need to be a charge, but could, for example, take the form of an assignment. Any security interest which gives the chargor the freedom to deal with the property may take effect as a floating charge.

charge is usually (but not necessarily[60]) created over a category of assets (such as the chargor's stock in trade) and automatically catches new assets which the chargor acquires from time to time which fall within the relevant category.

The existence of this form of security allows a company to use, as security, those assets which the company buys and sells as part of its ordinary business. Without the concept of a floating charge this would not be possible because the security would need to be discharged to allow sale.

A1.047

However, a floating charge has three significant disadvantages over a fixed charge.

- First, if a company gets into financial difficulties it is quite likely to find itself unable to replenish stock. So, when a charge enforces the security, there may be very few assets there.
- Second, unlike all other forms of security, the charge cannot keep all proceeds of the security but must (except in some circumstances where the security constitutes 'financial collateral'[61]) use part of the proceeds to pay certain other creditors.[62]
- Third, it may lose priority to a subsequent holder of a fixed charge over the assets of the chargor (see Box A1.12).

For these reasons, a floating charge should only be used for assets in respect of which no other form of security is realistically available.

---

[60] Goode, *Commercial Law* in 25.09.

[61] See Box A1.14.

[62] Under the Enterprise Act 2002 payments to tax authorities no longer have **preferential** status. However, under s252 of the Act a 'prescribed part' of a company's assets must be allocated to unsecured creditors, ahead of the holder of a floating charge. The amount of the prescribed part was fixed by SI 2003/2097 at a percentage of the net realized value of the floating charge assets, up to a maximum of £800,000.

488   Appendix 1: Some English Law Concepts

> **Box A1.12**
>
> A floating charge may lose priority to a later charge[63] because, by its nature, a floating charge does not prohibit dealings with the assets concerned, and so a subsequent fixed charge may be created and this charge will rank in priority to the previously created floating charge. The floating charge therefore usually includes a negative pledge. The registration of the floating charge with the Registrar of Companies will include a description of the charge and a statement as to whether or not the charge includes a negative pledge, so that anyone searching the register should become aware of the existence of the negative pledge. If a subsequent charge is aware of the existence of the negative pledge then their security would not have priority over the floating charge. However, there is uncertainty about the precise effect of security registration in terms of who is treated as having notice of the details which are available on the register.[64]

A1.048

Difficulties often arise in determining whether a given security document creates a fixed or a floating charge. The answer depends on the degree of control which the giver of the security has to deal with the asset—can they dispose of it in the ordinary course of business? Care therefore needs to be taken to ensure that any exceptions to a no disposals clause do not have the effect of changing what was intended to be a fixed security into a floating one by allowing disposals of charged assets in the ordinary course of business.[65]

A1.049

There are particular problems when security is taken over the borrower's income, either by taking an assignment of a stream of payments under a particular contract or by taking security over all of a borrower's present and future book debts without being more specific as to the source of those debts. This issue was considered by the House of Lords in 2005,[66] and it was held that the determining factor in deciding whether a security interest was fixed or floating was the degree of control which the borrower retained over the assets

---

[63] Unless the floating charge has crystallized at the time the fixed charge is created and the fixed charge holder has actual or **constructive notice** of the crystallization- see Goode, *Commercial Law* from 25.25 onwards.

[64] For more on this topic see Goode, *Commercial Law* from 24.46 onwards.

[65] See commentary on Clause 24.4 *(GENERAL UNDERTAKINGS: Disposals)* subclause (b) of the LMA Compounded/Term Rate Loan in 8.214.

[66] National Westminster Bank Plc v Spectrum Plus Limited (2005) 3 W.L.R. 58. In that case a borrower had given security over all its book debts, and agreed to pay those book debts to a specified bank account to which the borrower had free access. The court held that the security over the book debts was a floating charge.

Section 2: Security   **489**

which were the subject of the security. The case held that, in the context of security over debts, if the proceeds of the debts are required to be paid to a specified account, but the borrower is able to draw on that account in the ordinary way, the security over the debts is floating security. The case did not decide how much control the lender would need to have over the bank account in order to ensure that the security was fixed security.[67]

A1.050

Fixed Charge

A fixed charge (like a floating charge) is equitable. As such it may be defeated by a subsequent mortgage or by sale of the charged asset. This is because any equitable interest may be defeated by a bona fide purchaser for value without notice.[68] In practice, for many assets, this potential defect of a charge is not relevant since the existence of the charge is registered with the Companies Registry[69] and therefore subsequent purchasers and mortgagees will be put on notice of the existence of the charge when they search the register. If the subsequent purchaser or mortgagee did not search the register then they will be treated as having notice of the prior charge if they could reasonably be expected to have searched the register.[70] A charge may therefore be vulnerable if the assets over which the lender is taking security are assets of the type which purchasers may ordinarily be expected to buy without first doing a search of the Companies Registry (which would generally be the types of assets over which a floating charge would be taken).

A1.051

Assignment

In addition, security may be created over rights (such as rights under contracts) by way of assignment or by way of a charge.[71]

---

[67] See Goode, *Commercial Law* in 25.05 and 25.06.

[68] See A1.022.

[69] See A1.056.

[70] See Goode, *Commercial Law* in 24.45.

[71] A chose in action, like any other asset, may have security created over it either by passing title to the asset (as in a mortgage) until the secured debt is repaid, or by agreeing (as in a charge), that the asset may be taken and its proceeds used to pay the secured debt if there is a default in payment. If the route of passing title is to be used, the chose in action will be transferred by assignment, since

490   Appendix 1: Some English Law Concepts

A1.052

Assignment may be used either to sell a debt or to give security over it. The difference is that where the assignment is being given as security, the lender's interest in the debt will last only until the secured claim has been paid.

There are three main categories of assignment in England,[72] each of which may be used as a method of sale or as a method of creating security.

A1.053

A Statutory Assignment Under s136 Law of Property Act 1925

This form of assignment must be of the whole debt; notice must be given to the debtor and it must be absolute (see Box A1.13).

> **Box A1.13**
>
> The expression 'absolute' is used to mean a complete transfer, in which the assignor does not retain any interest in the property assigned. It is commonly compared with an assignment by way of charge. Nevertheless, this is not to suggest that just because an assignment is being used as a method of security, the result is that assignment cannot be absolute.[73]

This form of assignment results in the debtor having to make payment direct to the assignee. It has a minor procedural advantage over an equitable assignment of which notice has been given to the debtor (described in A1.054), in that, in order to take legal action against the debtor, the assignor does not need to be joined in the proceedings.

If any of the three requirements of a statutory assignment are missing then the assignment will still take effect in equity and its effect will depend on which of the three requirements are missing.

---

that is the only way to pass title to a chose in action. If assignment is not used, the security can be created by a charge, that is, an agreement which creates security but does not amount to a transfer of title.

[72] Ignoring assignments of proceeds of the debt and the different mechanisms by which equitable assignments can be created.

[73] See Treitel, *The Law of Contract*, in 15-011 on absolute assignments.

A1.054

An Equitable Assignment with Notice Given to the Debtor[74]

This form of assignment effectively[75] results in the debtor having to make payment direct to the assignee. It has a minor procedural disadvantage to a statutory assignment in that the assignor needs to be joined in to any proceedings against the debtor.

A1.055

An Equitable Assignment without Notice Given to the Debtor

This form of assignment results in the debtor having to make payment to the assignor, which will then be obliged to account for the moneys to the assignee.

There are three main disadvantages of this form of assignment—

- payment will be made to the assignor so that it will be necessary to make a claim against the assignor in order to be paid;
- priorities of competing assignments of the same debt depend on who gave notice to the debtor first.[76] Hence this assignment can be defeated by a subsequent assignment of the same debt which has been notified to the debtor;
- once notice is given the debtor cannot gain any new rights such as set off against the assignor. Not giving notice means that these types of rights may increase and so reduce the value of the assigned debt.

---

[75] In fact if the assignor objected then the debtor would need to pay the money into court and not to the assignee but any such objection would normally be a breach of the terms of the assignment.
[76] The rule in Dearle v Hall (1828) 3 Russ 1.

3. Registration requirements

A1.056

There are two potential registration requirements for security created by companies[77] under English law. One is registration against the asset and the second is registration against the company which created the security.

A1.057

Registration against the asset

In England there are asset registers for certain types of property including land, ships, aircraft and intellectual property. Security over any of these types of property needs to be registered in the asset register. Generally,[78] registration against the asset creates priority so that priority will be governed by the date of registration.

A1.058

Registration against the company

In addition to any applicable registration against the asset, charges (including mortgages) created by an English company (with certain limited exceptions) should be registered on the company's public records at the Companies Registry. That is the case wherever the asset which is the subject of the security happens to be.

Failure to register against the company in accordance with these requirements within 21 days of creation of the security has the effect of making the security void against an English liquidator, but, outside liquidation, as long as all security is registered within the required 21-day period, this registration has no effect on priorities.

Overseas companies do not need to register security at the Companies Register but they need to keep a register, available for inspection, of any security they give over land, ships, aircraft or intellectual property, and of any floating charge which covers assets in England.[79]

---

[77] Or by limited partnerships. Security created by individuals is beyond the scope of this book.

[78] Although there are special procedures for land.

[79] Overseas Companies *(Execution of Documents and* Registration of Charges*) (Amendments) Regulations 2011 (SI 2011/2194).*

4. What types of asset can security be created over?

A1.059
Under English law, security can be created over most types of assets. Some of these are discussed in the following paragraphs.

A1.060

Future property

This may be made the subject of floating security through a floating charge. It may also be made the subject of fixed security through an agreement now to create security when the property is owned. This is because of the equitable principle that 'equity treats as done that which ought to have been done'. So an agreement to create security is an effective (equitable) security.

A1.061

Intangible assets

Security can be created over intangible assets such as intellectual property by using an assignment as discussed from A1.051 onwards.

A1.062

Shares or other investments

Security can be created over shares or other investments in a company. How this is achieved and what effect it has depends on whether the security has been 'delivered' to the security holder (how much control does he have?) such that the security constitutes a 'financial collateral arrangement' (see Box A1.14) and on the nature of the investment, including, in particular, whether the investments are traded on a public market, and on whether the investments are held directly or through an intermediary.[80]

---

[80] See Ross Cranston et al., *Principles of Banking Law*, 3rd edn, 2018, from p551 onwards.

494 Appendix 1: Some English Law Concepts

> **Box A1.14**
>
> If the security constitutes a 'financial collateral arrangement' it will be governed by the Financial Collateral Arrangements (No 2) Regulations 2003. In that event it will benefit from a number of simplifications to the general law, including abolition of the need to register the security, continued ability to enforce the security despite the appointment of an administrator, and, broadly speaking, if the security is a floating charge which has been perfected by possession or control[81] abolition of the requirement to allocate a 'prescribed part' of the proceeds of realization of the security to other creditors. Additionally financial collateral can be enforced by simply 'appropriating' the security—that is, taking ownership. This method of enforcement is, under English law, unique to financial collateral arrangements although relief from forfeiture may still be available to the security provider—see Cukurova Finance International Ltd v Alfa Telecom Turkey Ltd 2013 UKPC 2.

A1.063

Moveable property

Security can be created over moveable property without the need for the lender to keep possession—this is achieved by way of creation of a fixed or floating charge over the property. But see Box A1.15.

A1.064

An entire business

This is achieved by a document (known as a debenture, or, more accurately, a mortgage debenture[82]) which contains a combination of mortgages, charges (fixed and floating) and assignments over all items of the company's property.

---

[81] See Principles of Corporate Insolvency Law 5th student edition 2019 by Roy Goode at 1.67.

[82] See 'debenture' in Appendix 2.

Section 2: Security   **495**

A1.065

A bank account

Security can be created over a bank account held by the borrower with the lender. There are four possible routes for a lender to take an interest in a bank account.[83] In practice, security documents usually provide for all the options to be available, so as to give greatest flexibility to lenders at the time of enforcement. The lender may:

- rely on general rights of set off;
- extend rights of set off by contract;
- use a conditional payment route (see Box A1.16)—note, this is particularly useful in countries which have limited rights of set off in insolvency;
- take a charge.

Box A1.15

The main problem with security over moveable property is the question of recognition of the security if the property moves into a different jurisdiction. Many jurisdictions have a conflict of law rule which recognizes interests in moveable property if those interests were validly created in accordance with the law of the jurisdiction where the property was at the time the interest was created. Other jurisdictions will not recognize interests in property if they cannot be 'translated' into an interest which is equivalent to some legal interest which could have been created under the local law. Even if the interest is recognized, it may be defeated for lack of registration.

For certain major assets, however, the issue of recognition (if not of registration) is addressed by international treaties[84] under which countries which are signatories to such conventions[85] agree to recognize 'foreign' security in those assets.

---

[83] See Goode, *Commercial Law* from 22.38 onwards.

[84] For example, Brussels Convention of 1926 relating to Maritime Liens and Mortgages, the Geneva Convention of 1948 on the International Recognition of Rights in Aircraft and the Cape Town Convention on International Interests in Mobile Equipment 2001.

[85] It should not be assumed that these conventions are worldwide in their operation, or anything like it. For example, the 1926 Brussels Convention was acceded to by only 19 countries.

496   **Appendix 1: Some English Law Concepts**

Box A1.16

In a conditional payment arrangement, (also referred to as a 'flawed asset') the documents provide that the obligations of the bank to pay the borrower the amount in the bank account is conditional on the borrower repaying the secured loan.

A1.066

There are a number of detailed differences between the effects of these arrangements, with some of the most significant being as follows:

- Security can be better than set off if the debt 'secured' is a contingent debt or is in a different currency than the bank account (each of which therefore requires valuation on an insolvency before a set off can be applied, and that valuation may not be accurate).
- Set off can be used without the consent of an administrator in the event of administration, while security cannot unless the security constitutes a 'financial collateral arrangement' as discussed in Box A1.14.
- If any security on the bank account is construed as a floating charge (see A1.046) then unless the security constitutes a 'financial collateral arrangement' the lenders will retain less funds through a security interest than they would through set off.
- Under English law, use of set off is not open to challenge, for example, as a transaction at an undervalue, while security may be.

For these reasons security on a bank account in England will usually include all the arrangements described here so as to give the lenders the option of choosing which rights to pursue at the time of enforcement.

A1.067

Comingled property

It is not however possible to give security over assets which have merged (or comingled) with assets belonging to a third party—such as gas in a pipeline. In this case the lender will need to take a pledge on a document of title or security over some other asset representing the merged property, such as the right to take delivery.

Section 2: Security   497

5. What can the security secure?

A1.068

Security can be given under English law for debts in any currency, for future loans,[86] for actual or contingent debts,[87] and without the need to specify a maximum secured amount.

A priority issue arises[88] if a lender has a security in an asset but another security interest is granted in the same asset to a different entity. The issue is that the first lender may find that even though their security purportedly secures future advances (e.g. as in an overdraft facility), nevertheless any advances made after the first lender becomes aware of the existence of the second security may rank behind the second security. For this purpose, registration of a subsequent mortgage does not give notice.[89] In the case of land, there is protection for the first lender if he was obliged to make the further advances, although in practice, this will rarely be the case—see Box A1.17.

Box A1.17

Invariably, security documents include a prohibition on the granting of additional security on the asset. So, if the borrower creates second security on the asset that will be an Event of Default. That Event of Default will release the lender from its obligation to advance funds. Any further advances may therefore lose priority to the second security.

An example may help—see Box A1.18.

Box A1.18

For example, assume

A lends $10 million to B taking security over assets which secure the $10 million plus any future advances.
C then lends $5 million to B taking second security over the same assets.
A then lends a further $2 million to C.

---

[86] Such as the new loans which are made on rollover under a revolving credit facility, or under a multicurrency loan which operates by re-payment and re-drawing.

[87] Such as the contingent liability in respect of the exposure which would arise if a swap were to terminate early.

[88] The issue is referred to as '**tacking**' of further advances.

[89] For more information on tacking see Goode, *Commercial Law* in 24.20.

498   Appendix 1: Some English Law Concepts

> If the advance of the additional $2 million was pursuant to an obligation binding on A then A's $2 million will have priority over C's $5 million.
> If A was not obliged to lend the additional $2 million, A will have priority if he was unaware of C's advance at the time he lent the additional $2 million. Otherwise, the additional $2 million will rank behind C's debt.

A1.069

Lenders should not advance further moneys against the security if they are aware of the existence of second priority security (unless, of course, they are obliged to do so or there are intercreditor agreements[90] documenting the position).

Section 3: Guarantees[91]

1. The nature of a guarantee

A1.070

The expression 'guarantee' may be used to describe a variety of instruments including suretyship guarantees, bank guarantees, demand guarantees and performance bonds. Moreover the names given to different instruments are not particularly helpful, particularly because they may be used differently in different jurisdictions. The clearest example of this is the expression 'demand guarantee' as discussed in A1.074.

This lack of clarity can easily lead parties to enter into documents which have quite a different effect from that which they intended, so it is important to focus on the various different characteristics of the different instruments rather than their names. The expression 'guarantee' when used here is used to mean a **suretyship** guarantee. The following paragraphs highlight the key differences between the different instruments.

---

[90] See Appendix 2.
[91] See Goode: *Commercial Law* Chapter 30.

Section 3: Guarantees 499

Guarantee versus indemnity

A1.071

A suretyship guarantee is an agreement to be answerable for the debt of another if that other does not pay.

An indemnity, on the other hand, is an agreement to make payment in certain circumstances (see Box A1.19).

Box A1.19

This can be illustrated by the difference between the following two situations

- A buys goods from B and C states 'If A does not pay you, I will'. That is a guarantee.
- A buys goods from B and C states 'I will make sure you are paid for those'. That is an indemnity.

In the first case, C is only liable to pay if A does not. In the second case, C must pay whether or not A is liable to pay.

A1.072

The indemnity is an independent debt; no underlying claim is necessary. In legal terms, it is a primary obligation, while a guarantee is a secondary obligation; it depends on the existence of an underlying debt.

A1.073

Primary versus secondary obligation

An indemnity is simply an example of a primary obligation. A primary obligation is any obligation which is not dependent on the existence of an underlying debt. Any undertaking to pay is usually a primary obligation (e.g. the undertaking to pay the price of goods ordered) (see Box A1.20).

Box A1.20

As discussed in the context of Clause 20.1 *(Guarantee and Indemnity)* subclause (b) in 7.002, English law guarantees commonly include indemnities as well as guarantees. Some English law guarantees do not do this but instead state

500 Appendix 1: Some English Law Concepts

> that the guarantor guarantees 'as primary obligor'. This shorthand approach is not recommended as it may have a number of different interpretations.[92] The clearest solution is to insert a primary undertaking to pay the debt on its due date as well as a guarantee.

Indemnity versus demand guarantee[93]

A1.074

A **demand guarantee** (sometimes also called a first demand guarantee, but see also the discussion in A1.077) is not a suretyship guarantee. Instead it is an instrument under which the guarantor must pay, regardless of whether there is an underlying debt, and, if applicable, regardless of whether the underlying debt is legally due and unpaid. Payment must be made by the guarantor on demand by the beneficiary of the demand guarantee and without looking into the merits of the claim against the debtor. A demand guarantee is similar to, but not the same as, an indemnity. One key difference is that under an indemnity the beneficiary needs to show that they have suffered a loss but even that is unnecessary under a demand guarantee. See Box A1.21. They are usually issued by banks and may, for example, take the form of a **standby letter of credit**.

> **Box A1.21**
>
> It may help to illustrate the nature of a demand guarantee to look at the example of a performance bond, which is an example of a demand guarantee. This is an instrument issued by a bank which states that if the bank's customer does not perform the relevant obligations to which the performance bond relates, then the bank will pay a specified sum of money to the holder of the performance bond. The bank must pay whenever the holder of the bond states that the relevant circumstances have arisen to trigger a payment. There is no defence to payment except fraud. The amount due does not need to reflect any loss suffered by the holder of the bond.

---

[92] See Philip Wood, *International Loans, Bonds, Guarantees and Legal Opinions*, 3rd edn, 37-015..

[93] See Goode, *Commercial Law*, 30.07 onwards, for further detail on the difference between suretyship guarantees and primary obligations such as indemnities and demand guarantees.

Section 3: Guarantees   **501**

A1.075

It is simply a question of construction as to whether any document takes effect as a suretyship guarantee (under which default must be demonstrated before demand may be made), a demand guarantee (under which there is no defence to payment except fraud and there is no need to prove a loss), or an indemnity (under which the amount of loss needs to be established in order to make a claim). However it is often very unclear as to whether a document is intended to be a suretyship guarantee or a demand guarantee, and this has resulted in a number of cases on the issue. Moreover, the simple fact that an English law guarantee is expressed to be payable 'on demand' does not make it into a 'demand guarantee', see Box A1.22.

> **Box A1.22**
>
> English law guarantees are expressed to be payable on demand so that the limitation period during which claim must be made only starts on the making of a demand. If these words were not there then the limitation period would start on the date of the borrower's default.

Courts will be reluctant to find that an instrument is a demand guarantee and, if that is the intention, the best way to achieve that is to incorporate the uniform rules for demand guarantees issued by the International Chamber of Commerce.[94]

A1.076

Need to claim against borrower

Another distinction which is sometimes made is as to whether the lender can claim under the guarantee without first having taken enforcement action against the borrower. Unfortunately, the expression 'first demand guarantee' is sometimes used to describe a guarantee under which a claim can be made on the guarantor without first enforcing rights against the borrower, but may also be used to describe the situation where there is no defence to payment except fraud, as in a standby letter of credit. Unsurprisingly this leads to confusion between this concept and the types of instrument described in A1.074.

A1.077

---

[94] Meritz Fire & Marine v Jan de Nul [2011] 2 Lloyds Rep 379.

502   Appendix 1: Some English Law Concepts

Continuing guarantees

Just as loans may be revolving in nature, with the amount outstanding both decreasing and increasing in accordance with the borrower's needs,[95] so also guarantees may be continuing in nature and may secure, not simply a fixed loan, but instead a loan, such as a revolving credit, which may be repaid and re-advanced from time to time. The guarantee relates to a fluctuating balance of the facility.

A1.078

A continuing guarantee may also be given on an 'all moneys' basis—to secure any money which is outstanding from the borrower when the guarantee is called on—whether under an agreement in place at the time the guarantee was entered into or under any subsequent arrangements. The guarantee relates to the amount outstanding when the demand is made under the guarantee. The question of what debts are covered by a guarantee is simply a question of interpretation of the wording of the guarantee.

Where the guarantee relates to advances which the lender is not committed to make at the time the guarantee is given (e.g. under an all moneys guarantee) the guarantor will be able to give notice terminating its liability in respect of advances not yet made at the time the notice of termination is given.[96]

A1.079

Guarantee versus third party charge

A guarantee is a right in personam.[97] A third party charge is a security interest (a right in rem) granted by a party which is not the borrower. The third party charge may be given as **security** for the third party's obligations under a guarantee or may be given directly for the borrower's obligations under the loan. Whichever route is chosen, the effect is that the third party is making its asset which is the subject of the charge available to meet the debts of the borrower. Since the third party is standing surety for the borrower to the extent of the value of the asset, it has the rights of a surety, and the various issues discussed in relation to guarantees (e.g. effect of discharge of security) apply equally to third party charges.

---

[95] As opposed to loans of a fixed sum, which, once advanced, must be repaid but are not available for re-drawing.

[96] See Goode, *Commercial Law*, in 30.20.

[97] See A1.010.

A1.080

Guarantee versus letter of comfort

A **comfort letter** is sometimes intended to create a legally binding commitment which is something short of a guarantee. Alternatively, it may not be intended to create a legal commitment of any kind. Commonly a comfort letter will contain assurances as to the shareholder's policy towards supporting its subsidiaries. The precise effect of the document will of course depend on its wording. If, as is common, the shareholder does not intend to enter into any commitments as to the future then words of promise such as 'agree' and 'undertake' should be avoided. Similarly any statements as to policies should clarify that they are only statements of 'current' policies or 'current' intentions so that they cannot be construed as implied representations as to the future.

If the intention is only to give a moral assurance then the document should clearly state that it is not intended to be legally binding. Simply calling it a letter of comfort does not result in it not being a legal commitment.[98]

2. Hazards with Guarantees

A1.081

Transactions at an undervalue[99]/commercial benefit

Under English law, guarantees may be vulnerable to be set aside as transactions at an undervalue[100] if

* given at a time when the company was insolvent[101] or if it became insolvent as a result of the guarantee;

---

[98] See Goode, *Commercial Law*, in 30.15. See also Chemco Leasing SpA v Rediffusion plc (1987) 1 FTLR 201, and Kleinwort Benson Ltd v Malaysian Mining Corp (1989) 1 AER 785.

[99] s238 Insolvency Act 1986. See further, Goode, *Commercial Law* in 31.40.

[100] A transaction under which a company gives substantially more than it receives. In a guarantee, an assurance is given and, in exchange the company receives the right to be indemnified by the original debtor if payment is made under the guarantee.

[101] That is, unable to pay its debts as they fall due or its liabilities exceed its assets, s123 Insolvency Act 1986. See also 8.253 onwards.

504   **Appendix 1: Some English Law Concepts**

- the company subsequently goes into liquidation or administration under a process which commenced during the hardening period[102] and
- the company cannot take advantage of the defence which is available. It is a defence if the guarantee was entered into in good faith and for the purpose of carrying on its business and there were reasonable grounds to believe it would benefit the company. In the case of a downstream guarantee[103] this benefit to the guarantor is often not hard to show—improving the financial position of a subsidiary generally improves the prospects of receiving dividends. In the case of an upstream or sister guarantee,[104] there may be more difficulty establishing this requirement.

A1.082

In addition to the hazards of transactions at an undervalue, payment under a guarantee may be challenged on the basis of a breach of the directors' duties under s172 Companies Act 2006. That section states that directors must act in the way that he or she considers, in good faith, will be most likely to promote the success of the company (see Box A1.23).

Box A1.23

The Companies Act duty was intended to be a codification and extension of existing common law rules and it expressly provides[105] that it is to be interpreted with regard to existing case law in relation to the equivalent common law provisions. The statutory duty to promote the success of the company is an extension of the pre-existing common law **fiduciary duty** of directors to act in the interests of the company. The principal case on the common law fiduciary duty is *Rolled Steel Products (Holdings) Ltd v British Steel Corp and others (1986) Ch 246* where a guarantee was set aside due to a lack of corporate benefit to the company itself. The case held that where a third party knowingly (including someone with **constructive notice**) received a payment which was made in breach of that duty, it would be obliged to refund that payment to the company. Lenders taking guarantees therefore remain concerned to ensure that directors do not act in breach of their duty outlined in *Rolled Steel* and therefore to ensure that they (the lenders) do not have constructive knowledge of a misuse of the company's assets. In the case of a solvent company it is thought that this duty may be waived by all the shareholders.

---

[102] That is, the period during which the transaction is open to challenge. The longest hardening period under English law (absent fraud) is two years.

[103] That is, a guarantee given by a parent for the benefit of a subsidiary.

[104] That is, a guarantee given by a subsidiary for the benefit of its parent or of a fellow subsidiary.

[105] At s170(4) Companies Act 2006.

A1.083

Lenders will therefore be concerned to ensure that the guaranteeing company obtains a benefit from the guarantee, or alternatively, in the case of a guarantor which will be solvent after the giving of the guarantee, to ensure that shareholder approval of the guarantee is obtained (see comments on Schedule 2 in 13.005).

A1.084

Guarantors will also need to consider the accounting impact of the giving of the guarantee, and whether a fee may need to be charged in order to avoid the guarantee being treated as a distribution.

A1.085

Subrogation/reimbursement

A guarantor which pays another's debt is generally entitled to be reimbursed by the debtor. The scope of this right depends on whether the debtor requested the issue of the guarantee. If the guarantee is entered into voluntarily by the guarantor (e.g. in a risk sub-participation) the right of the guarantor to be reimbursed is more limited than it otherwise would be.[106]

Guarantees usually require guarantors to agree that any claim for reimbursement which they have will be subordinate to the guaranteed debt.[107]

A1.086

A party which pays under a guarantee is also entitled to take over (or be subrogated to) the creditor's rights against the debtor, including any security held by the creditor. This right of subrogation (unlike the right of reimbursement discussed in A1.085) appears to be available to a guarantor whether or not the borrower requested the issue of the guarantee.[108]

Guarantees usually require guarantors to waive their right of subrogation until the lender is paid in full.[109]

---

[106] See Goode *Commercial Law* in 30.31 and 30.34.

[107] See comments on Clause 20.7 *(GUARANTEE AND INDEMNITY: Deferral of Guarantors' rights)* in 7.015.

[108] For further detail on the guarantor's rights see Goode *Commercial Law* in 30.31–30.38.

[109] See comments on Clause 20.7 *(GUARANTEE AND INDEMNITY: Deferral of Guarantors' rights)* in 7.015.

506 Appendix 1: Some English Law Concepts

A1.087

Discharge by amendment and other defences

As discussed in relation to Clause 20.4 (*GUARANTEE AND INDEMNITY*: *Waiver of defences*), care must be taken not to amend or waive the loan agreement or otherwise deal with it or any security for it, without obtaining the guarantor's confirmation that their guarantee will remain effective after the proposed action (or inaction) has been taken. See the discussion in Clause 20.4 (*GUARANTEE AND INDEMNITY Waiver of defences*) of the LMA Compounded/Term Rate Loan in 7.007.[110]

---

[110] See also Goode *Commercial Law* in 30.39–30.46 for a discussion of the factors which can discharge the guarantee.

Glossary of Terms

This glossary is intended to assist practitioners by giving brief explanations of certain words commonly encountered in international finance. It includes technical legal and banking expressions as well as colloquial terms.

Glossary of Terms

Acceleration The giving of notice to the borrower, following the occurrence of an Event of Default, requiring the loan to be repaid immediately.

Acceptance credit facility A facility under which the 'borrower' may issue bills of exchange or letters of credit which require 'acceptance' (or agreement to pay the amount specified in the relevant instrument) by the 'lender'. Amounts which the 'lender' has paid under the instrument are treated as loans made to the 'borrower'.

Accordion An uncommitted facility (included in a loan agreement for a committed loan) for the provision of further funds to the borrower on request, benefitting from the same guarantees and security as the existing debt.

Accrued interest The interest which, on any given day, has been earned (but is not yet due and payable) on a loan, bond or similar instrument.

Acquisition finance Finance provided for the purpose of funding a company acquisition.

© The Editor(s) (if applicable) and The Author(s), under exclusive license to Springer Nature Switzerland AG 2024
S. Wright, *The International Loan Documentation Handbook*, Global Financial Markets, https://doi.org/10.1007/978-3-031-38489-9

508   Glossary of Terms

Administration An English legal expression describing the legal situation which results from the issue of an administration order under the Insolvency Act 1986 as amended. Such an order may be issued in relation to a company which is in financial difficulties and allows the reorganization of the company's affairs or the realization of its assets for the benefit of creditors. While the order is in force, creditors cannot take action against the company, or enforce security against its assets, unless they obtain the consent of the court. Similar to 'Chapter 11' in the US.

Administrator The official who will take control of the business of a company while it is in administration.

Advance A drawing of money under a loan facility.

Agency fee A fee payable by the borrower to compensate the agent for the mechanical and operational work performed by it under the loan agreement.

Agent In the context of a syndicated credit facility, the Agent is the party which administers the facility, acting as a channel between the borrower and the syndicate for the purpose of communications and payments.

In other contexts, an agent is anyone who represents another (his 'principal') in a negotiation or other transaction.

Agreed Security Principles A set of principles used in acquisition finance to limit the security which lenders can request. The principles state that lenders will not request security or guarantees to the extent that the costs and legal and tax consequences involved would be disproportionate to the benefits.

Alphabet notes Debt which is divided into different tranches with different maturity dates and pricing where all the notes rank pari passu.

Amend and extend An amendment to a syndicated facility agreement where certain of the existing lenders agree in advance to extend the maturity of some or all of their loans.

Amortization In the context of a loan; the repayment of debt in stages. In the context of EBITDA, the writing down of goodwill.

Annuity A basis for repaying a loan which results in the total amount paid by the borrower on each payment date being the same. In the early years, this amount will be made up largely of interest, while in the later years it will constitute mostly principal.

Arbitrage Profiting from the difference in prices between markets, for example, between Tokyo and London.

Glossary of Terms

Arbitration A process for settling disputes without having recourse to courts of law. The dispute is decided either by a person appointed by the parties to the dispute or chosen by a third party they have nominated to make the appointment. See further Box 12.1.

Arranger The lender which is originally mandated by the borrower to arrange a syndicated loan.

Asset Any thing which has value. It may be physical, such as a ship; intellectual, such as a patent or otherwise intangible, such as a debt.

Asset backed securities Securities (such as those issued in a securitization) which are supported by assets such as credit card receivables (as opposed to normal debt securities issued by a company, which are often unsecured and pari passu with that company's general debts).

Asset finance Finance which is provided for the purpose of funding the acquisition of a major asset.

Asset stripping Sale of assets for cash instead of keeping them to generate income.

Assignment A method of transfer of 'choses in action'. An English law assignment may be used in an outright transfer, such as a sale, (as to which see 9.010 onwards), or as a method of security, (as to which see A1.051 onwards). An English law assignment may only be used to transfer rights, not obligations. In the US, the expression may also refer to a transfer (by assumption) of obligations.

Availability period The time during which a borrower may draw down advances under a loan.

Backstop facility A facility to be used in the event of a problem with alternative financing arrangements.

Back to back transactions A colloquial expression for two linked transactions on identical (or practically identical) terms—for example, a loan from X to Y and a corresponding loan from Y to Z.

Bail-in clause A provision in a contract with a systemically important financial institution, under which the counterparty contractually agrees to the powers granted to regulators by relevant legislation allowing them to convert claims against the relevant institutions into equity claims.

Balance sheet lending Lending on the strength of the borrower's balance sheet (as opposed to lending on the value of a particular asset or income stream).

Balloon repayment A final repayment of principal on a loan transaction which is substantially larger than earlier repayment instalments.

510   Glossary of Terms

Bankruptcy The situation which arises if a person has been declared by a court not to be able to pay his debts and whose affairs have been put into the hands of a receiver. In England, this term is applied only to persons. Companies go into liquidation as opposed to bankruptcy.

Base rate A fluctuating interest rate, peculiar to individual banks and used by them as a reference point for lending rates when lending on an inclusive (as opposed to a 'cost plus') basis. See Box 0.7.

Basel I Framework agreed in 1988 by the Basel Committee on Banking Supervision relating to supervisory regulations governing the capital adequacy of international banks.

Basel II The agreement reached in 2004 which updated the capital adequacy requirements which were originally set down in 1988. See 6.053.

Basel III The various documents issued by the Basel Committee on Banking Supervision following the 2007–2008 financial crisis and which, in the EU, was implemented via the 4th Capital Requirements Directive (commonly referred to as 'CRD IV') in 2013. See 6.054.

Basel IV also known as Basel 3.1. Amendments to Basel III introduced over time; principally the Post Crisis Reforms published by the Basel Committee in 2017 in 'Basel III: Finalising post-crisis reforms' See 6.055

Basis point 1/100 of one per cent (0.01%). It is the unit of measurement used to describe fees or spreads in most loan transactions.

Basket An exception to a loan undertaking (such as an undertaking not to borrow money) which allows the prohibited action to be done up to a monetary limit.

BBA British Bankers Association.

BBA LIBOR The London Interbank Offered Rate (*LIBOR*) as determined by the methodology of the British Bankers Association. It was replaced by ICE *LIBOR* in 2014 and subsequently by rates based on risk free rates. See 0.091.

Bells and whistles Unusual features of a transaction.

Beneficiary Any person for whose benefit assets are held in trust. See A1.019.

Bible Complete set of copy or conformed copy documents relating to a particular transaction.

Bid bond A bond provided by a bank which is payable if a bidder, on winning the bid, does not enter into a binding contract in accordance with the bid.

Bilateral facility A loan facility between one lender and one borrower.

Glossary of Terms   **511**

Bill of exchange A form of short-term promise to pay, widely used to finance trade and provide credit. It is an instruction by the drawer to the person accepting the bill of exchange to make a payment to a third party. It differs from a promissory note in that a promissory note is a promise by one party to make a payment. It differs from a letter of credit in that a letter of credit is payable only against presentation of documents (and is usually issued by a bank at the request of a customer).

Blocking Law A law[111] designed to limit the extraterritorial impact of the law of another country.

Bona fide A Latin expression meaning in good faith.

Bona fide purchaser for value An English legal expression meaning a person who, acting in good faith and acquiring, for a price, a legal interest in property, may defeat an equitable interest in the same property.[112]

Bond In the context of capital markets, means a medium- to long-term promise to pay a certain amount at a certain date in the future, traded in the capital markets. It may or may not be interest-bearing, (if it is, it is referred to as having a 'coupon'). In other contexts (as in bid bond or performance bond) some form of assurance given (in the form of a promise to pay a fixed sum in certain circumstances) that a person will perform as promised.

Book debts The items in a company's balance sheet which represent amounts owing to the company.

Book runner The bank(s) appointed to run the books during the primary syndication of the loan. Responsible for issuing invitations, passing information to interested banks and informing both the borrower and the management group of underwriters of daily progress.

Book value The value of a company's assets as shown in its balance sheet. It differs from the actual value because it simply shows the price paid less 'depreciation' which is a notional annual loss of value of an asset, based on its estimated valuable life.

Borrowing base finance A form of trade finance, typically a revolving credit, where the lender provides finance against the security of the borrower's trading assets—typically its receivables and inventory.

Break Costs See Broken funding costs.

Bridge financing Interim financing used as a short-term stop gap until the intended long-term financing facility is available.

---

[111] Such as the European Blocking Regulation (EC) 2271/96.

[112] See A1.023.

512 Glossary of Terms

Broken funding costs (or Break Costs) Costs (whether real or notional) which a lender might incur as a result of receiving payment of a sum on a date which is not its due date for payment. See 0.110.

Bullet repayment Repayment of a debt obligation in a single instalment at the date of maturity of the debt (i.e. with no amortization).

Business day A day on which relevant institutions are open for business in the relevant country. See discussion at 0.131.

Call option An agreement which gives the recipient the right, but not the obligation, to require the donor to transfer a specified asset to the recipient, normally at a specified price, on a specified date (or within a range of dates). The recipient of this right can be expected to exercise it if the value of the asset, on the date on which the option may be exercised, is higher than the price at which the option can be exercised. It therefore gives the recipient an option to participate in any increase in price of the relevant asset.

Cap A limit or ceiling, for example, setting the maximum interest rate on a loan.

Capital markets The markets for sale and purchase of tradeable financial instruments such as bonds and commercial paper.

Capitalized interest Interest which has accrued but which has been added to the principal amount of the loan and is itself bearing interest. Often interest is capitalized during the construction phase of a project finance transaction before there is any income to fund it.

Cashflow The difference, over a specified period of time, between the amount of cash flowing into the company and the amount of cash paid out.

CDS see Credit Default Swap.

Certain funds An English expression meaning funds with minimal conditions precedent to availability as necessary for meeting the requirements of the Takeover Code for financing the acquisition of a UK quoted company. See 0.279.

Chapter 11 US rules allowing a company a period of protection from its creditors while it seeks to reorganize its affairs and avoid winding up. Similar to English 'administration'.

Charge An English legal expression meaning a security interest under which the chargee does not get either title or possession but simply the right, in a default, to take the asset and apply its proceeds against the secured debt. See A1.045.

Glossary of Terms   **513**

Chinese wall An artificial barrier restricting communication between different areas within an organization, allowing them to act for parties who may have conflicting interests. The concept originated in securities houses. It is also commonly used within large firms of solicitors and accountants.

CHIPS A clearing system used in the US for settlement of large value payments.[113]

Chose in action An English legal expression meaning rights (such as rights under contracts) which can only be enforced by taking legal action.

Civil law Codified systems of law which have developed from Roman law—see A1.002.

Clawback clause A clause enabling one party to retrieve money already paid out. An example is the clause (Clause 31.4 *(PAYMENT MECHANICS: Clawback and pre funding)* of the LMA Compounded/Term Rate Loan) found in syndicated loan agreements enabling an agent to recover money already paid out by it to a party, without waiting to ensure that the agent has received the corresponding payment from another party. This allows an agent to distribute money (e.g. a repayment instalment) to the bank syndicate without confirming receipt of the payment from the borrower, knowing if it does not receive the monies from the borrower it may 'clawback' the monies paid out to the syndicate. Another example is Clause 15.4 *(TAX GROSS UP AND INDEMNITIES: Tax Credit)* of the LMA Compounded/Term Rate Loan, relating to withholding tax and allowing the borrower to 'clawback' some of the moneys paid under the grossing-up clause (Clause 15.2 *(TAX GROSS UP AND INDEMNITIES: Tax gross up)* subclause (c) of the LMA Compounded/Term Rate Loan) in the event that the relevant lender receives a tax credit which it attributes to those payments by the borrower.

Clean down period A requirement sometimes included in a revolving credit facility requiring the facility not to be used for a specified period in each year so as to demonstrate that it is not being used as part of the borrower's permanent capital.

Cleanup period used in leveraged finance—this is a period after the acquisition of the target company during which some of the provisions of the loan agreement are relaxed to give the borrower an opportunity to make the necessary arrangements to ensure compliance.

Clear market clause Clause in a term sheet by which a borrower undertakes, while its loan is being syndicated, not to put other offerings on sale which could compete with the syndication.

---

[113] See Ross Cranston, *Principles of Banking Law*, 3rd edn, p351.

514   **Glossary of Terms**

Closing The moment at which a loan is drawdown and conditions precedent satisfied—the completion of the commercial transaction.

Club A small group of banks which finance a loan without the need for a full syndication process.

CME Chicago Mercantile Exchange.

CME Term Sofr The daily set of forward looking interest rate estimates based on Sofr and published by The Chicago Mercantile Exchange for specific tenors (1, 3, 6 and 12 months).

Co-financing A financing where a number of different lenders or syndicates are involved, each providing a different facility to the borrower, under a different facility agreement, often with common undertakings and Events of Default as set out in a 'Common Terms Agreement'. Generally, the lenders will share any security in accordance with pre-agreed rules which are not simply based on one lender being senior in all circumstances to another. Distinct from a syndicated loan in that there are different facilities, to be used for different purposes, and with different pricing.

Collar A combination of a cap and a floor limiting movement (e.g. of interest rates) to stay within a defined range.

Collateral Assets used to secure a loan or other financing transaction.

Collateralized debt obligation (or 'CDO') A bond or other tradeable financial instrument issued by an SPV which is secured by a portfolio of debts purchased by that SPV. A CDO is a type of securitization.

Collateralized loan obligation A CDO where the debt obligations are loans.

Comfort letter a letter of support which is intended to give rise to a moral rather than a legal commitment, or, if intended to give rise to a legal commitment, to stop short of a guarantee—see A1.080.

Commercial paper Short-term promise to pay a specified amount at a future date, traded in the capital markets.

Commitment The specified amount of money agreed to be lent by a lender in a committed facility.

Commitment fee An annual percentage fee payable to a bank on the undrawn portion of its commitment under a committed facility. The commitment fee is usually paid periodically in arrears.

Committed facility A facility which the lenders are committed to make (or keep) available, subject only to the satisfaction of conditions precedent and non-occurrence of an Event of Default.

Common law Law as laid down by decisions of courts, rather than by statute. See A1.002.

Compound interest Interest charged on interest.

Glossary of Terms **515**

Conditions A word with many meanings. It may refer to

* the provisions of an agreement generally;
* things which need to be done in order for particular parts of an agreement to become, or to remain, operative (as in 'conditions precedent' or 'conditions subsequent') or
* those provisions of an agreement which are sufficiently important to warrant the termination of the agreement if there is a breach of the provision (as opposed to a warranty, breach of which gives rise only to damages).

Conformed copy A copy of a final executed document in which all signatures and any other handwritten words (e.g. dates or alterations) are printed in typed form. Conformed copies may be used to make up a transaction bible.

Consideration An English law expression meaning some benefit given in exchange for a promise in order for the promise to be legally enforceable.[114]

Constructive notice In many situations English law provides that a party's rights depend on whether or not it had notice of certain facts. In order to prevent parties from deciding not to enquire about things they might rather not know about, English law includes a concept of 'constructive notice'. Precisely what constitutes constructive notice in any given situation will depend on the facts of the case, but the concept is that a party will be treated as having notice (and will have constructive notice) if that party would have had notice if it had acted in a manner which the court decides that it should have acted, bearing in mind all the circumstances of the case.

Contingent debt A debt which may or may not mature. The obligation to pay it is dependent on the occurrence of some intervening event. An example is a guarantee, payment under which will only become due if the borrower defaults.

Contingent liability A liability which is dependent on the occurrence of an uncertain event (such as the liability under a guarantee).

Contra proferentem A rule of interpretation. The rule states that, where there is ambiguity in the wording of any provision of a contract, that provision is to be read against the party at whose instigation it was included in the contract and who is now seeking the benefit of the relevant provision.

Counterparty The other party to a contract.

Coupon The interest which is paid on a bond.

---

[114] See A1.024.

516   Glossary of Terms

Covenant A promise to do or not do specified acts. Same meaning as 'undertaking'.

Covenant lite Loans that have bond-like financial incurrence covenants rather than traditional maintenance covenants—see 8.078.

CP's Conditions precedent. The conditions (mostly documentary) which need to be satisfied in order for the loan funds to be released.

CRD IV EU Fourth Capital Requirements Directive implementing Basel III in the EU.

CRD VI EU Sixth Capital Requirements Directive published in 2021 and expected to come into effect in 2025 and which together with other proposed and existing EU regulations and directives is expected to implement Basel 3.1 in the EU. See 6.056.

Credit adjustment spread An additional spread (or price) charged if the baseline for charging interest is changed (e.g. from a rate of interest based on Euribor to one based on risk free rates). The spread is designed to compensate the lender for any difference in pricing between the historical baseline and the new baseline. See 0.107.

Credit default swap (or 'CDS') A financial instrument whereby, for valuable consideration, one party transfers credit risk to another party. Many CDSs have a pool of 'reference obligations' (i.e. the debts whose risk is transferred), which is often not static but may be changed over time. A CDS is a type of credit derivative.

Credit derivative A derivative relating to a particular credit risk, such as a credit linked note, total return swap or credit default swap. See 9.020.

Credit enhancement A guarantee or other form of support which will enable the rating of a particular issue of securities to be improved.

Cross default An Event of Default in a loan to a borrower which is triggered by a default in the payment, or the potential acceleration of repayment, of other indebtedness of the same borrower or of a member of its group see 8.238.

Cross security Security given for one loan also being given as security for another loan and vice versa.

Crystallization The termination of the freedom which a chargor has, under a floating charge, to deal with the assets which are the subject of the charge. See A1.046.

Cumulative Compounded RFR Rate The rate of interest (expressed as a rate per annum and applying to an Interest Period) inherent in the amount of growth which an investment would have seen if invested at the beginning of the Interest Period and rolled over (together with accrued interest) daily until the end of the Interest Period.

Glossary of Terms 517

Current asset Any asset which is not intended to be retained in a company and which is available to be turned into cash within one year.

Current liability A liability of a company which falls due within one year.

Daily Non-Cumulative Compounded RFR Rate In respect of any given day, the rate of interest (expressed as a rate per annum) inherent in the amount of growth seen in the Unannualised Cumulative Compounded Daily Rate on that day.

De minimis Too small to be concerned with.

Debenture This can be a document, such as a bond or promissory note, which evidences a debt. Often these securities are freely transferable and listed. They may be secured on the company's property ('mortgage debentures'). A debenture can also be a document which creates security over all of a company's business. The document contains, in the charging clause, mortgages, fixed and floating charges and assignments which together create the necessary security.

Debt service Payment of principal and interest in respect of the loan.

Deductible The amount which an insurer will deduct before making payment of a claim. The expression is also used in relation to tax, meaning the ability to deduct a particular payment from profits for the purpose of calculating tax liability.

Deed An English law expression meaning a document which will be enforced by the courts without the need for consideration.[115]

Default In its ordinary sense, this means a breach or a failure to perform as promised under a contract. It is usually also a defined term in the loan agreement, meaning something which may, or may not, result in an Event of Default. See commentary on 'Default' in 1.014.

Defaulting lender provisions see Lehman provisions.

Defeasance A structure which creates certainty that a payment obligation will be met from a specific source other than by the original debtor.

Demand guarantee An instrument such as a standby letter of credit or a performance bond under which the 'guarantor' must pay, regardless of whether there is an underlying debt unless they can establish fraud on the part of the person demanding payment—see A1.074.

Dematerialize To transfer to a system which is based on book entries.

Derivatives Assets (such as futures) which derive their value from underlying assets. See, for example, the discussion of credit derivatives from 9.020 onwards.

---

[115] See A1.024.

518   Glossary of Terms

Disbursement account The account to which the proceeds of a loan provided in a project finance transaction are paid. Money will be drawn from that account against approved invoices.

Disclosure regulation (also known as **'SFDR'**) Regulation (EU) 2019/2088 on sustainability-related disclosures in the financial services sector.

Distressed debt Debt which is, or which the lender believes will be, nonperforming (i.e. repaid late, partially or not at all) and which is usually sold for substantially less than the value of principal outstanding.

Distributable reserves The amount which a company is allowed to pay to its shareholders at any given time by way of dividend.

Dividend A payment by a company to its shareholders out of profits.

Double dipping Structuring a transaction in such a way that it becomes possible to utilize the tax benefits on capital investments in more than one jurisdiction.

Double taxation treaty An agreement between two countries intended to limit the double taxation of income and gains, under the terms of which an investor which is tax resident in one country but invests in another may be able to apply for an exemption or reduction in the taxes imposed on his income or gains by the country of his investment, on the basis that such income or gains will have tax levied on them in the country in which he is tax resident. This type of treaty encourages trade and financial transactions between countries. See 6.002.

Drawdown The borrowing of money under a loan facility.

Drop dead fee A fee payable to a lender in the event the proposed transaction does not proceed.

DTTP scheme or double taxation treaty passport scheme. This is an arrangement in the UK under which lenders may apply for a passport confirming their eligibility for treaty relief. Use of this passport significantly speeds up the process for obtaining clearance to pay interest to the lender without deduction of withholding tax. See 6.012

Due diligence The process of checking all relevant facts before entering into a transaction. Involves both financial and legal due diligence.

EBITDA Earnings before interest, tax, depreciation and amortization—see Box 8.18.

Encumbrance A general description of any restriction on rights of ownership. It includes all forms of security as well as other restrictions such as rights of way.

Engrossment The final version of a contract, ready for signature.

Glossary of Terms **519**

Equator principles A set of guidelines adopted by financial institutions to ensure that large scale development or construction projects such as those financed through project finance appropriately consider the associated potential impacts on the natural environment and the affected communities

Equity Has a number of meanings—

- Moneys invested into a company by its shareholders (including, perhaps, accumulated profits not yet distributed)
- The principles of law which are embodied in equitable principles (see A1.009)
- Fairness.

Equity cure These provisions allow the shareholders of issuers or borrowers to fix a breach of a financial covenant without having to request a waiver or amendment. Some agreements do not limit the number of equity cures, while others cap the number to, maybe, one per year or two over the life of the loan, with the exact details negotiated for each deal. See 8.124.

Equity kicker An option, often included in certain loan transactions, particularly in mezzanine finance and venture capital, to take a share in the profits arising from the transaction financed by the loan.

Equity of redemption A mortgagee's right to pay off the secured debt and obtain title back from the mortgagor.

ERISA Employee Retirement Income Security Act of 1974 in the US. Failure to comply with the requirements of the Act can result in penalties and security interests arising. US borrowers are therefore often asked to give representations and covenants as to compliance with ERISA.

Escrow arrangement Documents held in escrow are executed documents given by one executing party to a third party (usually a solicitor) to hold to its order until a certain condition is satisfied, or event occurs. The third party will usually be instructed that, on the satisfaction of such condition or occurrence of such event, the documents must be released out of escrow, usually to the other executing party. Money may also be held in escrow— that is, held by a third party with irrevocable instructions as to how to dispose of it in different circumstances.

ESG lending A general description of lending which aims to encourage an environmental, social or governance objective. The main types are Sustainability Linked Lending and Green Loans or Social Loans.

Estoppel An English law principle that, in certain circumstances, it would be unfair to allow a person to do something (such as enforcing their legal rights) and that he will therefore be 'estopped' from doing it. See 11.023.

520   Glossary of Terms

In the classic case[116] a landlord, having promised not to charge the full rent he was entitled to, was subsequently estopped from suing for the full rent.

€str Euro short-term rates—the overnight risk free rate for Euros.

Eurocurrency Traditionally, any currency held by a non-resident of the country of that currency.[117]

EU Taxonomy regulation Regulation (EU) 2020/852 on the establishment of a framework to facilitate sustainable investment.

Event of Default The circumstances listed in the loan agreement which entitle the lender to demand immediate repayment of the loan.

Evergreen A colloquial expression which means that the relevant thing is always there. For example, an evergreen repetition of the representations is one which requires them to be repeated daily and an evergreen facility is one which is renewable annually.

Exclusion clause A clause under which a person seeks to exclude the liability, which he would otherwise have had, to another.[118]

Execute Sign.

Exemption clause. See exclusion clause.

Export credit agency A government body created for the purpose of providing export credit.

Export finance (or export credit) Support provided by a country's government or an agency on behalf of the government, for the purpose of encouraging exports from that country. The support may take the form of guarantees, loans at subsidized interest rates, or other. The terms of export finance are regulated by the OECD Guidelines for Officially Supported Export Credit.

Facility A generic description for any form of financial support, whether by way of loan, guarantee, acceptance credit or other.

Factoring The sale and purchase of receivables, either on a recourse or non-recourse basis. In other words, the seller may or may not remain subject to the risk of default in relation to the receivables sold.

FATCA Foreign Account Tax Compliance Act—see 6.038.

FFI A 'foreign financial institution' for the purposes of FATCA.

Fiduciary duty This is the duty of the trustee or agent (including directors of companies, who are agents of the company by virtue of their position as directors) to act in the interests of those they represent. The existence

---

[116] Central London Property Trust Ltd v High Trees House Ltd (1947) KB 130.

[117] See Philip Wood, International Loans, Bonds, Guarantees, Legal Opinions, 3rd ed in 1-003.

[118] See A1.027.

Glossary of Terms 521

and exact scope of any fiduciary duty depends on the situation. In general, fiduciary duties include a duty

- not to make a secret profit,
- not to put oneself in a position where a conflict of interest may arise,
- not to sub-delegate and
- to act in good faith.[119]

Finance lease A means of financing involving a lease of an asset, the commercial effect of which is that the owner of the asset is in a similar position to a lender and the lessee is in a similar position to owner and borrower. Lease payments during the life of the lease are sufficient to enable the owner to recover the cost of the asset from the lessee, plus a return on its investment, regardless of any fluctuation in the value of the asset.[120]

Fixed charge Security over a specific asset which prevents the owner from dealing with the asset. See A1.045.

Floating charge Floating charges are security interests which allow the person giving the security to sell the items over which the security exists, free of the security until the security 'crystallizes'. They are often used to give security over categories of assets such as a trader's stock in trade from time to time. They have a number of disadvantages as against other forms of security; one of which is that the security holder cannot retain all the proceeds of the security. See A1.046.

Floor An agreed limit below which a particular figure, such as an interest rate, is not allowed to drop.

Force majeure A continental law concept meaning occurrences of a type (e.g. acts of God) which are outside the control of the parties and which justify the non-performance of obligations under a contract (without the contract itself having to set this out). Under English law, non-performance of a contract for reasons which are not specified in the contract but which are outside the control of the parties, is justified if the contract is 'frustrated'. This is a much narrower concept than the continental concept of force majeure. For this reason, many English law contracts contain force majeure clauses, specifically allowing non-performance in circumstances which would not amount to frustration.

Forward Start Facility A committed facility used to refinance (repay) an existing syndicated loan on maturity. It is signed some time in advance (several months to a year) of maturity of the existing loan and is provided by some of the existing lenders.

---

[119] See further Goode, *Commercial Law*, in 5.25.
[120] See Goode, *Commercial Law*, Chapter 28.

522   **Glossary of Terms**

Frustration The circumstances in which English law will release parties from further performance of a contract as a result of unanticipated occurrences. A contract is frustrated if it is incapable of being performed in a manner which will give the parties the same nature of benefit as they originally contracted for. Further performance is then excused.[121]

Full recourse In relation to an obligation, 'full recourse' means that the person who is owed the obligation has all the rights which the law gives in relation to enforcement of that obligation, for example, to sue the counterparty for all sums due and enforce any judgement against any of the assets of the counterparty.

Fungible assets Assets where the precise identity of the asset is irrelevant—each asset of that type is interchangeable. For example, in relation to cash, a deposit of £10 with a bank may be reimbursed by the bank returning £10—even though the precise notes are not the same as those originally deposited.

Futures Contracts to buy or sell specific assets for agreed prices on an agreed future date.

GAAP Generally accepted accounting principles—the common set of accounting principles, standards and procedures that companies use in any given country to compile their financial statements and reports.

Gearing The ratio of a company's debt to its equity.

Gilts Securities such as commercial paper issued by the British government.

Goodstanding A concept which is relevant in some (e.g. some US) jurisdictions where failure to pay taxes may jeopardize the company's existence or ability to do business.

Goodwill The value attributed in a company's balance sheet to certain of the company's non-physical assets such as its name, reputation and customer base.

Governing law See 'proper law'.

Grace period The period of time given to a borrower, in relation to the Events of Default in a loan agreement, in which it is allowed to remedy any given situation, and to avoid that situation becoming an Event of Default.

Green loan A loan which is provided for a green purpose (e.g. renewable energy) Use for a different purpose would be an Event of Default and the borrower should no longer be permitted to describe the loan as 'Green'

Greenwashing Giving the public impression of environmental and social responsibility without having genuine impact in those areas.

---

[121] See Chapter 19 of Treitel, *The Law of Contract*, 15th edn.

Gross-up A borrower may be required to gross up payments it has to make to the lenders, meaning it must make additional payments to compensate for withholding taxes, or similar deductions, which would otherwise reduce the amounts actually received by the lenders. See commentary on Clause 15.2 *(TAX GROSS UP AND INDEMNITIES: Tax Gross up)* subclause (c) of the LMA Compounded/Term Rate Loan in 6.004.

Guarantee A promise to pay a debt which has been made to another if that other defaults in payment. See A1.070 onwards.

Haircut A situation where a borrower has fallen into financial difficulties and lenders have agreed to accept a reduction in interest and or fees, or principal. Also a situation where a borrower has fallen into financial difficulty and a lender has decided to sell its exposure in the secondary market at a significant discount to its par value.

Hardening period The period of time before the commencement of an insolvency process (e.g. winding up) in respect of which a liquidator can challenge certain transactions entered into by the insolvent company. See 'Transactions at an undervalue' and 'Preference'. The longest hardening period in English law is two years (except in the case of fraud).

Hedge funds An investment vehicle that is privately organized and not widely available to the public. Hedge funds are generally not constrained by legal limitations on their investment discretion and can adopt a variety of trading strategies.

Hedging Arrangements made to protect against loss due to market or currency fluctuation.

Hell or high water clause A clause which requires payment regardless of any eventualities (e.g. to continue paying hire for an asset, regardless of its destruction, as will be contained in a finance lease).

Hire purchase A form of finance lease under which the lessee has the right to purchase the asset for a nominal sum at the end of the financing period.

ICE LIBOR The ICE Benchmark Administration Limited's (ICE) fixing of the London Interbank Offered Rate (*LIBOR*). It replaced *BBA LIBOR* in 2014 and has subsequently been replaced by risk free rates. See the discussion in 0.091

IFRS International Financial Reporting Standards created by the International Accounting Standards Board.[122]

---

[122] See also the comments in 1.037.

524   Glossary of Terms

IGA An agreement entered into between the US and another country, making compliance with FATCA much easier for FFIs in that country and enabling them to receive US source income in full, without deduction, and without breaching local bank confidentiality laws.

Indemnity An agreement to hold another harmless against loss. See A1.071.

Information memorandum A document prepared in connection with a proposed syndicated loan or issue of securities, providing information in relation to the proposed transaction for review by potential participants. See 'Prospectus'.

Initial public offering A flotation of a company on a stock exchange.

Insolvency A company is insolvent in the UK if either

- it cannot pay its debts as they fall due (the cash flow test) or
- its liabilities exceed its assets (the balance sheet test).[123]

Failure to meet either of these tests does not necessarily result in the company being wound up but it does give rise to additional duties for directors (see 'wrongful trading') and to the potential for certain transactions entered into (see 'transactions at an undervalue' and 'preference') being subsequently set aside if an insolvency process (such as a winding up or administration) starts during the hardening period. The expression is sometimes (inaccurately) used to mean the same as winding up. See also 8.259 onwards.

Institutional investor An organization whose function is to invest its assets, such as pension funds and investment funds.

Intangible assets Any asset which does not have a physical form. Examples are debts and patents.

Intercreditor agreement Any agreement made between different creditors (or groups of creditors, such as different syndicates) of a company. Such a document may deal with any issues which those creditors seek to regulate among themselves, but commonly covers such issues as priorities of debts, (perhaps prior to insolvency as well as in the event of insolvency of the debtor), priorities of security, agreement on the application of proceeds of sale of assets belonging to the debtor, rights (or restrictions on rights) to take action against the debtor or its assets, commitments relating to provision of further funding and/or provision of information and rights (or restrictions on rights) to adjust the existing contractual arrangements

---

[123] s123 Insolvency Act 1986.

Glossary of Terms 525

with the debtor. Such a document may also go by other names such as 'priorities deed', or 'subordination deed'.

Interest period The period(s) with reference to which interest is calculated for the purpose of a loan agreement. See commentary on Clause 12 *(Interest Periods)* of the LMA Compounded/Term Rate Loan from 5.013 onwards.

International Sustainability Standards Board founded in 2021 as an arm of the International Financial Reporting Standards Foundation with the aim of making sustainability reporting as consistent as financial reporting.

Inventory finance A form of trade finance used for the purchase of inventory. Usually takes the form of a revolving credit used for the purchase of inventory and secured against that inventory.

Investment grade Securities which are rated by the rating agencies at a specified rate high enough to be eligible for investment by certain organizations, such as pension funds.

ISDA International Swap and Derivatives Association. An association responsible for publishing standard terms for swaps and other derivatives.

Joint venture A business which is run by two or more companies in cooperation. The joint venture may take the form of a partnership between the companies, a separate legal entity or other contractual arrangements.

Judgement currency indemnity An indemnity sometimes included in credit facilities (e.g. Clause 17.1 (*OTHER INDEMNITIES: Currency indemnity*) of the LMA Compounded/Term Rate Loan) to protect the lenders against losses they may suffer if judgement is obtained against the borrower in a currency different to that in which the facility is denominated. Such an indemnity may not be enforceable in all circumstances and this is an issue for due diligence.

Jurisdiction The concept that any given court is only able to deal with certain issues, being those which fall within its 'jurisdiction'. The jurisdiction of any court may be limited with reference to the type of issue concerned (e.g. the family courts), the amount in dispute or the country or countries with which the dispute or the parties to it have a connection. Parties to a loan agreement will expressly submit to the jurisdiction of the courts of a specified jurisdiction. These need not be (but usually are) the courts of the country whose law has been chosen as the proper law of the agreement.

KPI Key performance indicators. Goals or objectives in sustainability linked loans, against which the borrower's performance will be measured.

KYC Various checks and investigations required to be made in relation to a bank's customers as part of the procedures to prevent money laundering.

Lag time See Lookback period.

526   Glossary of Terms

Lehman provisions (also known as the 'Defaulting Lender provisions'). The 'LMA Finance Party Default and Market Disruption Clauses' published by the LMA in June 2009, addressing lender default.

Lender of record A member of the syndicate, with direct claims against the borrower.

Lending office The branch or office of a lender through which the funds for a facility are provided.

Letter of credit (see also **standby letter of credit**) A document commonly used in connection with the sale and purchase of goods. It is a written undertaking by a bank (the Issuing Bank) given at the request of, and in accordance with the instructions of, the applicant (the buyer of the goods) to the beneficiary (the seller of the goods), to effect a payment of a stated amount of money, within a prescribed time limit, against the production of stipulated documents (such as evidence of shipment of the goods).

Leverage Ratio of debt to equity. Also known as gearing.

Liability A legal responsibility (may either be a responsibility to do a specified thing or to make a specified payment).

Libor London Interbank Offered Rate. Prior to its abolition this was the rate of interest quoted by banks in the London Interbank Market as the rate at which they were able to borrow money, that is, obtain deposits in a particular currency, for a particular period of time. See Box 0.7.

Lien A right to retain possession of an asset until paid where this right arises as a result of some commercial activity (such as repair of the asset) and was not created for the purpose of raising funds. In the US the expression may be used to mean all forms of security interest. See A1.044.

Limited recourse A limited recourse loan is one with limited comeback (or recourse) to the borrower. The comeback is usually limited to certain specified assets—usually the assets involved in, and income derived from, the project being financed. The expression may also be used in circumstances where there is full recourse to the borrower, but the borrower is an SPV, which only owns assets relating to the project being financed. In this case, the transaction is limited recourse to (or sometimes non-recourse to) the shareholders of the SPV. This is a structural limitation on recourse.

Liquidated damages A sum specified in a contract as being the amount to be paid by one party to the other in the event of a breach of (or of a specified provision of) the contract. Care needs to be taken in fixing the amount to ensure that it is not a penalty. See 'Penalty'.

Liquidation The winding up of a company and distribution of its assets.

Liquidator The official who will be responsible for collection and distribution of a company's assets in a liquidation.

Liquidity The ability of a company to pay its debts as they fall due. Often assessed by the liquidity ratio—the ratio of current assets to current liabilities. If a company is unable to pay its debts as they fall due, it is insolvent. See 'Insolvency'.

Liquidity coverage ratio the ratio between high quality liquid assets and expected outflows from a bank during periods of stress—see 6.054.

Liquidity premium The price charged by banks for taking a liquidity risk.

Liquidity risk The risk involved in the fact that banks borrow money on a short-term basis and on lend it on a long-term basis—see 6.049.

Listed A bond, note, company share or other instrument which is quoted on a recognized stock exchange.

Lookback Period The period of time by which the Observation Period precedes the Interest Period. See 0.102. It is the period allowed for administering and arranging the payment of interest.

Loss Given Default A measure of how much lenders lose when a borrower defaults. The loss will vary depending on the type of borrower and its value when it defaults. Secured creditors will of course lose less than unsecured creditors and senior creditors will lose less than subordinated creditors. Some calculations express loss as a nominal percentage of principal or a percentage of principal plus accrued interest. Others use a present value calculation using an estimated discount rate of an amount demanded by distressed investors.

Loss payee A person named on an insurance policy as the person to be paid in the event of a claim.

Mac Material Adverse change. A clause which states that it is an Event of Default in the event of the occurrence of something which could have or has had a material adverse effect on the borrower's business. Discussed in 8.272.

Mandate The authorization from one person to another to conduct the relevant transaction on the agreed terms. Usually given in the form of a letter signed by both parties.

Mandated Lead Arranger Mandated bank at the highest level. The MLA, or at least one MLA in cases when there is more than one MLA, will act as the bookrunner.

Margin In relation to floating interest rates, the rate of interest charged by the lender over and above the benchmark rate used in the determination of the interest rate (such as Term Sofr, or a compounded risk free rate)—see discussion in 1.041.

Mark to market Valuing an asset against its current market value (particularly used for swaps and other derivatives).

528   Glossary of Terms

Market disruption clause A clause dealing with what happens if the lender's actual funding costs for a currency are higher than its costs of borrowing that currency. See Box 0.13.

Market flex clause The clause in a term sheet which allows the Arranger to alter the terms if there are changes in market conditions.

Maturity The date upon which a debt is finally repayable.

Mezzanine finance or debt Usually high-interest-bearing debt, which ranks behind (i.e. is subordinate to) the 'senior debtors' so far as repayment and security is concerned. In terms of risk and reward it ranks between debt and equity. The debt may be structured as a subordinated loan or as preference shares, depending on the legal, regulatory and tax regime. See 'Subordinated debt'.

Misrepresentation An untrue statement inducing a contract. See A1.029.

Monoline insurer Insurer whose business is the provision of financial insurance.

Moratorium A period in which creditors agree to allow a borrower to delay payment of a debt, usually to allow negotiation of a rescue.

Mortgage A type of security interest. Under a common law mortgage, title passes to the mortgagee, subject to the mortgagor's equity of redemption. See A1.042.

Mulligan clause A clause that allows the borrower a second chance on the financial covenants. If, for example, a borrower does not comply with its financial covenants for one quarter but is back in line the following quarter, the previous quarter is disregarded as if it never happened.

Mutatis mutandis A Latin expression meaning 'with such changes as are necessary'. This is a shorthand expression, occasionally used in drafting. For example, the following statement may be used to avoid repetition. '*Clause [] (Agency) shall apply to the Security Trustee mutatis mutandis*'. This avoids the need to repeat the clause replacing all references to 'the Agent' with references to 'the Security Trustee'.

Negative pledge Undertaking by a borrower not to allow indebtedness to be maintained on a secured basis.

Net present value The current value of a given future payment or payments, discounted at a given rate (see Box A2.1).

> **Box A2.1**
>
> For example, if the current interest rate is 5% per annum, the net present value of a payment of $105 due to be made in 12 months' time is $100, since that is the amount which, if deposited in an account today and bearing interest at 5% for the year, would yield a payment of $105 in 12 months' time.

Net stable funding ratio The ratio between 'stable funding' of a bank and its mix of assets—see 6.054.

Netting a method of calculating a sum due from one party to another by taking into account the value of their rights against each other. Similar in effect to set off but the difference being that with netting only one payment obligation exists and netting is used to calculate the amount of that payment obligation.

Non-Cumulative Compounded RFR Rate see Daily Non-Cumulative Compounded RFR Rate.

Novation A method of transferring rights and obligations from one party to a contract to a third party.[124] This method involves the discharge of one contract and its replacement by a new, identical contract, with different parties.

Observation Period In relation to any given Interest Period, the period of time with reference to which interest rates for the Interest Period will be calculated. The Observation Period precedes the Interest Period by a period of days known as the 'Lookback Period'. See 0.102.

Observation Shift Using the number of RFR Banking Days in the Observation Period, rather than the number in the Interest Period, for the purpose of calculations of interest rates.

Offtaker A party which commits to purchase a quantity of the product produced in a project finance transaction.

Operating lease A lease which is not a finance lease.

Originator A party who sells its receivables in a securitization transaction.

Pari passu Equally and without preference in terms of entitlement to payment (as opposed to pro rata, which relates to actual payment, and requires that all receive the same percentage of what is due to them.) Two debts which are pari passu will, when payment is made, be paid pro rata. See also 8.052 onwards.

Participation A single lender's share of the overall loan facility.

---

[124] See 9.004.

530   Glossary of Terms

Performance bond A guarantee for a non-monetary obligation (such as due performance of a contract). The expression may be used in two entirely different ways. It may be used to describe a suretyship guarantee or, alternatively, to describe an instrument which is primary in nature.[125]

Penalty An English law expression. Under English law, any provision of a contract which deals with the consequences of a breach of contract will be unenforceable if the specified consequences are out of all proportion to the legitimate interests of the innocent party.[126] Common areas where this question arises are in relation to default interest and liquidated damages.

PIK notes Payment in kind, typically, does not provide for any payments from the borrower to the lender between the drawdown date and the maturity or refinancing date. PIK interest accrues and capitalizes periodically over the life of the debt, thus increasing the underlying principal (i.e. compound interest).

Plain vanilla A colloquial term used to describe loan facilities with no additional features such as call options.

Pledge The security created by the actual or constructive delivery of an asset to a lender where the possession of the asset was delivered for the purpose of raising funds (as opposed to a lien, where possession was delivered for some other purpose). See A1.043.

Pool A combination of assets into a single unit, such as a single investment (e.g. commercial paper) which is based on a number of investment instruments.

Poseidon Principles A framework for assessing the climate alignment of ship finance portfolios. Aimed at helping ensure that financial institutions providing finance to the maritime industry align their lending practices with responsible environmental objectives.

Power of attorney A legal document authorizing one person to act on behalf of another.

Preference An English law expression for a transaction which puts a person in a better position in the insolvency of another than they otherwise would have been (see Box A2.2). Any such step is vulnerable to be set aside as a fraudulent preference.[127]

---

[125] See Goode, *Commercial Law*, 5th edn in 35.154.

[126] See discussion in 5.010.

[127] s239 Insolvency Act 1986 (as amended).

Glossary of Terms **531**

> **Box A2.2**
>
> For example, assume a company has two loans, one of which has been personally guaranteed by the company's directors. If the company starts having financial difficulties, it might decide to pay off the guaranteed debt in order to obtain the release of the personal guarantees. If it subsequently goes into liquidation during the hardening period, the bank which had been repaid might be required to refund that sum to the company on the basis that the original repayment of the loan was a fraudulent preference. The only reason the company chose to pay off that loan was because it would result in the release of the personal guarantee and put the directors who had given the guarantees in a better position on an insolvency of the company than they otherwise would have been.

Preference shares Shares which receive their dividends before all other shares and are repaid first if the company goes into liquidation.

Preferential creditors Those creditors (such as, in many countries, employees) whose debts must be paid in priority to other unsecured creditors in a winding up.

Prepayment A payment made before it is scheduled to be made.

Pricing grid (or margin ratchet) A provision under which a borrower agrees to pay a margin which varies by reference to a specific financial ratio (e.g. leverage) or external credit rating, or other target such as in Sustainability linked loans see 0.316.

Principal This can be the amount which the lender advanced to the borrower and which the borrower must repay (as opposed to the interest due in respect of such amount), or, in relation to a person, the principal is the person for whom some other person acts as agent.

Privity The common law doctrine that no person is entitled to enforce a contract unless they are a party to it. See Box 1.17.

Pro forma accounts Financial statements that include the expected impact of the current transaction. For example, in the case of an acquisition, pro forma EBITDA will reflect the combined EBITDA of the two companies plus synergies from their merger. It could, for example, include cost savings generated by headcount reductions.

Pro rata In the same proportion (see Box A2.3).

532   **Glossary of Terms**

> **Box A2.3**
>
> If A owes $10 to B and $20 to C, and a sum of $6 is to be distributed pro rata between B and C, then A will recover $2 (20% of the amount due to it) and B will recover $4 (20% of the amount due to it).

Process agent The agent appointed by a non-English company to accept service of proceedings in the English courts on its behalf. See 12.007.

Project finance The financing of a specific project, the revenue from which will provide the lenders with repayment of their investment.

Promissory note A promise in writing to pay a fixed sum on demand or on a determinable future date.[128]

Proper law The law which applies to a contract. Sometimes referred to as the 'governing law'. This is the law which the court in which a dispute is heard decides should apply. In general a court in England or the European Union will give effect to the law chosen by the parties.[129]

Prospectus A document relating to investments (such as an issue of securities, or, potentially, participation in a syndicated loan) which sets out the relevant information in relation to the investment and is circulated to potential investors. See 'Prospectus legislation'.

Prospectus legislation The legislation which exists in many countries which regulates the contents of any prospectus distributed in that country and/or requires those issuing the prospectuses to be authorized to do so.

Put option An agreement which gives the recipient the right, but not the obligation, to require the donor to take title to a specified asset (e.g. shares) from the recipient, normally at a specified price on a specified date (or within a range of dates). The recipient can be expected to use this right if the value of the asset is less than the specified price on the specified date. Hence, such an agreement may be used to cap one party's potential losses in relation to an asset.

QFC Rules Rules in the US imposed on systemically important financial institutions requiring them to include provisions in relevant contracts

---

[128] See Goode, *Commercial Law*, 5th edn, in 21.02.

[129] This is governed by the Rome 1 Regulation 593/2008 and its English law equivalent The Law Applicable to Contractual Obligations and Non Contractual Obligations (Amendments etc.) (EU Exit) Regulations 2019. There are exceptions, for example, for rights relating to immovable property which must be governed by the law where the property is.

under which the counterparties expressly agree to specified restrictions on their rights so as to enable orderly resolution of the affairs of the institution—see 0.196.

Quasi security A transaction, such as a finance lease, which has the same commercial effect as security. Otherwise referred to as 'title financing'. See 0.286.

Rating Grading of a debt's quality as an investment.

Rating Agency Agencies which provide independently derived credit assessments on borrowers or on specific debt instruments issued by a borrower.

RCF Revolving credit facility.

Receivables Money which is owed to a company.

Receivables financing A type of trade finance in which a borrower can raise funds based on the amounts owing to it by customers under outstanding invoices.

Recharacterization The decision by a court not to take a transaction at face value but instead to look at its commercial effect in order to determine its validity. For example, a court in certain jurisdictions may determine that the true character of a transaction which involves quasi security is one of security, not ownership, and, as a result, may require that the transaction be registered as security or may treat the transaction as ineffective. Similarly, in England, a document may be expressed to be a fixed charge but a court may determine its effect to be that of a floating charge.

Redemption The repayment by a borrower of outstanding loans, in accordance with their terms, with the effect of extinguishing the outstanding debt.

Repo The sale of securities with an obligation to buy back at a future date.

Representation A statement. Statements made before another party enters into a contract (or as part of the contract as a condition to its effectiveness) may be 'mere representations' or they may be 'warranties'. Warranties go to the root of the contract and amount to promises that the statement is true, such that, if it is not, the other party is entitled to the contractual measure of damages. Representations do not go to the root of the contract. Generally speaking,[130] representations entitle the other party only to the tort level of damages[131] if untrue.

Repudiation Evidencing an intention no longer to be bound by a contract to which the person repudiating the contract is a party.

---

[130] There are four different categories of misrepresentation, each of which has different consequences.

[131] Which, unlike the contractual measure of damages, does not include loss of profit.

534   **Glossary of Terms**

Rescheduling In relation to debt obligations, the renegotiation and agreement of revised terms of a loan facility (usually involving the spreading of interest and capital repayments over a longer period).

Rescind or **Rescission** Treating a contract as at an end as a result of a breach by the counterparty.

Residual Value Guarantee A guarantee from one party that if the value of a given asset is less than a set figure at a particular date in the future (subject to specified conditions, such as the state of repair of the asset), that party will compensate the other for the shortfall in value.

Restitution An equitable remedy[132] under which a party which has been unjustly enriched at the expense of another will be required to refund the amount of that unjust enrichment.

Retention An ability by one person to keep moneys (or other assets) belonging to another, pending occurrence of a specified event.

Revolving credit A loan which may be drawn, repaid and redrawn as needed.

Ring fence To separate valuable assets or businesses[133] from others and limit transfers and other cash flows, out of the area where the valuable assets or businesses are situated, into other areas. For example, funds may be ring fenced if they are separated and allocated for use only in payment of given debts, or companies may be ring fenced in a group and payments out of the ring fenced companies restricted.

Risk Free rates. Rates of interest payable in overnight money markets. Examples are Sonia and Sofr. See 0.095.

Rollover The renewal of a drawing under a loan facility, for example, at the end of an Interest Period, or the reissue of a short-term commercial paper on its maturity.

Rollover loan In a revolving credit, any loan in respect of which the amount outstanding is equal to or less than the amount outstanding under the immediately preceding loan.

Same day funds Funds which will be available to the recipient with good value on the same day as that on which the instruction to transfer the funds is made.

SEC The Securities and Exchange Commission. A US agency whose role is to oversee the US securities market.

Second lien financing A European 2nd lien is a loan with a security on a borrower's assets ranking behind the 1st loan security.

---

[132] See A1.007.

[133] Or, indeed, assets which have the potential to give rise to extensive liabilities.

Secondary market the market where lenders trade loans among themselves as opposed to the primary market, where lenders make loans to borrowers directly.

Securities Tradeable financial assets such as bonds, notes and commercial paper.

Securitization Packaging assets (usually receivables such as credit card receipts) in such a way as to allow them to be used to back up an issue of securities.

Security An interest in property to secure a liability. See A1.041. Thus it would not include a guarantee, which does not give an interest in property. A guarantee is personal (not real) security. May also be used as in the singular version of 'Securities'.

Set off The right of a person who owes money to another but is also owed money by that other, to reduce the amount it pays by the amount it is owed. Set off is not a security, but a procedural right not to pay one debt to the extent that another is due from the payee to the payer.

Several liability Where there is more than one Obligor (such as in a guarantee where there are a number of guarantors) if their liabilities are several, they are completely independent of each other. Payment by one Obligor has no effect on the liability of other Obligors.

SFDR See Disclosure Regulation.

Shadow director Anyone in accordance with whose instructions the directors of a company are accustomed to act.[134] Such persons will have the same liabilities as directors.

Snooze you lose A clause in the loan agreement which disenfranchises a lender's voting right in relation to a specific amendment or waiver request if that lender has not responded to the agent within a certain predefined period of time. See Box 11.6.

Social loan A loan which is provided for a social purpose (e.g. affordable housing) Use for a different purpose would be an Event of Default and the borrower should no longer be permitted to describe the loan as 'Social'.

Sofr The Secured Overnight Financing Rate. The risk free rate for US Dollars.

Sonia Sterling Overnight Index Average. The risk free rate for Sterling.

Sovereign immunity In many countries, the assets of the sovereign government and organs of that government may not be seized by a court nor may the sovereign government or its organs be sued, but it may be possible for this immunity to be waived.

---

[134] S251 Companies Act 2006.

536   Glossary of Terms

SPC/SPV/SPE Special purpose company/vehicle/entity. A legal entity (it may not be a company) set up for a specific purpose (e.g. the project company in a project finance or the issuer of securities in a securitization) whose assets are limited to those relating to the transaction for which it was set up.

Sponsors In a project finance, the parties who join together to arrange the finance, being shareholders (usually) in the project company.

Spread In relation to securities—the difference between the offer and bid prices, that is, the price at which a broker would buy those securities and the price at which he would sell them. The word may also be used as another word for profit—in relation to a loan, the Margin may be referred to as the spread.

SPT Sustainability Performance Target The calibration of the KPIs in a Sustainability Linked Loan. The SPT is the target level for the KPI in question. So if for example the KPI is 'reduced carbon emissions' then the SPT will specify the amount of reduction to be achieved by when

Standby letter of credit A letter of credit issued by a bank but which is intended to be used as a fallback if there is a payment default under a specified instrument such as a loan agreement. A beneficiary of this arrangement is able to make a drawing on the letter of credit merely by providing a certificate of non-payment of the underlying debt. It is an example of a 'demand guarantee' discussed in A1.074.

Statutes Laws passed in Parliament. See A1.004.

Step-in rights Rights commonly given to lenders in the context of project finance, to step in and take over the performance of a particular contract, in place of the borrower.

Subordinated debt A debt which, in the event of the borrower's liquidation, ranks behind senior debt holders. See A1.033.

Sub-participation A method of transfer of the credit risk in the loan which does not result in the transferee having direct rights against the borrower, or becoming a lender of record. See 9.017.

Subrogation The right to take over the rights and security of another. In relation to a guarantee it is the right to take over the rights and security of the creditor on making payment under the guarantee—see A1.085. In relation to insurance, it is the right of the insurer to take over the claims of the insured on making payment of the claim.

Supplier credit Finance made available by a supplier by way of allowing delayed payments for the goods delivered or services provided. Supplier credit is often interest-bearing and with similar documentation to a loan.

Glossary of Terms **537**

Supranationals Entities set up by several sovereign states, for example, World Bank.

Surety A party (A) which agrees that, if a debt owed by another (B) is not paid, then A will pay B's debt or allow A's asset to be used towards payment of B's debt.

Sustainability Linked Loan A loan which is available for use for any purpose and under which borrowers are incentivized (invariably through a reduction in the Margin) to achieve specified sustainability targets (such as reduced emissions);

Swap The exchange of one asset for another, usually currencies, interest streams or securities.

Swingline facility A facility which is available immediately and without notice, and which will be used to overcome short-term liquidity issues. For example, it may be used to pay commercial paper if it cannot be rolled over. Such a facility can only be provided by lenders with access to immediate funds in the currency concerned.

Syndicated loan A loan made available by a group of lenders under a single loan agreement.

Synthetic Manufactured. In the context of loans or derivatives, it is used to denote the fact that the synthetic instrument has been created out of more than one underlying instrument (such as a combination of a fixed rate bond and a swap to create a stream of floating rate payments which may be represented by a synthetic instrument).

Tacking The right (or rather, the limits on the right) to advance further moneys against the security given for a debt in the event that there is a second security on the same asset. See A1.068.

Take or pay contract A contract which commits the counterparty to purchase a given quantity of a particular product at an agreed price, even if it does not, in the end, need that quantity.

Tangible net worth The book value of all the assets of a company minus its intangible assets such as goodwill.

TARGET Day A day when the Trans European Automated Real time Gross Settlement Express Transfer System is operating for payments of Euros.

Tax lease A finance lease under which the lessee benefits (by reduced rentals) from some part of the tax benefits available to the owner resulting from the owner's acquisition of the asset.

Taxonomy regulation Regulation (EU) 2020/852 on the establishment of a framework to facilitate sustainable investment

Tenor The period until maturity of a debt.

538 **Glossary of Terms**

Term out The conversion of a drawing (or part of a drawing) under a revolving credit into a term loan—see 4.004.

Thin capitalization Thin capitalization is the situation which exists if the capital injected into a company by way of shares is low in relation to the capital injected by way of shareholder loans. It is often more tax efficient for a company to be financed by debt rather than equity, because payments of interest are deductible in calculating the company's taxable profits, while payments of dividends are not deductible. As a result, subsidiaries are often capitalized by a combination of shares and shareholder loans.

Title financing Using title as an alternative to security. Otherwise known as quasi security. See 0.286.

Toggle A feature in some credit agreements which, at the discretion of the borrower, allows the borrower to switch periodically back and forth the payment of interest due on certain tiers of its debt between cash payments and PIK.

Tombstone An announcement, usually placed in the financial press, made by either the borrower or the lenders announcing provision of a loan facility. Tombstones are not intended as an advertisement to entice prospective lenders, they simply contain a brief description of the facility and a list of the participating banks.

Trade finance The financing of the manufacturing and selling process and of international trade generally

Transaction at an undervalue A transaction under which a company gives substantially more than it receives.[135]

Transfer fee The fee charged by an agent bank for transferring a portion of a loan from one lender of record to another lender of record.

Trust An English legal expression referring to the situation where the legal owner of property holds it on behalf of another (or others)—the beneficiary.[136] There are a number of different types of trust. Charities are an example where trusts are commonly used. The property of the charity belongs to the trustees who must use it for the benefit of those for whom the charity was established. Where someone wishes to create a trust, that trust will be created provided there is certainty as to:

* the intention to create a trust;
* the property vested in the trust and
* the beneficiaries of the trust.

---

[135] See A1.081.
[136] See A1.019.

Glossary of Terms **539**

A trust once created is irrevocable.

Trustee A person who holds ownership of an asset on behalf of another (the beneficiary). In the insolvency of the trustee, the trust property will not be available to the trustee's creditors. This compares with agency which is a purely contractual relationship.

Unannualised Cumulative Compounded Daily Rate In respect of any given day, the rate of interest inherent in the amount of growth which an investment would have seen if invested at the beginning of the then current Interest Period and rolled over (together with accrued interest) daily since then until that day. The rate of interest is expressed on the basis of the rate for the actual period of time covered by the calculation, as opposed to being expressed as a rate per annum.

Undertaking

* the business of a company, or
* a promise (as in covenant) to do or not to do, specified things.

Underwriter A lender which commits in advance of drawdown to take on a portion of the overall facility if it is not taken up in the initial syndication.

Venture capital Equity finance made available to, usually, newly established businesses to enable them to expand.

Warranty A word with many meanings. When used in connection with pre-contractual statements, a warranty is compared to a representation and means the more commercially important statement, which has contractual force and, if untrue, gives a right to the contractual level of damages.

When used in connection with provisions of the contract, a warranty is compared to a condition and means the less commercially important provision, which gives rise only to damages if breached, as opposed to a breach of condition which gives the right to terminate the contract.

Waterfall A provision in a document which sets out the order in which moneys are to be applied. A simple example is the clause in the loan agreement which specifies that monies received will be used to pay the Agent's fees and expenses before being applied to payment of interest.

Withholding tax A tax deducted at source on certain payments (e.g. interest or dividend payments). See 6.001.

Working capital Money required by a company to run its day-to-day activities, for example, to finance payment to employees and suppliers pending receipt of income from the sale of the product which the company supplies.

Workout Common term for the long-term rescue of a defaulting borrower by its lender(s) (and other creditors).

540   Glossary of Terms

Wrongful trading Carrying on trading after the point at which it should have been clear that insolvent liquidation was inevitable. Directors and shadow directors may[137] have to contribute to the company's assets on a winding up if the company has been guilty of wrongful trading.

Yank the bank A provision sometimes included in a loan agreement which allows the borrower to remove a lender which has voted against a waiver or amendment request under the loan agreement, which, but for that lender, would have been approved. See 4.023.

Yield The annual rate of return on an investment.

---

[137] Under s 214 Insolvency Act 1986 (as amended).

Index

Note: The page numbers followed by 'n' represents footnotes

A

acceleration 19, 228, 230, 256
  from Default to 321
  Events of Default and 384
  incorrect serving of notice of
    342n121
acceptance credit facility 12, 95
accession letter 427
acquisition finance 8
action in personam 471
action in rem 471
additional debt flexibility
  accordion 69
  extension option 69
  structural adjustments 69
administration 84
administrative provisions 16, 17,
    107–212
Agent
  agency clause 16
  agency fee 184
  amounts paid in error 392
  appointment of 385
  conduct of business by 393

confidentiality 390
distributions by 398
duties of 386
exclusion of liability 389
fiduciary duties of 387
impaired 73, 388, 392
instructions to 385
lenders' indemnity to 389
no duty to monitor 389
not responsible for credit
  appraisal 391
payments to 397
relationship with lenders 391
resignation of 390
responsibility for documentation
  388
rights and discretions of 388
role of 383
vs. trustee 483
Agent, security to 367–371
  as security for joint creditorship
    370
  as security for parallel debt 369

© The Editor(s) (if applicable) and The Author(s), under exclusive
license to Springer Nature Switzerland AG 2024
S. Wright, *The International Loan Documentation Handbook*, Global Financial Markets,
https://doi.org/10.1007/978-3-031-38489-9

542 **Index**

as security for underlying debts 368
'all moneys' guarantee 216
all reasonable endeavours 262
amendments and waivers 405–408
    exceptions to Majority Lenders principle 405, 406
anti-corruption laws 259
arbitration 415
arrangement fee 184
Arranger, role of 383, 386
asset finance 6, 82, 145
    conditions precedent in 110
    financial covenants in 271
asset risk 7
asset stripping 61, 305
asset types as security
    bank accounts 495
    businesses 494
    comingled property 496
    future property 493
    intangible assets 493
    moveable property 494
    shares and investments 493
assignments 84
    assignment agreements 379, 427
    assignment and assumption agreements 363
    vs. delegation 362
    effect on
        indemnities 361
        obligations 362
        security 362
    LMA assignment provisions
        for Lenders 375
        for Obligors 380
    loan transfers via 360
    notice of 316, 317
    types of assignment 469
Association of Corporate Treasurers 13, 191n5, 282, 283
automatic Events of Default 323
availability period 72, 153, 422

B

backstop facilities 149
balance sheet lending 7
base currency 111, 130, 283n54
Basel accords
    Basel I 203
    Basel II 204
    Basel III
        Liquidity coverage ratio 205
        Net stable funding ratio 205
    Basel 3.1. *See* Post Crisis Reforms
    Basel IV. *See* Post Crisis Reforms
    CRD IV 207
    CRD VI 206
    Post Crisis Reforms 206
    What are they for
        Capital adequacy 202
        Liquidity 202
    Who issues them 201
base rate 28
beneficial owner 474
beneficiary 474
best endeavours 262
bilateral facilities 11
bill of exchange 96
bona fide purchaser for value without notice 489
bonds 78, 80, 96
borrowers. *See also* Obligors
    additional 380
    key concerns of 19
    resignation of 382
Braganza implied term 386
break costs 36, 112, 169, 171, 184
bridge finance 9
British Bankers Association 27, 510
broken funding costs. *See* break costs

C

calculations and certificates 402–403
cancellation. *See* prepayment and cancellation
capital adequacy. *See* Basel accords

Index   **543**

capital expenditure restriction 272
capital markets 7
   convergence with 80
caps, on expenses 212
case law 469
cashflow 273, 336
cashless rollover 164
cash pooling 295
cash sweeps 278
centre of main interests (COMI) 314
certificates and determinations 402
change of business 308
change of control 167
charges
   fixed 489
   floating 486
choice of law and jurisdiction 461
chose in action 471
circularity of definitions 110
civil law 468
clawback and pre-funding clause 398
clawback clause 198, 513
clean down period 278
clean up period 15
club loans 11
CME 30
CME Term Sofr 30, 35–37, 41, 48,
     112, 129, 430, 431, 433,
     437
collateral 75
collateralized debt obligation (CDO)
   514
comingled property 496
commercial paper 10, 96
commitment fee 72, 168, 184
committed facility 5
commodification of debt 76–82
common law
   vs. civil law 468
   vs. equity 469
compliance certificate 128, 266, 428
compulsory prepayment events
   change of control 167
   and the cross default clause 333

"conclusive" evidence clause 402
conditions of utilization 146–152
   documentary conditions
      precedent 146, 148, 149
   factual conditions precedent 149
   maximum number of loans 152
   relating to Additional Obligors
     422
   relating to asset finance 422
   relating to optional currencies
     151
   relating to project finance 424
confidentiality 390, 408
confidentiality of funding rates 410
confidentiality undertaking 428
conflict of law 82
consideration 476
contingent debt 496, 497
continuing 109, 135
continuing guarantees 502
contra proferentem 404, 478
control 19
   change of 167
corporate reconstruction 308
cost-plus lending 27
costs and expenses clause 211
counterparts 411
covenant lite loans 262
covenants. *See* undertakings
credit default swaps (CDSs) 79
credit derivatives 4, 356, 364–366,
   371, 372
credit support arrangements 297
cross acceleration clause 332
cross default clauses 20, 249, 268,
   328, 333, 334
   compulsory prepayment events
     334
   consents 335
   cross acceleration clauses 332
   grace periods 335
   reducing impact of 334
Cumulative Compounded RFR Rate

544   Index

Comparison to Daily
Non-Cumulative
Compounded RFR Rate 40
Relevance for market disruption
40
currencies. *See also* multicurrency
loans
currency of account 400
Euro crisis 77, 136
symbols and definitions 136
currency indemnity 210

D

Daily Non-Cumulative
Compounded RFR Rate
Comparison to Cumulative
Compounded RFR Rate 40
The Formula 441
Principles for calculation of the
rate
Annualised Cumulative
Compounded RFR Rate
39, 441
Unannualised Cumulative
Compounded RFR Rate
40, 440
debentures 82
debt
claims in, vs. damages 230, 414
commodification of 76–82
security for
parallel debt 369
parallel debt, alternative to 369
subordination of 481. *See also*
subordination
underlying debt 368
types of
contingent 337
distressed 76, 80
prospective 337
short-term 319
sovereign 12, 252, 253
deeds 477

Default 54, 115. *See also*
acceleration; Events of
Default
acceleration and 321
notification of 269
stages of 322
defaulting lender provisions. *See*
Lehman provisions
default interest 176
deferral of guarantors' rights
222–225
definitions and interpretations
circularity 110
currency 136
in different contexts 109
in the LMA 111–139
operative provisions 111
out of context 108
rules of construction 134
uncapitalized definitions 109
demand guarantees 500, 501
demand loans 5
derivatives 328
credit 4, 355, 356, 365, 366,
371, 372
directors' duties 350, 420, 448
disruptions to payment systems 400
distressed debt 80
double taxation treaties 186
Double Tax Treaty Passport (DTTP)
Scheme 189, 194, 377
DTTP scheme. *See* Double Tax
Treaty Passport (DTTP)
Scheme
due diligence 17, 65, 91

E

EBITDA (Earnings before Interest,
Tax, Depreciation and
Amortization) 272–274,
281
Employee Retirement Income
Security Act (ERISA) 310

endeavours (degrees of) 262
enforceability opinions 450, 456, 460
enforcement expenses 211, 212
enforcement representations 245
English law
  basic concepts of 467–483
  guarantees 498–506
  legal concepts 475
  security and 484–498
  sources of 468–471
  types of claims and rights 471–475
'entire agreement' clause 478
equitable principles qualification 463
equity 9, 469
equity kicker 9
equity of redemption 485
ERISA. *See* Employee Retirement Income Security Act (ERISA)
ESG Lending
  consequences of failure to
    comply with reporting requirements 104
    meet targets 104
    use proceeds of Green Loan correctly 101
  Equator Principles 97
  Green Loan Principles 97
  Green Loans 99, 103
  Greenwashing 98
  Key Issues
    Choice of project 100
    Reporting 101
    Updating 102
    Verifying 102
  KPI's 100–103
  Poseidon principles 97
  SPT's 100, 101, 103
  Sustainability Co Ordinator 103
  Sustainability Linked loan 99, 102, 104
    Sustainability Linked Loan Principles 97
estoppel 404
€str 39
Euribor 27, 28, 112, 129, 431, 432
Events of Default 5, 14–16, 18, 20, 81, 87, 116, 319–351
  acceleration and 349
  automatic 323
  control over relevant events 321
  in the LMA Term Loan 324–351
    breach of financial covenant 325
    breach of other obligations 325
    creditors' process 339
    cross default 333
    insolvency 336
    insolvency proceedings 338
    material adverse change 341
    misrepresentation 326
    non-payment 324
    relationship with financial ratios 275
  notification of Default and 269
  objective vs. subjective 320
  ownership of the Obligors 341
  purpose of 319
exclusion clauses 378, 383, 389, 464, 478, 480
export credit 12

facility office 119
facility, types and nature 5, 139–144
  backstop 149
  finance parties' rights and obligations 141
  increase facility 140
  letter of credit 74
  revolving credit 6
FATCA. *See* Foreign Account Tax Compliance Act (FATCA)
fees 184, 399

546   Index

fiduciary duties 383, 387, 394
Finance Document 120
finance leases 90
Finance Parties
  rights and obligations 141–143
  sharing among 393
financial collateral 487
financial due diligence 391
financial indebtedness 92, 108, 120,
      121, 328
financial ratios 53, 279, 282, 347
  in asset finance transaction
      283–286
  breach of 327
  common ratios
    cashflow 273
    gearing 276
    interest cover 272
    leverage 274
    liquidity 275
    security cover 283
    tangible net worth 277
  consequence of breach of 280
  definition of words used in 282
  equity cure rights 281
  group level to run 278
  incurrence tests 279
  maintenance tests 279
  material adverse effect and 280
  periods for 279
  purpose of 276
  summary of 277
financial statements 250, 265
  original 130, 250, 251
  requirements as to 266
fixed charges 486, 489
floating charges 486
force majeure 87
Foreign Account Tax Compliance
      Act (FATCA) 199–201
  Model 1 intergovernmental
      agreement 200
  Model 2 intergovernmental
      agreement 200

form of assignment agreement 427
form of transfer certificate 426
forward purchase 94
forward sale 93, 97
frozen GAAP 267
funded sub-participation 364
further assurance clause 318
future property 493

G

GAAP 92, 124, 267
gearing ratio 276
geographical limitations 238
goodstanding 239
governing law 413
grace period 18, 115, 116, 335
gross up 52, 140, 187, 190, 193
  limitations 193
Group members
  changes in Group members 56
  changes in Obligors 56
  the Company 57
  group structure 318
  interactions between group
      members and Obligors 62
  Material Subsidiaries 62, 237,
      329
  Non recourse subsidiaries 62
  Obligor 54
  restricting non Obligors 56
  Subsidiaries 52
  Unrestricted Subsidiaries 55, 62
      and collateral stripping 55
guarantees 52, 62, 215–225
  'all moneys' 216
  appropriations 221
  continuing 217, 502
  deferral of guarantors' rights 222
  demand guarantees 500
  discharge by amendment 506
  in English law 499, 501, 503
  hazards of 503
  immediate recourse 221

Index **547**

vs. indemnity 215, 499, 500
interest and 225
vs. letter of comfort 503
nature of 498
need to claim against borrower
501
primary vs. secondary obligations
499
reinstatement 217
subrogation/reimbursement 505
transactions at an undervalue 503
vs. third party charge 502
upstream guarantees 483, 504
waiver of defences 218
guarantors 52, 53
additional 382
resignation of 382

H

hardening period 217, 359

I

illegality 165
impaired agent 73
provisions 392
inconsistencies, repeating
representations and
232–234
increased costs 206–208
claims 209
exceptions 209
mitigation of 211
incurrence tests 279
indemnities 16, 210, 217
currency 210
effect of assignment on 361
vs. guarantees 499, 50
guarantees and 215
tax 197
information memorandum 250
information undertakings 265–270
compliance certificate 266

financial statements 265
'know your customer' checks 270
miscellaneous 268
notification of Default 269
provision via websites 270
insignificant companies 58
insolvency 73, 335–337
balance sheet test 337, 524
cashflow test 524
directors' duties on 350
legal opinions and 446
proceedings as an Event of
Default 338
intangible assets 493
intellectual property rights 60, 307
interest. *See also* Libor: Reference
Rate Terms; and Risk free
rates
default 176
interest periods 32, 161
notification of rates of 175
payment of 176
pro rata interest settlement 380
interest cover ratio 273, 274
intergovernmental agreements
Model 1 agreement 200
Model 2 agreement 200
interpretation clause 109
Issuing Bank, role of 383

J

joint creditorship 370
joint (vs several) obligation 473
judgement currency indemnity 210
jurisdiction 16, 238, 414, 461

K

knowledge limitations 237
'know your customer' checks 270,
376, 379, 381

548 Index

L

legal concepts 475–483
legal opinions 421, 446–465
  assumptions in 452
  form of 451–465
  lawyers' role and 450
  limits on scope of 447
  locations of 449
  qualifications 462
  the opinions
    authority 454
    choice of law and jurisdiction 461
    due execution 455
    due incorporation and continued existence 453
    effectiveness of security 457
    enforcement of judgements 461
    no consents or filings needed 459
    no contravention of law or constitution 455
    no unexpected tax consequences 460
    pari passu 462
    power 454
    valid and enforceable obligations 456
  types of 447
legal owner 474
Lehman provisions 65, 67, 71, 73, 75, 141, 155, 164, 392, 408
lender default. *See* Lehman provisions
lender of record 79
lenders 22
  categories of, for tax purposes 188
  changes to. *See* loan transfers
  defaulting 118
  key concerns of 19
  majority 117, 126, 150, 385, 407
  non-bank 77

  number of 11
  of record 356, 372
  rights and obligations of 17
lending office 52
letter of comfort 503
letter of credit facilities 74
letter of credit utilization 155–156
  appointment of additional Issuing Banks 155
  indemnities 155
  part of facility B 155
  renewal of a letter of credit 156
  revaluation of letters of credit 156
Leveraged LMA 9, 15, 238, 305, 309, 375
leverage ratio 275
Libor
  Replacement of 27
liens 84, 292, 298, 302, 486
limitations to scope of representations
  companies covered 237
  geographical 238
  materiality 237
  with reference to knowledge 237
limited recourse financing 8
liquidity coverage ratio 145, 205
liquidity risk 202, 203
litigation proceedings as Event of Default 263, 264, 340
LMA. *See* Loan Market Association (LMA)
loan agreement overview 13
  hazards in reviewing 24
  key concerns for borrowers in 19
  key concerns for lenders in 22
  scope of 51–64
  structure 16
Loan Market Association (LMA) 2, 3
  recommended forms 13–16
loan markets, convergence with capital markets 77
loan stock 96

loan transfers 355–382
  assignments 360
  behind the scenes 371
  changes to lender of record 372
  conditions of 376
  consent to 371
  credit derivatives 364
  fees 378
  by lenders 375
  novation 357
  by Obligors 380
  procedure for 378
  restrictions on 373
  secured loans 366
  sub-participation 363

M

Majority Lenders 126, 407
Margin 9, 85, 126
Margin ratchet 127
market disruption clause 14, 36, 181
material adverse change clause
    341–349
  drafting points in 345
  financial condition and 347
  objections to
    excessive power to lenders 344
    fragility 343
    lack of use 342
    uncertainty 342
material adverse effect 129, 237,
    248, 255, 305, 345
materiality thresholds 237
material subsidiaries 237
mezzanine finance 9
minimum tangible net worth 332
misrepresentation 326, 478, 479
  as Event of Default 326
  liability in 227, 230
mitigation, of increased costs 211
money laundering 24

Moody's assessment framework for
    leveraged loan covenants
    287
mortgages 485
moveable property 494
multicurrency loans
  base currency 111
  change of currency 160
  documentary complexity 3
  Optional Currencies 161
  Reference Rate Terms 44, 129,
    130, 429
  selection of currency 160
multiple drawdown facilities 148

N

negative pledge 23, 123, 290–306
  consequences of breach 291
  content of 291
  exceptions to 295
  prohibition on quasi security 293
  prohibition on security 292
  purpose of 290
  security arising by operation of
    law 298
net stable funding ratio 205
netting arrangement 296
no disposals clause 287, 304
  exceptions to 295
non-bank lenders 77
non-recourse companies 59
notification of Default 269
novation 355, 375
  consents and 359
  effects of 358
  mechanics of 358
  security and 359

O

obligations
  effect of assignment on 362
  primary vs. secondary 499

550   Index

Obligors 52, 54, 62–64
assignments and transfers by 380
changes to 380
conditions precedent to
additional 422
distributions to 398
no set off by 400
ownership of the 341
operative provisions 111
Optional Currency 130, 154, 156,
161
ordinary course of business 299, 306
ordinary course of trading 299, 306
Original Borrowers 51
original financial statements 130,
251
Original Guarantors 51

P

parallel debt
alternative to 370
security for 369
pari passu 23, 251, 462, 480
partial invalidity 403
partial payments 399
payment letters 423
payment mechanics 397
penalty 177
PIK (payment in kind) financings
12, 275
pledges 485
pre-funding 398
prepayment and cancellation
163–171
change of control 167
illegality 165
restrictions 171
right in relation to single lender
170
voluntary cancellation 168
voluntary prepayment 169
primary obligation 499
privity 138

project finance 6, 84, 230, 234
conditions precedent in 424
disbursement accounts 86
distribution accounts 86
revenue accounts 86
promissory notes 96, 402
pro rata interest settlement 380
pro rata sharing clause 393, 405, 407
prospectus legislation 356

Q

qualifications in legal opinions
equitable principles 463
insolvency 462
qualifications to representations 237
qualifications to undertakings 261
quasi security 90–97
prohibition on 293
Quistclose trust 145

R

recharacterization 91
Reference Rate Terms
Compounded Rate Loan
Additional business day 46,
430
Baseline Cas 431
Break costs 431
Business Day Convention 47,
431
Central Bank Rate 431
Central Bank Rate Adjustment
432
Cost of funds as fallback 430
Daily Rate 432
Fallback Cas 432
Interest Periods 435
Lookback Period 433
Margin 433
Market Disruption Rate 433
Published Rate Contingency
Event 435

Index **551**

Rate Switch CAS 434
Reporting Day 434
RFR Banking Day 47, 434
Risk Free Rate 434
Term Rate Loan
Alternative Term Rate 436
Alternative Term Rate
Adjustment 436
Backstop Rate Switch Date
436
Central Bank Rate 437
Choice of Term Fallback
Option 436
Fallback Interest Period 437
Market Disruption Rate 437
Overnight Rate 437
Overnight Reference Rate 437
Primary Term Rate 438
Quotation Day 438
Rate Switch Currency 435
Term Reference Rate Cas 438
registration requirements for security
492
remedies and waivers 404–405
repeating representations 24, 26,
132, 231, 239, 248, 255
hazards of 232
Replacement of Libor, reasons 27
representations 14, 227–257
in different circumstances 257
disclosure and 228
drawstop/acceleration 228
liability in misrepresentation 230
limitations
geographical limitations 238
knowledge limitations 237
materiality thresholds 237
in the LMA Term Loan 238–257
binding obligations 240
financial statements 250
governing law and
enforcement 245
no Default 247
no filing or stamp taxes 247

no misleading information 249
non-conflict with other
obligations 242
no proceedings pending or
threatened 255
pari passu ranking 251
power and authority 243
status 239
tax deduction 246
validity and admissibility in
evidence 244
purpose of 227
repetition of 24, 26, 132, 231,
239, 248, 255
summary of 235
revolving credit 6, 126, 132, 139,
154, 158
clean down period 272, 278
repayment and 163, 164
Rollover Loans 151
Risk free rates 3, 27–36. *See also*
Reference Rate Terms
Backward looking compounded
rates
Daily Non-Cumulative
Compounded RFR Rate 33
Lookback period 31
ObservationShift 31
Zero floors 33
Break costs 36
Cost of funds 35
Credit Adjustment Spreads
Baseline 34
Fallback 35
Rateswitch 34
Term Reference Rate 35
Fallback provisions
For permanent problems 49
For temporary problems,
Compounded Rate Loans
49
For temporary problems, Term
Rate Loans 47
Forward looking term rates

552 Index

CME Term Sofr 30
Key Words in LMA
   Describing credit adjustment
      spreads 45
   Describing loan tranches 38
   Describing rate charged 39
   Describing schedules and
      supplements 44
   Relating to business days 46
   Summary 39
   Used in the calculation 42
market disruption 36
risk sub-participation 364

S

sanctions 166
scope of agreement 22
secondary market 70, 362, 409
secondary obligations 499
secured loans, transfers of 355, 362,
   366
securitization 10, 76
security 4
   for a syndicated loan
      to an agent 367
      for joint creditorship 370
      for parallel debt 369
      to trustee for covenant to pay
        367
      for underlying debt 368
   on different types of assets 493
   effect of assignment on 362
   in English law 484
   novation and 359
   prohibition on 292
   quasi 90, 293
   registration requirements 492
   subordinate 481
   tacking further advances 497
   third party charge as 502
   types of 485
security cover ratio 283
   release of additional security 286

   restrictions on acceptable assets
      285
   valuation of security 284
   value of cash 286
security over lenders' rights clause
   379
Security Trustee 51, 52, 366, 367
selection notice 426
separateness undertakings 319
service of process 416
set off 91, 94, 401
several obligation 473
shadow directors 260
'snooze you lose' provision 20
Sofr 30, 37, 43, 44
Sonia 30, 33, 37, 42, 44, 46, 49,
   180, 407, 434
sovereign debt 12, 252, 253
special resolution procedures for
      systemically important
      lenders 68
   bail in clauses 4
   QFC Rules 68
statute 135
subordination 481
   categories of 483
   of debt 481
   of security 481
   before winding up 224
   structural 482
   on winding up 224
sub-participation 371, 372
   funded 364
   risk 364
subrogation 219, 505
substantive consolidation 319
suspect period 217
swingline facilities 10

T

tangible net worth 58, 272, 277
TARGET Day 112, 133
tax

double taxation treaties 186
FATCA 196, 197
gross-up 187, 192
indemnities 197
lenders' tax status 188
tax credits 198
withholding 185
term loans 5, 139
third party charge 502
third party rights 137
title financing 83, 90, 91
title retention 92
tort 472
trade finance 10
transaction costs 324
transactions at undervalue 420
transfer certificate 358, 426
trustees 51, 483
   security 52, 366, 367
trusts 74, 367

U

undertakings 5, 14, 259–319
  covenant lite loans 262
  cumulative nature 264, 299
  in the LMA Term Loan 287–319
    authorization 288
    change of business 308
    compliance with laws 289,
      309, 310
    financial covenants 275–292.
      See also financial ratios
    information 265–270, 313
    mergers 308
    negative pledge 290–307
    no disposals clause 304–308
  other common 309–319

relating to assets given as
    security 315
relating to legal risks 314
restrictions on dealing with
    assets and security 311
restrictions on movement of
    cash 312
separateness 319
purpose of 259
qualifications 261
shadow directors and 260
utilization 153–161
  completion of utilization request
    153
  conditions of 146–152
  currency and amount 154
  delivery of utilization request 153
  utilization request 426

V

voluntary cancellation 170
voluntary prepayment 167, 171

W

waiver of defences to guarantee
    218–221
withholding tax 185, 187, 187, 190,
    192–194, 199, 209, 246,
    358, 364, 376, 377, 460.
    See also gross up
  documentation 190
wrongful trading 350

Y

'yank the bank' clause 20, 171, 417
yield protection clauses 201

Printed in the United States
by Baker & Taylor Publisher Services